Y0-AGU-692

MATHEMATICS PLUS

How I Balance My Meals

Breakfast	
Lunch	
Snack	
Dinner	

Plant Growth

Height in Inches

Time in Weeks

HBJ Harcourt Brace Jovanovich, Inc.

Orlando   Austin   San Diego   Chicago   Dallas   New York

Copyright © 1992 by Harcourt Brace Jovanovich, Inc.

All rights reserved. No part of this publication may be reproduced or transmitted in any form
or by any means, electronic or mechanical, including photocopy, recording, or any information storage
and retrieval system, without permission in writing from the publisher.

Requests for permission to make copies of any part of the work should be mailed to:
Permissions Department, Harcourt Brace Jovanovich, Publishers, 8th Floor, Orlando, Florida 32887

Printed in the United States of America
ISBN 0-15-300142-9
4 5 6 7 8 9 10   048   95   94   93   92

ACKNOWLEDGMENTS

Some computer lessons in this book are based on AppleWorks® by Claris Corporation.
© 1989 by Claris Corporation. All rights reserved. Claris is a registered trademark of Claris Corporation.
AppleWorks is a registered trademark of Apple Computer, Inc. licensed to Claris Corporation.
Apple is a registered trademark of Apple Computer, Inc.

Logo lessons in this book present the Terrapin Logo version. Terrapin
is a registered trademark of Terrapin Software, Inc.

AUTHORS

Grace M. Burton
Professor, Department of Curricular Studies
University of North Carolina at Wilmington
Wilmington, North Carolina

Jerome D. Kaplan
Professor of Education
Seton Hall University
South Orange, New Jersey

Martha H. Hopkins
Associate Professor
University of Central Florida
Orlando, Florida

Leonard Kennedy
Professor Emeritus
California State University at Sacramento
Sacramento, California

Howard C. Johnson
Chair, Mathematics Education
Professor of Mathematics and Mathematics Education
Syracuse University
Syracuse, New York

Karen A. Schultz
Professor, Mathematics Education
Georgia State University
Atlanta, Georgia

SENIOR EDITORIAL ADVISOR

Francis (Skip) Fennell
Professor of Education
Western Maryland College
Westminister, Maryland

ADVISORS

Janet S. Abbott
Curriculum Coordinator
Chula Vista Elementary School District
Chula Vista, California

Don S. Balka
Professor
Saint Mary's College
Notre Dame, Indiana

Gilbert Cuevas
Professor of Education
University of Miami
Miami, Florida

Michael C. Hynes
Professor
University of Central Florida
Orlando, Florida

Genevieve M. Knight
Professor of Mathematics
Coppin State College
Baltimore, Maryland

Charles Lamb
Associate Professor
University of Texas at Austin
Austin, Texas

Marsha W. Lilly
Mathematics Coordinator, K–12
Alief Independent School District
Alief, Texas

Sid Rachlin
Professor
University of Hawaii
Honolulu, Hawaii

Dorothy S. Strong
Director K–12 Mathematics
Chicago Public Schools
Chicago, Illinois

Steven Tipps
West Foundation Professor
Midwestern State University
Wichita Falls, Texas

David Wells
Retired Assistant Superintendent
for Instruction
Pontiac, Michigan

Contents

Geometry **106**
THEME: *Space*

**Dividing Whole Numbers
by 1-Digit Numbers   148**
THEME: *Recreation and Pastimes*

8   **Multiplying and Dividing Decimals**   **242**
THEME: *Consumer*

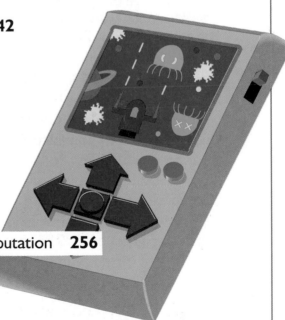

▶▶▶▶▶▶▶▶▶▶▶▶▶

 9

Number Theory and Fractions   274
THEME: *Gardening*

12 **Perimeter, Area, and Volume** **386**
THEME: *Carpentry*

13 **Ratio, Percent, and Probability** **420**
THEME: *Travel*

Computer Connection

Welcome to MATHEMATICS PLUS

Mathematics is an important part of your daily life. You use it at school, at home, and everywhere you go!

As you learn mathematics this year, look in your book for M.C. Lion. M.C. will give you hints for solving problems and tips for studying math.

This year you are going to use ideas you have already learned in interesting, new ways. You will learn more about solving problems. You will use the calculator and the computer as problem-solving tools. You will learn more about decimals and fractions. You will learn more about the perimeter and area of plane shapes and about the volume of solid shapes. You will work with very large and very small numbers. You will learn to do mental math and to estimate—so you can use numbers quickly to solve problems every day!

Math is fun! You will work in groups to share what you are learning. You will have fun solving the puzzles and problems in the **Math Fun Magazine** at the back of this book.

This year
you can make mathematics
a learning adventure!

The Authors

▶ ▶ ▶ ▶ ▶ ▶ ▶ ▶

How Do You Use Math Every Day?

People use math to help them do many things. Here are some of the things you do in which you use math.

shop	weigh
count	measure
share	save
build	cook
travel	tell time
compare	keep score
estimate	predict

Look at these pictures. Talk about how math is being used. Think of some ways you have used math to help you. Share your ideas with a classmate.

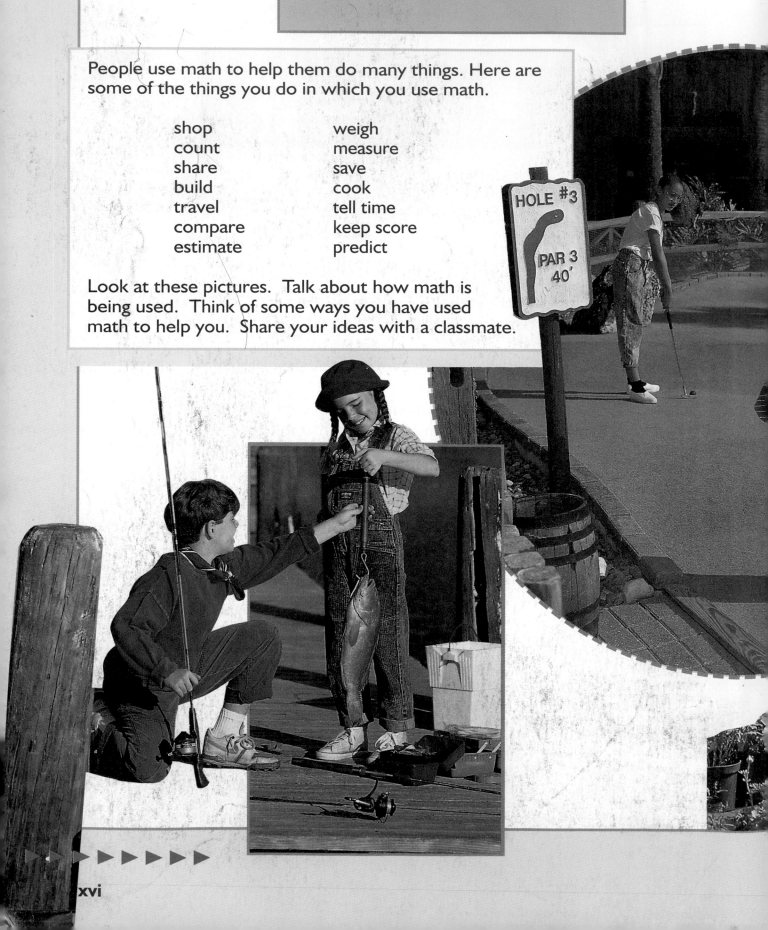

HOLE #3

PAR 3
40'

Solving Problems

You use math every day to solve problems. In this book you will learn how to solve problems by asking yourself questions. These questions will help you

- UNDERSTAND the problem.
- PLAN a solution.
- SOLVE the problem.
- LOOK BACK and check your solution.

Will has a problem to solve. Read his problem slowly and carefully.

Will plays the saxophone in a jazz band. Band practice is scheduled to begin at 7:15 P.M. at the Community Center. Will plans to arrive 15 minutes early to practice a duet with a friend. It will take 20 minutes for Will's grandfather to drive him to the Community Center. What time must Will and his grandfather leave the house?

How can Will decide what time to leave? Think along with Will as he solves the problem.

Understand the Problem

First, Will must UNDERSTAND the problem.

He restates the problem to himself. He wants to be sure he knows what the problem is about. Then he asks himself these questions.

What must I find? I must find the time when I should leave the house so I can meet my friend before band practice and be on time for practice.

What facts do I have? Band practice starts at 7:15 P.M. I need to meet my friend 15 minutes before practice. It takes 20 minutes to drive to the Community Center.

How would you restate Will's problem in your own words?

▶ ▶ ▶ ▶ ▶ ▶ ▶ ▶

Plan a Solution

Then, Will must PLAN how to solve his problem.

He thinks about the ways he solves problems. He chooses one of these strategies.

- Draw a picture
- Make a model
- Work backward
- Guess and check
- Act out the problem
- Write a number sentence

Then he makes a plan by asking himself this question.

How can I solve the problem? Since I know when practice starts, I can work backward from that time to find the time I must leave the house.

What other plan could Will have made?

Solve the Problem

Next, Will must SOLVE the problem.

He must decide how to solve the problem. He must decide whether to use a clock or mental math to work backward. For some other kinds of problems, Will might want to use a calculator or paper and pencil.

Will then thinks about how he will find the answer.

I can look at the clock and work backward from 7:15 to find the time I should leave the house.

Since I need to meet my friend 15 minutes before 7:15, I need to be at the Community Center at 7:00.

Since it takes 20 minutes to drive to the Community Center, my grandfather and I must leave the house at 6:40.

Why do you think Will worked backward to find the time? What method would you choose?

Look Back

Last, Will can LOOK BACK and check whether his answer is correct.

He thinks about a way to check his answer. He thinks about whether his solution answers the question.

He asks himself these questions.

How can I check my answer? I can add the number of minutes I will practice with my friend and the number of minutes it takes to drive to the Community Center. I can then count back the total number of minutes from 7:15.

15 min + 20 min = 35 min
35 minutes before 7:15 is 6:40.

Does my solution answer the question?
Since I found when I need to leave the house to arrive at band practice on time, my solution answers the question.

How else could Will check his answer?

Will solved his problem. He used math to help him get to band practice on time.

In Mathematics Plus you will learn to be a problem solver!

▶ ▶ ▶ ▶ ▶ ▶ ▶ ▶

How Will You Learn Math?

In Mathematics Plus you will learn math in different ways. All of the ways to learn involve *thinking*.

You will learn math by

- working with a group.
- modeling problems, using objects and diagrams.
- listening to your teacher and your classmates.
- talking about math ideas.
- writing about math ideas.
- recording the meanings of new words.
- choosing problem-solving strategies.
- making decisions about how to solve problems.
- using math in school, at home, and everywhere.

WORKING TOGETHER

- Listen carefully to other people's ideas.
- Encourage others to share their ideas.
- Discuss ideas in a friendly way.
- Plan how your group is going to share the work.

1

PLACE VALUE
WHOLE NUMBERS AND DECIMALS

Did you know ...

. . . that in 1833 Benjamin H. Day started the *New York Sun*, the first of many successful newspapers, and charged $0.01 per copy?

The number of United States newspapers peaked in 1909, when the country had about 2,600 different daily newspapers. Today the country has about 1,700 different daily newspapers. How does this number compare with the number of different daily newspapers in 1909?

EXPLORING
Place Value of Whole Numbers

WORK TOGETHER

Building Understanding

One way that number values can be shown is with base-ten blocks. If you let the unit represent 1, you can make the following chart.

Thousands	Hundreds	Tens	Ones
 cube	 flat	 long	 unit

Talk About It

▶ Show the block that represents 10×1.

▶ Show the block that represents 10×10.

▶ Show the block that represents 10×100.

▶ How could you represent $10 \times 1,000$ with base-ten blocks?

▶ What would be the value of this new block?

▶ What relationships do you see among all the blocks?

The blocks that represent numbers greater than 1,000 are too large to picture here. You can use the place-value chart to understand larger numbers.

Thousands			Ones			
Hundreds	Tens	Ones	Hundreds	Tens	Ones	
					1	= 1×1
				1	0	= 10×1
			1	0	0	= 10×10
		1,	0	0	0	= 10×100
	1	0,	0	0	0	= $10 \times 1,000$
1	0	0,	0	0	0	= $10 \times 10,000$

▶ How many times greater is 10 than 1? 100 than 10?

▶ What happens to the value of the digit 1 as you move to the left on the place-value chart?

▶ Describe what the chart shows.

2

Making the Connection

You can use **exponents** to express numbers as powers of ten.

exponent

10^4

base

Read: ten to the fourth power

4 is the exponent. It shows how many times the base is multiplied by itself.

10 is the base.

So, $10^4 = 10 \times 10 \times 10 \times 10 = 10,000$.

power of 10   multiplication sentence   number

Look at 10^3.

Talk About It

▶ What base-ten block represents 10^3?

▶ How many times greater is 10^3 than 10^2?

▶ What relationship do you see between the number of zeros in the number and the exponent for its power of ten?

This place-value chart shows the numbers expressed as powers of ten.

Thousands			Ones			
Hundreds	Tens	Ones	Hundreds	Tens	Ones	
					1	$= 10^0$
				1	0	$= 10^1 = 10 \times 1$
			1	0	0	$= 10^2 = 10 \times 10$
		1 ,	0	0	0	$= 10^3 = 10 \times 10 \times 10$
	1	0 ,	0	0	0	$= 10^4 = 10 \times 10 \times 10 \times 10$
1	0	0 ,	0	0	0	$= 10^5 = 10 \times 10 \times 10 \times 10 \times 10$

Checking Understanding

Complete.

1. $10 \times \blacksquare = 100$ 2. $10^2 = \blacksquare$ 3. $10^{\blacksquare} = 100,000$

	Number Name	Number	Multiplication	Power of Ten
4.	ten	$\blacksquare$	10×1	10^1
5.	hundred	100	10×10	$\blacksquare$
6.	thousand	1,000	$\blacksquare$	10^3
7.	<u> ? </u>	10,000	$10 \times 10 \times 10 \times 10$	10^4
8.	hundred thousand	100,000	$10 \times 10 \times 10 \times 10 \times 10$	$\blacksquare$

PLACE VALUE
to Hundred Thousands

The news media cover many athletic events in stadiums. This table shows the number of seats in some stadiums in the United States.

Seating Capacity in Stadiums	
Stadium	Number of Seats
Pontiac Silverdome	80,638
Rose Bowl	106,721
Astrodome	50,599

You can use the place-value chart to name the value of each digit in 106,721.

Thousands			Ones		
Hundreds	Tens	Ones	Hundreds	Tens	Ones
1	0	6	7	2	1

1×1	=	1
2×10	=	20
7×100	=	700
$6 \times 1,000$	=	6,000
$0 \times 10,000$	=	0
$1 \times 100,000$	=	100,000

A number can be expressed in different ways.

Standard Form: 106,721
Expanded Form:
$(1 \times 100,000) + (0 \times 10,000) + (6 \times 1,000) + (7 \times 100) + (2 \times 10) + (1 \times 1)$
$(1 \times 10^5) + (0 \times 10^4) + (6 \times 10^3) + (7 \times 10^2) + (2 \times 10^1) + (1 \times 10^0)$
$100,000 + 0 + 6,000 + 700 + 20 + 1$
Word Form: one hundred six thousand, seven hundred twenty-one

Check for Understanding

Write two other forms for each number.

1. $40,000 + 7,000 + 600 + 10 + 3$ **2.** 361,401

Write the value of each underlined digit.

3. 2_9_,416   **4.** 98,5_4_0   **5.** 380,2_5_6   **6.** _2_02,439

Practice

Write two other forms for each number.

7. 18,960   **8.** 68,582   **9.** 124,379   **10.** 207,503

11. one hundred fifteen thousand, four hundred eighty-seven

12. three hundred fifty-one thousand, five hundred twelve

13. 200,000 + 80,000 + 4,000 + 600 + 70 + 3

14. 400,000 + 6,000 + 10

> I can change the standard form into expanded form and word form.

Write the value of each underlined digit.

15. 6,7<u>9</u>5   **16.** <u>9</u>03   **17.** 1<u>6</u>,098   **18.** <u>7</u>60,439

19. 5<u>1</u>7,034   **20.** 807,<u>2</u>13   **21.** 32,<u>7</u>16   **22.** 1,00<u>6</u>

Mixed Applications

Write in two different forms.

23. I am a number greater than 99,999 but less than 100,001. What am I?

24. I am a number less than 150,000 but greater than 149,998. What am I?

SOCIAL STUDIES CONNECTION

Roman numerals can be found on clock faces, pages of books, and cornerstones. Where have you seen Roman numerals?

I	II	III	IV	V	VI	VII	VIII	IX	X	L	C
1	2	3	4	5	6	7	8	9	10	50	100

To find the value of a Roman numeral, add when the symbols are alike or when they decrease in value from left to right.

XVII = 10 + 5 + 1 + 1, or 17   CLXI = 100 + 50 + 10 + 1, or 161

Subtract when the value of a symbol is less than the value of the symbol to its right.

In the number CIX, C = 100, I is less than X, so IX = 10 − 1, or 9. So, CIX = 100 + 9, or 109.

Write the Roman numerals in standard form.

25. XVI   **26.** XXIII   **27.** XC   **28.** VL

Describe how the expanded form helps you understand the value of a number.

WRAP UP...

PLACE VALUE
to Hundred Millions

Professional sporting events attract millions of television viewers. A recent Super Bowl game was watched by about 42,000,000 households.

Use the place-value chart to help you read this number.

Millions			Thousands			Ones		
Hundreds	Tens	Ones	Hundreds	Tens	Ones	Hundreds	Tens	Ones
	4	2	0	0	0	0	0	0

← periods

Large numbers are separated into **periods**, each containing three place-value positions. Commas separate the periods and show where to use the period name.

Standard Form: 42,000,000

Expanded Form:

$(4 \times 10,000,000) + (2 \times 1,000,000)$
$(4 \times 10^7) \quad + \quad (2 \times 10^6)$
$40,000,000 \quad + \quad 2,000,000$

Word Form: forty-two million

Talk About It

Look at this number. 44,444,444

▶ How does the value of the digit 4 change as you look from right to left?

▶ How can you use a calculator to change the number to 54,444,444?

Check for Understanding

Use the number 784,251,060 for Exercises 1–4.

1. Write the value of the digit 8.

2. Write the word form of the number.

3. Name the period that includes the digits 251.

4. Name the place-value position of the digit 7.

Practice

Write the value of each underlined digit.

5. 1,982,435
6. 8,759,635
7. 75,927,643

8. 493,850,969
9. 790,263,485
10. 152,065,468

Write two other forms for each number.

11. 932,400
12. 8,210,100
13. 853,425,756

14. 100,000,000 + 50,000,000 + 400,000 + 20,000 + 5,000 + 700

15. 500,000,000 + 3,000,000 + 200,000 + 70,000 + 6,000 + 400

16. forty million, nine hundred thousand, five hundred eight

17. one hundred three million, six hundred eighty-five

18. two hundred thirty-five million, three thousand, ten

Mixed Applications

19. In a recent year, 50,241,840 homes had cable television. If 5 million more homes were added to this number, what would be the total number of homes with cable television?

20. A top television show was viewed in about fifty million homes. Write in two different forms the number that is one million less than fifty million.

EVERYDAY MATH CONNECTION

You can use the short word form to write a large number. First, write the digits in each period. Then, write the name of each period. It is not necessary to write the word form for the ones period.

Standard Form: 321,506,974
Short Word Form: 321 million, 506 thousand, 974

Write the short word form.

21. 250,725,697
22. 801,048,500
23. 900,000,050

Why is it important to remember the name of each period in a large number?

WRAP UP...

COMPARING AND ORDERING
Whole Numbers

Mr. Lucci turned a spinner five times and called out one digit each time. Sara and Ben each tried to write the greater number.

Sara 1 2 , 6 7 3   Ben 1 2 , 7 6 3

- How can you tell who wrote the greater number?

You can compare numbers by comparing the digits in each place-value position.

<	is less than
>	is greater than
=	is equal to

Compare 12,673 and 12,763. Start at the left. Check each place until the digits are different.

Step 1 Compare the ten thousands. 12,673 ↓ same number of ten thousands 12,763	**Step 2** Compare the thousands. 12,673 ↓ same number of thousands 12,763	**Step 3** Compare the hundreds. 12,673 ↓ 7 > 6 12,763

Since 12,763 > 12,673, Ben wrote the greater number.

You can order numbers by comparing them in the same way.
Order from greatest to least. 34,267; 35,764; 32,876

Step 1 Compare the ten thousands. 34,267 ↓ 35,764 same number of ↓ ten thousands 32,876	**Step 2** Compare the thousands. 34,267 ↓ 35,764 ↓ 32,876	**Step 3** Order the digits. 5 > 4 > 2	**Step 4** Order the numbers. 35,764 34,267 32,876

Talk About It

▶ Why do you start at the left to compare the digits?

▶ How could you order 34,267; 35,764; and 32,876 from least to greatest?

▶ How is comparing 13,425 and 7,289 different from the comparison above?

8

Connection, pages 462–463

Check for Understanding

Name the place-value position where the numbers differ.

1. 1,200; 1,500

2. 15,750; 15,740

3. 125,200; 120,500

Write whether the numbers are in order from *least to greatest* or from *greatest to least*.

4. 1,250; 1,500; 12,000

5. 18,525; 18,250; 1,850

6. 49,672; 49,762; 49,768

Practice

Write <, >, or = for ●.

7. 1,467 ● 1,376

8. 42,347 ● 42,437

9. 5,416,367 ● 5,416,367

Order from least to greatest.

10. 1,928; 1,856; 2,414

11. 26,430; 25,478; 26,413

12. 360,030; 306,600; 300,060

Order from greatest to least.

13. 4,645; 6,765; 6,583

14. 12,680; 13,200; 13,039

15. 458,608; 567,806; 485,304

Mixed Applications

Use the table to answer Exercises 16–18.

Network TV Program Viewing	
Evening Programs	**Number of Households**
Informational program	10,350,000
General drama	11,020,000
Suspense and mystery	13,040,000
Situation comedy	15,920,000
Feature film	14,580,000
Adventure	8,770,000

16. Which programs are viewed by the most households? the fewest households?

17. Which programs are viewed by fewer than 12,000,000 households?

18. Making Choices Which two kinds of TV programs would you choose to advertise a new product? Why?

How do you use place-value ideas when you compare numbers?

ESTIMATE
by Rounding Whole Numbers

A newspaper office reports a circulation of 36,475 newspapers. To the nearest ten thousand, about how many newspapers are circulated?

You can estimate 36,475 by rounding to the nearest ten thousand. You can use a number line to help you.

Notice that 36,475 is closer to 40,000 than to 30,000. So, about 40,000 newspapers are circulated.

To round a number, look at the digit to the right of the place to which you are rounding.

If that digit is less than 5, the digit being rounded remains the same.	If that digit is 5 or more, the digit being rounded increases by 1.

Examples

A. Round 36,475 to the nearest thousand.

digit to be rounded   4 < 5

36,475
↓
36,000

So, the thousands digit remains the same.

B. Round 36,475 to the nearest hundred.

digit to be rounded   7 > 5

36,475
↓
36,500

So, the hundreds digit increases by 1.

C. Round 36,475 to the nearest ten.

digit to be rounded   5 = 5

36,475
↓
36,480

So, the tens digit increases by 1.

Talk About It

▶ Why would the newspaper want to round its circulation to the nearest ten thousand rather than to the nearest thousand?

▶ What happens when you round 18,967 to the nearest hundred?

Check for Understanding

Round to the nearest thousand.

1. 2,816   **2.** 13,465   **3.** 238,716   **4.** 46,528

Round to the nearest hundred.

5. 3,621   **6.** 945   **7.** 20,835   **8.** 175,984

Practice

Round to the nearest ten.

9. 423   **10.** 549   **11.** 495   **12.** 834   **13.** 1,287

Round to the nearest hundred.

14. 874   **15.** 416   **16.** 764   **17.** 4,398   **18.** 1,952

Round to the nearest thousand.

19. 3,267   **20.** 8,090   **21.** 9,900   **22.** 15,123   **23.** 68,500

Round to the nearest ten thousand.

24. 37,205   **25.** 58,936   **26.** 324,520   **27.** 845,625

Round to the nearest hundred thousand.

28. 483,267   **29.** 678,090   **30.** 449,300   **31.** 12,786,500

Round to the nearest million.

32. 35,458,936   **33.** 20,843,267   **34.** 135,984,600

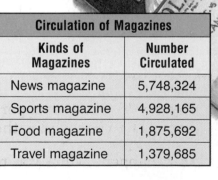

Mixed Applications

Use the table for Exercises 35–36.

35. Which kind of magazine has a circulation of about 5,000,000?

36. Round to the nearest million, and write about how many more news magazines are sold than travel magazines.

37. Number Sense The number 149 is the greatest three-digit number that can be rounded to 100. What is the greatest four-digit number that can be rounded to 1,000?

38. Number Sense The number 50 is the least two-digit number that can be rounded to 100. What is the least three-digit number that can be rounded to 1,000?

Circulation of Magazines	
Kinds of Magazines	Number Circulated
News magazine	5,748,324
Sports magazine	4,928,165
Food magazine	1,875,692
Travel magazine	1,379,685

In what kinds of situations are rounded numbers more useful than exact numbers?

WRAP
UP...

An ecologist has been studying fish near a coral reef. He wants to find out which of four species of fish was most affected by an oil spill. He has a list of the number of fish he observed in the area before and after the oil spill. Which species of fish was most affected by the oil spill?

Information, or **data,** about problems in the environment is often given in the news.

▶ **UNDERSTAND**

What is the problem about?

What does the ecologist want to find out?

▶ **PLAN**

How can the ecologist display his data?

First, he can make a table to organize the data. Then, he can compare the data.

▶ **SOLVE**

How will you carry out the plan?

Make a table of the data; then compare the fish counted before and after the spill.

Live Fish Counted		
Species of Fish	**Before Spill**	**After Spill**
Angelfish	238	58
Clownfish	434	391
Shark	9	9
Squirrel fish	168	159

← Name the table.
← Label the columns.

Fill in the data.

So, the species of fish most affected by the oil spill was the angelfish.

▶ **LOOK BACK**

How does the table help you find the answer?

WHAT IF... ... the ecologist had counted 500 angelfish before the spill? Would he be more worried or less worried about them?

Apply

Make a table and answer the questions.

Cats Are Top Dog

Coretta and her classmates gathered information about pets belonging to students. They found that the kindergarten students had 34 dogs, 41 cats, 23 tropical fish, 8 birds, and 6 hamsters. The first graders had 31 dogs, 27 tropical fish, 8 hamsters, 7 birds, and 38 cats.

A Day at the Beach

Three boys counted shells they saw at the beach. In the morning Bert counted 43 shells, Hank counted 52 shells, and Jerome counted 65 shells. That evening Bert counted 48 shells, Hank counted 37 shells, and Jerome counted 46 shells.

(1) Which kind of pet is owned by the most students?

(2) Which group of students owns more dogs?

(3) Do the first graders own more birds or more hamsters?

(4) Who counted the most shells in the morning?

(5) Did Bert count more shells in the morning or in the evening?

Mixed Applications ➤ **STRATEGIES** • Make a Table • Act It Out • Make a Drawing

Choose a strategy and solve.

Use the following information for Exercises 6–7.

Central School had a reading contest. The students from Room A read 20 books the first week, 35 books the second, and 27 books the third. The students from Room B read 27 books the first week, 30 books the second, and 35 books the third.

(6) Which class read the most books the first week?

(7) Which week did Room A students read more books than Room B students?

(8) Steven, David, Maria, Jon, and Chris sit in the same row in math class. Maria sits in front of Steven, and Jon sits four seats in front of Chris. David sits behind Steven. Who sits directly behind Jon?

(9) Each side of a square patio is 10 feet long. Starting at one corner, there is a plant every 2 feet around the border of the patio. How many plants are around the patio?

Make a table to answer each question.

Remember to name the table, label the columns, and fill in the data.

1. Tommy, Teresa, and David are collecting photos from magazines for a project. Before lunch Tommy found 10 photos, Teresa found 13, and David found 18. After lunch Teresa found 14 photos, Tommy found 12, and David found 8. Who found the most photos?

2. Sheila delivers newspapers on Mondays, Wednesdays, and Fridays. On Monday and Friday mornings, she delivers to 35 homes. On Wednesday mornings, she delivers to 30 homes. On Monday and Wednesday afternoons, she delivers to 25 homes. On which day does Sheila deliver the most papers?

Write two other forms for each number.

3. 18,960

4. 12,000,008

5. 30,000,000 + 80,000 + 4,000 + 50 + 8

6. one hundred fifteen thousand, four hundred eighty-seven

Name the place-value position where the numbers differ.

7. 13,574; 23,574

8. 17,524; 17,324

Write in order from least to greatest.

9. 4,568; 5,658; 5,458; 4,856

10. 1,250,000; 1,050,000; 1,025,000; 1,005,000

Round to the nearest million.

Round to the nearest thousand.

11. 153,849,400

12. 472,135

Round to the nearest ten thousand.

Round to the nearest hundred.

13. 85,473

14. 1,894

Complete.

15. $10 \times \blacksquare \times 10 = 1,000$

16. $10^6 = \blacksquare$

17. $10 \times 10 \times 10 \times 10 = \blacksquare$

18. $100 = 10^{\blacksquare}$

Spotlight ON
PROBLEM SOLVING

Understand
Plan
Solve
Look Back

Draw Conclusions

You can use a table to help you analyze and compare data. You can **draw conclusions** from data that has been collected.

The Cochran School has just finished the renovation of the school library. During the construction, the fifth-grade teachers stored library books in their classrooms. This table shows the number of books they stored.

FIFTH-GRADE TEACHER	NUMBER OF LIBRARY BOOKS STORED
Ms. Grove	1,346
Ms. Beasley	2,100
Ms. Good	1,643
Ms. Diaz	1,895
Ms. McCarty	1,238
Mr. Gordon	1,212
TOTAL	9,434

Apply

1-3. Study the following table. Write three questions that can be answered by using the table, and draw conclusions from the table. Share your questions and conclusions with the class.

Library Videos	
Travel	24
Sports	16
Literature	9
History	18
TOTAL	67

Talk About It

Using the data in the table above, answer the following questions.

- How many fifth-grade teachers stored library books in their classroom?

- Which teacher stored the most library books? the fewest?

- Which two teachers stored about the same number of books?

- There is now shelf space in the library for 15,000 books. About how many new books can the library hold?

- Write your own problem based on the table. Exchange with a partner. Solve.

15

Building Understanding

Decimal numbers can be modeled on decimal squares.

This square represents a whole, or 1.	The whole is divided into 10 equal parts. One part is shaded.	The whole is divided into 100 equal parts. One part is shaded.
Read: one **Write:** 1 or 1.0	**Read:** one tenth **Write:** $\frac{1}{10}$ or 0.1	**Read:** one hundredth **Write:** $\frac{1}{100}$ or 0.01

Decimal numbers can be modeled using money.

dollar (100 cents)	dime (10 cents)	penny (1 cent)

$1.00	$0.10	$0.01

Decimal numbers can be modeled using a meterstick.

meter (100 centimeters)	decimeter (10 centimeters)	centimeter
1.0 meter	0.1 meter	0.01 meter

Talk About It

▶ How is the whole represented in decimal squares, money, and metric units? the tenth? the hundredth?

▶ How many pennies equal a dime? dimes equal a dollar?

▶ How many centimeters equal a decimeter? decimeters equal a meter?

▶ What pattern do you observe in all three models?

Making the Connection

As with whole numbers, decimal numbers can be shown on a place-value chart.

Hundreds	Tens	Ones	.	Tenths	Hundredths	
1	0	0	.			= 100
	1	0	.			= 10
		1	.			= 1
		0	.	1		= 0.1 or $\frac{1}{10}$
		0	.	0	1	= 0.01 or $\frac{1}{100}$

↑ decimal point

Talk About It

▶ What is the purpose of the decimal point?

▶ Is 0.01 greater than or less than 0.1? Explain.

▶ Is 0.1 greater than or less than 1? Explain.

▶ What happens to the value of the 1 as it moves to the right on the place-value chart?

Checking Understanding

Write the amount as a decimal form of the whole unit.

1. 3 dimes
2. 3 decimeters
3. 3 tenths
4. 7 pennies
5. 7 centimeters
6. 7 hundredths

Complete.

7. 10 cents = ▨
8. 1 penny = ▨
9. ▨ = 100 pennies
10. 1 decimeter = ▨ meter
11. ▨ dimes = 1 dollar
12. 1 meter = ▨ centimeters
13. 1 dime = ▨ pennies
14. 1 dollar = ▨ pennies
15. 1 centimeter = ▨ meter

Use a calculator. Write in order the keys you can use to change the given numbers.

16. 6.78 to 6.08
17. 12.06 to 12.46

Decimals are used to name parts of a whole. You can use base-ten blocks to help you read and write decimals for 10 or 100 equal parts of a whole.

Tens	Ones	Tenths	Hundredths

cube	flat	long	unit
ten 10.0	one 1.0	one tenth 0.1	one hundredth 0.01

If you let the flat represent 1, you can make this chart.

You can use a place-value chart to find the value of each digit.

Tens	Ones	Tenths	Hundredths
3	4 .	6	5
			5 × 0.01 5 hundredths = 0.05
		6 × 0.1 6 tenths = 0.6	
	4 × 1 = 4.0 4 ones = 4.0		
3 × 10 = 30.0 3 tens = 30.0			

Standard Form: 34.65
Expanded Form: 30 + 4 + 0.6 + 0.05 = 34.65
Word Form: thirty-four and sixty-five hundredths

- How does a calculator display four tenths? fifty-two hundredths?

- Why do you use the word *and* to name the decimal point?

Check for Understanding

Write the decimal number.

1.   2.   3.

Write the value of each underlined digit.

4. 0.<u>2</u>   5. <u>1</u>8.37   6. 0.7<u>8</u>   7. 41.<u>0</u>3   8. <u>1</u>00.05

Monica Earp
Math pg 18-19 (1-29) Mixed review
9-22-97

① 0.27
② $0.15
③ 0.3
④ 0.06
⑤ 7.01

⑩ 8 longs, 2 units
⑪ 2 hundreds, 9 longs
⑫ 3 hundreds, 7 longs, 5 units
⑬ 0.3
⑭ fifteen hundredths

① 2.3
② 0.54
③ 1.07
④ 2 tenths
⑤ 10
⑥ 8 hundredths
⑦ one
⑧ hundred
⑨ 7 longs

Practice

Draw the base-ten blocks used to show each decimal number.

9. 0.7   **10.** 0.82   **11.** 2.9   **12.** 3.75

Copy and complete the table.

	Word Form	Decimal Form
13.	three tenths	▩
14.	?	0.15
15.	?	0.07
16.	four and nine tenths	▩
17.	?	82.49
18.	thirty hundredths	▩

$5.20

$0.50 $2.95

Look at the pictures to solve Exercises 19–20.

19. The price of which item has the digit 5 in the hundredths place?

20. The price of which item has the digit 2 in the tenths place?

Mixed Applications

21. Paper speeds through a printing press at a rate of three-tenths kilometer per minute. If a new printing press could print one-tenth kilometer more paper per minute, what would the new rate be?

22. What is the number that has the digit 8 in the hundredths place and the digit 6 in the ones and tenths places? Write this number in decimal form and in word form.

MIXED REVIEW

Write <, >, or = for ●.

1. 57 ● 65   **2.** 760 ● 758   **3.** 4,500 ● 4,500   **4.** 12,432 ● 10,891   **5.** 9,280 ● 19,280

Round to the nearest ten thousand.

6. 57,416   **7.** 82,620   **8.** 128,307   **9.** 923,415

How are decimals like fractions?

WRAP UP...

DECIMALS
Thousandths

This computer screen is made up of 1,000 small squares. What part of the screen is one square?

Word Form: one thousandth

Decimal Form: 0.001

There are 12 squares shaded in blue. What part of the screen are the 12 squares?

Word Form: twelve thousandths

Decimal Form: 0.012

There are 135 squares shaded in red. How much of the whole screen are the 135 squares?

Word Form: one hundred thirty-five thousandths

Decimal Form: 0.135

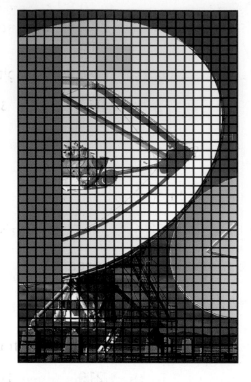

You can use the place-value chart to write 6.327 in expanded form.

Ones	Tenths	Hundredths	Thousandths
6	3	2	7
			7 × 0.001 7 thousandths = 0.007
		2 × 0.01 2 hundredths = 0.02	
	3 × 0.1 3 tenths = 0.3		
6 × 1 6 ones = 6.0			

Expanded Form: 6 + 0.3 + 0.02 + 0.007 = 6.327

Word Form: six and three hundred twenty-seven thousandths

Talk About It

▶ For numbers less than one, what does the zero written before the decimal point mean?

▶ How many times greater is hundredths than thousandths?

Check for Understanding

Write two other forms for each number.

1. fifty-three
thousandths

2. two and four
thousandths

3. four hundred
seventeen thousandths

Write the value of each underlined digit.

4. 6.4<u>5</u>9

5. 0.9<u>5</u>2

6. 1.48<u>6</u>

7. 0.<u>1</u>25

8. 6.05<u>8</u>

Practice

Write in standard form.

9. five hundred sixteen thousandths

10. two hundred thirty-one thousandths

11. seven and four hundredths

12. five and five thousandths

13. six and fifteen hundredths

14. nine thousandths

Write the place-value position of each underlined digit.

15. 0.3<u>1</u>

16. 1.2<u>1</u>9

17. 0.4<u>7</u>

18. 0.74<u>8</u>

19. 5.<u>1</u>06

20. <u>5</u>.608

21. 3.40<u>9</u>

22. 0.00<u>7</u>

23. 9.<u>7</u>83

24. <u>4</u>.859

Mixed Applications

Use the standard form for Exercises 25–26.

25. A record store sold 1,000 tapes one week. Of that number, 85 were country music tapes and 13 were classical music tapes. What part of the total sales were country music tapes and what part were classical music tapes?

26. One thousand people were asked to name their favorite radio station. The most popular station had 535 votes. What part of the people surveyed did not name the most popular station?

What would have to happen to the hundredths block to show thousandths?

PLACE VALUE
from Thousands to Thousandths

It was reported in the news that a new passenger jet reached a speed of 2,494.348 kilometers per hour.

You can use a place-value chart to show the value of each digit in 2,494.348. The value of each place-value position in a decimal is 10 times greater than the value of the place to its right.

Thousands	Hundreds	Tens	Ones	Tenths	Hundredths	Thousandths
1 × 1,000	1 × 100	1 × 10	1 × 1	1 × 0.1	1 × 0.01	1 × 0.001
2	4	9	4	3	4	8

Standard Form: 2,494.348

Expanded Form: 2,000 + 400 + 90 + 4 + 0.3 + 0.04 + 0.008

Word Form: two thousand, four hundred ninety-four *and* three hundred forty-eight thousandths

The whole-number part of the number is 2,494. The decimal part is 0.348. A decimal point separates the whole-number part from the decimal part, or the part less than 1.

Talk About It

Look at this number.   6,425.421

▶ Write the value of the digit 2 in both place-value positions. Explain how they are different.

▶ How many times greater is 4 hundreds than 4 tenths? Explain.

Check for Understanding

Use the number 3,910.246 for Exercises 1–4.

1. Write the value of the digit 9.

2. Write the word form of the number.

3. Name the place-value position of the zero.

4. What place-value position is 10 times greater than tens?

Practice

Write in standard form.

5. five thousand, one hundred forty-two and ninety-one hundredths

6. eighty-two and three hundred seven thousandths

7. six thousand and seven hundredths

8. one thousand, two hundred and two hundred fifteen thousandths

Write the place-value position of each underlined digit.

9. 36.4<u>7</u>

10. 98.30<u>2</u>

11. 103.<u>5</u>

12. <u>9</u>,008.409

13. <u>2</u>5.43

14. <u>7</u>40.56

Write the value of the digit 4 in each number.

15. 46.39

16. 506.402

17. 358.047

18. 4.906

19. 428.72

20. 4,013.8

Mixed Applications

21. Jan lives 35.6 miles from the radio station. Raul lives one-tenth mile farther away. How far does Raul live from the radio station?

22. A radio commercial is timed at 15.2 seconds. Another commercial is two-tenths second longer. How long is this commercial?

23. Write a decimal number using the digits 9, 8, 7, 6, 5, and 4. It must have a 9 in the tenths place, 6 ones, 8 tens, and 7 hundreds. The digit 4 is a whole number. The number is less than 5,000.

24. What number has a 9 in the thousands and thousandths places, a 7 in the hundreds and hundredths places, a 5 in the tens and tenths places, and a 3 in the ones place?

PATTERNS AND RELATIONSHIPS

Write the next three numbers for each pattern.

25. 0.2, 0.4, 0.6, ▓, ▓, ▓

26. 0.03, 0.06, 0.09, ▓, ▓, ▓

27. 0.25, 0.20, 0.15, ▓, ▓, ▓

28. 0.498, 0.499, 0.500, ▓, ▓, ▓

How can you compare the thousands place to the thousandths place?

WRAP UP...

COMPARING AND ORDERING
Decimals

Suppose you turn on the radio with the dial set at FM 102.0. Which station is closer to the 102.0 setting, 101.1 or 101.9?

You can use a number line to compare decimals.

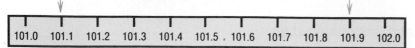

| 101.0 | 101.1 | 101.2 | 101.3 | 101.4 | 101.5 | 101.6 | 101.7 | 101.8 | 101.9 | 102.0 |

The number 101.9 is to the right of 101.1. This means 101.9 is greater than 101.1. So, 101.9 is closer to 102.0.

Compare 2.135 and 2.137.

Step 1	Step 2	Step 3	Step 4
Compare the ones.	Compare the tenths.	Compare the hundredths.	Compare the thousandths.
2.135 ↓ 2.137 same number of ones	2.135 ↓ 2.137 same number of tenths	2.135 ↓ 2.137 same number of hundredths	2.135 ↓ 2.137 $5 < 7$

So, $2.135 < 2.137$.

You can order decimals by comparing them in the same way. Order from least to greatest. 5.46, 5.39, 5.20

Step 1	Step 2	Step 3	Step 4
Compare the ones.	Compare the tenths.	Order the digits.	Order the numbers.
5.46 ↓ 5.39 same number of ones ↓ 5.20	5.46 ↓ 5.39 ↓ 5.20	$2 < 3 < 4$	5.20 5.39 5.46

• Order the numbers from greatest to least.

Check for Understanding

Name the place-value position where the numbers differ.

1. 1.26; 1.06
2. 12.14; 12.41
3. 129.023; 129.025

Order from greatest to least.

4. 2.09, 2.01, 2.15
5. 57.18, 56.99, 57.81, 57.80
6. 97.62, 97.26, 99.78, 100.26

Connection, pages 462–463

Practice

Write <, >, or = for ●.

7. 36.49 ● 36.46

8. 742.45 ● 742.54

9. 1.02 ● 1.020

10. 0.610 ● 0.600

11. 0.080 ● 0.008

12. 0.73 ● 0.70

13. 0.05 ● 0.50

14. 35.350 ● 35.35

15. 438.563 ● 438.536

Order from least to greatest.

16. 3.26, 3.19, 3.07, 3.70

17. 9.345, 93.450, 9.354, 93.540

18. 24.051, 42.015, 24.060, 24.560

19. 396.78, 39.78, 39.87, 396.87

Order from greatest to least.

20. 12.50, 12.40, 12.54, 12.45

21. 0.70, 0.77, 7.70, 7.07

22. 32.050, 32.150, 32.155, 32.515

23. 234.627, 243.625, 243.007, 234.067

In which number of each pair does the digit 6 have the greater value?

24. 26.7 or 62.7

25. 208.6 or 218.16

26. 5.06 or 5.65

27. 3.136 or 0.06

28. 6.02 or 0.16

29. 16.15 or 162.7

30. 51.6 or 37.26

31. 23.96 or 5.306

Mixed Applications

Use the table for Exercises 32–33.

32. According to the radio store's price list, which radios cost less than $9.00?

33. Which radio costs more than the portable radio but less than the clock radio?

34. Jim's favorite radio station is between 105.5 and 106.0. What is a good estimate for the station number?

Radio Store Price List	
Portable radio	$8.99
Radio headset	$9.05
AM radio	$8.89
Clock radio	$9.98

105.0	105.5		106.0

How is comparing and ordering decimal fractions like comparing and ordering whole numbers?

WRAP UP...

ESTIMATE
by Rounding Decimals

Newspaper ads can vary in size from less than 2.5 centimeters in length to a full page. Suppose Sally wants to place three ads at the lengths given in the table. Estimate each length to the nearest centimeter.

Newspaper Ads	
Display Ad	Length (in cm)
Car	12.3
Grocery	12.5
Tire	12.7

A number line can help you estimate decimals by rounding to the nearest whole number.

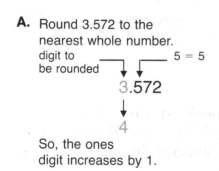

```
  12              Car    Grocery   Tire        13
◄──┼───┼───┼───┼───┼───┼───┼───┼───┼───┼──►
  12.0 12.1 12.2 12.3 12.4 12.5 12.6 12.7 12.8 12.9 13.0
```

Car ad: 12.3 is closer to 12, so it is rounded to 12 centimeters.
Grocery ad: 12.5 is halfway between 12 and 13, so it is rounded to the next larger number, or 13 centimeters.
Tire ad: 12.7 is closer to 13, so it is rounded to 13 centimeters.

You can use the rules for rounding whole numbers to round decimals.

Examples

A. Round 3.572 to the nearest whole number.

digit to be rounded ⟶ 3.572   5 = 5

↓

4

So, the ones digit increases by 1.

B. Round 3.572 to the nearest tenth.

digit to be rounded ⟶ 3.572   7 > 5

↓

3.6

So, the tenths digit increases by 1.

C. Round 3.572 to the nearest hundredth.

digit to be rounded ⟶ 3.572   2 < 5

↓

3.57

So, the hundredths digit remains the same.

Talk About It

▶ Why are the digits to the right of the rounding place dropped?

▶ The price of gasoline at a pump may appear as $1.239. Why is the total amount rounded to the nearest cent?

Check for Understanding

Round to the nearest whole number.

1. 18.4   **2.** 26.3   **3.** 3.9   **4.** 7.05

Round to the nearest tenth and the nearest hundredth.

5. 5.387   **6.** 14.876   **7.** 1.072   **8.** 29.708

Practice

Round to the nearest tenth.

9. 84.07 **10.** 89.93 **11.** 0.98 **12.** 0.32

13. 103.506 **14.** 165.094 **15.** 2,045.055 **16.** 1,390.039

Round to the nearest hundredth.

17. 0.934 **18.** 7.783 **19.** 37.839 **20.** 45.005

21. 0.014 **22.** 0.996 **23.** 93.097 **24.** 198.894

Round to the nearest dollar.

25. $2.93 **26.** $11.67 **27.** $0.98

28. $4.02 **29.** $32.39 **30.** $199.49

Round to the nearest whole number.

31. 3.75 **32.** 87.42 **33.** 18.9

34. 42.09 **35.** 100.54 **36.** 99.99

Mixed Applications

37. Number Sense Write a number that can be rounded to 0.65 using the digits 4, 6, and 8.

38. Number Sense If a number is rounded to 5.55, what digits could be in the thousandths place in 5.54▪?

MIXED REVIEW

Write <, >, or = for ●.

1. 0.20 ● 0.02 **2.** 4.238 ● 4.230 **3.** 12.85 ● 12.85 **4.** 5.2 ● 8.5

Write the word name for each decimal number.

5. 0.045 **6.** 0.98 **7.** 1.123 **8.** 205.106

What place-value position do you look at when you want to round to the nearest dollar? the nearest dime?

W R A P
U P . . .

PROBLEM *Solving*

As an editor for her school newspaper, Suzanne needs to purchase some writing supplies. She selects 2 pens for $1.15 each and a writing pad for $1.35. How much will she spend?

Making a diagram or drawing can help you solve some problems.

▶ **UNDERSTAND**

What are you asked to find?

What facts are given?

▶ **PLAN**

What strategy can Suzanne try?

She can draw coins and bills to represent the amount of money she will spend.

▶ **SOLVE**

Which coins and bills can Suzanne draw to find the solution?

Pens =

How can she use these drawings to find the solution? She can count $1.00, $2.00, $3.00, $3.25, $3.35, $3.45, $3.55, $3.60, $3.65.

Writing Pad =

So, Suzanne will spend $3.65 for her supplies.

▶ **LOOK BACK**

What other strategy can she use to help her find the solution?

WHAT IF... ... the pens cost $0.85 each and the writing pad costs $0.75? Which coins could Suzanne draw to find the solution?

Apply

Solve. Make a drawing or diagram.

1. School newspapers were sold for $0.25 each. If Vince collected 7 quarters, 4 dimes, and 2 nickels from his class, what is the total amount of money he collected?

2. The school reporter wanted to list the starting lineup of five swimmers. She remembered that Kim was in the first lane. If Jane was between Mary and Renee, and Mary was next to Kim, in which lane was Carol?

Mixed Applications ➤ **STRATEGIES** • Make a Table • Act It Out • Make a Drawing

Choose a strategy and solve.

Use the following information to solve Exercises 3–4.

Suzanne is reporting the scores from the gymnastics competition. She knows the Longwood team had a total score of 38.275 on the vault and 42.750 on the floor exercise. Westridge had a total team score of 38.450 on the vault and 42.655 on the floor exercise.

3. Which team had a higher total score for the floor exercise?

4. Which team scored higher than 38.30 on the vault?

Use the following information to solve Exercises 5–6.

It was reported that one gymnast scored 7.90 on the vault. A second gymnast scored 0.50 of a point higher. A third gymnast scored 0.20 of a point higher than the second.

5. What was the highest score for the vault?

6. Suppose another gymnast scored 0.05 of a point higher than the first. What would that gymnast's score be?

WRITER'S CORNER

7. Choose any two decimal numbers to represent scores in a school event. Write a short article for your school newspaper comparing these two numbers.

Vocabulary Check

Choose a word or words from the box to complete each sentence.

> data
> decimal
> expanded form
> exponents
> million
> number line
> period
> rounded
> standard form
> thousandths

If you do not remember a definition, look at the page listed in the chapter.

1. You can use __?__ to express numbers as powers of ten.
   (page 3)

2. The usual way of writing a number is called the __?__.
   (page 4)

3. The number 200,000 + 30,000 + 100 + 60 + 9 is written in __?__. *(page 4)*

4. Each group of three digits in the number 738,109,869 is called a(n) __?__. *(page 6)*

5. The value of the 9 in the number 9,480,321 is nine __?__.
   (page 6)

6. A __?__ can be used to help you round numbers. *(pages 10, 26)*

7. The number 23,492 can be __?__ to 23,500. *(page 10)*

8. Another name for information is __?__. *(page 12)*

9. Seven tenths can be written in __?__ form as 0.7. *(page 16)*

10. The value of the 6 in the number 4,325.026 is six __?__.
    (page 20)

Concept Check

Write in standard form. *(pages 4, 18)*

11. five thousand, six hundred twelve

12. fourteen and thirty-two hundredths

Complete. *(page 16)*

13. 20 cents = ■

14. 2 meters = ■ centimeters

Write the value of each underlined digit. *(pages 4, 6, 18)*

15. 75<u>5</u>,096

16. 90.7<u>5</u>

17. <u>2</u>,800,750

18. 4,638.4<u>5</u>

Complete. *(page 3)*

19. $100 = 10 \times 10 = 10^{\blacksquare}$

20. $10^3 = 10 \times 10 \times 10 = \blacksquare$

Skill Check

Use commas to separate periods. *(page 6)*

21. 18346

22. 609352

23. 4258691

24. 97459132

Write <, >, or = for ●. *(pages 8, 24)*

25. 4,586 ● 5,311

26. 89,247 ● 9,246

27. 456,000 ● 456,000

28. 0.6 ● 0.6

29. 31.021 ● 3.102

30. 0.37 ● 0.73

Write in order from least to greatest. *(pages 8, 24)*

31. 2,415; 2,400; 2,410

32. 6,070; 15,707; 6,000; 15,600

33. 0.123, 1.23, 0.12, 1.234

34. 14.6, 14.060, 14.63, 14.36

Round to the nearest ten thousand. *(page 10)*

35. 43,927

36. 839,124

37. 1,653,109

38. 1,075,400

Round to the nearest tenth and hundredth. *(page 26)*

39. 0.937

40. 6.921

41. 9.546

42. 0.899

Problem-Solving Check

Solve. *(pages 12, 28)*

43. A farmer has 28 meters of fence. He wants to enclose a rectangular piece of land that is 8 meters long and 6 meters wide. If fence posts are placed 4 meters apart on the long side and 3 meters apart on the short side, how many posts will he need?

44. Last month our veterinarian treated 112 dogs, 75 cats, and 15 hamsters. This month she treated 76 dogs, 89 cats, and 2 hamsters. Make a table for the set of data. Which kind of animal did she treat the most often during the past two months?

45. Chang asked 20 fourth graders and 20 fifth graders about their favorite fruits. Of the fourth graders, 9 chose apples, 5 chose pears, and 6 chose oranges. Of the fifth graders, 13 chose apples, 4 chose pears, and 3 chose oranges. Which fruits did more fourth graders than fifth graders like?

46. Mike's goal was to run the 200-meter race in less than one minute. The first day he recorded his time as 60.12 seconds. The next day his time was 0.05 second faster. The third day his time was 0.08 second faster than the second day. Did Mike reach his goal? (HINT: When he runs faster, he takes less time.)

CHAPTER TEST

Write two other forms for each number.

1. 10,000 + 8,000 + 900 + 60

2. 270,404

3. three hundred sixty-one million, four hundred thousand, twenty

In standard form use a comma to separate the periods.

Write in word form.

4. 0.3

5. 0.157

Write in standard form.

6. thirty hundredths

7. four and nine tenths

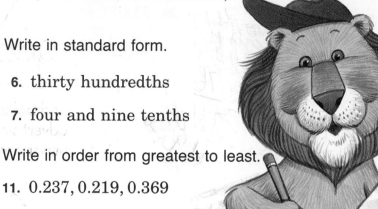

Write <, >, or = for ●.

8. 1,575 ● 1,575

9. 137,632 ● 157,676

10. 7.542 ● 7.531

Write in order from greatest to least.

11. 0.237, 0.219, 0.369

12. 4.132, 10.278, 5.238

13. 15.42, 14.42, 15.24

Round to the nearest tenth.

14. 0.254

Round to the nearest hundredth.

15. 0.279

Round to the nearest thousand.

16. 3,742

Round to the nearest whole number.

17. 87.42

Complete.

18. ■ $= 10 \times 10 = 10^2$

19. $1,000 = 10 \times 10 \times$ ■

20. $10,000 = 10$■

Write the amount as a decimal form of the whole unit.

21. 1 penny = ■ dollar

22. 1 decimeter = ■ meter

23. 7 hundredths = ■

Make a diagram to solve.

24. Mrs. Romero needs a fence around a square garden. It must be 10 meters on each side. If she places a fence post every 2 meters, how many posts will she need?

Make a table and solve.

25. Before lunch Devon found 47 rocks, Eli found 42 rocks, and Mark found 53 rocks. After lunch Devon and Mark each found 12 more. Eli found 15 more. Who found the most rocks?

Make an Advertisement for a Product

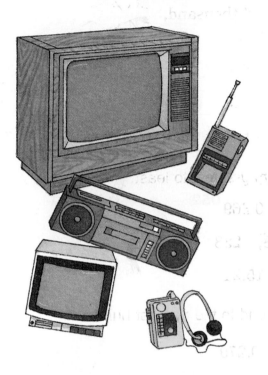

A high fee paid for a 30-second television commercial was $1,500,000. Costs of advertising vary a great deal depending on the product being advertised and the media used. With your teammates, research and analyze data about various advertising media. Decide what product you want to advertise and which media would be best to use.

Decide Talk about how you can use an encyclopedia and books from the library to compare advertising costs for television, radio, and newspapers.

Do Work with your teammates. Use a reference book to find costs for a 30-second radio commercial, a 30-second television commercial, and a 1-page newspaper display advertisement. You may wish to call a local television station, radio station, or newspaper for the information. Record the information in a table.

Share Show your table. Describe the difference in cost of using different media for advertising.

TALK ABOUT IT

a. How can you use your table to compare the cost of advertising in a magazine?

b. Describe everyday situations in which whole numbers and decimals are used to compare.

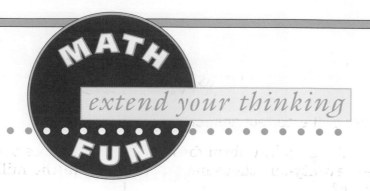

extend your thinking

Activity

CREATE A NUMBER

1. You can write 6 three-digit numbers using these 3 digits.

7 8 9

Two of the numbers are 789 and 798. Write the other 4 numbers.

2. You can write 18 three-digit numbers using these 3 digits and a decimal point.

7 8 9

Three of the numbers are 7.89, 78.9, and 789. Write the other 15 numbers.

3. You can write 24 four-digit numbers using these 4 digits.

6 7 8 9

Write the numbers.

4. Write as many four-digit numbers as you can using these 4 digits and a decimal point.

6 7 8 9

Challenge

Number Sense

Look at the underlined digit in each number. Decide which digit has greater value.

1. 76.052 or 34.652
2. 3.985 or 3.589
3. 45.783 or 67.834

Challenge

Calculator

Write a number to tell how many times greater the first number is than the second number.

1. 70 and 0.007
2. 5,000 and 0.05
3. 300 and 0.3

CUMULATIVE REVIEW

CHAPTER 1

Write the letter of the correct answer.

1. Which is the standard form for two hundred seventy-one thousand, sixty-three?

A. 271,063   **B.** 271,630
C. 271,063,000   **D.** not here

2. Choose the number with the digit 6 in the millions place.

A. 705,643,218   **B.** 706,143,852
C. 715,362,084   **D.** 715,430,426

3. What is the standard form for $400,000 + 7,000 + 100 + 90 + 2$?

A. 407,129   **B.** 407,192
C. 470,192   **D.** 4,700,192

4. Which is the standard form for one hundred forty-six thousandths?

A. 0.0146   **B.** 0.146
C. 1.46   **D.** not here

5. Write the value of the underlined digit in the number 631.54<u>8</u>.

A. 0.008   **B.** 0.08
C. 0.8   **D.** 8

6. What is 0.23 in word form?

A. twenty-three thousandths
B. two and three tenths
C. twenty-three hundred
D. not here

7. Which number is greater than 0.75?

A. 0.079   **B.** 0.725
C. 0.749   **D** 0.76

8. Which is true?

A. $6,114 = 6,124$ **B.** $6,114 > 6,124$
C. $6,354 < 4,536$ **D.** $6,354 > 4,536$

9. Order the numbers from greatest to least.

A. 61.25; 62.21; 61.52
B. 61.25; 61.52; 62.21
C. 61.52; 62.21; 61.25
D. 62.21; 61.52; 61.25

10. Round 613.89 to the nearest whole number.

A. 600.00   **B.** 610.00
C. 613.00   **D.** 614.00

11. $10^3 = \blacksquare$

A. 10×10 **B.** 100
C. 1,000   **D.** not here

12. 5 pennies $= \blacksquare$

A. $0.005   **B.** $0.05
C. $0.50   **D.** $5.00

13. Jeff ran a race in 61.32 seconds on Monday, in 61.25 seconds on Tuesday, and in 62.21 seconds on Wednesday. On what day did he run the fastest?

A. Monday   **B.** Tuesday
C. Wednesday   **D.** Thursday

14. Mr. Jones wants to enclose a square piece of land that is 6 meters on each side. If the fence posts are 3 meters apart, how many posts will there be?

A. 4 posts   **B.** 8 posts
C. 10 posts   **D.** 12 posts

ADDING AND SUBTRACTING
WHOLE NUMBERS AND DECIMALS

Did you know ...

... that the Olympic athletes of Greece are first to march into the opening ceremonies, in honor of the original Olympics held in ancient Greece?

Suppose the seating capacity of an arena for an event is 15,400 seats. On Monday 8,250 tickets were sold, and on Tuesday 5,690 tickets were sold. How can you find the number of tickets that are still available?

OF THE XXIVTH OLYMPIAD SEOUL 1988

CONNECTING ADDITION AND SUBTRACTION

Chris scored 26 points in the first half of the basketball game and 38 points in the whole game. How many points did she score in the second half?

The problem can be solved by finding the missing addend.

points scored in first half		points scored in second half		total points scored
26	+	▪	=	38
26	+	12	=	38

Or, you can use this subtraction sentence.

total points scored		points scored in first half		points scored in second half
38	−	26	=	▪
38	−	26	=	12

So, Chris scored 12 points in the second half.

Addition and subtraction are **inverse** operations. This means that one operation undoes the other operation.

You can see this in the diagram.

$$38 - 26 = 12 \qquad 12 + 26 = 38$$

The inverse relationship allows you to check an addition computation by using subtraction and to check subtraction by using addition.

Problem	Check	Problem	Check
13	27	754	253
+14	−14	−501	+501
27	13	253	754

• Opening a door is the inverse of closing a door. What other inverse actions can you name?

Check for Understanding

Complete.

1. Write a missing-addend sentence for $38 - 19 = $ ▪.

2. Write a subtraction sentence for $52 + $ ▪ $ = 83$.

Solve. Use the inverse operation to check each number sentence.

3. $56 - 15 = $ ▪

4. $89 = 32 + $ ▪

5. $76 + $ ▪ $ = 189$

6. $134 - 38 = $ ▪

Practice

Write a missing-addend sentence for each.

7. $42 - 12 = $

8. $25 - 16 = $

9. $78 - 14 = $

10. $85 - 56 = $

11. $145 - 97 = $

12. $158 - 95 = $

Write a subtraction sentence for each.

13. $18 + \blacksquare = 74$

14. $32 + \blacksquare = 98$

15. $\blacksquare + 45 = 90$

16. $\blacksquare + 58 = 123$

17. $49 + \blacksquare = 154$

18. $142 + \blacksquare = 174$

Write the inverse operation sentence for each. Solve.

19. $18 + \blacksquare = 78$

20. $\blacksquare + 42 = 98$

21. $146 = 32 + \blacksquare$

Mixed Applications

22. The soccer team plays 14 games each season. They have already played 3 games. How many more games will they play this season? Write a missing-addend sentence and solve.

23. Write at least three number sentences using only the numbers 13, 15, and 28. Are any two of these sentences inverse operation sentences? Explain.

Use the table for Exercises 24–25.

Soccer Team Records			
School	Wins	Losses	Total Games
Westwood Elementary	6	$\blacksquare$	8
Lake Silver Elementary	7	$\blacksquare$	8
Princeton Elementary	$\blacksquare$	5	8

24. Write a missing-addend sentence for each team's record. Solve.

25. **Make Up a Problem** Use the table to write a word problem. Solve.

How would you enter this number sentence in a calculator? $\blacksquare + 49 = 83$

WRAP UP...

Jose collects baseball cards for four teams. He has 42 Astros cards, 86 Cubs cards, 13 Giants cards, and 61 Dodgers cards. About how many baseball cards does Jose have in his collection?

When an exact answer is not needed, you can estimate.

You can use **front-end estimation** to find an estimate.

$$\begin{array}{r} 4\,2 \\ 8\,6 \\ 1\,3 \\ +\ 6\,1 \\ \hline 19\ \blacksquare \end{array}$$

Add the lead, or front-end, digits in the group of numbers.

So, Jose has about 190 baseball cards in his collection.

- When you add only the front-end digits, is your estimate greater or less than the sum?

- How would a rounded estimate differ from your front-end estimate?

Another way to estimate is by using **compatible numbers.** These numbers are easy to compute mentally.

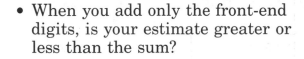

$$\begin{array}{r} 42 \\ 86 \\ 13 \\ +61 \end{array}$$

$$42 + 61 \approx 100$$
$$86 + 13 \approx \underline{+100}$$
$$200$$

$\approx$ is the symbol for "is approximately equal to."

So, $42 + 86 + 13 + 61 \approx 200$.

So, another estimate is about 200 baseball cards.

- Why is the estimate using compatible numbers different from the estimate with front-end digits?

Check for Understanding

Estimate each sum with a method you choose.

1.	2.	3.	4.	5.
89	15	52	116	103
12	34	18	110	268
72	22	77	133	214
+ 26	+ 26	+ 49	+ 142	+ 327

Practice

Estimate each sum. Tell which method you used.

6. 68
  +19

7. 24
  +62

8. 403
  +113

9. 613
  +294

10. 8,013
  + 956

11. 52
  89
  46
  +12

12. 18
  43
  59
  +75

13. 205
  122
  540
  +616

14. 349
  728
  634
  +426

15. 114
  219
  205
  +410

16. $431 + 625 \approx$

17. $3,091 + 515 + 2,125 \approx$

18. $8,975 + 9,607 + 9,830 \approx$

Mixed Applications

Use the table for Exercises 19–21.

19. In Weeks 3 and 4, it was estimated that 1,200 tickets were sold. What estimation method was used?

20. About how many tickets were sold in the first two weeks?

Baseball Ticket Sales	Week 1	Week 2	Week 3	Week 4	Week 5
	327	412	629	685	879

21. **Number Sense • Estimation** How can you use compatible numbers to find the ticket sales for all five weeks?

NUMBER SENSE • ESTIMATION

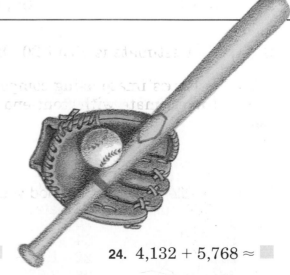

You can estimate by **finding a range**.

845 845 is between 800 and 900.
+683 683 is between 600 and 700.

Round low.	Round high.
800	900
+ 600	+ 700
1,400	1,600

The range is 1,400 to 1,600.

Find a range for each.

22. $635 + 473 \approx$

23. $987 + 269 \approx$

24. $4,132 + 5,768 \approx$

Why is it important to estimate in more than one way?

WRAP UP...

ADDING
Whole Numbers

Astro Airlines flew 5,368 passengers to the Olympic Games in 1984. In 1988 the airline flew 3,425 passengers to the Olympics. How many people flew to the Olympics on Astro Airlines?

$$\begin{array}{r} 1 \\ 5{,}368 \\ +3{,}425 \\ \hline 8{,}793 \end{array}$$

Regroup 13 ones as 1 ten 3 ones.

So, 8,793 people flew to the Olympics on Astro Airlines.

More Examples

A. 845 + 796 + 897 = ■

$$\begin{array}{r} 21 \\ 845 \\ 796 \\ +\ \ 897 \\ \hline 2{,}538 \end{array}$$

B. 46 + 213 + 1,508 = ■

$$\begin{array}{r} 1 \\ 46 \\ 213 \\ +1{,}508 \\ \hline 1{,}767 \end{array}$$

Line up the addends so that digits of the same place value are in the same column.

Another Method

Use estimation and a calculator to add large numbers. Choose an estimation strategy.

$$\begin{array}{r} 52{,}738 \rightarrow \ \ 50{,}000 \\ +34{,}214 \rightarrow +30{,}000 \\ \hline \text{about} \ \ 80{,}000 \end{array}$$

You can use a calculator to find the sum.

5 2 7 3 8 + 3 4 2 1 4 =   86952.

Since 86,952 is close to the estimate of 80,000, the sum is reasonable.

Check for Understanding

Estimate the sum. If the estimated sum is greater than 5,000, find the sum.

1. $\begin{array}{r} 916 \\ +584 \\ \hline \end{array}$

2. $\begin{array}{r} 1{,}439 \\ +2{,}678 \\ \hline \end{array}$

3. $\begin{array}{r} 11{,}507 \\ +18{,}468 \\ \hline \end{array}$

4. $\begin{array}{r} 52{,}708 \\ +43{,}695 \\ \hline \end{array}$

Practice

Estimate the sum. If the estimated sum is greater than 10,000, find the sum.

5. 235
    + 742

6. 404
    + 91

7. 7,303
    + 2,143

8. 5,127
    + 795

9. 9,478
    + 2,603

10. 24,305
    + 15,594

11. 37,498
    + 61,537

12. 72,830
    + 4,786

13. 40,340
    + 39,689

14. 92,216
    + 11,595

15. 213
    341
    + 724

16. 321
    196
    + 254

17. 310
    236
    + 134

18. 5,207
    3,584
    + 2,671

19. 9,726
    5,403
    + 25,312

Complete the table.

Number Sentence	Estimate	Sum
3,583 + 8,312 =	20.	21.
4,034 + 968 =	22.	23.
3,078 + 11,935 =	24.	25.
11,224 + 30,867 =	26.	27.

Mixed Applications

28. Jimmy and his family drove their car from their home in Utah to the Winter Olympics in Calgary, Alberta. On Monday they drove 219 miles in the morning and 182 miles in the afternoon. On Tuesday they drove 245 miles in the morning and 167 miles in the afternoon. On which day did they drive farther?

29. The Dutch team skated 134 laps the first day of practice, 167 laps the second day, and 241 laps the third day. The Swiss team skated 251 laps the first day, 142 laps the second day, and 121 laps the third day. Which team skated more laps?

Look at Exercise 16. Estimate with front-end digits and by rounding. Which estimate is closer to the sum?

The track coach has 36 students try out for her team, and the swimming coach has 14. The softball coach has 15 more students try out than the swimming coach. If no student is on more than one team, how many students try out in all?

Writing a number sentence may help you solve problems. A number sentence can show how the facts in the problem are related.

▶ UNDERSTAND

What are you asked to find?

What facts are given?

▶ PLAN

What strategy can you use?

You can write a number sentence, using n for the number of students who try out in all.

▶ SOLVE

What number sentence can you write?

track tryouts		swimming tryouts		softball tryouts		all tryouts
36	+	14	+	(14 + 15)	=	n
↓		↓		↓		↓
36	+	14	+	29	=	79

So, a total of 79 students try out in all.

▶ LOOK BACK

Estimate the sum. How can you use your estimate to check the reasonableness of your answer?

How can you check your addition?

WHAT IF... ... the track coach has 52 students try out? What number sentence can you write to find how many more students try out for track than for softball?

Apply

Write a number sentence and solve.

1 At swim practice on Monday, Alicia swam 47 laps, Nora swam 62 laps, and Lily swam 10 laps more than Alicia. How many laps did the three girls swim?

2 Brian wants 2 pairs of track shoes that cost $35 a pair. He has a coupon for $10 off the price of one pair. What price will Brian pay for both pairs of shoes?

Mixed Applications ➤ **STRATEGIES**
- Make a Table
- Write a Number Sentence
- Make a Drawing

Choose a strategy and solve.

3 There were 98,965 people at the track stadium and 74,930 people at the soccer stadium. How many more people were at the track stadium than at the soccer stadium?

4 Linda swam the freestyle in 52.43 seconds. Wendy's time was 0.05 second slower than Linda's. Patty's time was 0.04 second slower than Wendy's. What was Patty's time for swimming the freestyle?

5 Consuelo spent $14 for shorts, $12 for knee pads, and $27 for track shoes. How much did she spend?

6 A ticket to the soccer game costs $8.75. If Ray has only a $20.00 bill, how much change will he receive?

7 A square bulletin board is 24 inches on each side. If there is a picture of a soccer ball every 8 inches along the edge, including one in each corner, how many soccer balls are on the bulletin board?

8 Eastbrook Community Center has 27 fifth graders and 31 fourth graders on its track team. There are 21 fifth graders and 24 fourth graders on its swim team. How many more fourth graders than fifth graders are on the track and swim teams?

ESTIMATING
Whole-Number Differences

Scott is on the bowling team. The scores for his first three games were 78, 97, and 126. Estimate the difference between his highest score and his lowest score.

Sometimes, an estimate is all that is needed. You can estimate by **rounding** each number before subtracting.

$$126 \rightarrow 130 \quad \text{Round to the nearest ten.}$$
$$-\;78 \rightarrow -\;80 \quad \text{Round to the nearest ten.}$$
$$50$$

So, the estimated difference is 50.

Find the difference.

- What would happen if you rounded each number to the nearest hundred?

Another Example   Estimate. $3,617 - 2,392 \approx n$

Round to the nearest thousand.	$3,617 \rightarrow 4,000$ $-2,392 \rightarrow -2,000$ $2,000$	Round to the nearest hundred.	$3,617 \rightarrow 3,600$ $-2,392 \rightarrow -2,400$ $1,200$

Find the difference.

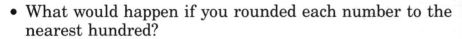

Talk About It

Compare the estimates.

▶ Which estimate is closer to the difference? Why?

▶ What reasons can you give for needing a closer estimate?

Check for Understanding

Estimate the difference by rounding each to the nearest thousand and to the nearest hundred.

1. 5,298 − 1,172	2. 6,425 − 4,236	3. 9,943 − 8,835	4. 15,782 − 12,313	5. 12,874 − 9,818

Estimate the difference.

6. $\begin{array}{r} 475 \\ -284 \end{array}$
7. $\begin{array}{r} 947 \\ -\ 34 \end{array}$
8. $\begin{array}{r} 982 \\ -525 \end{array}$
9. $\begin{array}{r} 852 \\ -\ 34 \end{array}$
10. $\begin{array}{r} 1,962 \\ -\ 953 \end{array}$

11. $\begin{array}{r} 2,685 \\ -\ 518 \end{array}$
12. $\begin{array}{r} 8,748 \\ -3,978 \end{array}$
13. $\begin{array}{r} 6,979 \\ -4,204 \end{array}$
14. $\begin{array}{r} 29,327 \\ -18,419 \end{array}$
15. $\begin{array}{r} 15,734 \\ -\ 8,319 \end{array}$

16. $\begin{array}{r} 7,832 \\ -2,643 \end{array}$
17. $\begin{array}{r} 9,840 \\ -1,298 \end{array}$
18. $\begin{array}{r} 18,479 \\ -\ 9,521 \end{array}$
19. $\begin{array}{r} 32,205 \\ -12,084 \end{array}$
20. $\begin{array}{r} 36,231 \\ -12,059 \end{array}$

21. $8,918 - 693 \approx n$
22. $13,561 - 3,801 \approx n$
23. $18,793 - 659 \approx n$

24. $8,230 - 4,956 \approx n$
25. $21,857 - 12,104 \approx n$
26. $35,938 - 11,321 \approx n$

27. $16,432 - 3,768 \approx n$
28. $28,697 - 18,430 \approx n$
29. $49,782 - 24,516 \approx n$

Mixed Applications

Use the table for Exercises 30–32.

30. If you round to the nearest ten, is the estimated difference between Randy's first-game score and Rhonda's first-game score greater than or less than 25?

31. **Analyze Data**   Round to the nearest ten to estimate the total score of each bowler. Which two bowlers have about a 50-point difference in their total scores?

32. James had about 250 total points for two games. If his first-game score was 130, what are the lowest and highest scores he might have bowled in the second game?

Bowling Scores		
Bowler	**First Game**	**Second Game**
Rhonda	124	118
Randy	94	117
Billy	128	132

Name situations in which an estimated answer is all you need when you subtract.

WRAP UP...

SUBTRACTING
Whole Numbers

The Olympic Committee received 5,230 requests for tickets in the reserved section for the opening ceremonies. There are 3,592 seats available. How many people will not receive tickets?

Subtract. 5,230 − 3,592 = n

Step 1	**Step 2**	**Step 3**	**Step 4**
Decide whether to regroup. 2 > 0. So, regroup 3 tens 0 ones as 2 tens 10 ones. Subtract the ones.	9 > 2 So, regroup 2 hundreds 2 tens as 1 hundred 12 tens. Subtract the tens.	5 > 1 So, regroup 5 thousands 1 hundred as 4 thousands 11 hundreds. Subtract the hundreds.	3 < 4 So, subtract the thousands.
2 10 5, 2 3̸ 0̸ − 3, 5 9 2 ——— 8	12 1 2̸ 10 5, 2̸ 3̸ 0̸ − 3, 5 9 2 ——— 3 8	1112 4 1̸ 2̸ 10 5̸ 2̸ 3̸ 0̸ − 3, 5 9 2 ——— 6 3 8	1112 4 1̸ 2̸ 10 5̸, 2̸ 3̸ 0̸ − 3 5 9 2 ——— 1, 6 3 8

So, 1,638 people will not receive tickets.

Another Method

A calculator is useful for subtracting large numbers. First, estimate the difference.

$$
\begin{array}{ccc}
87{,}546 & \rightarrow & 90{,}000 \\
-48{,}579 & \rightarrow & -50{,}000 \\
\hline
& & 40{,}000
\end{array}
$$

Then, use a calculator to find the difference.

8 7 5 4 6 − 4 8 5 7 9 = | 38967. |

Since 38,967 is close to the estimate of 40,000, the difference is reasonable.

Check for Understanding

Estimate the difference. If the estimated difference is greater than 1,000, subtract to find the difference.

1. 923 − 367	2. 2,476 − 529	3. 5,208 − 1,759	4. 37,413 − 14,826	5. 58,428 − 39,745

Practice

Estimate each difference. If the estimated difference is greater than 40,000, subtract to find the difference.

6. 7,735
    − 3,634

7. 2,168
    − 1,409

8. 61,213
    − 9,692

9. 57,434
    − 14,765

10. 68,253
    − 19,867

11. 78,531
    − 4,781

12. 42,869
    − 34,739

13. 76,839
    − 17,499

14. 97,467
    − 67,859

15. 89,562
    − 37,619

Complete the table.

Number Sentence	Estimate		Difference	
28,476 − 14,825 = n	16.		17.	
56,123 − 27,316 = n	18.		19.	
89,967 − 30,856 = n	20.		21.	
25,406 − 15,399 = n	22.		23.	

Mixed Applications

24. In the Heptathlon of the 1988 Olympics, Jackie Joyner-Kersee scored 7,215 points. Her closest competitor scored 5,715 points. How many more points did Jackie Joyner-Kersee score than her competitor?

25. During the Olympics, attendance for the indoor and outdoor track-and-field events was 36,885. The outdoor events were attended by 22,103 people. How many people attended the indoor events?

Use the table for Exercises 26–28.

26. In what year were the most points scored?

27. How many more points were scored in 1976 than in 1988?

28. How many more points did Daley Thompson score in 1984 than in 1980?

Decathlon		
Year	Athlete	Points
1976	Bruce Jenner	8,617
1980	Daley Thompson	8,495
1984	Daley Thompson	8,798
1988	Christian Schenk	8,488

Why is it important to estimate first when you use a calculator to find a difference?

William and Harry are competing in the track-and-field events at their school. William ran 3,000 meters. Harry came late and ran only 1,650 meters. How much farther did William run than Harry?

To compare the two numbers, you subtract.

Subtract. $3,000 - 1,650 = n$

Step 1	**Step 2**	**Step 3**	**Step 4**
Subtract the ones.	5 > 0 So, regroup 3 thousands 0 hundreds as 2 thousands 10 hundreds.	Regroup 10 hundreds 0 tens as 9 hundreds 10 tens.	Subtract.
3,0 0 0 −1,6 5 0 ――――― 0	2 10 3̸,0̸ 0 0 −1,6 5 0 ――――― 0	9 2 1̸0 10 3̸,0̸ 0̸ 0 −1,6 5 0 ――――― 0	− 9 2 1̸0 10 3̸,0̸ 0̸ 0̸ −1,6 5 0 ――――― 1,3 5 0

So, William ran 1,350 meters farther than Harry.

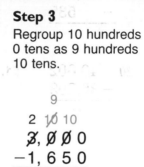
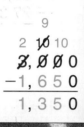

You can regroup in different ways.

A.　　3 9 9 10
　　5̸4̸,0̸0̸0̸　You can regroup
　−5 1 , 8 6 3　400 tens as
　――――――――　399 tens 10 ones.
　　2 , 1 3 7

B.　7 9 10
　8̸0̸0̸
　−7 6 2
　――――
　　　3 8

C.　6 9 17 13
　7̸,0̸ 8̸ 3̸
　−5 , 4 9 6
　――――――
　1 , 5 8 7

D.　2 9 9 11
　3̸,0̸ 0̸ 1̸
　−2 , 5 6 7
　――――――
　　　4 3 4

E.　6 9 9 9 10
　7̸0̸,0̸0̸0̸
　−5 9 , 4 3 1
　――――――――
　1 0 , 5 6 9

Check for Understanding

Show how you regrouped for each problem. Solve.

1.	2.	3.	4.	5.
5 0 0 −2 1 3	4 0 8 −3 5 7	7 , 0 0 1 −5 , 8 2 3	4 , 0 1 0 −2 , 4 8 5	9 0 , 0 0 0 −6 1 , 7 6 4

Practice

Show how you regrouped for each problem. Solve.

6.	7.	8.	9.
600 − 532	1,002 − 983	20,005 − 17,416	50,004 − 48,756

Find the difference.

10. 505 − 98	11. 300 − 137	12. 502 − 224	13. 830 − 543

14. 1,000 − 168	15. 3,002 − 1,765	16. 13,004 − 537	17. 7,500 − 726

18. 9,090 − 8,987	19. 36,000 − 27,379	20. 40,002 − 35,803	21. 52,001 − 49,502

Mixed Applications

22. Don plays professional basketball. In one year he scored a total of 1,002 points. One teammate scored 150 fewer points. Another teammate scored 234 points fewer than Don. How many points did each of the other players score?

23. **Analyze Data** A leading professional basketball player has made 3,005 free throws in his career. Another leading player has made a total of 1,654. Is 2,351 a reasonable difference between the totals? Explain.

MIXED REVIEW

Compare. Write <, >, or = for each ●.

1. 4.36 ● 4.63
2. 0.20 ● 0.20
3. 1.07 ● 1.70
4. 43.2 ● 42.3

Write each group of numbers in order from least to greatest.

5. 8.9, 7.6, 8.8
6. 1.0, 0.7, 0.5
7. 9.4, 9.1, 8.9
8. 5.3, 2.3, 3.5
9. 3.56, 3.49, 3.4
10. 10.3, 1.03, 1.3
11. 0.01, 1.1, 0.1
12. 0.51, 0.05, 0.5

WRAP UP...

1. The first tournament hockey game attracted 4,290 fans, the second game had 1,785 fans, and the third game had 6,840 fans. How many fans attended hockey games?

2. Each wall of a square meeting room is 40 feet long. If loudspeakers are placed 20 feet apart around the room, how many loudspeakers are in the room?

I can draw a diagram to solve some problems.

Write in decimal form.

3. nine tenths

4. four and eighteen thousandths

5. sixty-five hundredths

6. seventeen and twenty-one hundredths

Write the value of the underlined digit.

7. 6.9<u>8</u>

8. 0.37<u>5</u>

9. 12.0<u>4</u>

10. 3.<u>4</u>09

Order from greatest to least.

11. 8.745, 8.675, 8.750

12. 13.094, 13.940, 13.900, 13.904

Round to the nearest hundredth.

13. 10.609

14. 5.976

15. 13.054

16. 5.546

Write the amount as a decimal form of the whole unit.

17. 30 cents

18. 8 hundredths

19. 4 decimeters

Write the inverse operation sentence for each. Solve.

20. $25 + \blacksquare = 78$

21. $\blacksquare - 85 = 14$

22. $16 + \blacksquare = 98$

23. $\blacksquare - 18 = 56$

24. $\blacksquare + 29 = 63$

25. $\blacksquare - 43 = 69$

Estimate the sum or difference.

26. 489 + 314

27. 2,968 − 1,296

28. 27,569 − 12,084

29. 46,469 + 53,796

30. 68,312 + 9,839

Practice

Estimate the sum or diff

6. $5.84
    + 6.28

10. $26.43
    − 9.58

14. $74.59 + 25.42 \approx n$

Estimate the sum or di
each ●.

16. $5.13 + 6.87 ● 4.8$

18. $6.48 − 3.36 ● 6.7$

Mixed Applicatio

20. Juan ran a race
    Karen finished
    Juan estimates
    3 seconds faster
    Karen estimate
    difference. Who
    closer?

NUMBER SE

Sometimes, sums
Clustering is a me
clustered around,

Estimate. 24.8 +
    ↓
    25 +

Estimate each sum

22. $9.86 + 10.4 +$

Spotlight ON
PROBLEM SOLVING

Visualize the Solution

When you visualize the solution, you take a mental snapshot of how the problem can be solved.

Baseball is sometimes referred to as the national pastime. Baseball is played on an infield shaped like a diamond. The bases are 90 feet apart. There are players at each base, one at shortstop, some in the outfield (left, center, and right), and one on the pitcher's mound.

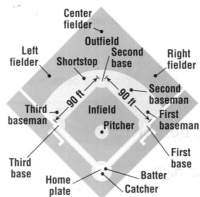

Talk About It ■ ■ ■ ■ ■ ■ ■ ■ ■

Study the baseball diamond and the positions. Visualize solutions to the problems. Discuss the results with a partner.

♦ The left fielder threw the ball to first base. Did the fielder throw to the left or to the right?

♦ Which player would have the shortest throw to the catcher? the longest?

♦ A player hit a home run. How far did the player run?

♦ The center fielder ran to the right to help a fallen outfielder field a ball. Where was the ball?

♦ A ball traveled about 150 feet from home plate. Where could the ball have gone?

Apply

Visualize the results. Draw a picture if needed. Solve.

1 The Roadrunners Club ran a race. They ran north for 3 miles, then west for 4 miles, then 2 miles south, then 5 miles east. How far had they run when they crossed their own path?

2 The outfield fence at the baseball field is 340 feet from one foul line to the other. The part of the fence in center field measures about 110 feet. The left and right parts of the fence are each the same length. How long are the fences in left field and right field?

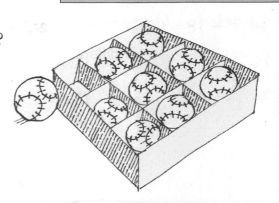

53

Sara is saving for a
$42.47 during the su
About how much has

Front-end estimatior

Step 1	St
Add the front-end, or lead, digits.	Ad est
$4 2. 4 7 + 1 1. 4 9 $5■.■■	+

So, Sara has saved

Another Method

Round to the nearest whole

42.47 → 42
+11.49 → +11
53

• How do the roun
front-end adjuste

Rounding can be u

Round to the near

8.3 → 8
− 5.6 → −6
2

Check for Und

Estimate the sum d

1. $8.97
+ 3.78

At a concession stand, the small cup of popcorn holds 1.7 ounces. The medium box holds 2.8 ounces. The jumbo tub holds as much as both the small and medium containers. How many ounces does the jumbo tub hold?

You can use base-ten blocks to model decimal place value.

Flat = 1 whole   Long = 0.1   Unit = 0.01

First, estimate. $2.8 + 1.7 \approx n \rightarrow 3 + 2 = 5$
Use base-ten blocks to model $1.7 + 2.8 = n$

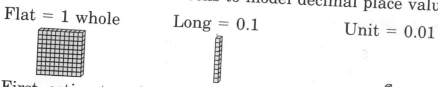

Step 1
Model

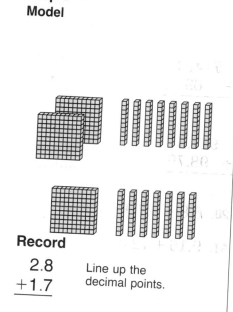

Record

2.8   Line up the
+1.7   decimal points.

Step 2
Model

Regroup 10 tenths as 1.

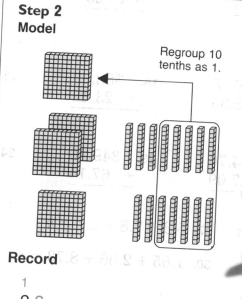

Record

1
2.8   8 tenths + 7 tenths =
+1.7   15 tenths or
4.5   1 one 5 tenths

Place the decimal point in the sum.

So, the jumbo tub holds 4.5 ounces of popcorn. Since 4.5 ounces is close to the estimate of 5, the answer is reasonable.

More Examples

A.
1
6.7
+ 7.5
14.2

B.
1
0.27
+0.56
0.83

C.
1 1
0.89
+0.35
1.24

D.
1 1
$9.78
+ 5.94
$15.72

Check for Understanding

Use base-ten blocks to model. Write the sum.

1. 1.4
    + 3.5

2. 2.7
    + 0.8

3. 4.91
    + 2.32

4. 1.42
    + 2.76

5. 3.53
    + 1.68

Practice

Estimate the sum to the nearest whole number.

6. 1.6
    + 3.9

7. 4.4
    + 0.6

8. 6.19
    + 8.20

9. 5.05
    + 14.80

10. 19.82
    + 6.03

11. $26.86
    + 0.92

12. 84.7
    + 69.8

13. 29.83
    + 14.29

14. $49.82
    + 27.41

15. $ 4.45
    + 99.89

Find the sum.

16. $9.57
    + 7.90

17. $29.75
    + 8.65

18. $82.68
    + 23.42

19. $140.37
    + 69.90

20. 106.76
    + 18.28

21. 100.22
    + 99.89

22. 234.76
    + 817.09

23. 349.26
    + 67.14

24. 917.61
    + 98.79

25. 987.96
    + 145.34

26. $0.96 + 0.30 + 0.05 = n$

27. $5.3 + 7.8 + 2.1 = n$

28. $6.8 + 3.7 + 9.3 = n$

29. $0.42 + 9.27 + 0.35 = n$

30. $1.65 + 2.86 + 8.73 = n$

31. $9.16 + 72.34 + 29.07 = n$

Mixed Applications

32. At the concession stand, a small drink sells for $0.75, and a large drink sells for $1.15. If Anna purchases two small drinks and two large drinks, what is the total cost?

33. Cora received $1.65 from Elena and $1.45 from Earl. She already had $0.75. Does she have enough money to buy 3 boxes of popcorn if each box costs $1.30?

34. At Bay High, there were 315 fans in the lower seats and 128 fans in the upper seats. The other school had 218 fans in each of the upper and lower seats. Estimate which school had the most fans.

35. **Mental Math** Felicia bought 2 bags of peanuts for $1.05 each. Tommy bought a hot dog for $2.25. How much more did Tommy spend?

How is adding decimals like adding whole numbers?

ADDITION PROPERTIES

Addition properties are helpful in finding whole-number sums. You can use the same properties to find decimal sums.

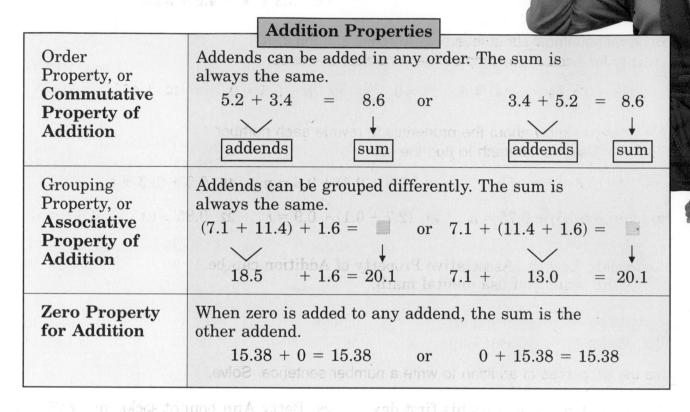

Addition Properties

Order Property, or **Commutative Property of Addition**	Addends can be added in any order. The sum is always the same. $5.2 + 3.4 = 8.6$ or $3.4 + 5.2 = 8.6$ addends sum addends sum
Grouping Property, or **Associative Property of Addition**	Addends can be grouped differently. The sum is always the same. $(7.1 + 11.4) + 1.6 = $ ▇ or $7.1 + (11.4 + 1.6) = $ ▇ $18.5 + 1.6 = 20.1$ $7.1 + 13.0 = 20.1$
Zero Property for Addition	When zero is added to any addend, the sum is the other addend. $15.38 + 0 = 15.38$ or $0 + 15.38 = 15.38$

Talk About It

▶ How is the Commutative Property different from the Associative Property?

▶ Does the Commutative Property work for subtraction? Explain.

Check for Understanding

Write the name of the addition property used in each number sentence.

1. $12.5 + 5.4 = 5.4 + 12.5$

2. $3.1 + (8.2 + 6.3) = (3.1 + 8.2) + 6.3$

3. $0 + 16.12 = 16.12$

4. $5.78 + 0 = 5.78$

5. $106.7 + 98.2 = 98.2 + 106.7$

6. $(0.5 + 1.5) + 3.9 = 0.5 + (1.5 + 3.9)$

Practice

Complete. Identify the property used.

7. $\blacksquare + 2.5 = 2.5 + 1.4$

8. $4.5 + (\blacksquare + 6) = (4.5 + 1.2) + 6$

9. $1.3 + 7.4 = \blacksquare + 1.3$

10. $(1.3 + 0.7) + 6.8 = 1.3 + (\blacksquare + 6.8)$

11. $14.5 + 0 = \blacksquare$

12. $25.2 + \blacksquare = 4.6 + 25.2$

Use what you know about inverse operations and the Zero Property for Addition to complete each number sentence.

13. $7.25 - 0 = \blacksquare$ **14.** $4.8 - \blacksquare = 0$ **15.** $\blacksquare - 2.5 = 0$ **16.** $1.4 - \blacksquare = 1.4$

Use what you know about the properties to rewrite each number sentence. Use mental math to find the sum.

17. $0.5 + (0.5 + 5.6) = n$

18. $(0.8 + 0.4) + 0.6 = n$

19. $0.2 + (0.8 + 4.5) = n$

20. $(9.50 + 0.25) + 0.75 = n$

21. $(2.7 + 0.1) + 0.9 = n$

22. $0.85 + (0.15 + 0.45) = n$

23. Explain how the Associative Property of Addition can be helpful when you use mental math.

Mixed Applications

Use the properties of addition to write a number sentence. Solve.

24. Carlos ran 0.5 mile on his first day of training, 0.5 mile on the second day, and 1.25 miles on the third. How many total miles did he run?

25. Betty Ann bought socks for $4.25, a shirt for $5.75, and shorts for $7.50. How much did she spend on the three items?

26. Julia bought some watches for her friends. She spent $6.85 for one watch, $5.50 for another, and $4.15 for a third one. How much did she spend on all three watches?

27. The four girls on the 400-meter relay team each ran 100 meters. Their times were 15.6 seconds, 15.1 seconds, 15.4 seconds, and 14.9 seconds. What was their combined time?

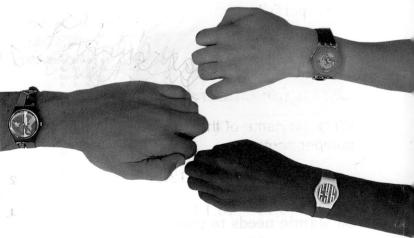

Why is there no Associative Property for subtraction?

WRAP UP...

EXPLORING

Equivalent Decimals

You know that numbers have many names.

24 can be expressed in many ways:
10 + 10 + 4, 20 + 4, 12 + 12,
3 × 8, 6 × 4, 24.00, and 24 ones

Equivalent decimals are different names for the same number.

WORK TOGETHER

Building Understanding

Use decimal squares to model each decimal.

1 tenth (0.1)   10 hundredths (0.10)   100 thousandths (0.100)

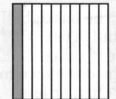  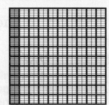

Talk About It

▶ How many tenths are shaded?

▶ How many hundredths are shaded?

▶ How many thousandths are shaded?

▶ How are the shaded parts of the decimal squares related?

▶ Are 0.1, 0.10, and 0.100 equivalent decimals? Why or why not?

Use your decimal squares to model these decimals. Then decide whether they are equivalent decimals.

a. 0.6 and 0.60

b. 0.80 and 0.08

c. 0.3 and 0.300

d. 0.002 and 0.02

▶ What happens to the size of the parts when additional zeros are to the right of a decimal number as in Exercise **c**?

▶ What happens to the value of the digit 3?

▶ What happens to the size of the parts when additional zeros are to the left of the decimal number as in Exercise **b**?

▶ What happens to the value of the digit 8?

Making the Connection

You can make equivalent decimals by **annexing** zeros. Use them to rewrite addition and subtraction problems.

Find the sum of 0.6 and 1.32.

$$\begin{array}{r} 1.3\,2 \\ +\ 0.6\ \blacksquare \\ \hline \end{array} \rightarrow \begin{array}{r} 1.32 \\ +\ 0.60 \\ \hline 1.92 \end{array} \leftarrow \text{Annex a zero.}$$

You can use a place-value chart to form equivalent decimals. Then, rewrite by aligning the decimal points.

A. Find $6.9 + 1.452 + 0.68 = n$.

Ones	Tenths	Hundredths	Thousands
6	9	0	0
1	4	5	2
0	6	8	0

$$\begin{array}{r} \overset{2\ \ 1}{} \\ 6.900 \\ 1.452 \\ +0.680 \\ \hline 9.032 \end{array}$$

B. Find $9.82 - 4.3 = n$.

Ones	Tenths	Hundredths
9	8	2
4	3	0

$$\begin{array}{r} 9.82 \\ -4.30 \\ \hline 5.52 \end{array}$$

Talk About It

▶ Does annexing zeros change the value of the numbers? Explain.

▶ Why is it helpful to annex zeros to the right of a decimal number when adding or subtracting?

Checking Understanding

Write two equivalent decimals for each.

1. 0.9   **2.** 5.800   **3.** 1.3   **4.** 2.40

Use equivalent decimals to rewrite each problem.

5. $4.8 + 3.64 = n$ **6.** $9.32 - 2.6 = n$ **7.** $7.1 - 4.82 = n$ **8.** $3.68 + 0.9 = n$

Rewrite each problem. Then solve.

9. $0.62 - 0.4 = n$ **10.** $2.7 + 33.85 = n$ **11.** $48.1 + 35 + 17.3 = n$

3

MULTIPLYING
WHOLE NUMBERS

Did you know ...

... that the heat energy that makes a hot-air balloon rise comes from a propane gas burner?

A hot-air balloon can travel at about 11 miles per hour. Jane and Marc have recorded 235 hours in their balloon log this year. How can Jane and Marc find how many miles they have traveled in their hot-air balloon this year?

MULTIPLICATION PROPERTIES

Multiplication properties can help you find products.

Multiplication Properties	
Commutative Property of Multiplication	You can multiply numbers in any order. The product is always the same. **Example** 4×6 = 24 6×4 = 24 factors product factors product
Associative Property of Multiplication	You can group factors differently. The product is always the same. **Example** $(2 \times 5) \times 3$ = $2 \times (5 \times 3)$ 10×3 = 2×15 $30 = 30$
Property of One	When one of the factors is 1, the product equals the other factor. **Example** $5 \times 1 = 5$ $1 \times 5 = 5$
Zero Property for Multiplication	When one factor is 0, the product is 0. **Example** $7 \times 0 = 0$ $0 \times 7 = 0$

Talk About It

▶ How is the Commutative Property different from the Associative Property?

▶ Explain how the Associative Property of Multiplication can be helpful when you use mental math.

Check for Understanding

Write the name of the multiplication property used in each number sentence.

1. $5 \times (8 \times 3) = (5 \times 8) \times 3$ **2.** $37 \times 6 = 6 \times 37$ **3.** $(7 \times 25) \times 4 = 7 \times (25 \times 4)$

4. $(247 \times 0) \times 8 = 0$ **5.** $5 \times 9 = 9 \times 5$ **6.** $3,857 \times 1 = 3,857$

Practice

Solve. Identify the property used.

7. $68,390 \times \blacksquare = 0$

8. $144 \times 1 = \blacksquare$

9. $6 \times 28 = \blacksquare \times 6$

10. $(25 \times 4) \times \blacksquare = 25 \times (4 \times 5)$

11. $7,468 \times \blacksquare = 7,468$

12. $5 \times (4 \times 7) = (5 \times 4) \times \blacksquare$

Use the Associative Property to find the product. Show your work.

13. $2 \times (50 \times 9) = n$

14. $2 \times (500 \times 7) = n$

15. $(3 \times 5) \times 200 = n$

16. $(8 \times 50) \times 2 = n$

17. $(6 \times 25) \times 4 = n$

18. $50 \times (4 \times 8) = n$

Solve.

19. $5,416 \times 0 = \blacksquare$

20. $35 \times (2 \times 5) = \blacksquare$

21. $(500 \times \blacksquare) \times 6 = 6,000$

22. $(4 \times \blacksquare) \times 8 = 160$

23. $145 \times \blacksquare = 123 \times 145$

24. $6,340 \times \blacksquare = 6,340$

Mixed Applications

25. Lee conserves gasoline by walking to and from school instead of riding in a car. He walks 5 miles a day, 5 days a week. He has done this for 3 weeks. How many miles has he walked?

26. Luis rode his bike 3 miles round-trip to the library one day. He also rode his bike to baseball practice 4 miles round-trip each day for 5 days. How many miles did he ride his bike?

27. Using the factors 3, 6, and 9, give an example of the Associative Property of Multiplication.

28. Using 4 as a factor, give an example of the Commutative Property of Multiplication.

HISTORY CONNECTION

Leonardo Fibonacci (1170–1250) was an Italian mathematician who studied patterns of numbers. These numbers, called the Fibonacci numbers, can be found in nature. The sequence of numbers is: 1, 1, 2, 3, 5, 8, 13 . . . . Look for a pattern in the numbers.

29. Find the next three numbers in the pattern.

Why does the Zero Property for Multiplication give a different answer than the Zero Property for Addition?

USING MENTAL MATH
with Multiples of 10

The average person uses about 40 gallons of water to take a shower. If each of 5 family members takes a shower daily, about how much water do they use for showers in one day?

You know about how much water 1 person uses. Multiply to find about how much a family of 5 uses.

Multiply. $5 \times 40 = n$

So, a family of 5 uses about 200 gallons of water each day for showers.

$$\begin{array}{r} 4 \text{ tens} \\ \times\ 5 \\ \hline 20 \text{ tens} \end{array} \longrightarrow \begin{array}{r} 40 \\ \times\ 5 \\ \hline 200 \end{array}$$

Think:
Since $5 \times 4 = 20$,
$5 \times 40 = 200$.

You can use a calculator to find patterns with multiples of 10.

Entry	Display
6 M+ × 7 =	M 42.
MRC × 7 0 =	M 420.
MRC × 7 0 0 =	M 4200.
MRC × 7 0 0 0 =	M 42000.

The M+ key stores one factor in memory.

The MRC key recalls that factor from memory.

More Examples

A.
$8 \times 1 = 8$
$8 \times 10 = 80$
$8 \times 100 = 800$
$8 \times 1,000 = 8,000$

B.
$9 \times (3 \times 1) = 9 \times 3 = 27$
$9 \times (3 \times 10) = 9 \times 30 = 270$
$9 \times (3 \times 100) = 9 \times 300 = 2,700$
$9 \times (3 \times 1,000) = 9 \times 3,000 = 27,000$

Talk About It

▶ How is the pattern in **B** different from the pattern in **A**?

▶ How can you use mental math to find $5 \times 7, 5 \times 70, 5 \times 700,$ and $5 \times 7,000$?

Check for Understanding

Use mental math to find the product.

1.	2.	3.	4.	5.
$\begin{array}{r} 80 \\ \times\ 7 \end{array}$	$\begin{array}{r} 500 \\ \times\ 8 \end{array}$	$\begin{array}{r} 4,000 \\ \times\ 3 \end{array}$	$\begin{array}{r} 9,000 \\ \times\ 5 \end{array}$	$\begin{array}{r} 300 \\ \times\ 9 \end{array}$

Practice

Use mental math to find the product.

6.	50 × 5	7.	30 × 7	8.	800 × 2	9.	900 × 4	10.	500 × 6

11.	400 × 8	12.	900 × 3	13.	4,000 × 6	14.	2,000 × 7	15.	7,000 × 9

Complete each number sentence by using mental math.

16. $700 \times 9 = n$ 17. $400 \times 5 = n$ 18. $n \times 30 = 240$ 19. $50 \times n = 350$

20. $3 \times 200 = n$ 21. $500 \times 6 = n$ 22. $800 \times n = 4,800$ 23. $n \times 200 = 1,200$

24. $2 \times n = 600$ 25. $n \times 40 = 320$ 26. $6 \times n = 3,000$ 27. $800 \times 9 = n$

Multiply each number by 10, 100, and 1,000.

28. 2   29. 4   30. 5

31. 7   32. 9

Mixed Applications

Use the table to solve Exercises 33–34.

Cost of Gas and Electricity	
Month	Amount
January	$150
April	$ 95
July	$200
October	$ 90

33. How much more was the cost of gas and electricity for January and July than the cost of gas and electricity for April and October?

34. **Find Data** There are 8 houses on the block. If each household paid the same amount for gas and electricity in October, how much did all the households on the block pay?

How many zeros are in each product when you multiply 5 × 500, 3 × 7,000, and 8 × 90?

WRAP UP...

Modern windmills, called turbines, are used to produce electricity. One type can produce 6 megawatts of electricity in a strong wind. About how many megawatts can 254 of these turbines generate in a strong wind?

Estimate. $6 \times 254 \approx n$

Find the lead, or front-end, digit. Multiply.	Count the places after the lead digit.	Write that number of zeros in the product.
254 $\times$ 6 — 12	254 $\times$ 6 — 12	254 $\times$ 6 — 1,200

So, about 1,200 megawatts can be generated.

- Is the estimate *greater than* or *less than* the actual answer?

—————————————————

Another way to estimate is by rounding.

254 $\rightarrow$ 300   Round one of the factors
$\times$ 6 $\rightarrow$ $\times$ 6   and multiply.
————
about 1,800

So, another estimate is about 1,800 megawatts.

Talk About It

▶ Why is the front-end estimate different from the rounded estimate?

▶ Is the rounded estimate *greater than* or *less than* the exact answer? How do you know?

Check for Understanding

Estimate by using front-end digits.

1. $3 \times 83 \approx n$ 2. $7 \times 543 \approx n$ 3. $9 \times 6,512 \approx n$ 4. $8 \times 9,345 \approx n$

Estimate by rounding.

5. $9 \times 48 \approx n$ 6. $4 \times 679 \approx n$ 7. $8 \times 3,207 \approx n$ 8. $5 \times 9,879 \approx n$

Practice

Estimate each product. Tell which method you used.

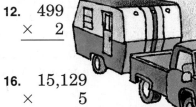

9. 35
    × 5

10. 78
    × 3

11. 212
    × 9

12. 499
    × 2

13. 64
    × 8

14. 429
    × 2

15. 2,648
    × 3

16. 15,129
    × 5

17. 2,238
    × 4

18. 8,729
    × 5

19. 11,132
    × 7

20. 19,549
    × 9

Estimate the product.

21. $678 \times 3 \approx n$

22. $498 \times 5 \approx n$

23. $1,827 \times n \approx 4,000$

24. $10,582 \times n \approx 50,000$

Mixed Applications

Use the table for Exercises 25–28.

Fuel Economy in Cars: Comparing Miles per Gallon			
Size	City	Highway	Average Yearly Fuel Cost
Subcompact	53	58	$287
Compact	37	43	$338
Midsize	23	34	$562
Large	21	30	$657

25. If a midsize car, driven in the city, used 8 gallons of gasoline, about how many miles did it travel?

26. About how many miles can a compact car travel on the highway on 4 gallons of gasoline?

27. **Analyze Data** If a family owned a large car and a compact car, about how much did they spend on fuel in 2 years?

28. If a subcompact car is driven for 6 years, about how much is spent on fuel?

Why are front-end and rounded estimates both acceptable estimates?

WRAP
UP...

More Practice, Lesson 3.3, page H42

EXPLORING
the Distributive Property

Sometimes, you can break apart numbers to make multiplication with larger numbers easier.

WORK TOGETHER

Building Understanding

Use centimeter graph paper to model a rectangle.

Outline a rectangle that is 8 units high and 17 units wide.

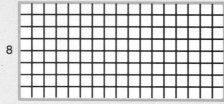

Talk About It

▶ How many units are there inside the rectangle?

▶ How did you find the number of units inside the rectangle?

▶ What multiplication number sentence does the rectangle represent?

Move across the top, count off 10 units, and draw a line to break apart the rectangle.

▶ How many units are in each of the two rectangles?

▶ What multiplication number sentence can you write for each rectangle?

▶ What is the sum of the products for the two smaller rectangles?

▶ Is the product for the large rectangle the same as the sum of the products for the two smaller rectangles?

▶ How can you use mental math to solve this problem?

Making the Connection

There is an easier way to multiply numbers. You can use the
Distributive Property, which allows you to break apart
numbers to make them easy to multiply.

Compare the two methods.

Multiply. $6 \times 24 = n$

Method 1
Model 6×24 on centimeter graph paper.
Move across the top, count off 20 squares, and
draw a line. Write a multiplication sentence for
each rectangle. Add the two products.

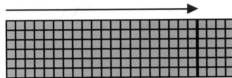

$(6 \times 20) = 120$ $(6 \times 4) = 24$ $120 + 24 = 144$

Method 2
Break apart 24 into $20 + 4$.
Rewrite as $6 \times (20 + 4)$.
Multiply. $(6 \times 20) = 120$
            $(6 \times 4) = \ \ 24$

Add the two products.
            $120 + 24 = 144$
            $6 \times 24 = 144$

Talk About It

▶ How is Method 2 like Method 1?

▶ Why does breaking apart the number make the
multiplication easier?

▶ What two operations did you use in both methods?

Checking Understanding

Use centimeter graph paper to find each product.

1. $3 \times 25 = n$

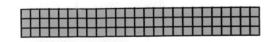

2. $5 \times 37 = n$

Complete. Find each product.

3. Find 3×25.
$$3 \times 20 = n$$
$$3 \times \ \ 5 = n$$
Add.
$$60 + 15 = n$$
$$3 \times 25 = n$$

4. Find 5×37.
$$5 \times 30 = n$$
$$5 \times \ \ 7 = n$$
Add.
$$150 + 35 = n$$
$$5 \times 37 = n$$

More Practice, Lesson 3.4, page H43

PROBLEM Solving

Mr. Davis wants to use less electricity to heat his home. He bought 3 electric blankets for $32 each, 4 air filters for $2 each, and 2 cords of logs for $95 each. How much money did he have left if he had $350 to start?

Sometimes, you need to use more than one step or operation to solve a problem. There may be hidden data to find first.

▶ UNDERSTAND

What are you asked to find?

What facts are given?

▶ PLAN

What plan can you make?

First, find the total cost of each kind of item. Then, subtract the total cost of all the items from $350.

▶ SOLVE

How can you solve the problem?

First, estimate the cost.

blankets	filters	logs
32	2	95
× 3	× 4	× 2
about 90 +	about 10 +	about 200 = about 300

Use this number sentence to find the total cost of the purchases, and then subtract to find the amount left from $350.

$$(3 \times 32) + (4 \times 2) + (2 \times 95) = n$$

$$\begin{array}{r} \$350 \\ - \ 294 \\ \hline \$ \ 56 \end{array}$$

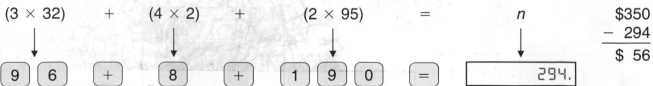

9 6 + 8 + 1 9 0 = 294.

So, Mr. Davis had $56 left.

▶ LOOK BACK

How can you check your computation? Is this answer reasonable? How does it compare with the estimate?

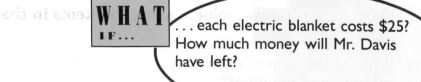

WHAT IF... ...each electric blanket costs $25? How much money will Mr. Davis have left?

Apply

1. Mr. Gomez wants to conserve energy. He bought 3 ceiling fans for $75 each and 4 window fans for $60 each. He had budgeted $500 for the fans. How much money did he have left after his purchases?

2. Mr. Gomez hired 2 people to help him install the fans. He paid each of them $10 an hour. One person worked 3 hours, and the other person worked 11 hours. What is the total amount he paid the workers?

Mixed Applications	**STRATEGIES**	• Make a Drawing • Make a Table • Write a Number Sentence

Choose a strategy and solve.

3. A carpenter has one piece of molding 8 feet long, one piece 9 feet long, and one piece 13 feet long. How much more molding does she need to complete a job that requires 45 feet of molding?

4. Billy rode his bicycle 9 kilometers each day for 5 days. Jim rode his bicycle 8 kilometers each day for 5 days. How many more kilometers did Billy ride than Jim?

5. A car averages 32 miles to a gallon of gas. Its tank holds 12 gallons of gas. How far can the car be driven on one tank of gas?

6. Diane counted the fence posts in a fenced-in back yard that was 25 meters long and 15 meters wide. If the posts were 5 meters apart, how many posts were there?

WRITER'S CORNER

7. Write a multistep problem about the items in the table.

Energy-Saving Items

Fluorescent bulbs	$ 4
Window shades	$12
Light-dimmer control	$10

REVIEW AND MAINTENANCE

1. In the first three weeks of selling cookies, Carol sold 319 boxes. If she sold 103 boxes the first week and 98 boxes the second week, how many boxes did she sell the third week?

2. Susan saved $50.00 to buy tennis supplies. She needed 2 cans of tennis balls at $3.45 for each can, a tennis racket for $22.98, and a tennis skirt for $11.95. Did Susan have enough money to buy these items?

Order from least to greatest.

3. 7.23; 8.73; 7.08   4. 1.0; 0.97; 1.07   5. 3.34; 3.034; 3.403

Round to the nearest tenth.

6. 29.07   7. 4.18   8. 6.92   9. 20.455   10. 0.35

I compare the digits in each place-value position when I put numbers in order.

Find the sum or difference.

11. 507
   − 283

12. 24,792
   + 1,034

13. 46,093
   + 78,111

14. 37,014
   − 12,983

15. 0.904
   + 0.725

16. 9.06
   − 5.78

17. 40.156
   − 13.877

18. 79.815
   + 33.245

Complete. Identify the multiplication property used.

19. $4,392 \times \blacksquare = 0$

20. $648 \times 1 = \blacksquare$

21. $5 \times 29 = 29 \times \blacksquare$

22. $(15 \times \blacksquare) \times 9 = 15 \times (23 \times 9)$

Estimate.

23. 895
   × 4

24. 4,291
   × 4

25. 925
   × 8

26. 18,470
   × 5

27. 29,562
   × 9

Multiply.

28. 430
   × 5

29. 6,752
   × 7

30. 4,978
   × 8

31. 9,086
   × 6

32. 8,965
   × 4

33. $5 \times 923 = n$

34. $3 \times 3,097 = n$

35. $2 \times 7,915 = n$

36. $7 \times 6,893 = n$

Analyze Data

Apply

Work with a partner to solve each problem. Write the relevant information only. Then discuss the results.

1 The Martings were sorting aluminum cans and paper products for their weekly trash collection. They accumulated 6 bags of paper trash and 26 cans. Trash collection cost $3 for each bag. How much did the Martings pay to have their paper trash collected?

2 A restaurant is switching from plastic cups to paper cups. Each box of plastic cups costs $10, and each box of paper cups costs $20. There are 500 cups in each box. How much will the restaurant pay in a 6-month period for 3 boxes of paper cups per month?

Problems may contain relevant and irrelevant information. Relevant information is information that is useful in solving the problem. Irrelevant information is *not* useful in solving the problem. Copy the problem below. Underline only the relevant information.

Landfills are used for solid-waste disposal. Paper products make up over one third of the solid waste discarded. Yard waste accounts for about one fifth of the solid waste discarded. A local landfill will allow solid-waste deposits at a rate of $20 for each deposit of 50 pounds (lb) or less. If a landfill operator receives separate solid-waste deposits of 27 lb, 43 lb, 35 lb, 50 lb, and 40 lb, how much will he collect in fees?

Talk About It

● **What is the problem?**

● **What do you need to know to solve this problem?**

● **Is there irrelevant information in the problem? If so, what is irrelevant?**

● **How can you solve this problem? Be prepared to discuss the solution with your classmates.**

During one month an employee at the hydroelectric power plant worked 10 hours each day for 20 days. How many hours did the employee work that month?

Multiply. $20 \times 10 = n \longrightarrow$ 2 tens $\times$ 10 = 20 tens
$20 \times 10 = 200$

So, the employee worked 200 hours.

Look for the pattern.

20×1	= 20	60×7	= 420
20×10	= 200	60×70	= 4,200
20×100	= 2,000	60×700	= 42,000
$20 \times 1,000$	= 20,000	$60 \times 7,000$	= 420,000

Another Example

Look at the multiplication table. Observe the pattern.

x	40	400	4,000
20	800	8,000	80,000
40	1,600	16,000	160,000
50	2,000	20,000	200,000
60	2,400	24,000	240,000

Talk About It

▶ What pattern do you see?

▶ What do you observe in the pattern of zeros in the products of 50×40, 50×400, and $50 \times 4,000$?

▶ Why are there more zeros in the products?

▶ How can you use mental math to multiply $60 \times 40,000$?

Check for Understanding

Use mental math to find the product.

1. $10 \times 40 = n$ **2.** $30 \times 700 = n$ **3.** $50 \times 7,000 = n$ **4.** $60 \times 50 = n$ **5.** $40 \times 500 = n$

Practice

Use mental math to find the product.

6. 20 $\times\,30$	**7.** 40 $\times\,40$	**8.** 500 $\times\;70$	**9.** 300 $\times\;50$	**10.** 600 $\times\;40$
11. 800 $\times\;50$	**12.** 900 $\times\;10$	**13.** 4,000 $\times\;\;\;30$	**14.** 2,000 $\times\;\;\;50$	**15.** 9,000 $\times\;\;\;80$

16. $50 \times 30 = n$ **17.** $20 \times 40 = n$ **18.** $90 \times 50 = n$

19. $400 \times 60 = n$ **20.** $3,000 \times 80 = n$ **21.** $800 \times 70 = n$

22. $700 \times 60 = n$ **23.** $5,000 \times 40 = n$ **24.** $60,000 \times 50 = n$

Complete each number sentence.

25. $20 \times 50 = n$ **26.** $40 \times n = 1,200$

27. $n \times 60 = 2,400$ **28.** $600 \times n = 6,000$

29. $4,000 \times n = 200,000$ **30.** $30 \times 6,000 = n$

31. Multiply the number 60 by the numbers 60, 600, and 6,000.

Mixed Applications

32. A science teacher received 20 reports on energy from her class. Each report was 20 pages long. What was the total number of pages in all the reports?

33. At Midway Elementary each of 300 students brought in 20 aluminum cans for recycling. What was the total number of cans brought in?

34. **Number Sense** How many zeros will be in the product of the numbers 500 and 7,000? What is the product?

35. **Number Sense** Write a two-digit number and a four-digit number that have a product of 490,000.

Will there be more or fewer zeros in the product when you multiply 30×800 than when you multiply 50×800? Explain.

WRAP UP...

Complete.

Check your answer.

1. $7 \times 35 = \blacksquare \times 7$ 2. $(4 \times 25) \times 3 = 4 \times (\blacksquare \times 3)$

3. $185 \times 1 = \blacksquare$ 4. $6,732 \times \blacksquare = 0$

5. $(8 \times 4) + (8 \times 7) = \blacksquare \times (4 + 7)$

Estimate.

6. $\begin{array}{r} 378 \\ \times\ \ 4 \\ \hline \end{array}$
7. $\begin{array}{r} 4,250 \\ \times\ \ \ \ 5 \\ \hline \end{array}$
8. $\begin{array}{r} 17,985 \\ \times\ \ \ \ \ \ 7 \\ \hline \end{array}$
9. $\begin{array}{r} 840 \\ \times\ \ 52 \\ \hline \end{array}$
10. $\begin{array}{r} 965 \\ \times\ \ 67 \\ \hline \end{array}$

Multiply.

11. $\begin{array}{r} 300 \\ \times\ \ \ 5 \\ \hline \end{array}$
12. $\begin{array}{r} 4,000 \\ \times\ \ \ \ \ 3 \\ \hline \end{array}$
13. $\begin{array}{r} 70 \\ \times\ 40 \\ \hline \end{array}$
14. $\begin{array}{r} 600 \\ \times\ \ 50 \\ \hline \end{array}$
15. $\begin{array}{r} 8,000 \\ \times\ \ \ \ \ 60 \\ \hline \end{array}$

16. $\begin{array}{r} 57 \\ \times\ 2 \\ \hline \end{array}$
17. $\begin{array}{r} 652 \\ \times\ \ \ 5 \\ \hline \end{array}$
18. $\begin{array}{r} 4,305 \\ \times\ \ \ \ \ 6 \\ \hline \end{array}$
19. $\begin{array}{r} 9,760 \\ \times\ \ \ \ \ 5 \\ \hline \end{array}$
20. $\begin{array}{r} 8,978 \\ \times\ \ \ \ \ 7 \\ \hline \end{array}$

21. $\begin{array}{r} 84 \\ \times 17 \\ \hline \end{array}$
22. $\begin{array}{r} 95 \\ \times 32 \\ \hline \end{array}$
23. $\begin{array}{r} 486 \\ \times\ \ 51 \\ \hline \end{array}$
24. $\begin{array}{r} 369 \\ \times\ \ 75 \\ \hline \end{array}$
25. $\begin{array}{r} 907 \\ \times\ \ 48 \\ \hline \end{array}$

26. $46 \times 23 = n$ 27. $87 \times 79 = n$ 28. $86 \times 125 = n$ 29. $98 \times 206 = n$

Solve.

30. Bob and Fern unpacked boxes of new books in the library. They unpacked 13 boxes that held 28 books each. How many books did they unpack?

31. Shing put 136 packages of construction paper on a shelf. Each package held 48 sheets of paper. How many sheets of construction paper did he put on the shelf?

32. Lisa had $50.00. She bought 4 books for $3.00 each, 3 magazines for $1.50 each, and 6 bookmarks for $1.00 each. How much money did she have left after her purchases?

33. Carl likes mystery stories. One day he read 46 pages. The next day he read 55 pages, the third day 63 pages, and the fourth day 70 pages. If this pattern continues, how many pages will he read on the sixth day?

Make a Model of Solar Collectors

Solar energy may be captured by solar collector cells, sometimes placed on the roof of a building. It takes 28 panels of 37 cells to produce 1 kilowatt of electricity. With your teammates, model the solar collectors needed to produce 1 kilowatt of electricity.

Talk about how you can use index cards, glue, and markers to model the solar collectors needed to produce 1 kilowatt of electricity.

Work with your teammates. Glue 28 index cards onto a large sheet of colored paper to represent solar collector panels. Use a marker to show 37 "dot" solar collector cells inside each panel.

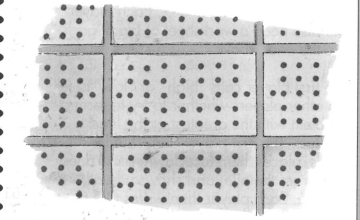

Show your model. Describe how the number of solar collector cells needed to produce 1 kilowatt of electricity can be calculated.

Talk About It

a. How can you use your model to imagine the number of cells needed to produce 77 kilowatts of electricity?

b. In your everyday activities, what other multiplication situations that involve large products have you noticed?

4

GEOMETRY

Did you know ...

... that on space flights, astronauts wear monitoring devices that help specialists learn how the human body reacts to conditions in space?

Talk About It

Isabel is fascinated with space technology. She describes a space picture over the telephone to her friend. How can Isabel use what she knows about three-dimensional figures to describe the picture's features?

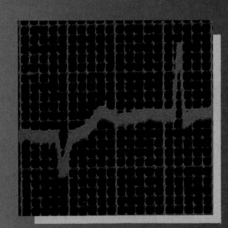

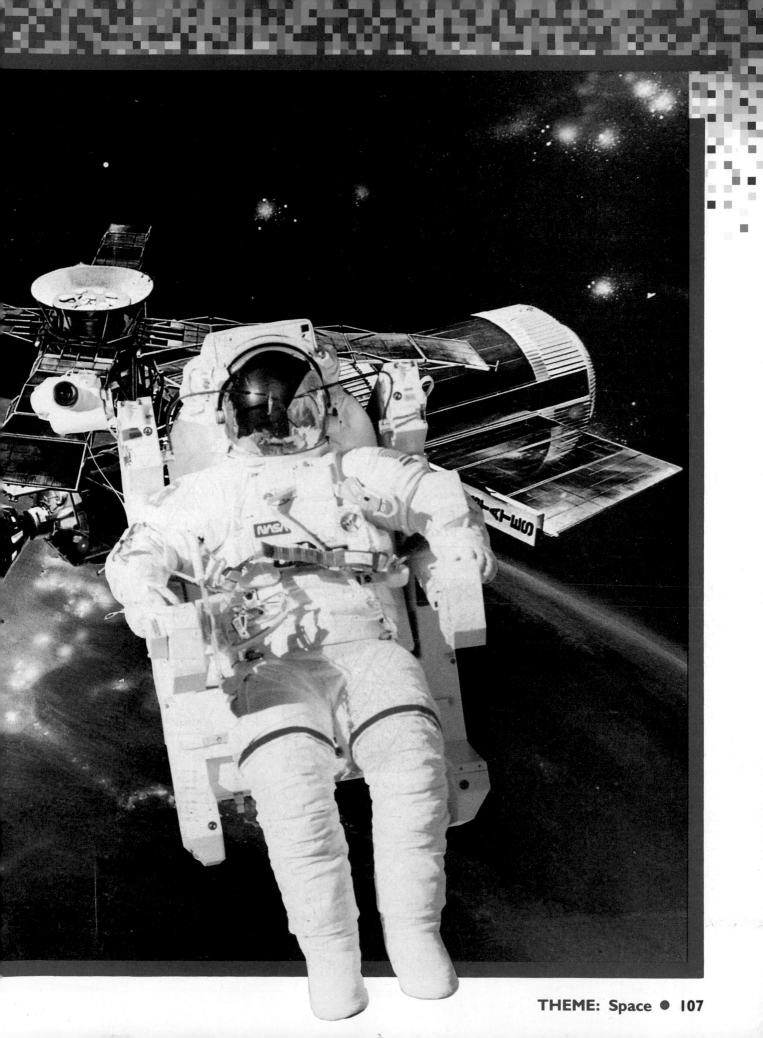

LINE RELATIONSHIPS

The astronauts who explore space discuss the size, shape, and position of things. They use basic ideas from geometry.

A **point** is used to describe an exact location in space.	*P*	Use a capital letter to name a point. *P* • Point *P*, or *P*
A **line** is a straight path made up of points in a plane. A line goes on forever in both directions.	*A* *C*	Use any two points on a line to name a line. Line *AC*, or $\overleftrightarrow{AC}$ Line *CA*, or $\overleftrightarrow{CA}$
A **line segment** is part of a line. It is a straight path with two endpoints.	*E* *F*	Use the endpoints to name a line segment. Line segment *EF*, or $\overline{EF}$ Line segment *FE*, or $\overline{FE}$
All the points that form a flat surface are called a **plane**. A plane extends in all directions.	*E* *F* *A* *B*	Use 3 points to name this plane. Plane *AEF*

- Is line segment *EF* vertical or horizontal?

You can use a sheet of paper to represent a plane and 10 toothpicks to represent line segments.

Drop 10 toothpicks on the paper. Look for different ways the toothpicks can touch or cross. Draw all the different ways you see. Then repeat the process.

Talk About It

▶ How can you describe the positions of the toothpicks?

▶ Name a point where the line segments touch or cross.

Within a plane, lines can be either intersecting or parallel.
Look at the drawings.

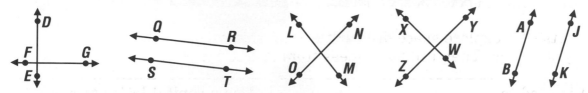

Lines that meet or cross each other at one point are called
intersecting lines.

- Name the intersecting line segments.

Lines that intersect at one point to form square corners are
called **perpendicular** lines.

- Name the perpendicular line segments.

Lines in a plane that will never intersect are the same
distance from each other. They are called **parallel** lines.

- Name the parallel line segments.

Talk About It

▶ When you dropped the toothpicks, did
you draw any line relationships you
do not see in the drawings above?

▶ Do perpendicular lines always
intersect? If so, at how many points
do they intersect?

▶ Are all intersecting line segments
perpendicular? Explain.

▶ How do you know that parallel lines
will never intersect?

Imagine that the toothpicks are lines
that extend in both directions.

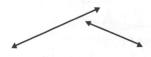

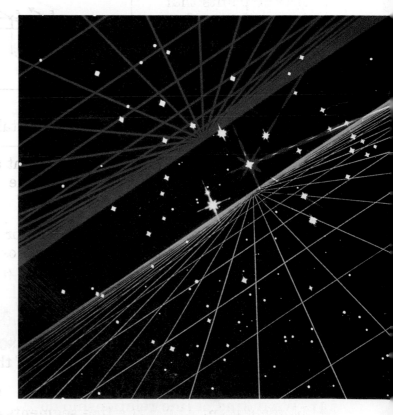

- Are there some lines in the same plane that are neither
intersecting nor parallel? Explain your answer.

Check for Understanding

Complete. Write *always*, *sometimes*, or *never*.

1. A line segment ___?___ forms a straight path.

2. Intersecting lines ___?___ cross each other at one point.

3. Intersecting lines are ___?___ perpendicular.

4. Parallel lines ___?___ intersect.

5. Lines in a plane ___?___ intersect if they are not parallel.

Practice

Choose the sentence that describes the relationship of the lines. Write **a**, **b**, or **c**.

6.

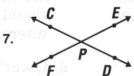

a. $\overleftrightarrow{AB}$ is not perpendicular to $\overleftrightarrow{DC}$.

b. $\overline{AB}$ is parallel to $\overline{DC}$.

c. $\overline{AB}$ is perpendicular to $\overline{DC}$.

7.

a. $\overleftrightarrow{CD}$ is parallel to $\overleftrightarrow{EF}$.

b. $\overleftrightarrow{CD}$ intersects $\overleftrightarrow{EF}$.

c. $\overleftrightarrow{DC}$ is perpendicular to $\overleftrightarrow{FE}$.

8.

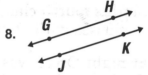

a. $\overleftrightarrow{GH}$ is perpendicular to $\overleftrightarrow{JK}$.

b. $\overleftrightarrow{GH}$ intersects $\overleftrightarrow{JK}$.

c. $\overleftrightarrow{GH}$ is parallel to $\overleftrightarrow{JK}$.

Mixed Applications

Use the map for Exercises 9–12.

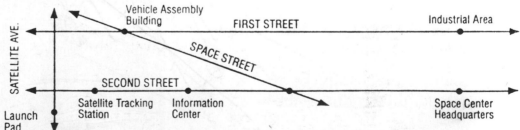

9. Which streets run horizontally? vertically?

10. Explain the relationship between First Street and Space Street.

11. What kind of line relationship do First Street and Second Street represent?

12. **Write a Question** Use the map to write a question about a line segment.

What line relationships have you noticed in your everyday world?

More Practice, Lesson 4.1, page H46

Oscar's family lives in Spaceville, Earth. Solve each problem to find out about a day in the life of Oscar.

1. Oscar takes the school shuttle to Big Dipper School, located 125.6 space miles away. On the path from his home to school, the shuttle stops to pick up Venus. She lives 27.8 space miles from Oscar. How far does Venus live from Big Dipper School?

2. While at school, Oscar decides to buy some lunch pellets with his starbucks at the spaceteria. He buys a red food pellet for $0.25, a green food pellet for $0.50, 2 blue food pellets for $0.75 each, and an asteroid apple for $0.60. How much change will he receive from $5.00?

3. Henry and Hugo are in Oscar's first class at school. Henry, Hugo, and Venus are in his second class. Hugo and Venus are in Oscar's third class, and Henry, Hugo, and Venus are in his fourth class. Who has the most classes with Oscar?

4. After school Oscar plays spaceball. Oscar imagines that a straight path from first base to second base and one from second base to third base are line segments. At what point would these two line segments intersect?

5. That night Oscar was first to arrive at the intergalactic gig. During the first 5 minutes of the gig, 5 more spacemates arrived. After 10 minutes 12 spacemates were at the gig, and after 15 minutes 24 spacemates were there. If the pattern continued, how long was it before all 96 spacemates were at the gig?

6. Oscar's space pad is located on a path between his friends Henry and Hugo. Venus also lives between Henry and Hugo. If Venus lives next door to Hugo, who lives next door on both sides of Oscar?

NAMING RAYS AND ANGLES

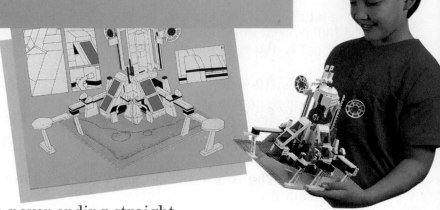

The drawing of a plan for a space station shows the many angles that are formed by its structure.

You have learned that a line is a never-ending straight path that extends in both directions.

A **ray** is part of a line that has one endpoint and goes on forever in one direction.

A ray is named by its endpoint and any other point on the ray. The endpoint is always named first.

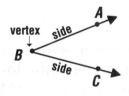

Ray BC, or $\overrightarrow{BC}$

Talk About It

▶ Name another ray on line *AC*.

▶ Is a line segment part of a ray? Why or why not?

▶ Name some real things that are examples of rays.

When two rays have the same endpoint, they form an **angle**. The common endpoint is the **vertex** of the angle. The rays are the **sides** of the angle.

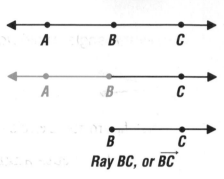

Angle *ABC*, Angle *CBA*, or Angle *B*
$\angle ABC$, $\angle CBA$, or $\angle B$

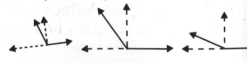

Angles that form square corners are called **right** angles.

Angles that fit inside a right angle are called **acute** angles.

Angles that fit between a right angle and a straight line are called **obtuse** angles.

Talk About It

▶ Can angles be formed by line segments that have the same endpoint? Why or why not?

▶ Name some real things that show examples of angles.

Check for Understanding

Choose a word from the box to complete each sentence.

acute
obtuse
ray
right
vertex

1. An angle smaller than a right angle is a(n) __?__ angle.

2. An angle larger than a right angle is a(n) __?__ angle.

3. An angle that forms a square corner is a(n) __?__ angle.

4. Part of a line that has one endpoint is a(n) __?__ .

5. The common endpoint of an angle is the __?__ .

Practice

Identify the angle. Write *right, acute,* or *obtuse.*

6.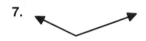

7.

8.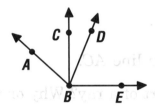

Use the figure for Exercises 9–11.

9. Name two acute angles.

10. Name a right angle.

11. Name an obtuse angle.

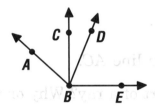

Mixed Applications

12. A launch is scheduled for 2:00 P.M. Classify the angle formed by the hands on a clock for this time.

13. The shuttle will lift off at 3:00 P.M. What angle is formed by the hands on a clock for this time?

14. Clara's family drove 5 hours to reach the launch site. If they drove 55 miles each hour, how many miles did they drive?

15. Ralph bought a model of the shuttle for $12.50 and 2 calendars for $5.95 each. How much change did he receive from $25.00?

VISUAL THINKING

In this figure, ∠RQT is in a plane. Point S is in the **exterior** of the angle. Point W is in the **interior** of the angle.

16. Draw and name an angle in a plane. Name a point in the interior and exterior of the plane.

Find three angles in your classroom that are right, acute, and obtuse. Describe and draw a picture of each angle.

EXPLORING

Angle Measurement

Just as there are unit names for measuring time or length, there is a unit name for measuring angles. It is called a **degree** (°). A circle is divided into 360 degrees.

A **protractor** is a tool used for measuring the size of the opening of an angle. Its scale is marked from 0° to 180°.

WORK TOGETHER

Building Understanding

Use a protractor to measure these angles.

Make sure ray *EF* passes through zero (0).

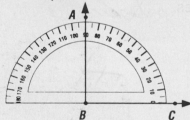

Read the measure of the angle where ray *BA* passes through the scale.

∠*ABC* is a right angle. Its measure is 90°.

Place the center at the vertex of the angle.

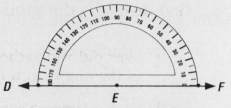

∠*DEF* is a **straight** angle. Its measure is 180°.

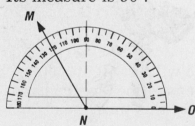

Make sure the rays pass through the marks on the scale.

Obtuse angles measure more than 90° but less than 180°.

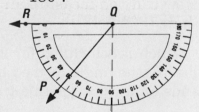

Acute angles measure less than 90°.

Talk About It

▶ What can you conclude about the measure of right angles?

▶ What are the measures of ∠*MNO* and ∠*PQR*?

▶ Suppose you have a ray *PQ*. How can you use a protractor to draw an angle of 45°?

▶ If the rays are extended, will the angle measure be changed? Why or why not?

 Connection, pages 450–451

Making the Connection

Study this diagram. Use what you know about angle measures to explore the angles formed by intersecting lines.

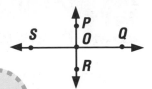

Talk About It

► Describe the angles formed by these lines.

► What is the measure of each of the angles formed?

► What relationship do you see between a right angle and a straight angle?

► What is the sum of the degrees of all four angles?

Make a table showing types of angles. Draw two of each type of angle. First, estimate and record the estimated measures. Then, find their actual measures and record.

Talk About It

► How did you estimate the measures of the angles you drew in your table?

► How do your estimates compare with the actual measures of the angles?

► How can you measure an angle greater than 180°?

Checking Understanding

Trace each angle. First, estimate the angle measure. Then, use a protractor to measure each angle. You may need to extend the rays.

1.
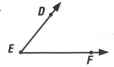

2.
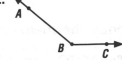

3.
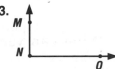

4. Draw an acute angle. Use a protractor to measure the angle. Record the measure.

5. Draw an obtuse angle. Use a protractor to measure the angle. Record the measure.

6. Use a protractor to draw an angle of 60°.

More Practice, Lesson 4.3, pages H46–H47

EXPLORING
Polygons

WORK TOGETHER

Building Understanding

Look at the diagrams. Since they lie on a flat
surface, they are called plane figures. They
are made up of points that are all in the same plane.

These are **open** figures.   These are **closed** figures.

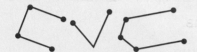 

Use a geoboard or dot paper to make several closed figures.

Talk About It

▶ Describe some of the closed figures you made.

▶ How many line segments does each of your shapes have? angles?

▶ What is the relationship between the number of line segments
and the number of angles of each shape?

Special closed plane figures are called **polygons**.
Polygons are made up of line segments that meet
at vertices, but do not cross.

A polygon is modeled on each of these geoboards.

• Pentagon •

• Hexagon •

Use a geoboard or dot paper to model six different polygons.

Talk About It

Look at your models.

▶ What relationship can you find between the number of sides and
the number of angles of each of your models?

▶ Name some examples of real objects with polygon shapes.

Making the Connection

Copy and complete the table using your polygon models.

Polygons			
Name of Polygon	Number of Sides	Number of Angles	Picture of Your Model
Triangle	3	■	◁
Quadrilateral	■	4	■
Pentagon	5	■	■
Hexagon	■	■	⬡
Octagon	8	■	■

Use the table to give you some clues about regular polygons.

These are regular polygons.

These are irregular polygons.

Talk About It

▶ Look at the regular and irregular triangles. Describe the angles in both. Describe the sides.

▶ How are regular polygons different from irregular polygons?

So, a **regular** polygon has all sides the same length and all angles the same measure, while an **irregular** polygon has sides of various lengths and angles of different measures.

Checking Understanding

Name a polygon represented by each object.

1. pennant   2. baseball diamond   3. chalkboard   4. stop sign

Write *true* or *false*.

5. A triangle is an open plane figure.

6. A hexagon has six angles and six sides.

7. A regular pentagon has two sides of unequal length.

8. A polygon has the same number of sides and angles.

More Practice, Lesson 4.4, page H47

CLASSIFYING TRIANGLES

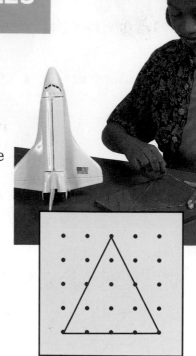

The *Columbia* is a space shuttle. It moves like a rocket and uses triangular wings to glide to a landing.

A **triangle** has three sides and three angles. Triangles can be classified according to the lengths of their sides.

Use the geoboard, a geoband, and a piece of string to explore triangles. Use your geoband to form a triangle.

Start on the top row of the geoboard. Place the geoband on the center peg. Then loop it around the corner pegs at the bottom.

• How many sides are formed? how many angles?

Use a piece of string to measure the lengths of the sides.

• How many sides are the same length?

A triangle that has at least two sides of equal length is called an **isosceles** triangle.

Form a new triangle by moving the geoband from the center peg to two spaces up from the bottom left corner. Use your string to measure the lengths of the sides.

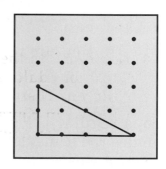

• Is this an isosceles triangle? How do you know?

• What did you find out about the lengths of the three sides?

A triangle in which each side is a different length is called a **scalene** triangle.

Some geoboards have pegs on the back side. These pegs form a circular pattern. Look at the triangle in the example. Measure the lengths of the sides.

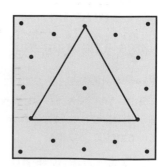

• What did you find out about the length of the three sides?

A triangle with all sides of equal length is called an **equilateral** triangle.

Use a geoboard to model each kind of triangle in three different sizes. Check the lengths of the sides with your string. Record your results, and classify your triangles in a table.

Idea Bank, page 464, Exercise 3

Check for Understanding

Identify the triangle. Write **a**, **b**, or **c**.

1. equilateral   a. ◺   b. △   c. ◹

2. scalene   a. ▽   b. ▽   c. ◁

3. isosceles   a. △   b. ◁   c. ◺

Practice

Name each triangle. Write *equilateral, scalene,* or *isosceles.*

4. △   5. ◁   6. ▽   7. ◿

Mixed Applications

8. Admission to the science center is $3.25 for adults and $2.75 for children. There are 2 adults and 2 children in Kay's family. What will they pay for admission?

9. Models of rockets were on exhibit in 4 different rooms. Tony counted about 39 people in one room. If each room had about the same number of people, about how many people were viewing the exhibit?

LOGICAL REASONING

Complete the activity to discover the sum of the number of degrees of all angles in a triangle.

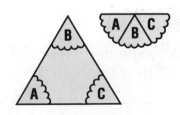

Use a ruler to draw a picture of a large triangle. Label each vertex with the letters *A, B,* and *C.* Tear the corners as shown. Place the angles together at a point on a straight line.

10. What is the total measure of the three angles of the triangle?

11. Draw another triangle and repeat the activity. What are your results?

Name the polygon with the fewest sides and angles.

WRAP UP...

The angles of triangles can be used to classify triangles.

Use dot paper and a ruler to explore the angles of triangles.

To draw a triangle on your dot paper, start on a corner dot. Count across three spaces and mark the vertex. Count up three spaces and mark the vertex. Draw line segments between each pair of vertices.

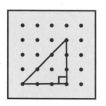

- How many angles are formed inside the triangle?

- How can you estimate the measure of each angle?

- Name each type of angle in the triangle.

A triangle that has a right angle is a **right** triangle.

Draw a triangle that matches this model.

- How do these angles compare with right angles?

- Name each type of angle in the triangle.

A triangle that has three acute angles is an **acute** triangle.

Use the dot paper again.
Draw a triangle that matches this model.

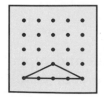

- How do these angles compare with right angles?

- What do you call an angle greater than a right angle?

- Name each type of angle in the triangle.

A triangle that has one obtuse angle is an **obtuse** triangle.

 Idea Bank, page 464, Exercise 2

Check for Understanding

Identify the triangle. Write **a**, **b**, or **c**.

1. right a. 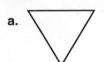 b. c.

2. acute a.  b. c.

3. obtuse a. 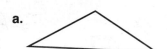 b. 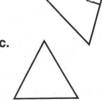 c.

Practice

Name each triangle. Write *right*, *acute*, or *obtuse*.

4. 　　5. 　　6. 　　7.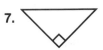

Mixed Applications

8. A Titan vehicle can lift 8,600 pounds into a low orbit of Earth. With two solid-fuel boosters, it can lift 27,000 pounds. How much more weight can the Titan lift with the boosters?

9. **Logical Reasoning** Jenny said the wings of a space shuttle were right triangles, and her brother said they were scalene triangles. Could both be correct? Explain.

10. **Logical Reasoning** Draw a triangle. By drawing one line, can you divide the triangle into two right triangles? Explain.

11. A spacecraft 200 miles high must travel at a speed of 17,000 miles per hour. At 22,000 miles high, it must travel 6,900 miles per hour. What is the difference in the speeds?

MIXED REVIEW

Complete.

1. Round 16.547 to the nearest tenth, hundredth, and whole number.

Express each as a part of the whole unit.

2. 9 centimeters = ■ meter　　3. 5 decimeters = ■ meter　　4. 8 hundredths = ■

Name the three words used to classify angles.

More Practice, Lesson 4.6, page H47

EXPLORING
Quadrilaterals

Quadrilaterals are polygons with four sides and four angles. There are several different quadrilaterals. Some of them you already know.

WORK TOGETHER

Building Understanding

Make larger drawings of these figures. Make cardboard strips from your drawings. Punch holes in the cardboard strips and connect them with fasteners. Record the figures on a sheet of paper.

Make a rectangle.   Make a square.   Make a trapezoid.

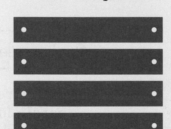

Talk About It

▶ How many different shapes did you make?

▶ Which figures have four right angles?

▶ Which figure has acute and obtuse angles?

▶ Which figures have two pairs of parallel sides?

▶ Which figure has only one pair of parallel sides?

Adjust the cardboard strips of the square and the rectangle to form a different kind of quadrilateral for each. Trace these new figures on a sheet of paper.

▶ Describe the new figures you made.

▶ Do your new figures have any right angles?

▶ Do any of your figures have parallel sides? If so, how many?

Making the Connection

Here are names and examples of some different types of quadrilaterals. Make a table of quadrilaterals. Describe the relationship between the sides and angles.

Quadrilateral	Description	Example
Rectangle	?	▭
Square	?	◻
Rhombus	?	▱
Parallelogram	?	▱
Trapezoid	?	⏢

Checking Understanding

1.  parallelogram   trapezoid

Compare the sides of a parallelogram with the sides of a trapezoid. How are they different?

2. parallelogram   rectangle

Compare the sides of a parallelogram with the sides of a rectangle. How are they the same?

3. rhombus   trapezoid

Compare the sides of a rhombus with the sides of a trapezoid. How are they different?

4. rectangle   square

Compare the angles of a rectangle with the angles of a square. What are their measures?

VISUAL THINKING

5. A tangram is a famous puzzle. Copy the seven closed plane figures of a tangram. Cut out the pieces. Rearrange all seven pieces to form different quadrilaterals. How many different quadrilaterals can you make? Name them.

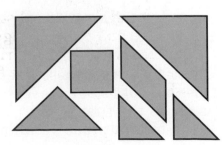

PROBLEM *Solving*

The rocket used to launch a space probe has 4 stages. Each stage goes up twice as many miles as the stage before it. The total altitude reached is 75 miles. If the last stage travels 8 times as far as the first stage, how far does each stage travel?

Often problems can be solved by using the strategy *guess and check*. If the first guess is not correct, use the information learned and guess again.

▶ **UNDERSTAND**

What are you asked to find?
What facts are given?

▶ **PLAN**

What plan can you make?

Make a guess for the altitude reached by the first stage.

▶ **SOLVE**

How can you solve the problem?

First, guess 4 miles. Then, check the number by doubling the 4 to get the distance for the second stage. Continue doubling the distance to find the distances for the other stages.

$$4 + 8 + 16 + 32 = 60$$
Stage 1 Stage 2 Stage 3 Stage 4

Is the sum 75? No, it is less than 75.
Guess again. Try a larger number. Guess 5.

$$5 + 10 + 20 + 40 = 75$$
Stage 1 Stage 2 Stage 3 Stage 4

Is the sum 75? Yes.
So, the 4 rocket stages travel 5, 10, 20, and 40 miles.

▶ **LOOK BACK**

How can you check your answer?

Check by asking these questions:
Does the last stage travel 8 times as far as the first?
Is the total altitude 75 miles?

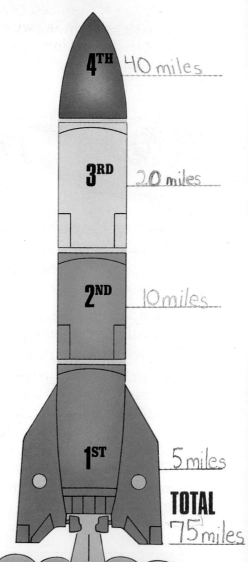

4TH 40 miles

3RD 20 miles

2ND 10 miles

1ST 5 miles

TOTAL 75 miles

WHAT IF... ...the rocket only reaches an altitude of 45 miles? How far will each stage travel?

Apply

Solve. Use the strategy guess and check.

(1) A rocket is divided into 4 sections. On the launch pad, the rocket stands 90 feet tall. The second section is twice as long as the first section, the third section is twice as long as the second section, and the fourth section is twice as long as the third section. How long is each section of the rocket?

(2) On a space station miles above the earth, a rocket has been assembled with 3 stages. The rocket is designed so that each stage will go 3 times as far as the one before it. If the total altitude to be reached is 6,500 miles, how far will each stage travel?

Mixed Applications	**STRATEGIES**	• Guess and Check • Make a Drawing
		• Find a Pattern • Write a Number Sentence

Choose a strategy and solve.

(3) Nine planets travel around the sun. Of the five planets closest to the sun, Earth is between Venus and Mars. If Mercury is between Venus and the sun, what planet is next to Jupiter?

(4) Suppose each stage of a rocket could carry it 80,000 miles. The moon is about 240,000 miles away. If you wanted to go to the moon and return, how many stages would a rocket need?

(5) A shuttle crew released a satellite into orbit. After 1 minute the satellite was 80 yards from the launch vehicle. After 2 minutes it was 160 yards away. After 3 minutes it was 240 yards away, and after 4 minutes it was 320 yards away. If the pattern continues, how far away will the satellite be after 6 minutes?

(6) Mercury is 57,040,000 miles from Earth, and Mars is 48,360,000 miles from Earth. How much farther is Mercury from Earth than Mars is from Earth?

WRITER'S CORNER

(7) Write a *guess-and-check* problem. Add two numbers, and give only the sum of the numbers to a partner. Give one additional clue (the product or difference of the numbers), and ask your partner to find the numbers.

REVIEW AND MAINTENANCE

1. A baseball team won 8 more games than it lost. If it played 56 games, how many games did it win?

2. On the first day of practice, Paul did 3 sit-ups. On the second day he did 5, on the third day he did 8, and on the fourth day he did 12. If this pattern continued, how many sit-ups did he do on the sixth day of practice?

I can look for patterns to help me solve problems.

Write two other forms for each number.

3. 1.35　　4. 0.678　　5. 14.209　　6. 0.003　　7. 12.12

Complete.

8. $10^{\blacksquare} = 1{,}000$　　9. $10 \times 10 \times 10 \times 10 = \blacksquare$　　10. $10^{\blacksquare} = 10{,}000$

Estimate.

11. $\begin{array}{r} 495 \\ + \ 47 \\ \hline \end{array}$　12. $\begin{array}{r} 780 \\ + 115 \\ \hline \end{array}$　13. $\begin{array}{r} 1{,}423 \\ + \ \ 397 \\ \hline \end{array}$　14. $\begin{array}{r} 28{,}125 \\ + 31{,}084 \\ \hline \end{array}$　15. $\begin{array}{r} 41{,}095 \\ + \ 6{,}154 \\ \hline \end{array}$

Complete. Identify the addition property used.

16. $7{,}985 + \blacksquare = 7{,}985$　　　　17. $4.25 + 5.73 = 5.73 + \blacksquare$

18. $275 + 450 = \blacksquare + 275$　　　　19. $(50 + 75) + 125 = \blacksquare + (75 + 125)$

Multiply.

20. $\begin{array}{r} 60 \\ \times \ 3 \\ \hline \end{array}$　21. $\begin{array}{r} 700 \\ \times \ \ 5 \\ \hline \end{array}$　22. $\begin{array}{r} 300 \\ \times \ \ 8 \\ \hline \end{array}$　23. $\begin{array}{r} 8{,}000 \\ \times \ \ \ \ 4 \\ \hline \end{array}$　24. $\begin{array}{r} 4{,}000 \\ \times \ \ \ \ 9 \\ \hline \end{array}$

25. $\begin{array}{r} 83 \\ \times \ 8 \\ \hline \end{array}$　26. $\begin{array}{r} 254 \\ \times \ \ 5 \\ \hline \end{array}$　27. $\begin{array}{r} 4{,}397 \\ \times \ \ \ \ 6 \\ \hline \end{array}$　28. $\begin{array}{r} 6{,}592 \\ \times \ \ \ \ 4 \\ \hline \end{array}$　29. $\begin{array}{r} 8{,}543 \\ \times \ \ \ \ 6 \\ \hline \end{array}$

Identify the angle. Write *acute*, *obtuse*, or *right*.

30. 　31. 　32. 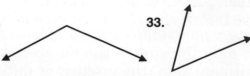　33.

Spotlight ON PROBLEM SOLVING

Analyze Data

You can use patterns to solve some problems. Study the situation. See whether you can determine the pattern that will solve the problem.

The astronauts in a space-station simulator receive their mail every 5 days. They receive fresh food every 4 days. How often do they receive their mail and fresh food on the same day?

Talk About It

Work with a partner to answer the questions.

- How can you use the drawing to help you solve the problem?

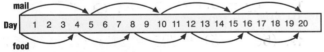

- What is delivered on day 12? on day 15?

- When is the first time that the mail and the food are delivered on the same day?

- Predict what will be delivered on day 28. How do you know?

- When is the second time that the mail and the food will be delivered on the same day?

- Is there a pattern of days when the astronauts receive their mail and food on the same day? Explain.

- Is there another way to solve the problem? Explain.

Apply

Solve. Be prepared to describe the patterns in the problems.

1 During a 4-week mission, an astronaut does exercises every other day. She also works out with weights every third day. How many times during the mission will she do exercises and work out with weights on the same day?

2 A mission specialist checks his plant experiments every 3 days, fungus experiments every 4 days, and crystal experiments every 6 days. During a 30-day mission, how many times will he check all 3 experiments on the same day? On what days?

127

A figure has a line of **symmetry** if it can be folded so that the two parts of the figure are identical.

Look at the cutout letters. Each letter is marked with a dotted line of symmetry. Place a mirror along the dotted line to show a **mirror image** of each letter.

- What do you see?

- Which letters have both a vertical and a horizontal line of symmetry?

A figure may have more than one line of symmetry. Use scissors and a regular-hexagon pattern to explore lines of symmetry. Cut out a regular hexagon, and follow these steps:

- Fold the pattern in half so that one side exactly covers the other side.

- Open the pattern and fold in half another way.

- Repeat the process to make as many folds in the pattern as possible.

- Count the number of folds you made.

- How many lines of symmetry does a regular hexagon have?

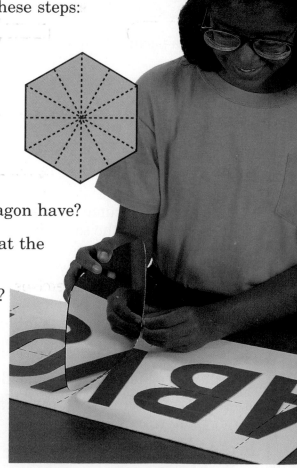

Cut out a square and an equilateral triangle. Repeat the steps above.

- How many lines of symmetry does a square have? an equilateral triangle?

Record your results. Draw the lines of symmetry.

- Compare the number of sides of the square and the equilateral triangle with the number of lines of symmetry. What do your results tell you about regular polygons and lines of symmetry?

Idea Bank, page 464, Exercise 1

Check for Understanding

Trace each drawing. Draw all the lines of symmetry for each regular polygon.

1.
2.
3.
4.

Practice

Tell whether the picture shows a mirror image. Write *yes* or *no*.

5.
6.
7.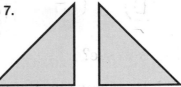

Trace each figure. Draw all the lines of symmetry for each figure.

8.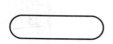
9.
10.
11.

Trace each drawing and complete the design to make a symmetrical figure.

12.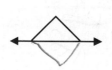
13.
14.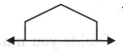
15.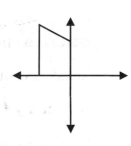

Mixed Applications

Use the list of letters for Exercises 16–19.

N   O   P   Q   R   S   T   U   V   W   X   Y   Z

16. Which of the letters have no lines of symmetry?

17. Which of the letters have only one line of symmetry?

18. Which of the letters have more than one line of symmetry?

19. **Analyze Data** Use only symmetrical letters to write a word.

Name some things found in nature that have line symmetry.

EXPLORING
Congruence and Motion

Figures that have the same shape and size are **congruent**.

$\overline{AB}$ is congruent to $\overline{CD}$.

$\triangle GHI$ is congruent to $\triangle LMN$.

Figure X is congruent to Figure Y.

WORK TOGETHER

Building Understanding

Use pattern blocks and graph paper to explore different ways to move congruent polygons on a flat surface.

Place a trapezoid on graph paper as shown. Trace around it to record a starting position. **Slide**, or move the trapezoid along the line, going up 8 units and right 5 units.

- Did the trapezoid change its size or shape?

- What is changed when you slide the trapezoid?

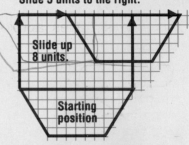

Slide 5 units to the right.
Slide up 8 units.
Starting position

Return the trapezoid to the starting position. **Flip**, or turn over, the trapezoid across a line of symmetry.

- Are the two trapezoids congruent?

- How has the starting position of the trapezoid changed?

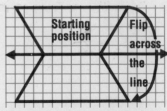

Starting position
Flip across the line

Return the trapezoid to the starting position. This time, **turn**, or rotate, the trapezoid around a vertex as shown.

- What changed this time?

- What did not change?

- Turn the trapezoid around another vertex. What happened?

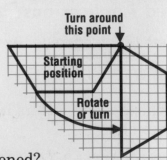

Turn around this point
Starting position
Rotate or turn

Choose several other polygons. Try sliding, flipping, and turning them.

- What can you say about one figure if you can slide, flip, or turn it to make it look like another figure?

130

Making the Connection

Look at the figures. Decide whether the second figure is a result of a move.

A.
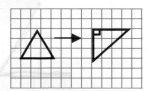

B.
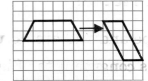

C.
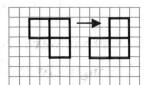

> **Talk About It**
>
> ▶ Which of the figures shows motion?
>
> ▶ If any figures do not show motion, explain why.
>
> ▶ Does motion change a figure's shape? Explain.

Checking Understanding

Copy the figures in Exercises 1–3 on graph paper.

1. Flip the squares across the line.

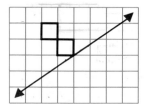

2. Turn the rectangle around this vertex until it sits on another side.

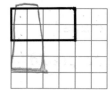

3. Slide the rhombus down 3 units and left 7 units.

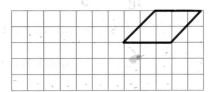

Write *slide*, *flip*, or *turn* to indicate how each figure was moved.

4.
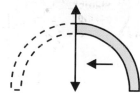

5.

6.

7.
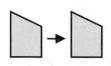

8.
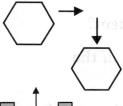

9.
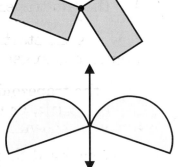

Use Figures *a, b, c,* and *d* for Exercises 10–12.

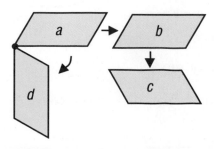

10. Name the motion when *a* is moved to *b*.

11. Name the motions when *a* is moved to *c*.

12. Name the motion when *a* is moved to *d*.

IDENTIFYING SIMILAR FIGURES

Figures that have the same shape are called **similar** figures. They may or may not have the same size.

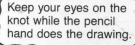
Keep your eyes on the knot while the pencil hand does the drawing.

Use a large sheet of paper, tape, a pencil, and two identical rubber bands to create a similar figure.

- Knot together two rubber bands.

- Tape a large sheet of paper to the desk.

- Place the figure to be traced on one side of the paper.

- Loop the rubber band around your finger to act as an anchor.

- Stretch the rubber band from the anchor point so that the knot is directly over the figure.

- Place your pencil at the other end of the rubber band, and move the pencil as the knot traces the figure.

Talk About It

▶ Do the two figures have the same shape? the same size?

▶ Is the new figure similar to the first figure?

▶ What will happen if you change the anchor point to another point?

Compare the groups of polygons.

These are similar.　　　　These are not similar.

Talk About It

▶ How can you tell whether two polygons are similar?

▶ Are a pair of regular hexagons always similar? Why or why not?

▶ Are all circles similar? How do you know?

Check for Understanding

Use dot paper to draw a similar figure. Double the length of each side.

1.
2.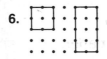
3.
4.

Practice

Are the figures similar? Write *yes* or *no*.

5.
6.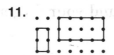
7.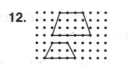
8.

9.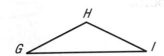
10.
11.
12.

Use a larger dot pattern to draw a similar figure.

13.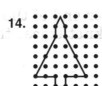
14.

15. Explain why triangle *DEF* and triangle *GHI* are not similar.

16. Is a baseball similar to a basketball? Explain.

17. If a rocket travels 25,000 miles per hour, how many miles does it travel in 8 hours?

MIXED REVIEW

Multiply.

1. 382
   × 2

2. 475
   × 3

3. 693
   × 5

4. 4,325
   × 4

5. 6,871
   × 8

Multiply each by 10, 100, and 1,000.

6. 7
7. 18
8. 23
9. 36
10. 49

When the sides of a 2 x 2 square on graph paper are doubled, how many squares are in the new figure?

WRAP UP...

EXPLORING

Circles

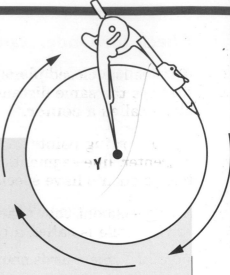

WORK TOGETHER

Building Understanding

A **compass** is a tool for constructing circles.

Use a compass or two pencils and a paper clip to draw a circle. Place a point, *Y*, on a sheet of paper. Place the tip of the compass on the point, and swing the pencil around to form the circle.

The point *Y* is the center of the circle. A circle is named by its center. The point *X* is one of many points on the circle.

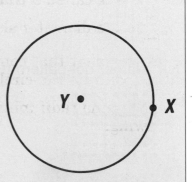

- Using the compass, how can you make larger or smaller circles?

Trace and cut out the circle you have made.

- How many ways can you fold the circle so that the fold passes through the center, *Y*?

- What do you call these folds?

Using this information about circles, construct a circle on a large sheet of paper. The circle must be larger than one that can be drawn with a compass.

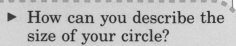

Talk About It

▶ How can you describe the size of your circle?

▶ How did you make the circle?

A circle is a closed plane figure formed by all points that are the same distance from a given point in the plane called a **center**.

By connecting points on the circle, or in its center, line segments are formed. These line segments have special names.

A line segment that connects two points on the circle is called a **chord**.

• Name some chords shown in the drawing.

A chord that passes through the center of the circle is called a **diameter**.

• Name the diameter shown in the drawing.

A line segment that connects the center with a point on the circle is called a **radius.**

• Name some radii (plural) shown in the drawing.

Checking Understanding

Write *sometimes, always,* or *never* for Exercises 1–4.

1. A chord is __?__ shorter than a diameter.   2. A chord is __?__ longer than a diameter.

3. There are __?__ two radii in a diameter.   4. A radius is __?__ part of a diameter.

Complete.

5. What is the longest chord that can be drawn in a circle?

6. If you know the radius of a circle, how can you determine the diameter?

7. If you know the diameter of a circle, how can you determine the radius?

8. Name some items you could use to draw a circle if you did not have a compass.

9. What line segments in a circle determine the size of the circle?

10. Suppose you draw a circle by tracing around a cylinder. How could you locate the center point? (HINT: Use a cutout circle.)

WORK TOGETHER

Building Understanding

Use patterns to model solid figures.

Use the pattern on page H91 to model a figure that looks like a shoebox.

Your model represents a solid figure called a **rectangular prism.**

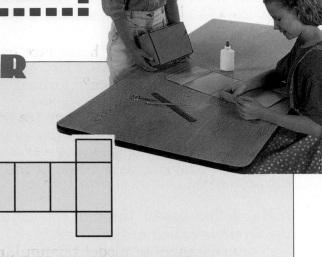

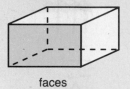
faces

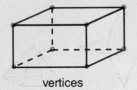
vertices

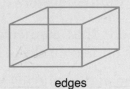
edges

• How many **faces** does the model have?

• What is formed where two faces intersect?

• How many **vertices** does the model have? how many **edges**?

Use the pattern on page H92 to model another prism.

• What do you notice about the lengths of the edges?

• What shape are the faces?

• How is this prism like the rectangular prism above?

• How is it different from the rectangular prism?

This special prism is called a **cube.**
A prism has two congruent faces, called **bases**. Here are other prisms.

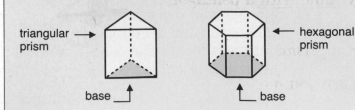

triangular prism

hexagonal prism

base

base

Talk About It

▶ What shapes are the bases of these prisms?

▶ What relationship does the name of each prism have with the shape of its base?

Use pipe cleaners to make four congruent equilateral triangles and one square. Use wire ties to hold the polygons together at the vertices to make a **pyramid**. Since the square is the base of the pyramid, this is a square pyramid.

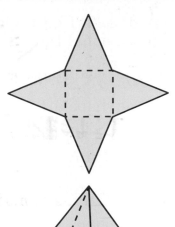

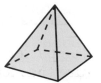

- How many faces does the square pyramid have?

- What shape is each face?

- How many edges does the square pyramid have?

- How do the faces, edges, and vertices of the square pyramid compare with those of the rectangular prism? the cube?

Use pipe cleaners to model triangular and rectangular pyramids.

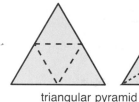

triangular pyramid   rectangular pyramid

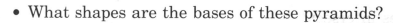

- What shapes are the bases of these pyramids?

- How are these pyramids like the square pyramid?

- How are these pyramids different from the square pyramid?

- What relationship does the name of each pyramid have with the shape of its base?

Talk About It

Use what you know about pyramids and prisms.

▶ What do all pyramids have in common?

▶ What name can you give to a prism with two pentagonal bases?

▶ What name can you give to a pyramid with a pentagonal base?

▶ How is a pyramid different from a prism?

▶ What other pyramids or prisms can you name?

Not all solid figures have flat surfaces. Some 3-dimensional figures have curved surfaces.

Use the pattern on page H96 to make a cylinder.

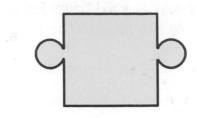

- What shape are the bases of a cylinder?

- How is a cylinder different from a pyramid or a prism?

Use the pattern on page H97 to make a cone.

- What shape is the base of a cone?

- How are a cone and a cylinder alike?

- How are a cone and a cylinder different?

- How are a cone and a pyramid alike?

Look at this model of a sphere.

- Does a sphere have any flat surfaces?

- How is a sphere different from a cone and a cylinder?

Look at the solid figures from the views given.

Figure A	Figure B	Figure C

Top View   Side View   Side-View

Talk About It

▶ Which solid figures could be represented by Figure A?

▶ Which solid figures could be represented by Figure B?

▶ In Figure B, what view would you be looking at if this were a triangular prism?

▶ Which solid figures could be represented by Figure C?

138

Making the Connection

Think about the solid figure formed by each pattern.

A.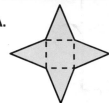

B.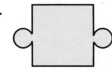

C.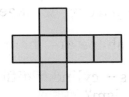

D.

E.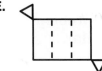

F.

Talk About It

▶ Which figures represent pyramids? prisms?

▶ Name each pyramid and prism.

▶ Which figures represent curved surfaces?

▶ Describe how the figures with curved surfaces differ from those with flat surfaces.

Checking Understanding

Copy and complete the table.

Solid Figure	Name	Number of Faces	Number of Vertices	Number of Edges
1.	Cube	6	8	■
2.	Square pyramid	■	5	8
3.	■	4	4	6
4.	Triangular prism	5	■	9
5.	Cylinder	2	■	0

6. Name the shapes needed and the number of each shape you would use to build a square pyramid.

7. Name at least two objects that have a shape like a cylinder.

8. Name two solid figures that have at least four triangles.

More Practice, Lesson 4.13, page H49

Marlene has a painted cube made up of 64 smaller cubes. Some have 3 faces painted, some have 2 faces painted, some have 1 face painted, and some have 0 faces painted. How many cubes of each type are there?

Sometimes you can solve a more difficult problem by first *solving a simpler problem* that is similar.

▶ UNDERSTAND

What are you asked to find?

What facts are given?

▶ PLAN

How can you do an easier problem first?

One way is to build several simpler cubes. Decide whether the paint will be on 3 faces, 2 faces, 1 face, or 0 faces. Make a table of the results.

▶ SOLVE

What simpler cubes can you make?

First, make a cube of $2 \times 2 \times 2$, or 8, smaller cubes and a cube of $3 \times 3 \times 3$, or 27, smaller cubes. Count the painted faces and complete the table.

Number of Cubes	3 Faces Painted	2 Faces Painted	1 Face Painted	0 Faces Painted
8	8	0	0	0
27	8	12	6	1
64	▇	▇	▇	▇

What cube can you make to complete the table? You can make a cube of $4 \times 4 \times 4$, or 64, smaller cubes. So, there are 8 cubes with 3 faces painted, 24 cubes with 2 faces painted, 24 cubes with 1 face painted, and 8 cubes with 0 faces painted.

▶ LOOK BACK

In what other way could you make a simpler problem?

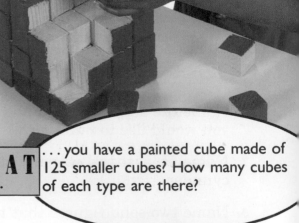

WHAT IF... ...you have a painted cube made of 125 smaller cubes? How many cubes of each type are there?

Apply

Use a simpler problem to solve.

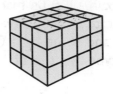

1 Find the number of cubes with 3 painted faces, 2 painted faces, 1 painted face, and 0 painted faces in this rectangular prism.

2 Find the number of cubes with 3 painted faces, 2 painted faces, 1 painted face, and 0 painted faces in this rectangular prism.

Mixed Applications	**STRATEGIES**	• Find a Pattern • Guess and Check • Write a Number Sentence • Solve a Simpler Problem

Choose a strategy and solve.

3 Ema's family visited the space museum. Her father purchased 2 adult's tickets and 3 child's tickets. Each adult's ticket sold for $1 more than a child's ticket. If her father paid a total of $22 for the tickets, how much was 1 adult's ticket and how much was 1 child's ticket?

4 Luis began a science club with 2 members. At the end of the first week, he brought in 3 members. At the end of the second week, he brought in 4 more members. If this pattern continued for two more weeks, what was the total membership?

5 The museum is arranging 15 square tables for seating the students. Each table can seat 1 student on each side. If the tables are pushed together to make one long table, how many students can be seated?

6 Barry is trying to save $200 so he can attend camp next summer. He has $20 in a savings account. If Barry can deposit $5 a week, how long will it take him to save the $200 he needs for camp?

7 Each student who plans to attend the field trip needs to pay $8.50. If 125 students are planning to go on the trip and a total of $1,011.50 has been collected, how many students have not yet paid?

8 While on a field trip, Kitty bought a book for $1.45. She used quarters, dimes, and nickels to pay for the book. If there were 9 coins in all, how many of each type of coin did she use?

Vocabulary Check

Choose a word from the box to complete each sentence.

chord —
diameter —
equilateral —
intersecting
isosceles —
parallel —
prism —
radius —
scalene —

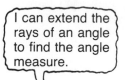

I can extend the rays of an angle to find the angle measure.

1. Lines that never intersect and that are always the same distance from each other are called __?__ lines. *(page 109)*

2. A triangle with all sides of equal length is called an __?__ triangle. *(page 118)*

3. A triangle that has at least two sides of equal length is called an __?__ triangle. *(page 118)*

4. A line segment that has one endpoint on the circle and one endpoint in the center of the circle is called a __?__. *(page 135)*

5. A chord that passes through the center of the circle is called a __?__. *(page 135)*

6. A figure that has two congruent bases is called a __?__. *(page 136)*

7. A triangle in which each side is a different length is called a __?__ triangle. *(page 118)*

8. A line segment inside a circle with endpoints on the circle is called a __?__. *(page 135)*

9. Lines that meet or cross each other at one point are called __?__ lines. *(page 109)*

Concept Check

Trace each angle. First, estimate the angle measure. Then, use a protractor to measure each angle. *(page 114)*

10. 11. 12. 13.

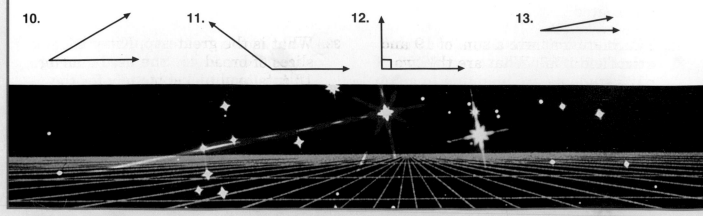

Draw all the lines of symmetry for each regular polygon. *(page 128)*

14.

15.

16.

17.

Write *slide, flip,* or *turn* to indicate how each figure was moved. *(page 130)*

18.

19.

Identify the solid figure. *(pages 136–138)*

20.

21.

22.

23.

Skill Check

Identify the angle. Write *right, acute,* or *obtuse.* *(page 112)*

24.

25.

26.

27.

Are the figures similar? Write *yes* or *no.* *(page 132)*

28.

29.

30.

31.

Problem-Solving Check

Solve. *(pages 124, 140)*

32. Two numbers have a sum of 19 and a product of 88. What are the two numbers?

33. What is the greatest number of slices of bread you can get by using 12 cuts to slice the bread?

34. A Boy Scout troop had 6 more 13-year-old boys than 12-year-old boys. If there were 24 boys in the troop, how many were 13 years old?

35. A square table can seat one person on each side. How many people can be seated at 10 square tables if the tables are pushed together in a line?

CHAPTER TEST

Use the figure for Exercises 1–4.

1. What line is parallel to $\overleftrightarrow{AB}$?

2. What line intersects $\overleftrightarrow{AB}$?

3. What line is perpendicular to $\overleftrightarrow{AB}$?

4. Name a right angle.

> Within a plane, lines can be either intersecting or parallel.

Write the number of sides and the number of angles of each polygon.

5. pentagon   6. quadrilateral   7. hexagon   8. octagon

Name each triangle. Write *equilateral, isosceles,* or *scalene.*

9.    10.   11.   12.

Trace each figure. Draw all the lines of symmetry for each figure.

13.   14.   15.

Use the circle for Exercises 16–18.

16. Name the diameter.

17. What type of line segment is $\overline{CD}$?   18. What type of line segment is $\overline{BA}$?

Write the number of faces of each solid figure.

19. triangular pyramid   20. triangular prism   21. cube

Solve.

22. Jo and Sue wrote their spelling words. It took a combined time of 17 minutes for them to write the words. The product of their time was 70 minutes. What were their individual times?

23. The sum of the times it took two students to solve a math problem was 14 minutes. The product of their times was 48 minutes. What were their individual times?

24. How many cuts would you need to make in a loaf of bread to get 25 slices?

25. A table seats one person on each side. To seat 14 people, how many tables can be pushed together to form one long table?

Teamwork P-R-O-J-E-C-T

MAKE A MODEL

Space-shuttle systems began to operate in the early 1980's. Unlike other space vehicles, a space shuttle can make more than one flight. With your teammates, model a space shuttle.

DECIDE

Talk about how you can use oak tag, tracing paper, and tape to model the solid and plane figures that compose the space shuttle.

DO

Work with your teammates. Trace and cut out the plane figures shown.

Use the traced patterns to cut the same shapes out of oak tag.

Fold along the dotted lines to form cones and cylinders. Tape the edges together.

Tape the solid figures and plane triangles together to form a model of the space shuttle.

SHARE

Show your model. Describe how the shuttle compares with other solid figures you know about.

TALK ABOUT IT

How can you use your model to imagine how a space station could be built from a combination of solid figures?

In your everyday activities, what other solid-figure combinations have you noticed?

5

DIVIDING
WHOLE NUMBERS
BY 1-DIGIT NUMBERS

Did you know ...

... that the world's largest carousel, located in Santa Clara, California, is a double-deck carousel that is as tall as a ten-story building?

In one day a carnival carousel runs 104 times. It runs the same number of times each hour. If the carnival is open for 8 hours, how can you find the number of times the carousel runs each hour?

EXPLORING

Divisibility

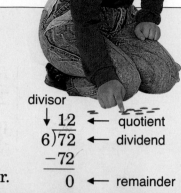

WORK TOGETHER

Building Understanding

Because there is a remainder of zero when you divide 72 by 6, 72 is **divisible** by 6.

You can use counters to check for divisibility. Look for numbers that divide into groups with no counters left over.

$$\begin{array}{r} \text{divisor} \\ \downarrow\ 12 \leftarrow \text{quotient} \\ 6\overline{)72} \leftarrow \text{dividend} \\ -72 \\ \hline 0 \leftarrow \text{remainder} \end{array}$$

Divide into Groups of	2	5	10
Number 10	●● ●● ●● ●● ●●	●●●●● ●●●●●	●●●●●●●●●●
12	●● ●● ●● ●● ●● ●●	●●●●● ●●●●● ●●	●●●●●●●●●● ●●
15	●● ●● ●● ●● ●● ●● ●● ●	●●●●● ●●●●● ●●●●●	●●●●●●●●●● ●●●●●

Talk About It

▶ Which numbers in the table have no counters left over when divided into groups of 2? 5? 10?

▶ What do you call numbers that are divisible by 2? Explain.

▶ Is 15 divisible by 2? Explain.

▶ Why are both 10 and 15 divisible by 5?

▶ Guess which of the following numbers are divisible by 2, 5, or 10. Then use a calculator to test your answers.

218   125   450   360

Use the counters to model the numbers in the table. Divide the counters into groups of three.

▶ Is 10 divisible by 3? Explain.

▶ Which numbers are divisible by 3?

▶ What is the sum of the digits in the number 12?

▶ Is this sum divisible by 3? Explain.

▶ What is the sum of the digits in the number 15?

▶ Is this sum divisible by 3? Explain.

▶ What rule can you write to show that a number is divisible by 3?

Making the Connection

There are rules of divisibility that tell whether a number is divisible by 2, 3, 5, or 10.

Even numbers are divisible by 2. These numbers end in 2, 4, 6, 8, or 0. These numbers are divisible by 2.	10, 24, 32, 46, 58
If the sum of the digits is a multiple of 3, then the number is divisible by 3. These numbers are divisible by 3.	12, 15, 33, 42, 54
If there is a 0 or a 5 in the ones place, then the number is divisible by 5. These numbers are divisible by 5.	15, 20, 35, 50, 65
If there is a 0 in the ones place, then the number is divisible by 10. These numbers are divisible by 10.	10, 20, 30, 40, 50, 60

1. Why are all numbers that are divisible by 10 also divisible by 2?

2. Are all numbers that are divisible by 5 also divisible by 2? Explain.

3. Are all numbers that are divisible by 5 also divisible by 3? Explain.

4. Are any numbers that are divisible by 10 also divisible by 3? Explain.

Checking Understanding

Use the rules to decide whether the first number is divisible by the second. Write *yes* or *no*.

5. 8, 2

6. 34, 3

7. 80, 10

8. 95, 5

Use the rules to decide whether each number is divisible by 2, 3, 5, and 10. Complete the table. Write *yes* or *no*.

9.

Divisible by	25	36	38	45	92	100	125
2	?	?	?	?	?	?	?
3	?	?	?	?	?	?	?
5	?	?	?	?	?	?	?
10	?	?	?	?	?	?	?

10. If a number is divisible by 5, is it always divisible by 10?

11. If a number is divisible by 10, is it always divisible by 2 and 5?

Babs rode in a hot-air balloon 134 times. If she rode the same number of times in each of 7 months, about how many times did she ride in a balloon each month?

Estimate. $134 \div 7 \approx n$

To estimate a quotient, you can use compatible numbers. **Compatible numbers** are numbers close to the actual numbers that can be divided evenly. Compatible numbers for 7 are numbers divisible by 7, such as 14, 21, or 28.

$7\overline{)134}$ **Think:** Since there are not 7 or more hundreds, divide the 13 tens. The first digit will be in the tens place.

$\overset{20}{7\overline{)140}}$ ← estimate **Think:** $7 \times 2 = 14$

So, Babs rode in a balloon about 20 times each month.

More Examples

A. Estimate. $93 \div 4 \approx n$

$4\overline{)93}$ **Think:** $4 \times 2 = 8$ $\overset{20}{4\overline{)80}}$

B. Estimate. $364 \div 5 \approx n$

$5\overline{)364}$ **Think:** $5 \times 7 = 35$ $\overset{70}{5\overline{)350}}$

- Name some other compatible numbers for Examples **A** and **B**.

- What compatible numbers can you use to estimate a quotient for $902 \div 4$? What is the estimated quotient?

- How do compatible numbers help you estimate mentally?

Check for Understanding

Choose the better estimate. Write **a** or **b**.

1. $145 \div 3 \approx n$
   a. 40   **b.** 50

2. $298 \div 9 \approx n$
   a. 30   **b.** 40

3. $443 \div 5 \approx n$
   a. 60   **b.** 90

4. $375 \div 6 \approx n$
   a. 30   **b.** 60

Estimate each quotient.

5. $64 \div 3 \approx n$

6. $193 \div 6 \approx n$

7. $295 \div 7 \approx n$

8. $337 \div 4 \approx n$

Practice

Choose the better estimate. Write **a** or **b**.

9. $65 \div 8 \approx n$
    a. 7 **b.** 8

10. $138 \div 6 \approx n$
    a. 20 **b.** 30

11. $642 \div 7 \approx n$
    a. 80 **b.** 90

12. $700 \div 9 \approx n$
    a. 30 **b.** 70

Estimate each quotient.

13. $3\overline{)16}$ **14.** $7\overline{)58}$ **15.** $5\overline{)32}$ **16.** $4\overline{)29}$

17. $8\overline{)70}$ **18.** $2\overline{)13}$ **19.** $4\overline{)85}$ **20.** $6\overline{)63}$

21. $3\overline{)95}$ **22.** $7\overline{)152}$ **23.** $5\overline{)267}$ **24.** $9\overline{)908}$

25. $4\overline{)832}$ **26.** $2\overline{)795}$ **27.** $6\overline{)850}$ **28.** $3\overline{)701}$

29. $46 \div 6 \approx n$ **30.** $29 \div 3 \approx n$ **31.** $68 \div 5 \approx n$

32. $137 \div 5 \approx n$ **33.** $396 \div 4 \approx n$ **34.** $657 \div 8 \approx n$

35. $428 \div 2 \approx n$ **36.** $615 \div 7 \approx n$ **37.** $909 \div 9 \approx n$

Mixed Applications

38. A group of 23 students has signed up to learn hang gliding. If there are 4 instructors, about how many students will be with each instructor?

39. Yoko's kite has a tail 325 inches long. If the tail is about 7 times as long as the kite, about how long is the kite?

40. At a public park, 175 people want to take part in a kite festival. Only 8 kites are allowed in each area of the park. Will 16 areas be enough for 175 people to fly kites?

41. Write a Question There are 7 hot-air balloons and 18 people waiting to ride them.

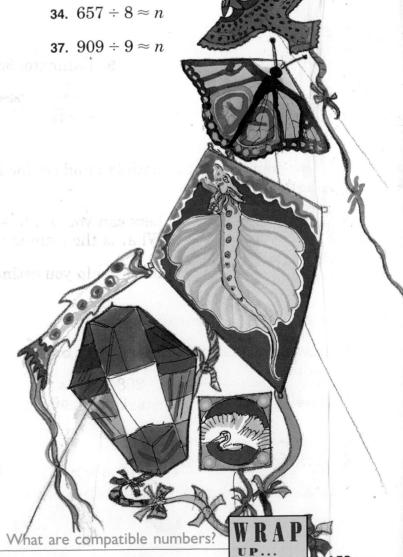

What are compatible numbers?

WRAP UP...

DIVIDING
Two-Digit Numbers

Many people enjoy playing marble games. Patricia, Regina, and Eduardo are dividing a collection of 71 marbles. If each person gets the same number of marbles, how many marbles will each one get?

First, estimate. **Think:** $3\overline{)71}$ $3 \times 2 = 6$ 20 $3\overline{)60}$ Since 7 tens can be divided by 3, the first digit of the quotient will be in the tens place.

Divide. $71 \div 3 = n$

Step 1	**Step 2**	**Step 3**
Divide the tens. $3\overline{)7}$ Think: $3 \times n \approx 7$.	Bring down the ones. Divide the 11 ones. Think: $3 \times n \approx 11$. Record the remainder.	Multiply to check.
$\begin{array}{r} 2 \\ 3\overline{)71} \\ -6 \\ \hline 1 \end{array}$ Multiply. Subtract. Compare. $1 < 3$	$\begin{array}{r} 23\ \text{r2} \leftarrow \text{remainder} \\ 3\overline{)71} \\ -6\downarrow \\ \hline 11 \\ -9 \\ \hline 2 \end{array}$ Multiply. Subtract. Compare. $2 < 3$	$\begin{array}{r} 23 \leftarrow \text{quotient} \\ \times\ 3 \leftarrow \text{divisor} \\ \hline 69 \\ +\ 2 \leftarrow \text{remainder} \\ \hline 71 \leftarrow \text{dividend} \end{array}$

Since there is a remainder of 2, the marbles cannot be shared equally. So, each person will get 23 marbles, and 2 marbles will be left over.

• Compare the answer to the estimate. Is the answer reasonable?

Talk About It

▶ How can you decide how many digits will be in the quotient?

▶ Why can you use multiplication to check division?

Check for Understanding

Estimate the number of digits in each quotient. Then find the quotient.

1. $39 \div 6 = n$ **2.** $62 \div 7 = n$ **3.** $47 \div 4 = n$ **4.** $87 \div 5 = n$

Practice

Estimate. Write the number of digits in each quotient.

5. $6\overline{)39}$ 6. $7\overline{)62}$ 7. $2\overline{)28}$ 8. $5\overline{)37}$ 9. $4\overline{)49}$

10. $9\overline{)59}$ 11. $8\overline{)95}$ 12. $5\overline{)28}$ 13. $8\overline{)75}$ 14. $6\overline{)74}$

Estimate. Then find the quotient.

15. $3\overline{)69}$ 16. $7\overline{)46}$ 17. $6\overline{)35}$ 18. $9\overline{)48}$ 19. $4\overline{)76}$

20. $3\overline{)33}$ 21. $8\overline{)78}$ 22. $7\overline{)67}$ 23. $4\overline{)48}$ 24. $5\overline{)92}$

Divide. Then check each quotient.

25. $54 \div 8 = n$ 26. $58 \div 7 = n$ 27. $55 \div 5 = n$ 28. $75 \div 6 = n$

29. $63 \div 3 = n$ 30. $29 \div 7 = n$ 31. $74 \div 8 = n$ 32. $37 \div 3 = n$

Mixed Applications

33. **Logical Reasoning** There are 18 students in Carmen's ballet class. The teacher is planning a dance for the recital and wants the same number of students in each row. What arrangements would have the same number of students in each row?

34. Four friends want to play jacks. They have 38 jacks. If each player gets the same number of jacks, how many jacks will each have? How many extra jacks will there be?

NUMBER SENSE

If the sum of the digits in a number is a multiple of 9, then the number is divisible by 9.

Example 216
$2 + 1 + 6 = 9$ $9 \div 9 = 1$
So, 216 is divisible by 9.

Tell whether the number is divisible by 9. Write *yes* or *no*.

35. 63 36. 531 37. 138 38. 1,260 39. 4,312

Explain how estimating first is helpful when you divide.

WRAP UP...

Baseball and softball are favorite pastimes of many people. The youth baseball league has 283 games scheduled. The 9 umpires want to share the games equally. At how many games will each umpire work?

First, estimate.

$9\overline{)283}$ Think: $9 \times 3 = 27$ $9\overline{)270}$ ^30 Since 28 tens can be divided by 9, the first digit of the quotient is in the tens place.

Divide. $283 \div 9 = n$

Step 1	Step 2	Step 3
Divide the hundreds. $9\overline{)2}$ Since there are not enough hundreds, divide the 28 tens. Think: $9 \times n \approx 28$.	Bring down the ones. Divide the 13 ones. Think: $9 \times n \approx 13$. Record the remainder.	Multiply to check.

Step 1:
$$9\overline{)283} \quad \frac{3}{} $$
−27 Multiply.
Subtract.
1 Compare. $1 < 9$

Step 2:
$9\overline{)283}$ ^31 r4
−27↓
13
− 9 Multiply. Subtract. Compare.
4 $4 < 9$

Step 3:
$$\begin{array}{r} 31 \\ \times\ 9 \\ \hline 279 \\ +\ 4 \\ \hline 283 \end{array}$$

So, each umpire will work at least 31 games. The remaining 4 games can be shared by 4 of the umpires.

More Examples

A.
$$\begin{array}{r} 123\ r3 \\ 5\overline{)618} \\ -5 \\ \hline 11 \\ -10 \\ \hline 18 \\ -15 \\ \hline 3 \end{array}$$
Since 6 hundreds can be divided by 5, the first digit of the quotient is in the hundreds place.

B.
$$\begin{array}{r} 74\ r5 \\ 7\overline{)523} \\ -49 \\ \hline 33 \\ -28 \\ \hline 5 \end{array}$$
Since 5 hundreds are not enough, divide the 52 tens. The first digit of the quotient is in the tens place.

Check for Understanding

Estimate each quotient. If the estimate is greater than 50, find the quotient.

1. $159 \div 4 \approx n$ 2. $247 \div 3 \approx n$ 3. $589 \div 6 \approx n$

Practice

Estimate each quotient.

4. $8 \overline{)546}$ **5.** $7 \overline{)589}$ **6.** $5 \overline{)495}$ **7.** $3 \overline{)129}$ **8.** $4 \overline{)358}$ **9.** $6 \overline{)713}$

Divide.

10. $7 \overline{)291}$ **11.** $8 \overline{)746}$ **12.** $9 \overline{)909}$ **13.** $7 \overline{)590}$ **14.** $6 \overline{)555}$ **15.** $4 \overline{)854}$

16. $167 \div 7 = n$ **17.** $296 \div 3 = n$

18. $510 \div 8 = n$ **19.** $195 \div 2 = n$

20. $296 \div 2 = n$ **21.** $687 \div 6 = n$

22. $895 \div 9 = n$ **23.** $485 \div 5 = n$

24. Without dividing, tell whether the quotient of $438 \div 3$ has two digits or three digits. Explain.

Mixed Applications

25. A total of 100 people are traveling to a softball tournament. If each car holds 5 people, how many cars will be needed to take everyone to the tournament?

26. Sabrina wants to put her collection of baseball cards in a new album. She has 248 cards, and each page of the album will hold 8 cards. How many pages will she need?

27. There are 18 players on a softball team. At practice, every player is at bat 6 times. If 9 players take turns pitching to each player, how many times will each one get to pitch?

28. Make Up a Problem Write a division problem that has a divisor of 6 and a quotient with a remainder of 4.

MIXED REVIEW

Write two other forms for each number.

1. 42,700 **2.** 130,680 **3.** 2,800,050 **4.** 12,009,005

Estimate each sum. Tell which method you used.

5. $\begin{array}{r} 61 \\ + 42 \\ \hline \end{array}$ **6.** $\begin{array}{r} 185 \\ + 327 \\ \hline \end{array}$ **7.** $\begin{array}{r} 4,540 \\ + 5,450 \\ \hline \end{array}$ **8.** $\begin{array}{r} 6,342 \\ + 2,105 \\ \hline \end{array}$

Explain how you can tell whether the quotient of $489 \div 6$ will have 2 or 3 digits.

WRAP UP...

SHORT DIVISION

Diane likes to read whenever she has time. She has 4 days to read a 112-page book. How many pages does she need to read each day?

You can use the short form of division to find $112 \div 4$. Multiply and subtract mentally, and write the remainders in the dividend. Write the last remainder as part of the quotient.

First, estimate. $4\overline{)112}$ **Think:** $4 \times 3 = 12$ $\quad \dfrac{30}{4\overline{)120}}$

Divide. $112 \div 4 = n$

Step 1	**Step 2**
Divide the 11 tens. Think: $4 \times n \approx 11$.	Divide the 32 ones. Think: $4 \times n = 32$.
$\dfrac{2}{4\overline{)1\,1^{3}2}}$ **Think:** $2 \times 4 = 8$ $\quad 11 - 8 = 3$ Place the remainder in the dividend.	$\dfrac{2\,8}{4\overline{)1\,1^{3}2}}$

So, Diane needs to read 28 pages each day.

- How do you know whether your answer is reasonable?

More Examples

A. $\dfrac{2\,4\,9\,r1}{4\overline{)9^{1}9^{3}7}}$
B. $\dfrac{1\,4\,8\,r3}{5\overline{)7^{2}4^{4}3}}$

Talk About It

▶ How is short division different from long division?

▶ Why is the estimate of the quotient especially useful in short division?

Check for Understanding

Use short division to find each quotient.

1. $5\overline{)63}$
2. $7\overline{)125}$
3. $8\overline{)532}$
4. $6\overline{)976}$
5. $4\overline{)395}$

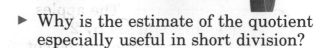

Practice

Use short division to find each quotient.

6. $4\overline{)57}$ 7. $5\overline{)43}$ 8. $3\overline{)85}$ 9. $5\overline{)435}$ 10. $2\overline{)638}$

11. $4\overline{)459}$ 12. $7\overline{)952}$ 13. $7\overline{)837}$ 14. $6\overline{)941}$ 15. $5\overline{)267}$

16. $2\overline{)857}$ 17. $8\overline{)936}$ 18. $5\overline{)828}$ 19. $3\overline{)742}$ 20. $9\overline{)858}$

21. $169 \div 7 = n$ 22. $952 \div 8 = n$ 23. $837 \div 6 = n$

24. $378 \div 4 = n$ 25. $289 \div 9 = n$ 26. $859 \div 7 = n$

27. $981 \div 9 = n$ 28. $857 \div 5 = n$

29. Dave likes to help in the school library. He has 435 books to put back on the shelves. He uses 3 carts to carry the books, and each cart can hold 125 books. Will he need another cart? Explain.

30. Megan is making a quilt out of 4 different fabrics. She has cut out a total of 664 pieces. She cut the same number of pieces from each fabric. How many pieces did she cut from each fabric?

EVERYDAY MATH CONNECTION

Some things are commonly separated into parts, while other things are never divided. A remainder in division must be handled according to the situation.

Examples

A. There are 71 apples to make 2 batches of applesauce. The apples are to be shared equally by 2 classes. The extra apple can be cut in half. How many apples are in each batch?

B. There are 71 paper cups to be shared equally by 2 classes. The extra cup would not be cut in half. How many cups does each class get? How many cups are left over?

Divide the items equally among 6 people. Then write how many each person gets.

31. 140 pencils   32. 105 cookies   33. 81 books

1. The c
square
Benea
How n
were 6

2. A pair
paints
123 ca

Write two

3. 87,953

Estimate.

7. 6.231
   + 5.897

Find the su

11. 3,085
    + 2,974

Estimate the

16. 186
    × 4

Use the figu

21. Name tv

22. Name tv

23. Name th

24. Name th

Divide.

25. 4)75

29. 3)287

CHAPTER 6

DIVIDING
WHOLE NUMBERS
BY 2-DIGIT NUMBERS

Did you know . . .

. . . that the St. Bernard is a dog famous for rescuing lost travelers? It was trained in the Alps of Switzerland to rescue people who were lost.

Suppose a St. Bernard eats 1,800 pounds of dog food in a 12-month period. How can you find the amount of food it eats each day?

DIVISION PATTERNS

Ginny wanted to set a record by growing the largest watermelon. After trying for several years, Ginny grew a watermelon that weighed 160 pounds. If she cut the watermelon into 40 equal pieces, how much did each piece weigh?

Divide.

Think:

weight of the watermelon	number of equal pieces	weight of each piece
160	÷ 40	= n

You know that multiplication and division are inverse, or opposite, operations. So, you can use a multiplication sentence to help find a quotient.

Since $4 \times 40 = 160$, you know that $160 \div 40 = 4$. So, each piece of Ginny's watermelon weighed 4 pounds.

Look at these division patterns.

A.
$$60 \div 30 = 2$$
$$600 \div 30 = 20$$
$$6,000 \div 30 = 200$$

B.
$$420 \div 70 = 6$$
$$4,200 \div 70 = 60$$
$$42,000 \div 70 = 600$$

C.
$$600 \div 20 = 30$$
$$6,000 \div 20 = 300$$
$$60,000 \div 20 = 3,000$$

Talk About It

▶ What pattern do you see?

▶ How can the pattern help you determine the number of zeros in the quotient?

▶ How many zeros will be in the quotient of $40,000 \div 50$? How does this differ from the pattern?

Check for Understanding

Complete the pattern.

1.
$$80 \div 40 = 2$$
$$800 \div 40 = n$$
$$8,000 \div 40 = 200$$

2.
$$90 \div 30 = 3$$
$$900 \div 30 = 30$$
$$9,000 \div 30 = n$$

3.
$$250 \div 50 = n$$
$$2,500 \div 50 = 50$$
$$25,000 \div 50 = 500$$

4.
$$180 \div 60 = 3$$
$$1,800 \div 60 = n$$
$$18,000 \div 60 = 300$$

Write the number of zeros in the quotient.

5. $60\overline{)1,200}$ **6.** $70\overline{)14,000}$ **7.** $60\overline{)30,000}$ **8.** $80\overline{)160,000}$ **9.** $50\overline{)50,000}$

(31) 80,000 ÷ 80 = 2,000   (32) 150,000 ÷ 50 = 3,000

(33) 1,800 ÷ 30 = 60 inches

(34) 30
$\times$60
‾‾‾‾
00
+1800
‾‾‾‾‾
1,800 newspapers

(35) 800 ÷ 20 = 40 dominoes

Mixed Review

(1) ⁵6.8
   −4.9
   ‾‾‾‾
   1.9

(2) 78.²85⁷5
   −5.46
   ‾‾‾‾‾
   2.89

(3) 12.³48⁷
   −9.39
   ‾‾‾‾‾
   3.09

(4) 123.⁸75
   −106.57
   ‾‾‾‾‾‾
   17.18

(5) ²28
   × 3
   ‾‾‾
   84

(6) ¹2⁴³8
   × 4
   ‾‾‾
   992

(7) ⁶⁴197
   × 7
   ‾‾‾
   1379

(8) ¹6,503
   × 2
   ‾‾‾‾
   13,006

Monica Earp
Math pg. 180-181 # 1-35 Mixed Review
3-3-98   # 1-8

① 80 ÷ 40 = 2   ② 90 ÷ 30 = 3
  800 ÷ 40 = 20   900 ÷ 30 = 30
8,000 ÷ 40 = 200   9,000 ÷ 30 = 300

③ 250 ÷ 50 = 5   ④ 180 ÷ 60 = 3
2,500 ÷ 50 = 50   1,800 ÷ 60 = 30
25,000 ÷ 50 = 500   18,000 ÷ 60 = 300

⑤ 1,200 ÷ 60 = 20   ⑥ 14,000 ÷ 70 = 200

⑦ 30,000 ÷ 60 = 3,000   ⑧ 160,000 ÷ 80 = 2,000

⑨ 50,000 ÷ 50 = 1,000   ⑩ 60 ÷ 20 = 3   ⑪ 80 ÷ 40 = 2

⑫ 540 ÷ 60 = 9   ⑬ 640 ÷ 80 = 8   ⑭ 560 ÷ 80 = 7

⑮ 2,400 ÷ 30 = 80   ⑯ 3,600 ÷ 40 = 90

⑰ 36,000 ÷ 30 = 1,200   ⑱ 80 ÷ 20 = 4

⑲ 90 ÷ 30 = 3   ⑳ 90 ÷ 10 = 9   ㉑ 50 ÷ 50 = 1

㉒ 210 ÷ 70 = 3   ㉓ 800 ÷ 40 = 20   ㉔ 160 ÷ 80 = 2

㉕ 270 ÷ 90 = 3   ㉖ 360 ÷ 60 = 6   ㉗ 4,000 ÷ 20 = 200

㉘ 4,900 ÷ 70 = 70   ㉙ 6,000 ÷ 20 = 300   ㉚ 1,800 ÷ 30 = 60

→ over

Practice

Find the quotient.

10. $60 \div 20 = n$ **11.** $80 \div 40 = n$ **12.** $540 \div 60 = n$ **13.** $640 \div 80 = n$

14. $560 \div 80 = n$ **15.** $2{,}400 \div 30 = n$ **16.** $3{,}600 \div 40 = n$ **17.** $36{,}000 \div 30 = n$

18. $20\overline{)80}$ **19.** $30\overline{)90}$ **20.** $10\overline{)90}$ **21.** $50\overline{)50}$ **22.** $70\overline{)210}$

23. $40\overline{)800}$ **24.** $80\overline{)160}$ **25.** $90\overline{)270}$ **26.** $60\overline{)360}$ **27.** $20\overline{)1{,}000}$

28. $70\overline{)4{,}900}$ **29.** $20\overline{)6{,}000}$ **30.** $30\overline{)1{,}800}$ **31.** $80\overline{)80{,}000}$ **32.** $50\overline{)150{,}000}$

pg. 180-181
#1-35 and
Mixed Review
#1-8

5. $1200 \div 60 = 20$
c. $14{,}000 \div 70 = 200$

© Hmk. Cds.

...d a
...classroom
...he
...ents
...inches.
...ght of the

...nts in her
...hool
...g. If there
...h student
...how many
...nt set up?

34. Mrs. Ramsey's class set a school record by collecting the most newspapers for recycling. If each of her 30 students collected 60 newspapers, how many newspapers did they collect in all?

36. Mental Math Is 60 a reasonable quotient for $480 \div 80$? Explain.

MIXED REVIEW

Find the difference.

1. $\begin{array}{r} 6.8 \\ -\,4.9 \\ \hline \end{array}$ **2.** $\begin{array}{r} 8.35 \\ -\,5.46 \\ \hline \end{array}$ **3.** $\begin{array}{r} 12.48 \\ -\,9.39 \\ \hline \end{array}$ **4.** $\begin{array}{r} 123.75 \\ -\,106.57 \\ \hline \end{array}$

Find the product.

5. $\begin{array}{r} 28 \\ \times\,3 \\ \hline \end{array}$ **6.** $\begin{array}{r} 248 \\ \times\,4 \\ \hline \end{array}$ **7.** $\begin{array}{r} 197 \\ \times\,7 \\ \hline \end{array}$ **8.** $\begin{array}{r} 6{,}503 \\ \times\,2 \\ \hline \end{array}$

Explain how to determine the number of zeros in a quotient.

WRAP
UP...

Karen Stevenson holds the record for eating the most baked beans in the least amount of time. Using a toothpick, she ate 2,780 beans in 30 minutes. About how many baked beans did she eat each minute?

Since an exact number is not needed, estimate the quotient. Choose compatible numbers that are close to the original numbers that divide easily.

Estimate. $2,780 \div 30 \approx n$

Think: $30 \times n = 2,700$
$30 \times 90 = 2,700$

$$\begin{array}{r} 90 \longleftarrow \text{estimate} \\ 30\overline{)2,700} \end{array}$$

So, Karen ate about 90 baked beans each minute.

- Is 90 greater than or less than the actual quotient? How can you tell?

Another Method

Sometimes you can use more than one pair of compatible numbers to estimate a quotient. Finding more than one estimate will give you two possible quotients.

Estimate. $43\overline{)2,752}$

Talk About It

▶ Does $2,400 \div 40$ give a good estimate? Why or why not?

▶ Does $2,800 \div 40$ give a good estimate? Why or why not?

▶ What are the two possible estimates?

▶ Name two pairs of compatible numbers for $1,572 \div 35$.

Check for Understanding

Name two pairs of compatible numbers.

1. $158 \div 34 \approx n$

2. $620 \div 87 \approx n$

3. $1,425 \div 27 \approx n$

Estimate the quotient.

4. $18\overline{)178}$

5. $23\overline{)138}$

6. $28\overline{)627}$

7. $32\overline{)7,120}$

8. $68\overline{)6,216}$

Practice

Write two pairs of compatible numbers for each. Give two possible estimates.

9. $153 \div 34 \approx n$

10. $640 \div 87 \approx n$

11. $153 \div 18 \approx n$

12. $275 \div 32 \approx n$

13. $1,425 \div 27 \approx n$

14. $3,050 \div 56 \approx n$

Estimate the quotient.

15. $17\overline{)163}$

16. $33\overline{)315}$

17. $57\overline{)305}$

18. $28\overline{)281}$

19. $46\overline{)379}$

20. $37\overline{)162}$

21. $59\overline{)382}$

22. $75\overline{)540}$

23. $92\overline{)790}$

24. $72\overline{)581}$

25. $26\overline{)809}$

26. $48\overline{)470}$

27. $12\overline{)789}$

28. $24\overline{)812}$

29. $43\overline{)736}$

30. $53\overline{)2,470}$

31. $13\overline{)4,900}$

32. $74\overline{)5,780}$

33. $31\overline{)2,650}$

34. $64\overline{)1,738}$

35. $530 \div 72 \approx n$

36. $625 \div 27 \approx n$

37. $4,680 \div 47 \approx n$

38. $5,716 \div 81 \approx n$

39. $3,469 \div 43 \approx n$

40. $6,250 \div 87 \approx n$

41. $6,321 \div 34 \approx n$

42. $9,800 \div 97 \approx n$

Mixed Applications

43. The largest cucumber on record weighed 66 pounds. There are 73 calories per pound in cucumbers. If the largest cucumber was divided into 50 equal slices, about how many calories were in each slice?

44. Number Sense The largest pecan pie ever baked weighed 40,266 pounds. If 4 pounds of pecan pie can feed about 10 people, about how many people could the record-setting pie have fed?

45. Write a Question The longest continuous loaf of bread ever baked was about 2,350 feet long. Aluminum foil comes in rolls of 75 feet.

46. The largest gingerbread house ever made was 52 feet high. If 1,650 pounds of icing were used, about how many pounds of icing were used for each foot?

How does using compatible numbers help you estimate quotients?

Each year thousands of runners enter the New York City Marathon. Ellen is a paramedic who assists runners who are injured. She needs to set up 16 first-aid stations along the course. She has 96 volunteers. How many volunteers should Ellen assign to each station if she wants an equal number at each station?

First, estimate. $96 \div 16 \approx n$

Think: $20 \times n = 100$ or
$15 \times n = 90$, so $n = 5$ or 6.

Then, divide. $16\overline{)96}$

Step 1 Since the estimate is a one-digit number, divide the 96 ones.	**Step 2** Since the remainder is equal to the divisor, increase the quotient.
$\begin{array}{r} 5 \\ 16\overline{)96} \\ -80 \\ \hline 16 \end{array}$ Multiply. Subtract. Compare. $16 = 16$	$\begin{array}{r} 6 \\ 16\overline{)96} \\ -96 \\ \hline 0 \end{array}$ Multiply. Subtract. Compare. $0 < 16$

So, Ellen should assign 6 volunteers to each station.

More Examples

A. Estimate. $18\overline{)84}$

Think: $20 \times n = 80$ or
$15 \times n = 75$, so $n = 4$ or 5.

$\begin{array}{r} 4 \text{ r12} \\ 18\overline{)84} \\ -72 \\ \hline 12 \end{array}$ Write the remainder next to the quotient.

Check
$\begin{array}{r} 18 \leftarrow \text{divisor} \\ \times 4 \leftarrow \text{quotient} \\ \hline 72 \\ +12 \leftarrow \text{remainder} \\ \hline 84 \leftarrow \text{dividend} \end{array}$

B. Estimate. $26\overline{)67}$

Think: $30 \times n = 60$ or
$25 \times n = 75$, so $n = 2$ or 3.

$\begin{array}{r} 2 \text{ r15} \\ 26\overline{)67} \\ -52 \\ \hline 15 \end{array}$

Check
$\begin{array}{r} 26 \leftarrow \text{divisor} \\ \times 2 \leftarrow \text{quotient} \\ \hline 52 \\ +15 \leftarrow \text{remainder} \\ \hline 67 \leftarrow \text{dividend} \end{array}$

Talk About It

▶ How can you determine the place value of the first digit in the quotient?

▶ How is your estimate part of the division process?

Check for Understanding

Estimate. Then find the quotient.

1. $12\overline{)62}$ **2.** $18\overline{)41}$ **3.** $37\overline{)84}$ **4.** $48\overline{)95}$ **5.** $53\overline{)167}$

Practice

Estimate.

6. $52 \div 12 \approx n$ **7.** $82 \div 38 \approx n$ **8.** $90 \div 25 \approx n$ **9.** $45 \div 13 \approx n$

10. $65 \div 32 \approx n$ **11.** $73 \div 40 \approx n$ **12.** $49 \div 17 \approx n$ **13.** $89 \div 26 \approx n$

Divide. Check with multiplication.

14. $22\overline{)88}$ **15.** $34\overline{)94}$ **16.** $16\overline{)80}$ **17.** $21\overline{)62}$ **18.** $12\overline{)79}$

19. $51\overline{)58}$ **20.** $32\overline{)96}$ **21.** $27\overline{)81}$ **22.** $42\overline{)88}$ **23.** $34\overline{)86}$

24. $12\overline{)70}$ **25.** $48\overline{)98}$ **26.** $65\overline{)72}$ **27.** $13\overline{)99}$ **28.** $13\overline{)97}$

29. $85 \div 32 = n$ **30.** $74 \div 12 = n$

31. $57 \div 22 = n$ **32.** $49 \div 19 = n$

33. $90 \div 18 = n$ **34.** $98 \div 47 = n$

Mixed Applications

35. Logical Reasoning When a two-digit number is divided by a two-digit number, is the quotient ever a two-digit number? Explain.

36. Robert's van can hold 11 people plus the driver. If Robert plans to transport 40 friends to see a race, how many trips will he need to make?

37. At the marathon race, T-shirts were sold for $14 each. The vendor had purchased the shirts in packages of 15 at a cost of $120 per package. How much profit did the vendor make on sales of 75 shirts?

38. Amy wants to buy some jogging suits to wear for practice. She has $74, and the suits cost $28 each. How many jogging suits can Amy buy? How much money will she have left over?

Explain why you sometimes get a remainder when you divide.

CORRECTING QUOTIENTS

A group of students at a high school set a record for the longest volleyball game. The game lasted a little more than 118 hours. How many continuous days did the students play volleyball?

Since there are 24 hours in a day, divide 118 hours by 24 hours.

Estimate. $118 \div 24 \approx n$

Think: $20 \times n = 100$ or $30 \times n = 120$, so $n = 5$ or 4.

Divide. $24 \overline{)118}$

Try 5.

$$
\begin{array}{r}
5 \\
24\overline{)118} \\
-120 \\
\end{array}
$$
Since $120 > 118$, this estimate is too large.

Try 4.

$$
\begin{array}{r}
4 \ \ r22 \\
24\overline{)118} \\
-96 \\
\hline
22 \\
\end{array}
$$

So, the students played for 4 days and 22 hours.

Another Example

Estimate. $269 \div 38 \approx n$

Think: $40 \times n = 240$ or $40 \times n = 280$, so $n = 6$ or 7.

Divide. $38\overline{)269}$

Try 6.

$$
\begin{array}{r}
6 \\
38\overline{)269} \\
-228 \\
\hline
41 \\
\end{array}
$$
Since $41 > 38$, the estimate is too small.

Try 7.

$$
\begin{array}{r}
7 \ \ r3 \\
38\overline{)269} \\
-266 \\
\hline
3 \\
\end{array}
$$

Talk About It

► How do you know when an estimated quotient is too large?

► How do you know when an estimated quotient is too small?

► What can you do to correct an estimate that is too large? too small?

► How do you know when an estimated quotient is correct?

Check for Understanding

Look at each estimated quotient. Write whether the estimated quotient is *too large, too small,* or *just right.*

1. $15\overline{)76}^{\ 6}$

2. $86\overline{)351}^{\ 4}$

3. $53\overline{)349}^{\ 7}$

4. $65\overline{)336}^{\ 4}$

5. $78\overline{)496}^{\ 6}$

Practice

Choose the correct estimate to use in the quotient. Write **a** or **b**.

6. $22\overline{)185}$ **a.** 8   **b.** 9

7. $54\overline{)194}$ **a.** 3   **b.** 4

8. $42\overline{)352}$ **a.** 8   **b.** 9

9. $37\overline{)268}$ **a.** 6   **b.** 7

10. $16\overline{)150}$ **a.** 9   **b.** 10

Divide.

11. $19\overline{)74}$ 12. $25\overline{)85}$ 13. $33\overline{)80}$

14. $14\overline{)94}$ 15. $27\overline{)134}$ 16. $44\overline{)175}$

17. $54\overline{)235}$ 18. $65\overline{)342}$ 19. $46\overline{)456}$

20. $38\overline{)270}$ 21. $22\overline{)119}$ 22. $49\overline{)489}$

23. $29\overline{)234}$ 24. $36\overline{)191}$ 25. $52\overline{)335}$

Mixed Applications

26. A total of 84 students signed up for a volleyball tournament. The principal asked 6 teachers to coach one team each. If there are 12 students on each team, is another coach needed?

27. The volleyball team practices each Monday, Wednesday, and Friday after school. If each practice is 2 hours long, how many hours does the team practice in 8 weeks?

28. The captain of the volleyball team has collected $140 to buy new balls for the tournament. If the balls cost $32 each, how many can he buy?

29. **Analyze Data** The uniforms for the 12 team members cost $42 each. If the players have earned $360 at a car wash to be used toward the purchase of the uniforms, how much additional money will each player have to pay for a uniform?

How do you know whether your first estimate in the quotient is too large or too small?

WRAP UP...

DIVIDING
Three-Digit Numbers

Collecting postcards is a popular hobby. One of the largest collections in the world has 1,000,265 postcards.

Ted's grandmother has a collection of 579 postcards. She wants to divide them equally among her 17 grandchildren. How many postcards can she give to each of her grandchildren?

Estimate. $579 \div 17 \approx n$ **Think:** $20 \times n = 600$ or
$15 \times n = 600$, so $n = 30$ or 40.

Divide. $17\overline{)579}$

Step 1	**Step 2**	**Step 3**
Since the estimate is a two-digit number, divide the 57 tens.	Bring down the ones. Divide the 69 ones.	Since the remainder is greater than the divisor, correct the quotient.

Step 1

$$\begin{array}{r} 3 \\ 17\overline{)579} \\ -51 \\ \hline 6 \end{array}$$ Multiply. Subtract. Compare. $6 < 17$

Step 2

$$\begin{array}{r} 33 \\ 17\overline{)579} \\ -51\downarrow \\ \hline 69 \\ -51 \\ \hline 18 \end{array}$$ Multiply. Subtract. Compare. $18 > 17$

Step 3

$$\begin{array}{r} 34 \text{ r1} \\ 17\overline{)579} \\ -51 \\ \hline 69 \\ -68 \\ \hline 1 \end{array}$$ Multiply. Subtract. Compare. $1 < 17$

So, Ted's grandmother can give 34 postcards to each of her grandchildren. She will have 1 postcard left.

More Examples

A. Estimate. $35\overline{)843}$

Think: $40 \times n = 800$ or
$30 \times n = 900$, so $n = 20$ or 30.

$$\begin{array}{r} 24 \text{ r3} \\ 35\overline{)843} \\ -70 \\ \hline 143 \\ -140 \\ \hline 3 \end{array}$$

B. Estimate. $28\overline{)720}$

Think: $30 \times n = 600$ or
$25 \times n = 750$,
so $n = 20$ or 30.

$$\begin{array}{r} 25 \text{ r20} \\ 28\overline{)720} \\ -56 \\ \hline 160 \\ -140 \\ \hline 20 \end{array}$$

• How can you tell whether your answer is reasonable?

Check for Understanding

Estimate. Then find the quotient.

1. 31)975   **2.** 41)820   **3.** 28)564   **4.** 87)931

Practice

Find the quotient.

5. 21)875   **6.** 35)842   **7.** 16)850   **8.** 24)521

9. 12)706   **10.** 30)275   **11.** 42)168   **12.** 54)302

13. 53)968   **14.** 63)567   **15.** 31)618   **16.** 47)987

17. 23)385   **18.** 34)400   **19.** 23)414   **20.** 13)415

21. $819 \div 39 = n$ **22.** $500 \div 14 = n$ **23.** $605 \div 52 = n$

Mixed Applications

24. Alex started his rock collection with 4 rocks. He collected 6 more rocks the first week, 8 rocks the next week, and 10 rocks the third week. If this pattern continues, how many rocks will he have after 6 weeks?

25. Flora collects dolls from different countries. She has 132 dolls in her collection. If she can place 15 dolls on a shelf, how many shelves will she need to display all her dolls?

26. Lloyd has the largest baseball-card collection in his class. He collected 15 cards each week for 18 weeks. If he divided these cards evenly into the 30 pages of his album, how many cards were on each page?

27. Mental Math Edith has 200 shells in her collection. She wants to make 6 wind chimes and use 50 shells for each. How many more shells does she need to collect?

LOGICAL REASONING

28. Using the digits 1, 3, 5, 7, and 9, write a division problem that has a two-digit divisor, a three-digit dividend, and the greatest possible quotient. Make sure that you use each digit at least once.

Why is it helpful to have more than one estimate?

WRAP UP...

PROBLEM *Solving*

The Grand Canyon is one of the largest land gorges in the world. Tim and his family have saved $1,235 to spend on a visit to Grand Canyon National Park. If their expenses will average $185 per day, will they have enough money for a 6-day visit?

Sometimes an exact answer is not needed to solve a problem. In such a situation, you can decide whether to overestimate or to underestimate.

▶ **UNDERSTAND**

What are you asked to find?

What facts are given?

▶ **PLAN**

Do you need an exact answer to solve the problem?
No, an estimate is reasonable.

Do you need to overestimate or to underestimate to find the solution?

You need to overestimate the cost per day and underestimate the amount saved to be sure that Tim and his family will have enough money.

▶ **SOLVE**

How will you carry out the plan?

To estimate the quotient, increase the divisor and decrease the dividend. Choose compatible numbers to divide.

$1,235 ÷ $185 = n   The exact quotient will be more
  ↓   ↓   ↓   than the estimated quotient.
$1,200 ÷ $200 = 6

So, Tim and his family will have enough money to stay about 6 days.

▶ **LOOK BACK**

What would happen if you estimated by using $1,200 ÷ $100?

WHAT IF... ... Tim and his family have saved $1,020 and expect expenses to average $175 per day? Will they have enough money for a 5-day visit?

Apply

Tell whether an exact answer is needed. Solve.

1. Some tourists plan to spend 5 days traveling about 400 miles in Grand Canyon National Park. They will travel about 185 miles in a minibus for 1 day. They will bicycle for 4 days. About how many miles will they travel each day on bicycles?

2. Jack and his family will spend 10 days touring the Grand Canyon. They purchased 8 rolls of film with 36 exposures on each roll. About how many pictures can they take on each of the 10 days if they take about the same number every day?

Mixed Applications ➤ **STRATEGIES** • Write a Number Sentence • Guess and Check • Find a Pattern • Work Backward

Choose a strategy and solve.

3. Lake Superior is in both the United States and Canada. Its surface area of about 31,800 square miles is the greatest of any freshwater lake. About how many square miles are in Canada if about 20,700 square miles are in the United States?

4. Rudy was the first to board a tour bus at the stop. It stopped at the next corner, and 3 passengers got on. At the third stop, 5 passengers got on. If the pattern continues, how many people will be on the bus after 5 stops?

5. The Carsons used traveler's checks on their vacation. By the end of the fourth day, they had spent $185.74 for lodging, $212.48 for food, and $56.91 for gas. They had $340.00 in traveler's checks and about $5.00 in change left. How many dollars worth of traveler's checks did they begin with?

6. There are 350 burros in the park. The park rangers want to move them to another area. They plan to move 30 burros the first month. If they move 20 more burros each month than the month before, how many months will it take to move all the burros?

1. When Janice deposited her birthday money in her savings account, her total savings increased from $484.96 to $522.56. Janice received $15.00 from her aunt and the rest from her parents. How much did her parents give her?

2. Luis went grocery shopping and bought 2 chickens for $2.12 each, milk for $1.05, potatoes for $1.69, and eggs for $0.89. About how much change did he receive from $20.00?

Watch for hidden data in problems.

Find the sum or difference.

3.
$$12.45$$
$$+ 17.57$$

4.
$$45.78$$
$$- 28.95$$

5.
$$236.705$$
$$+ 874.365$$

6.
$$485.932$$
$$- 269.064$$

Multiply.

7.
$$498$$
$$\times \ 14$$

8.
$$6,725$$
$$\times \ \ \ 6$$

9.
$$16,430$$
$$\times \ \ \ \ 25$$

10.
$$45,893$$
$$\times \ \ \ \ \ 3$$

Name each triangle. Write *equilateral*, *isosceles*, or *scalene*.

11.

12.

13.

14.

Estimate each quotient.

15. $6\overline{)55}$ 16. $8\overline{)333}$ 17. $4\overline{)1,789}$ 18. $5\overline{)4,345}$

19. $17\overline{)380}$ 20. $29\overline{)875}$ 21. $42\overline{)3,300}$ 22. $62\overline{)4,605}$

Divide.

23. $7\overline{)64}$ 24. $9\overline{)238}$ 25. $3\overline{)976}$ 26. $8\overline{)1,875}$

27. $16\overline{)83}$ 28. $35\overline{)79}$ 29. $24\overline{)194}$ 30. $32\overline{)580}$

Find the average.

31. 45, 57, 68, 74, 76   32. 139, 275, 398, 420   33. 1,275; 1,485; 1,803

34. 2,575; 3,012; 4,985   35. 3,576; 1,475; 1,288   36. 7,648; 4,875; 5,327

Check the Reasonableness of the Solution

An important part of the problem-solving process is to check whether your solution is reasonable.

Kyle set the high-jump record for the ten-year-olds. He jumped 4 feet 6 inches. His sister Becky asked their father, "Does this mean that when Kyle is 20 years old, he will be able to high-jump 9 feet?"

Talk About It

Work with a partner. Answer the questions.

● What is the Olympic or world record for the high jump?

● Is Becky's question reasonable? Explain.

● What do you think is a reasonable high jump for Kyle when he is 20 years old?

● How does the world-record information help you arrive at a reasonable high jump for Kyle?

Apply

Decide whether each solution is reasonable. Be prepared to discuss your responses.

1 Zack holds the class record for a perfect score of 100 on 7 spelling tests. He will make a score of 45 on the next test.

2 Terry's record for running a half mile is 3 minutes. This means she can run a mile in about 6 minutes.

3 The local pizza-eating record is 10 slices in 10 minutes. This means that the record setter can eat 60 slices in an hour.

4 Janine and Leon are having a rope-jumping contest. Janine jumped for 5 minutes, and Leon jumped for 6 minutes. This means that Leon will always jump longer than Janine.

Karting is a sports event in which people try to set records. In one such event, the most mileage recorded in 24 hours on a closed, twisting circuit was 1,018 one-mile laps. On the average, how many laps were completed in an hour?

Estimate. $1,018 \div 24 \approx n$

Think: $25 \times n = 1,000$ or $20 \times 50 = 1,000$, so $n = 40$ or 50.

Divide. $24\overline{)1,018}$

Step 1	**Step 2**
Since the estimate has two digits, divide the 101 tens.	Bring down the 8 ones. Divide the 58 ones.
	Think: $25 \times n = 50$.

Step 1

$$\begin{array}{r} 4 \\ 24\overline{)1,018} \\ -96 \\ \hline 5 \end{array}$$

Multiply.
Subtract.
Compare. $5 < 24$

Step 2

$$\begin{array}{r} 42 \text{ r}10 \\ 24\overline{)1,018} \\ -96\downarrow \\ \hline 58 \\ -48 \\ \hline 10 \end{array}$$

Multiply.
Subtract.
Compare. $10 < 24$

So, on the average, 42 laps were completed each hour. The remainder of 10 represents only parts of laps.

Another Method

A calculator can help you divide large numbers.

Estimate. $14,304 \div 48 \approx n$

Think: $50 \times n = 15,000$
$50 \times 300 = 15,000$

So, $14,304 \div 48 = 298$.

Talk About It

▶ Compare your estimate with the quotient. Is your answer reasonable? Explain.

▶ Is your estimate an overestimate or an underestimate? Why?

 Idea Bank, page 464, Exercise 5

Check for Understanding

Choose the correct answer. Write **a**, **b**, or **c**.

1. $16\overline{)3,568}$
   a. 22
   b. 222
   c. 223

2. $27\overline{)1,382}$
   a. 51
   b. 51 r5
   c. 515

3. $42\overline{)8,904}$
   a. 21
   b. 221
   c. 212

4. $53\overline{)2,385}$
   a. 45
   b. 450
   c. 455 r5

Practice

Estimate. Then find the quotient.

5. $5,751 \div 81 = n$

6. $6,050 \div 93 = n$

7. $3,620 \div 27 = n$

8. $8,589 \div 11 = n$

9. $2,398 \div 46 = n$

10. $4,580 \div 32 = n$

Divide.

11. $37\overline{)1,036}$

12. $23\overline{)2,185}$

13. $54\overline{)5,508}$

14. $68\overline{)4,624}$

15. $24\overline{)68,976}$

16. $12\overline{)45,984}$

17. $17\overline{)55,403}$

18. $32\overline{)33,024}$

Mixed Applications

19. The original Ferris wheel was erected in 1893 at the World's Columbian Exposition in Chicago. The wheel carried 36 cars, each seating 60 people. What was the total number of passengers that could be seated?

20. **Number Sense** What is the smallest four-digit number that can be divided by 20 and leave a remainder of 15?

21. **Number Sense** If a motorcycle traveled 1,502 miles in 24 hours, was its average speed more than 50 miles per hour?

NUMBER SENSE

Compare. Use < or > for ●.

22. $6,539 \div 13$ ● $6,539 \div 19$

23. $8,250 \div 12$ ● $6,250 \div 12$

24. $1,034 \div 24$ ● $3,098 \div 24$

25. $4,195 \div 27$ ● $4,195 \div 17$

Why is an estimate needed when you use a calculator to find quotients?

WRAP UP...

ZEROS IN THE QUOTIENT

The largest barbecue ever recorded, at the May Festival in Memphis, Tennessee, was attended by 80,000 people. Rosa and her friends are planning a smaller barbecue to be held on Saturday. Over a period of 12 hours, a team of cooks will prepare 1,248 pounds of beef. What is the average number of pounds of beef they will prepare each hour?

Estimate. $1,248 \div 12 \approx n$

Think: $12 \times n = 1,200$ or
$10 \times n = 1,200$, so $n = 100$ or 120.

Divide. $12\overline{)1,248}$

Step 1	**Step 2**	**Step 3**
Since the estimate is three digits, divide the 12 hundreds. $12 \times n = 12$	Bring down the tens. Divide the 4 tens. **Think:** Since $12 > 4$, write 0 tens in the quotient.	Bring down the ones. Divide the 48 ones.
$\begin{array}{r} 1 \\ 12\overline{)1,248} \\ -12 \\ \hline 0 \end{array}$	$\begin{array}{r} 10 \\ 12\overline{)1,248} \\ -12{\downarrow} \\ \hline 04 \\ -0 \\ \hline 4 \end{array}$	$\begin{array}{r} 104 \\ 12\overline{)1,248} \\ -12 \\ \hline 04{\downarrow} \\ -0{\downarrow} \\ \hline 48 \\ -48 \\ \hline 0 \end{array}$

So, on the average, the cooks will prepare 104 pounds of beef each hour.

- What would happen if you did not write a zero in the tens place?

Check for Understanding

Choose the correct answer. Write **a**, **b**, or **c**.

1. $26\overline{)5,382}$ **a.** 27   **b.** 207   **c.** 270

2. $34\overline{)3,604}$ **a.** 16   **b.** 160   **c.** 106

3. $53\overline{)6,364}$ **a.** 120 r4   **b.** 12 r4   **c.** 102 r4

4. $47\overline{)4,841}$ **a.** 13   **b.** 103   **c.** 130

Practice

Divide.

5. $25\overline{)500}$ 6. $12\overline{)360}$ 7. $13\overline{)390}$ 8. $29\overline{)585}$

9. $58\overline{)2,900}$ 10. $56\overline{)5,040}$ 11. $38\overline{)4,066}$ 12. $11\overline{)7,812}$

13. $93\overline{)9,594}$ 14. $41\overline{)4,141}$ 15. $35\overline{)14,070}$ 16. $41\overline{)16,769}$

17. $240 \div 12 = n$ 18. $155 \div 15 = n$ 19. $3,570 \div 34 = n$ 20. $4,769 \div 23 = n$

21. $9,421 \div 31 = n$ 22. $31,310 \div 62 = n$ 23. $17,650 \div 44 = n$ 24. $16,082 \div 52 = n$

Mixed Applications

25. A county set a record in its state for having the largest barbecue. Lonnie sold a total of 1,350 tickets in two weeks. If he sold 100 more tickets the second week than he sold the first week, how many tickets did he sell each week?

26. There were 3,000 people who attended the barbecue. There were supposed to be enough tables to seat half that number at one time. If 70 tables were ordered and each table seated 20 people, how many more tables should have been ordered?

27. **Making Choices** If the tickets to the barbecue are sold for $10 each or 5 for $40, how much money can 120 people save if they buy their tickets as a group?

28. **Number Sense** Explain why a quotient of 15 is incorrect for $3,150 \div 30$.

MIXED REVIEW

Write in standard form.

1. six tenths 2. twelve hundredths 3. five hundredths

Find the sum.

4. 398
   $+ 876$

5. $2,187$
   $+ 7,950$

6. 89.50
   $+ 64.98$

7. 264.20
   $+ 857.95$

Explain why the zero in a quotient is important.

WRAP
UP...

EXPLORING

Division with a Calculator

A calculator is a useful tool. Use a calculator to explore division.

WORK TOGETHER

Building Understanding

Estimate. $45,236 \div 16 \approx n$

Think: $20 \times n = 50,000$
$15 \times n = 45,000$,
so $n = 2,500$ or $3,000$.

Divide. $16\overline{)45,236}$

Talk About It

▶ How do you read $16\overline{)45,236}$?

▶ When you enter division on a calculator, does the divisor or the dividend come first?

$\boxed{4}$ $\boxed{5}$ $\boxed{2}$ $\boxed{3}$ $\boxed{6}$ $\boxed{\div}$ $\boxed{1}$ $\boxed{6}$ $\boxed{=}$

▶ When you press the $\boxed{=}$ key, what shows on the display?

▶ Name the whole-number part of the display.

▶ How does your quotient compare with your estimate?

▶ What does the decimal part of the display represent? How do you know?

▶ How can you find 0.25 of 16?

▶ If you do this division by paper and pencil, what is the remainder?

Making the Connection

When you use a calculator for division and there
is a remainder, the display shows a decimal.
Suppose you need to know the whole number
this decimal represents.

Do this division on a calculator.

$$\boxed{3}\ \boxed{0}\ \boxed{4}\ \boxed{2}\ \boxed{0}\ \boxed{\div}\ \boxed{4}\ \boxed{7}\ \boxed{=}\quad \boxed{647.23404}$$

The whole-number part of the display is the quotient. Use
this number to find the remainder. Multiply this number
by the divisor, 47. Then subtract the product from the
dividend, 30,420.

You can use the **memory keys** on your calculator to do this.

Step 1 $\boxed{6}\ \boxed{4}\ \boxed{7}\ \boxed{\times}\ \boxed{4}\ \boxed{7}\ \boxed{=}\quad \boxed{30409.}\ \boxed{M+}\quad ^M\ \boxed{30409.}$

Step 2 $\boxed{3}\ \boxed{0}\ \boxed{4}\ \boxed{2}\ \boxed{0}\ \boxed{-}\ \boxed{MRC}\ \boxed{=}\quad ^M\ \boxed{11.}$

So, the remainder is 11.

⌐ recalls the product from memory

Some calculators use
$\boxed{MR}$ for memory recall.

Talk About It

▶ How can you check that this
remainder is correct?

▶ What happened when you pressed the
$\boxed{M+}$ key?

▶ What does the *M* on the display represent?

▶ What happened when you pressed the $\boxed{MRC}$
key?

▶ What happens when you press $\boxed{MRC}$ $\boxed{MRC}$
$\boxed{ON/C}$?

Checking Understanding

Use a calculator to divide. Then find the remainder.

1. $16\overline{)26,136}$ 2. $25\overline{)48,920}$ 3. $63\overline{)56,850}$ 4. $58\overline{)28,720}$

Choose a Strategy

The most extensive cave system in the world is under Mammoth Cave National Park in Kentucky. Many visitors tour the caves. Rod and his father are purchasing tickets for one of the tours. The cost is $7.50 for one child and one adult. The adult's ticket costs $3.00 more than the child's ticket. What is the cost of each ticket?

| Understand |
| Plan |
| Solve |
| Look Back |

You have learned many problem-solving strategies. It is important to remember that some problems can be solved by using more than one strategy.

One strategy you can use is *guess and check*.

Guess. $2.00 for the child's ticket

child's ticket	+	child's ticket		
		plus $3	=	n
$2	+	($2 + $3)	=	n
$2	+	$5	=	$7

Is this sum $7.50? No, it is less than $7.50. Guess again. Try a larger number.

Guess. $2.25 for the child's ticket

| $2.25 | + | ($2.25 + $3.00) | = | n |
| $2.25 | + | $5.25 | = | $7.50 |

Another strategy you can use is *work backward*.

| child's ticket ? | → | × 2 tickets | → | + $3.00 for adult | → | $7.50 |

| ? | ← | ÷ 2 | ← | − $3.00 | ← | $7.50 |

| $2.25 | | $2.25 | | $4.50 | | $7.50 |

So, the child's ticket costs $2.25, and the adult's ticket costs $5.25.

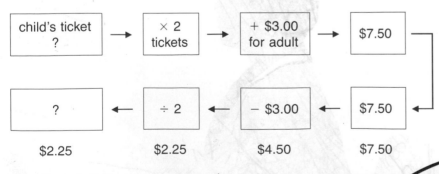

WHAT IF... ...the total cost of admission is $10.00? What is the cost of each ticket?

- Make a Table   • Find a Pattern
- Guess and Check   • Write a Number Sentence
- Work Backward

Choose a strategy and solve.

1. The largest cake ever baked was made from 31,026 boxes of cake mix. If each box required 2 eggs, how many dozen eggs were used in the cake?

2. You are to find two 2-digit numbers. The sum of the two numbers is 50, and the difference is 22. What are the two numbers?

3. Otis is practicing to set a new record with his yo-yo. The first day he practiced, he made 70 loops. The second day he made 100 loops, and the third day he made 140 loops. If he continues at this rate, how many days of practice will it take before he makes 400 loops?

4. Sue Ann now has 15,000 postcards in her collection. On her twelfth birthday, she received half of this total from her brother, 500 cards from her aunt, and 125 cards from friends. How many cards did she have before her twelfth birthday?

5. The heaviest cat on record weighed about 47 pounds, and the lightest adult cat weighed about 2 pounds. The heaviest dog on record weighed about 338 pounds, and the lightest adult dog weighed about 1 pound. What is the difference in weight between the heaviest cat and dog? between the lightest cat and dog?

6. Jack and Lucinda played a number game. Jack told Lucinda to choose a number. Then he told her to multiply it by 4, add 6, divide by 2, and subtract 5. When Lucinda said that her answer was 6, Jack told her what number she began with. What was Lucinda's starting number?

WRITER'S CORNER

7. Write a brief news article about an imaginary record-breaking event at school. Include several number facts. Then make up a problem based on those number facts. Exchange your article and problem with a partner. Solve.

Vocabulary Check

Choose a word from the box to complete each sentence.

| memory |
| pattern |
| reasonable |
| remainder |
| strategy |

1. When 40, 400, and 4,000 are divided by 50, you can see a __?__ in the quotients. *(page 180)*

2. The [M+] key on the calculator is a __?__ key. *(page 199)*

3. Some problems can be solved by using more than one problem-solving __?__ . *(page 200)*

4. If you multiply the whole-number quotient in the display of a calculator by the divisor and subtract this product from the dividend, you can find the __?__ . *(page 199)*

5. An important part of the problem-solving process is to check whether your solution is __?__ . *(page 188)*

Concept Check

> Compatible numbers are close to the original numbers, and they divide easily.

Complete the pattern. *(page 180)*

6. $60 \div 20 = 3$
   $600 \div 20 = 30$
   $6,000 \div 20 = n$

7. $120 \div 60 = n$
   $1,200 \div 60 = 20$
   $12,000 \div 60 = 200$

8. $240 \div 30 = 8$
   $2,400 \div 30 = n$
   $24,000 \div 30 = 800$

Name a pair of compatible numbers for each. *(page 182)*

9. $260 \div 77 \approx n$ 10. $475 \div 58 \approx n$ 11. $1,697 \div 26 \approx n$

12. $146 \div 43 \approx n$ 13. $317 \div 26 \approx n$ 14. $1,587 \div 68 \approx n$

Estimate the quotient. *(page 182)*

15. $18\overline{)83}$ 16. $13\overline{)47}$ 17. $29\overline{)85}$ 18. $43\overline{)78}$

19. $47\overline{)287}$ 20. $32\overline{)936}$ 21. $24\overline{)389}$ 22. $53\overline{)997}$

23. $36\overline{)3,750}$ 24. $27\overline{)2,792}$ 25. $42\overline{)8,106}$ 26. $61\overline{)5,500}$

Look at each estimated quotient. Write whether the estimated quotient is *too large*, *too small*, or *just right*. *(page 186)*

27. $21\overline{)86}$ with quotient 5 28. $73\overline{)149}$ with quotient 2 29. $45\overline{)287}$ with quotient 5 30. $86\overline{)317}$ with quotient 4

Skill Check

Find the quotient. *(page 180)*

31. $20\overline{)60}$ **32.** $30\overline{)90}$ **33.** $10\overline{)800}$ **34.** $40\overline{)160}$

35. $50\overline{)250}$ **36.** $60\overline{)480}$ **37.** $70\overline{)6,300}$ **38.** $40\overline{)2,800}$

Estimate the quotient. *(page 182)*

39. $41\overline{)825}$ **40.** $12\overline{)710}$ **41.** $25\overline{)595}$ **42.** $71\overline{)139}$

43. $60\overline{)4,328}$ **44.** $54\overline{)3,050}$ **45.** $82\overline{)2,500}$ **46.** $93\overline{)8,000}$

Find the quotient. *(pages 184, 186, 188, 194, 196)*

47. $15\overline{)67}$ **48.** $25\overline{)85}$ **49.** $24\overline{)72}$ **50.** $36\overline{)547}$

51. $56\overline{)896}$ **52.** $35\overline{)770}$ **53.** $45\overline{)1,043}$ **54.** $19\overline{)986}$

55. $1,470 \div 42 = n$ **56.** $2,890 \div 65 = n$ **57.** $5,602 \div 12 = n$

58. $640 \div 32 = n$ **59.** $9,246 \div 23 = n$ **60.** $10,285 \div 17 = n$

Problem-Solving Check *(pages 190, 200)*

61. Heather needs to make 150 hearts for the crafts fair. She has made 48. If she completes 10 each day, about how many days will it take her to finish making the hearts?

62. Larry worked a total of 18 hours on Monday and Tuesday. If he worked 4 more hours on Tuesday than he did on Monday, how many hours did he work each day?

63. At a crafts fair, Alma sold 7 baskets for $15 each, 3 wreaths for $12 each, and a rug for $24. The cost of entering the fair was $15. After deducting the cost of her materials, Alma made $95. How much did her materials cost?

64. Ryan and his family will travel a total of 1,870 miles in 6 days. The first day they will drive 430 miles. To divide the travel evenly, about how many miles will they have to travel each of the remaining days?

CHAPTER TEST

Estimate.

1. $23\overline{)78}$

2. $18\overline{)56}$

3. $33\overline{)88}$

4. $42\overline{)290}$

5. $27\overline{)235}$

6. $49\overline{)444}$

7. $13\overline{)5,750}$

8. $37\overline{)3,509}$

9. $52\overline{)4,567}$

Find the quotient.

10. $20\overline{)80}$

11. $30\overline{)270}$

12. $50\overline{)300}$

13. $40\overline{)1,600}$

14. $17\overline{)85}$

15. $23\overline{)96}$

16. $35\overline{)315}$

17. $28\overline{)560}$

18. $52\overline{)987}$

19. $14\overline{)2,884}$

20. $42\overline{)5,690}$

21. $23\overline{)4,823}$

Choose a strategy and solve.

22. Diane has an order to weave 103 baskets. If she already has 19 baskets made and can weave 9 baskets each day, about how many days will it take her to complete the order?

23. During his vacation, Brett plans to visit 5 cities in 29 days. If he spends 10 days traveling, about how many days can he spend in each city?

24. One day Bruce spent $6 for a tape, $10 for gas, and $3 for lunch. A friend paid him $5 that she owed him. Bruce now has $12. How much money did he have at the beginning of the day?

25. Liona worked a total of 78 hours in 2 weeks. If she worked 12 hours more the second week than she worked the first week, how many hours did she work each week?

Copy each problem carefully.

Teamwork P-R-O-J-E-C-T

ORGANIZE A SPORTS ACTIVITY

There are many record-setting events in the sports world. One such event was the longest roller-skating marathon. The winner skated continuously for more than 344 hours.

Find out about some other record-setting events. With your teammates, organize a sports activity for your team.

Alvarez Takes First In Skate Race

On June 25, Seminole County sponsored the first ever roller-skate race. There were 48 skaters participating in the 2-mile race down Sand Lake Road. The street was closed to traffic, and fans lined the road to cheer on the competitors.

SHARE

Prepare a booklet describing the event. Explain how the activity was set up, what the rules were, and how the record-keeping was done. You can relate stories about the participants' experiences and give a statistic of a team member's record-setting performance.

Discuss interesting information about each team's event. Compare record-keeping methods. Combine the team booklets into one book of class records.

DECIDE

Create a sports activity in which all of your teammates can participate. Discuss the materials you will need and the way you will conduct the competition.

DO

Gather the necessary materials. Schedule times when individuals will perform the activity. Design record-keeping sheets. Carry out the planned event.

TALK ABOUT IT

☐ What interesting facts did you learn?

☐ If the class chooses to sponsor a school-wide sports activity, which event would work best for the school?

☐ Based on the performances of the participants, could an average time for an event be calculated?

☐ How was multiplication or division used in this project?

STATISTICS AND GRAPHING

Did you know ...

... that the earliest restaurant was opened in 1725 in Madrid, Spain?

Talk About It

The owner of a restaurant keeps track of his sales each month. He wants to determine his busiest months. How can the data be graphed to show the pattern of sales for the year?

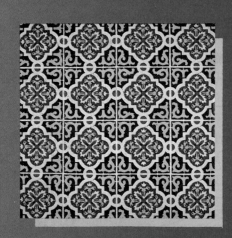

EXPLORING
Sample Groups

WORK TOGETHER

Building Understanding

Brian's favorite sport is soccer. He thinks most fifth graders' favorite sport is soccer. He predicted 15 students in his class would name soccer as their favorite sport. He surveyed his class and organized the data in a frequency table.

Brian's Prediction					
Choice	Archery	Baseball	Basketball	Football	Soccer
Votes	1	5	4	5	15

Brian's Survey					
Choice	Archery	Baseball	Basketball	Football	Soccer
Votes	8	7	3	10	2

◄— Frequency tables show how often events occur.

Talk About It

► Why do you think his prediction was so different from the survey?

► What do you think would happen if Brian surveyed a different fifth-grade class?

One way to find the sport that most fifth graders like best is to ask a small group, or **sample group,** of fifth graders. You can use data collected from a sample group to help you predict the favorite sport of fifth graders. The larger your sample group is, and the more it is like most fifth graders, the better it is.

One way to choose a sample group is to choose names at **random.** When names are selected at random, all students have the same chance of being chosen. One way to select a random group is by drawing names from a bag.

	Susan	Bill	Andre
Suggestions for sample groups were given by these students:	10 Art Club members 10 chorus members 10 girls	10 eleven-year-olds 10 boys 10 Math Club members	50 fifth graders chosen at random

• Which sample group is best? Why?

Making the Connection

A fifth-grade class won $50 in a safety contest. Predict how most of the class would spend the money. Then survey a sample group from your class.

- With a partner, select a sample group.

- Decide what choices to include in your survey.

- Decide how you will record the data.

- Conduct your survey.

- Organize the data.

Talk About It

▶ How large is your sample group and how did you select it?

▶ What was the most frequent choice of your sample group?

▶ How do the results of your sample group differ from those of other sample groups?

▶ How do you think the results would have differed if you had surveyed only students who participate in sports?

Checking Understanding

1. Tell which sample group would better predict the choice of fifth graders. Defend your answer.

   30 Math Club members or 50 fifth-grade students chosen at random

Choose a word or words from the box to complete each sentence.

predict
random
sample group
survey

2. When you choose a group at ? , all students have the same chance of being chosen.

3. A ? can be conducted to find the most frequent choice of a group.

4. Data collected from a ? can help you ? the most frequent choice of a larger group.

RANGE, MODE, MEDIAN, AND MEAN

Carla surveyed fifth-grade students to find out how many hours a week they watch television. The frequency table shows the results of Carla's survey.

Weekly Hours of TV Watched					
Student	Kyle	Leandra	Tanya	Jody	Steven
Hours	8	10	5	2	5

Use connecting cubes to model the number of hours each student watches television. Find the difference between the number of cubes in the tallest and the shortest stacks. This is called the **range.**
10 − 2 = 8   So, the range is 8.

Look for stacks that have the same number of cubes. The number that appears most often is 5. So, 5 is the **mode.**

Place the stacks of cubes in order from greatest to least. The number in the middle stack contains 5 cubes. So, 5 is the **median**.

Put the cubes in one stack. Separate the stack into five equal stacks. Count the cubes in each new stack. This number, called the **mean,** is the average number of cubes in the original stacks. You can compute the mean.

Find the total number of cubes.	Divide by the number of stacks.
8 + 10 + 5 + 2 + 5 = 30	30 ÷ 5 = 6

Talk About It

▶ In what ways are the median and the mode different?

▶ In what ways do the median and the mode differ from the mean? the range?

Check for Understanding

Find the range, mode, median, and mean for each set of data.

1. 7, 3, 2, 3, 5

2. 19, 9, 7, 5, 5

3. 6, 10, 18, 6, 25

Practice

Find the range, mode, median, and mean.

4. 27, 31, 34, 31, 32

5. 55, 59, 60, 59, 57

6. 15, 20, 25, 15, 30

7. 30, 45, 50, 45, 65

8. 24, 37, 42, 15, 42

9. $28, $42, $59, $42, $64

10. $271, $298, $271

11. 575, 630, 720, 575, 525

12. 13, 22, 13, 15, 12

Mixed Applications

13. A football team has scored 14 points, 7 points, 10 points, and 17 points in its last four games. Find the mean of the points scored in the four games.

14. **Logical Reasoning**   Sheila scored 95, 82, 90, and 83 on four tests. After the fifth test, the mode of her scores was 83. What did she score on the fifth test?

15. Buses will be used to take students to a football game. How many buses will be needed if 225 tickets are sold and each bus holds 48 people?

16. A math quiz has 25 problems. If each problem has a value of 4 points, how many problems did Pedro miss if he scored 84?

CALCULATOR

You can use a calculator to find the mean of a set of data.

Example   Sharon scored 86, 92, 95, 100, and 92 on five tests. What is her average score?

Press 86 + 92 + 95 + 100 + 92 =

465. ÷ 5 = 93.

Find the mean of each set of data.

17. 59, 63, 53, 75, 65

18. 135, 375, 450

19. 13, 19, 28, 13, 17

How can a set of data have more than one mode?

WRAP UP...

PICTOGRAPHS

Loren surveyed students at Lakeview School to find out how many participate in chorus and band. She recorded the results in a frequency table. She made a pictograph to compare the data she counted.

A pictograph uses a **key** to tell how many students are shown by each symbol in the graph.

Talk About It

▶ How many students are represented by one symbol in Loren's key?

▶ What problems will Loren have if she uses one symbol to represent each student?

▶ How many students does half a symbol represent?

▶ How can Loren show 30 if she chooses one symbol to represent 12 students?

▶ What is the greatest number that Loren can use as her key if she wants to have all whole symbols?

Check for Understanding

Use the data that shows each grade's Computer Club membership. Plan a pictograph.

1. What title would you use?

2. Tell what you would label each column.

3. Where would you write the grade levels?

4. What symbol would you use to represent the number of students?

5. How many students would each symbol represent?

6. What two questions could be answered by using your graph?

Lakeview Students in Chorus and Band	
Grade	Number of Students
K	12
1	24
2	36
3	30
4	40
5	48

Lakeview Students in Chorus and Band	
Grade	Number of Students
K	●●●
1	●●●●●
2	●●●●●●●●●
3	●●●●●●●◖
4	●●●●●●●●●●
5	●●●●●●●●●●●●

Key ● = 4 students

Computer Club Data	
Grade	Number of Club Members
K	4
1	7
2	10
3	10
4	12
5	8
6	3

Practice

Use the pictograph for Exercises 7–9.

7. Which type of book was checked out most often in one week?

8. How many joke books were checked out?

9. How many fiction and science fiction books were checked out in one week?

10. Use the data from the table to make a pictograph. Title and label your graph and choose a key.

Types of Books Checked Out from Library in One Week	
Type of Book	**Number of Books**
Biography	📖📖📖📖📖📖📖
Fiction	📖📖📖📖📖📖📖📖📖
Science fiction	📖📖📖📖📖
Puzzles	📖📖📖📖
Joke book	📖📖📖
History	📖📖📖📖

Key 📖 = 2 books

Students Playing Musical Instruments							
Type of Instrument	Guitar	Piano	Accordion	Recorder	Flute	Organ	Violin
Number of Students	8	48	6	14	16	4	12

Mixed Applications

11. **Write a Question** Make up a question that can be answered by using the pictograph you made in Exercise 10.

12. If the key in a pictograph has a symbol that represents 6 students, how many symbols will be used to show 75 students?

13. A flute sells for $450. If the rental fee, $25 a month, can be used toward the purchase of the flute, how many months will it take to pay for the flute?

14. There were 65 students in the band at the end of the year. If twelve students joined and seven left the band, how many students were in the band at the start?

VISUAL THINKING

The symbols used in some pictographs indicate the subject of the graphs.

For each symbol shown, describe the kind of information that might be on the graph.

15.

16.

17.

18.

When would a pictograph be useful?

WRAP UP...

The table shows the data Miss Whittier's class collected from fifth graders about their family homes.

Miss Whittier's students tallied and then counted their data. They wanted to display the data so that it could be read quickly and easily. They decided to make a bar graph. A bar graph has these parts.

- A bar graph has a **title.**

- Each part of the graph has a **label.**

- A **scale** is used on the graph to tell what each unit length represents.

- Bars can be drawn either vertically or horizontally.

Bar graphs make it easy to compare data that can be counted. The title, labels, and scale help you understand the information on the bar graph.

Family Homes of Fifth Graders		
Type of Home	**Number of Students**	
Apartment	⌿⌿⌿ ⌿⌿⌿ ⌿⌿⌿ ⌿⌿⌿ ⌿⌿⌿	25
Condominium	////	4
Duplex	⌿⌿⌿ ⌿⌿⌿	10
House	⌿⌿⌿ ⌿⌿⌿ ⌿⌿⌿ ⌿⌿⌿ ⌿⌿⌿ /	26
Mobile home	⌿⌿⌿ ///	8

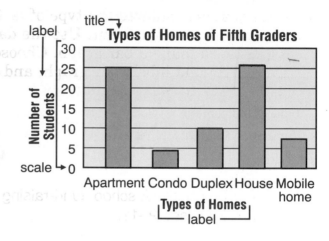

Talk About It

▶ Is a bar graph a reasonable way to show the data? Explain.

▶ How does a bar graph make the data easy to read?

▶ How many students does each unit length represent?

▶ How do you read a bar that ends between unit lengths?

Check for Understanding

Use the bar graph for Exercises 1–3.

1. About how many more students live in houses than in apartments?

2. About how many more students live in apartments than in mobile homes?

3. About how many students do not live in a house?

Practice

Use the bar graph about Longwood Elementary School for Exercises 4–7.

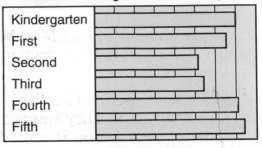

Students at Longwood Elementary

4. What is each unit length shown on the scale?

5. Are there more students in first grade or fourth grade?

6. Which grades have fewer than 120 students?

7. How many students are in kindergarten?

8. A class survey showed the type of fast food preferred by each student. Use the data from the table to make a bar graph. Choose a scale, title and label your graph, and then color in the bars.

Favorite Fast Food	
Food	Number of Students
Chicken	1
Hamburgers	8
Pizza	12
Tacos	4
Other	3

Mixed Applications

Use the bar graph about school fund-raising projects for Exercises 9–11.

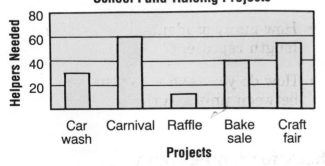

School Fund-Raising Projects

9. Which project needs the most helpers?

10. **Analyze Data** How many more helpers are needed at the carnival than at the bake sale?

11. Which project represents the median for all helpers needed?

Solve.

12. At the bake sale, 120 cookies were sold. Half of the cookies were oatmeal. The rest were raisin or carob-chip. If there were 10 more carob-chip cookies than raisin, how many cookies were carob-chip?

13. At the car wash, 5 cars were washed the first hour, 10 cars the second hour, and 15 cars the third hour. If the pattern continues, how many cars will be washed the sixth hour?

Would you rather read a pictograph or a bar graph? Explain.

WRAP UP...

CHOOSING
the Appropriate Scale

My data includes numbers from 4 to 63. If I start my scale at zero and number each line to 63, I'll run out of room on my paper.

There are 179 fifth graders in Jay's school. Jay surveyed them to find how they travel to and from school. The frequency table shows his results. He wants to choose a scale so he can display his data on a graph.

Transportation					
Type	Car	Bicycle	School bus	Walk	Van
Number of Students	43	30	63	39	4

The scale is made up of **intervals**, or units that are equal in number.

Jay drew three different scales:

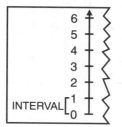

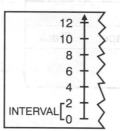

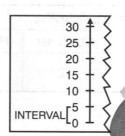

Jay's First Attempt
Each interval stands for 1 person.

Jay's Second Attempt
Each interval stands for 2 persons.

Jay's Third Attempt
Each interval stands for 5 persons.

Talk About It

▶ With what number should you start each scale?

▶ How are Jay's attempts different? How are they similar?

▶ What is a reasonable scale for Jay's set of data? Explain.

Check for Understanding

Choose the most reasonable scale for the set of data. Write **a, b,** or **c.** Explain your choice.

1.

Favorite Kinds of Books				
Books	Poetry	Biography	Fiction	Science Fiction
Number of Students	15	19	25	10

a.
```
100
 80
 60
 40
 20
  0
```
b.
```
25
20
15
10
 5
 0
```
c.
```
20
14
12
 8
 2
 0
```

Practice

Choose the most reasonable scale for each set of data. Write **a**, **b**, or **c**.

2.

Fifth-Grade Girls					
Bicycle Color	Green	Pink	Purple	White	Other
Number of Students	10	20	25	5	18

a. 10 8 6 4 2 0   b. 25 20 15 10 5 0   c. 15 12 9 6 3 0

3.

Favorite Types of Television Shows					
Shows	Cartoon	Comedy	Drama	News	Sports
Number of Students	5	8	4	2	3

a. 100 80 60 40 20 0   b. 75 60 45 30 15 0   c. 10 8 6 4 2 0

4.

After-School Activities					
Activity	Band	Chorus	Computer	Newspaper	Track
Number of Students	75	36	12	21	53

a. 25 20 15 10 5 0   b. 100 80 60 40 20 0   c. 30 24 18 12 6 0

Mixed Applications

5. Tyrone is taking a survey of 125 fifth-grade students. If there are 15 more boys than girls, how many students are boys and how many are girls?

6. **Logical Reasoning** Would it be reasonable to mark a scale off in ones if the graph is going to show the numbers of different kinds of books in a library? Explain.

7. **Making Choices** If a graph is to show the number of pets owned by students in a class of 30, do you think the scale should be marked off in ones, tens, or fifties? Explain.

8. Pauline wants to know how many copies of her survey she should make. Each student will receive one copy. If there are 29 students in each of 3 classes and 32 students in each of 2 classes, how many copies should she make?

What is true of the intervals of all scales?

WRAP UP...

PROBLEM *Solving*

Mr. Snyder's class exchanged letters and computer messages with a class in Panama. As a gift to the class in Panama, the students made a friendship quilt. First, the students made 36 small quilt squares. Then, they sewed the small squares together to make the quilt. It took 18 minutes to sew 4 of the small squares together into 1 larger square. How long did it take to sew all the small squares into larger squares?

Sometimes you can look for a pattern in the numbers that are used in a problem. A pattern can help you set up a table to solve the problem.

▶ **UNDERSTAND**

What are you asked to find?

What facts are given?

▶ **PLAN**

What strategy can you use?

A table is useful to display a pattern of numbers. Since there is a pattern of 4 small squares for every 18 minutes, you can *make a table* to solve the problem.

▶ **SOLVE**

How can you solve the problem?

Make a table showing the number of small squares and the number of minutes needed to sew them into larger squares.

	× 2	× 3	× 4	× 5	× 6	× 7	× 8	× 9
Squares Used	4	8	12	16	20	24	28	32	36
Time in Minutes	18	36	54	72	90	108	126	144	162
	× 2	× 3	× 4	× 5	× 6	× 7	× 8	× 9

So, the table shows it took 162 minutes to sew the larger squares.

▶ **LOOK BACK**

What is another way to solve the problem?

 WHAT IF... ...the class made 64 small squares? How long would it take the class to sew them into larger squares?

Apply

Make a table and solve.

1. At the opening of a school carnival, a booth has 108 prizes to give away. If every 15 minutes 9 prizes are given away, how long will it take to give away all the prizes?

2. Sonia is making a pot holder with 42 loops. If her pattern uses 4 red loops for every 6 loops in the design, how many red loops will be used for the pot holder?

Mixed Applications ➤ **STRATEGIES** • Work Backward • Make a Drawing • Make a Table • Guess and Check • Write a Number Sentence

Choose a strategy and solve.

3. A pottery booth sold a total of 32 pieces of pottery. If 8 more pieces were sold in the afternoon than in the morning, how many pieces were sold in the afternoon?

4. An industrial arts class can complete 5 projects every 9 weeks. How many projects can 5 classes complete in the 36 weeks of the school year?

5. Construction paper is sold in packages of 24 sheets. An art teacher has 3 classes with 28 students in each class and 2 classes with 30 students in each class. How many packages of paper should she buy if each student needs one sheet?

6. When Neil arrived home after purchasing art supplies, he had $4.35. He bought paper for $3.89, paint for $5.19, and brushes for $4.12. He received a $2.00 discount on his total bill. How much money did he have to start?

7. Two buses will transport people to an art festival. Each bus holds 52 people. A total of 1,248 people will be transported. If each bus makes the same number of trips, how many trips will each bus make?

8. At an outdoor art show, there were five different booths on a block. Photography was on the corner, and pottery was between photography and woodworking. Jewelry was between woodworking and pottery. If the oil paintings were next to jewelry and pottery, in what order were the five booths on the block?

Choose a strategy and solve.

1. Jason took some baseball cards to Matt's house. Matt gave Jason 12 cards. Jason gave Matt 5 cards. Jason then had 23 cards. How many cards did Jason have when he went to Matt's house?

2. It takes Meredith about 25 minutes to type 2 pages of her report. If she has a total of 10 pages to type, about how long will it take her to type the report?

Some problems can be solved using more than one strategy.

Write the value of the underlined digit.

3. 4.5̲27

4. 12.40̲6

5. 15.28̲5

6. 25.7̲50

Complete each number sentence.

7. 6.55 + ▢ = 6.55

8. 9.8 + 6.3 = ▢ + 9.8

9. 7.25 + (3.75 + 2.50) = (7.25 + ▢) + 2.50

Multiply.

10. 485
× 4

11. 7,081
× 8

12. 5,902
× 8

13. 6,875
× 16

14. 809
× 25

Identify each angle. Write *right, acute,* or *obtuse.*

15.

16.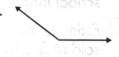

17.

18.

Use the rules for divisibility to decide whether the first number is divisible by the second. Write *yes* or *no.*

19. 794; 2

20. 534; 3

21. 507; 5

22. 6,480; 10

23. 642; 3

Estimate.

24. 8)555

25. 3)259

26. 6)3,780

27. 9)8,000

28. 7)6,498

Divide.

29. 12)348

30. 36)2,358

31. 25)2,515

32. 43)5,762

33. 28)2,688

Spotlight ON
PROBLEM SOLVING

Make Inferences

You can use a graph to help you compare data. You can also use a graph to answer questions whose solutions are not directly shown by the data. When you do this kind of thinking, you are **making an inference.** Study the graph.

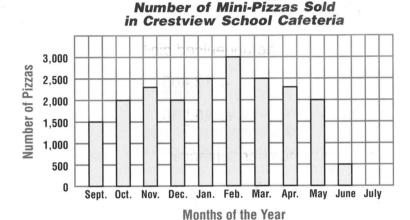

Number of Mini-Pizzas Sold in Crestview School Cafeteria

Number of Pizzas (y-axis): 0, 500, 1,000, 1,500, 2,000, 2,500, 3,000

Months of the Year (x-axis): Sept., Oct., Nov., Dec., Jan., Feb., Mar., Apr., May, June, July

Talk About It • • • • • • • • • • • • • • • • • •

▢ In which month were the most pizzas sold?

▢ Why do you think the difference in the number of pizzas sold was so great between May and June?

▢ What inferences can be made about pizza sales in July?

▢ Is it possible to infer from the data that pizza was the favorite school lunch?

▢ Estimate the number of pizzas sold at Crestview School in a year.

Apply

Work together. Find the number of students in your class who participate in a sport each day after school during one week. Make a graph of your data. Use your graph for Exercises 1–5.

1. On which day did the most students participate in a sport?

2. On which day did the fewest students participate in a sport?

3. Use the data from your graph to make an inference about the class's participation in sports.

4. What do you think is a reason that few students participate in a sport?

5. What do you think causes more students to participate in a sport?

223

LINE GRAPHS

Cher went on a bicycle trip. She made a table to record her average miles per hour for each hour of her trip.

Average Miles Per Hour for Each Hour of Cher's Trip					
Hours	1	2	3	4	5
Average Miles Per Hour	15	10	0	15	5

She recorded the data in a line graph. **Line graphs** are used to make comparisons and show changes over time. Bar graphs and pictographs are used to compare data that is counted. A bar graph has one scale, and a pictograph has a scale and a key. A line graph has a scale on the vertical and the horizontal axis.

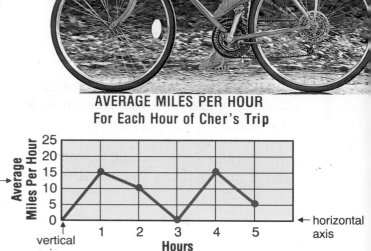

AVERAGE MILES PER HOUR
For Each Hour of Cher's Trip

Talk About It

▶ Why is a line graph a good choice to compare the average miles per hour Cher rode for each hour of her trip?

▶ What does each mark on the **vertical axis,** or left side of the line graph, represent?

▶ What does each mark on the **horizontal axis,** or bottom line, represent?

▶ How do you think Cher chose the scale on the vertical axis?

▶ What does each point on the graph represent?

▶ Which part of the graph shows whether there is an increase, a decrease, or no change in the miles?

Check for Understanding

Use the line graph for Exercises 1–2.

1. What is represented by the scale on the vertical axis?

2. What does the line show?

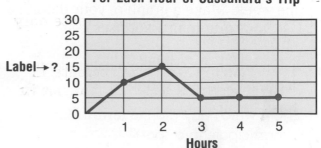

AVERAGE MILES PER HOUR
For Each Hour of Cassandra's Trip

Practice

Use the line graph for Exercises 3–8.

3. In which month did the most new members join?

4. In which two months did the same number of new members join?

5. How many new members were there in May?

6. Between which two months was there the greatest increase in new members?

7. How many new members were there for the first two months of the year?

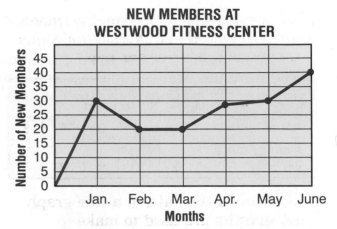

NEW MEMBERS AT WESTWOOD FITNESS CENTER

8. **Analyze Data** In which month was there a decrease in membership growth and in which months was there an increase in membership growth?

Mixed Applications

9. One day each week, 48 students participate in an aerobics class. If 3 different students lead the class each week, how many weeks will it take for all the students to lead the class?

10. Mario joined a running club that meets 3 days a week. He runs for 15 minutes each day the club meets. Mario also runs on weekends for 20 minutes each day. For how many minutes does he run each week?

LOGICAL REASONING

A Venn diagram uses geometric shapes to show relationships.

Use this Venn diagram of student participation in school sports for Exercises 11–13.

11. How many students participate only in basketball?

12. How many students participate in both soccer and baseball, but not in basketball?

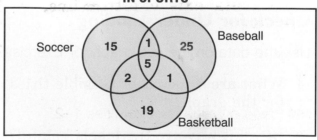

STUDENTS PARTICIPATING IN SPORTS

13. What is the total number of students participating in these three sports?

Why do you think it is important for the distance between the lines on a line graph's grid to be the same?

WRAP UP...

MAKING A LINE GRAPH

Paula's family bought a rowing machine. Paula could easily row 200 times in the first 5 minutes. She made a table showing her rate of rowing in 5-minute intervals for 30 minutes. You can make a line graph using the data from the table to show the changes in her rowing rate over time.

Rowing rate per 5 minutes	200	200	150	150	0	200
Time in minutes	5	10	15	20	25	30

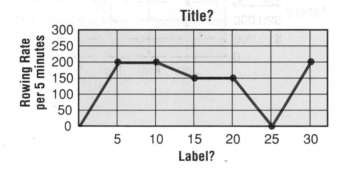

Talk About It

▶ What should the title of the graph be?

▶ What does each unit on the horizontal axis represent? on the vertical axis?

▶ How should you label the horizontal axis?

▶ What do you think happened after 25 minutes?

Check for Understanding

Use the data on the line graph for Exercises 1–3.

1. What are some other possible titles for the graph?

2. In what way are the labels helpful?

3. What are the unit lengths of the horizontal axis and the vertical axis?

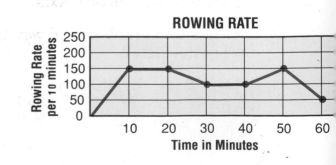

Practice

4. Use the data in the table to make a line graph.

Average Yearly Muffin Sales					
Year	1987	1988	1989	1990	1991
Average Sales	$18,000	$25,000	$43,000	$35,000	$60,000

Use the line graph for Exercises 5–7.

5. What should the label be on the vertical axis? on the horizontal axis?

6. What happened to the total sales between January and February?

7. Would it be reasonable to use a scale of $1,000? Explain.

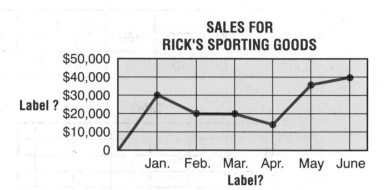

SALES FOR
RICK'S SPORTING GOODS

Mixed Applications

Solve.

8. Mai's mother is going to buy Mai and her sister each a pair of skates. If the total price for each pair of skates is $23.45, how much change will Mai's mother receive from $50.00?

9. Mental Math Estimate to determine whether $30.00 will be enough for Angelo to buy a tennis racket for $18.95, tennis balls for $0.99, and a shirt for $10.99.

Use the data in the table for Exercises 10–12.

10. If you make a line graph of the data, what will the intervals be in the scale on the vertical axis?

11. Why is a line graph a good way to display this data?

12. Analyze Data In which hours did the amount of rain that fell measure more than 0.10 cm?

Rainfall During 5-Hour Storm	
Hour	Amount
1	0.25 cm
2	0.12 cm
3	0.5 cm
4	0.3 cm
5	0.1 cm

What would you think had happened if a line between two points on a line graph showed a sharp drop?

WRAP
UP...

EXPLORING
Circle Graphs

WORK TOGETHER

Building Understanding

Miss Colletti's class has 36 students. She gave them a choice of vegetables for lunch. Of the students, $\frac{1}{2}$ chose green beans, $\frac{1}{4}$ preferred corn, and $\frac{1}{4}$ selected beets.

The data from Miss Colletti's class can be shown on a **circle graph.** Fraction-circle pieces can be put together to show a whole circle. Use circle pieces to help you understand and make a circle graph.

- Mark and cut out a circle.

- Cut the circle in half.

- Color one half of the circle green. Cut the other half in half to make fourths.

- Color one fourth red and the other yellow.

- Put the pieces together to make a whole circle.

- Trace around the whole circle. Remove the pieces.

- Put the red and yellow pieces on the circle you traced.

- Put the green piece on the circle you traced.

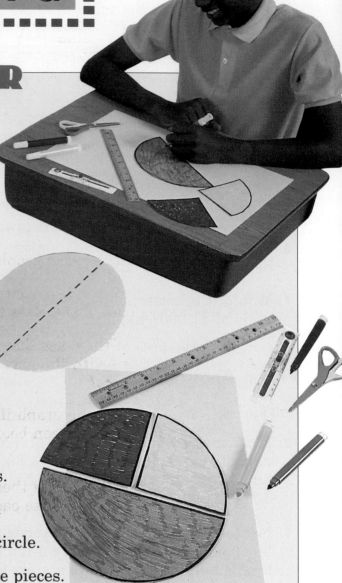

Talk About It

▶ How is the whole class represented?

▶ What section of the circle shows the part of the class that chose green beans?

▶ What do you think the red and the yellow sections of the circle represent?

Making the Connection

A circle graph shows how parts are related to the whole. It also shows how the parts are related to each other.

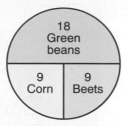

Vegetable Choices of 36 Students

Talk About It

▶ What is the title of this graph?

▶ How is each part of the circle graph labeled?

▶ How does the part of the class that prefers corn compare with the part of the class that prefers beets?

▶ How does the part of the class that prefers green beans compare with the part of the class that prefers beets?

▶ How would you change the graph if the same number of students liked green beans, corn, and beets?

▶ How would the graph change if there were 6 vegetable choices and some students chose each?

Checking Understanding

Use circle pieces to draw graphs that show the number of people represented by each part of the circle.

1. Miss Colletti brought juice for the 36 students at the class picnic. Of the students, $\frac{3}{4}$ wanted apple juice and $\frac{1}{4}$ wanted grape juice. Show this in a circle graph.

2. During the picnic, $\frac{1}{4}$ of the students entered sack races, $\frac{1}{4}$ played horseshoes, $\frac{1}{4}$ played softball, and $\frac{1}{4}$ ran in the three-legged race. Show this in a circle graph.

3. The picnic was attended by 24 parents who helped Miss Colletti. Of the parents, $\frac{1}{2}$ helped serve food, $\frac{1}{4}$ helped with games, and $\frac{1}{4}$ read stories to the students. Show this in a circle graph.

COMPARING GRAPHS

You can use graphs to present facts in different ways. Graphs are often easier to understand than written descriptions because they show a large amount of information in picture form. While graphs have some things in common, each type has advantages and disadvantages.

Bar Graphs

Advantages
- used with countable data
- used to compare facts about groups
- show patterns in data

Disadvantages
- bars nearly the same length are difficult to compare
- scale can be used to make small differences look large

FAVORITE SPORTS

Number of Students: 35 30 25 20 15 10 5 0
Football Baseball Basketball Gymnastics Soccer

Pictographs

Advantages
- used with countable data
- used to compare facts about groups

Disadvantages
- parts of pictures may be needed to show exact amounts
- calculations may be needed for exact amounts

FAVORITE SPORTS

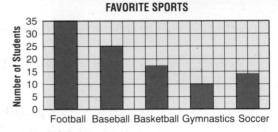

● = 2 students

Line Graphs

Advantages
- show patterns in data
- show changes over time

Disadvantage
- not the best to use when counting objects

AMOUNT OF PRACTICE TIME

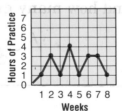

Hours of Practice: 7 6 5 4 3 2 1 0
1 2 3 4 5 6 7 8
Weeks

Circle Graphs

Advantage
- good when comparing part of a group to whole group

Disadvantage
- difficult to use when the parts of the number to be graphed can not be shown by simple fractions

STUDENTS' FAVORITE CLUBS

Science
Music
Library
Computer
Math

Check for Understanding

1. Which type of graph would you use to show how you usually spend all 24 hours of a weekday?

2. Which type of graph would you use to show the number of pages read during a year?

Practice

Choose a type of graph for Exercises 3–6. Explain your choice.

3. yearly incomes for several different jobs

4. height development for boys

5. types of books preferred by a fifth-grade class

6. how a student spends $10

Mixed Applications

Use the data in the table for Exercises 7–9.

7. Would you use a line graph to display this data? Explain.

8. Analyze Data What type of graph would you use to display this data? Explain.

9. What is the total number of students surveyed?

10. Maureen's test scores in math are 95, 92, 83, and 78. What is the mean of her test scores?

11. There are 53 students in the chorus. If there are 15 more girls than boys, how many boys and how many girls are in the chorus?

Favorite Subject	
Subject	**Number of Students**
English	6
Math	8
Social studies	7
Science	5
Music	4

MIXED REVIEW

Estimate.

1. $12\overline{)230}$

2. $18\overline{)395}$

3. $38\overline{)150}$

4. $41\overline{)280}$

5. $28\overline{)3,217}$

Find the sum or difference.

6. 2.345
   + 9.745

7. 8.975
   − 5.896

8. 12.427
   + 89.582

9. 14.312
   + 38.721

10. 25.602
   − 7.093

Could a circle graph be used for the data in the Favorite Subject table? Explain.

WRAP UP...

	Jeep	Station Wagon	Moped
Leah			NO
			NO
	NO	NO	yes
	NO		NO

Leah, Dennis, Dena, and Eli own one vehicle each. Altogether, they own a moped, a station wagon, a jeep, and a van. Eli does not own a van or a jeep. Leah went to a restaurant with the owner of the van. Dena owns a moped. Which vehicle does Dennis own?

▶ UNDERSTAND

What are you asked to find?

What facts are given?

▶ PLAN

How can you solve the problem?

You can make a table to organize the data.

▶ SOLVE

How can you carry out your plan?

Use logical reasoning to show all the possibilities. Since each person owns one vehicle, there can be only one *yes* in each row and column.

A.	Van	Jeep	Station Wagon	Moped
Leah				No
Dennis				No
Dena	No	No	No	Yes
Eli				No

B.	Van	Jeep	Station Wagon	Moped
Leah			No	No
Dennis			No	No
Dena	No	No	No	Yes
Eli	No	No	Yes	No

C.	Van	Jeep	Station Wagon	Moped
Leah	No	Yes	No	No
Dennis	Yes	No	No	No
Dena	No	No	No	Yes
Eli	No	No	Yes	No

A. Dena owns a moped.

B. Since Eli does not own the van, jeep, or moped, he must own the station wagon.

C. Since Leah does not own the van, she must own the jeep.

So, Dennis must own the van.

▶ LOOK BACK

How can you make sure your answers make sense?

WHAT IF... ...the problem did not state that Dena owns a moped? Could you solve the problem? Explain.

Apply

Organize the information in a table. Use logical reasoning to solve.

1. Diego, Becky, Leon, and Lonnie won the first four prizes in an art contest. Diego won second prize. Lonnie did not win third prize. Leon won fourth prize. What prize did Becky win?

2. Andy, Pete, and Bea each bring a different type of sandwich for lunch. One brings peanut butter, one brings cheese, and one brings meat. Andy does not like meat, and Pete does not like meat or cheese. Who brings each sandwich?

Mixed Applications → **STRATEGIES**
- Write a Number Sentence
- Use Estimation
- Find a Pattern
- Work Backward

Choose a strategy and solve.

3. Molly wants to buy a sweater that costs $38. If she saves $7 each week from her baby-sitting job, how many weeks will it take her to earn enough money?

4. Brian earns $2.75 an hour for baby-sitting. If he baby-sits from 7:00 P.M. to 12:45 A.M., about how much will he earn?

5. Tomas mows lawns for 2 hours the first week, 4 hours the second week, and 6 hours the third week. If he follows this pattern, for how many hours will he mow lawns in the eighth week?

6. Leslie wants to earn $1,000 mowing lawns this summer. If she works for 10 weeks and mows 5 lawns each week, how much should she charge for each lawn?

WRITER'S CORNER

7. Make a graph of the temperatures 98°, 85°, 75°, and 82°, and the data Monday, Tuesday, Wednesday, and Thursday. Write a question that can be answered by using the graph, and exchange with a partner. Decide whether the data could be shown in another kind of graph.

Vocabulary Check

Choose a word or words from the box to complete each sentence.

> coordinates
> horizontal axis
> key
> mean
> median
> mode
> ordered pair
> range
> sample group
> scale
> vertical axis

1. The left side of a line graph is called the __?__. *(page 224)*

2. The bottom of a line graph is called the __?__. *(page 224)*

3. The difference between the greatest and least numbers is the __?__. *(page 212)*

4. You can locate points on a map or grid by using an __?__. *(page 234)*

5. The two numbers in an ordered pair are the __?__. *(page 234)*

6. The number that appears most often in a set of numbers is the __?__. *(page 212)*

7. The middle number in an ordered set of numbers is the __?__. *(page 212)*

8. The average of the numbers is the __?__. *(page 212)*

9. You can collect data from a __?__ to help you make predictions. *(page 210)*

10. The unit length on a line compared with the number it stands for is the __?__. *(page 218)*

11. A __?__ tells how many are represented by each picture in a pictograph. *(page 214)*

Read each problem carefully.

Concept Check

Use the data to find the range, mode, median, and mean. *(page 212)*

12. 12, 1, 4, 9, 4

13. 10, 20, 15, 20, 30

Tell which sample group would better predict the choice of fifth graders. Write **a** or **b**. *(page 210)*

14. favorite after-school activity
    a. members of a fifth-grade class
    b. members of a football team

Choose a type of graph for Exercises 15–18. Explain your choice. *(page 230)*

15. careers chosen by your classmates

16. how a fifth grader spent $20

17. changes in enrollment at your school during the past five years

18. favorite movies seen this year by your classmates

Skill Check

Use the data in the table for Exercises 19–20.
(pages 214, 218)

19. Decide on a scale and labels for the vertical and horizontal axes, and make a bar graph.

20. Make a pictograph using the data in the table.

Bicycle Colors	
Colors	Number of Students
White	3
Red	12
Blue	24
Pink	15

Use the grid to find the coordinates for each point. *(page 234)*

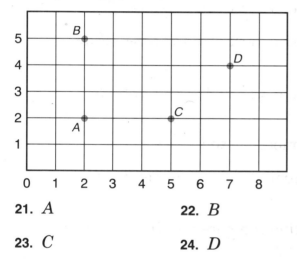

21. A

22. B

23. C

24. D

Use the line graph for Exercises 25–26.
(page 224)

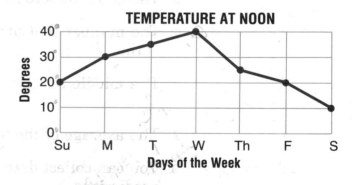

25. For which two days was the temperature at noon the same?

26. How much warmer was it on Thursday than on Saturday?

Problem-Solving Check *(pages 220, 232)*

27. Mr. Suarez plans to walk 35 city blocks. He decides to rest for 3 minutes after every 7 blocks he walks. For how many minutes will he rest on the 35-block walk?

28. Each of 20 large squares was made by gluing 9 small squares together. It took 4 minutes to make 1 large square. How long did it take to make all 20 large squares?

29. Chris, Wes, and Alicia each caught a fish. The fish they caught are a grouper, snapper, and a grunt. Chris did not catch the grunt or the snapper. Alicia did not catch the snapper or the grouper. Who caught each fish?

30. Phil, Kenesha, and Darryl finished first, second, and third in a gymnastics tournament. Phil did not finish first or third. Kenesha finished third. In what place did Darryl finish?

CHAPTER TEST

Use the data to find the range, mode, median, and mean.

1. 70, 95, 90, 75, 70   **2.** 16, 22, 18, 22, 27

Use the bar graph for Exercises 3–5.

3. How should you label the vertical axis? the horizontal axis?

4. How many more meals were served on Tuesday than on Monday?

5. What was the total number of meals served Monday through Friday?

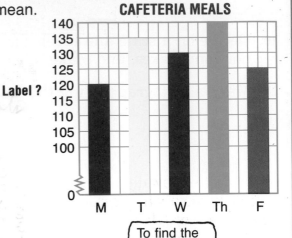

CAFETERIA MEALS

Label ?

Use the grid to find the coordinates for each point.

6. A

7. B

8. C

9. D

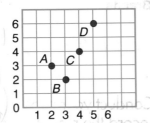

To find the coordinates, I move right and then up.

Use the line graph for Exercises 10–12.

10. In which two months was the amount of sales the same?

11. In which month was the amount of sales the lowest?

12. Between which two months did the greatest increase in sales occur?

Sales Record

Amount of Sales $350 $300 $250 $200 $150 $100 $50 0

J F M A M J
Months

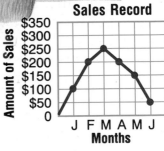

Solve.

13. A family is planning to travel 1,380 miles on a trip. If the family can travel 276 miles on 12 gallons of gasoline, how many gallons of gasoline will the family use for the trip?

14. Sixty students were asked to name their favorite food. For every 6 students asked, 4 chose hamburgers. How many students chose hamburgers as their favorite food?

15. Alyson, John, and Amy each play a musical instrument. The instruments are the piano, the guitar, and the flute. Alyson does not play the guitar or the piano. John does not play the guitar or the flute. Who plays each instrument?

Make a Survey

"**M**ore people like Brand A than Brand B." How do people find out who likes one thing more than another? They can use a survey. A survey is a set of questions that a group of people are asked.

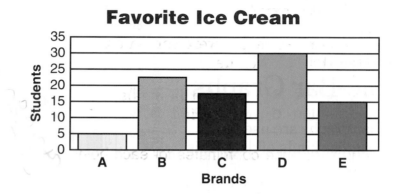

Decide Work with your team. Talk about making a survey of the class. Decide how you can learn about other students' likes and dislikes. Decide what kind of information will be learned from the survey. Determine what questions will be asked on the survey and who will ask them.

Choose at random the people your team will question, and decide how you will record their answers.

Do Conduct your survey, and record the results. Choose the type of graph you think would best show your data. Determine the title, labels, and scale, and then make your graph.

Share Let the other teams examine your graph, and ask them to tell you what conclusions they can draw from your data. Ask them to make predictions by using the data from your graph.

TALK ABOUT IT

a. How many questions were in your survey?

b. How many people were in your sample group?

c. Do you think the number of people in your sample group affected your data? Explain.

d. What type of graph did you use, and why did you choose it?

e. How could a business use the data from your survey?

8

MULTIPLYING AND DIVIDING DECIMALS

Did you know ...

... that in many places cash registers are terminals that are connected to a computer? The system is called a *point-of-sale*, or *POS*, system.

Talk About It

Crystal bought 3 pairs of socks at $1.79 each while shopping at the mall. She also purchased a belt for $5.99. How can she find the cost of the socks and belt?

EXPLORING
Decimal Multiplication

WORK TOGETHER

Building Understanding

You can use graph paper to show decimal products.

Work with a partner. Use a 10-by-10 section of graph paper and three different-colored markers. Remember that the model represents 100 squares. Each square is $\frac{1}{100}$, or 0.01.

Multiply. $3 \times 0.16 = n$

Show 3 of the 16 hundredths. Shade 0.16 of the section three times. Use a different color each time.

Talk About It

▶ What is the product? How do you know?

▶ Is the product greater than or less than one whole?

▶ How is multiplying 3×0.16 similar to multiplying 3×16?

Work with a partner. Use another 10-by-10 section of graph paper. Remember that 1 column or 1 row is each 0.1 of the square.

Multiply. $0.4 \times 0.3 = n$

Shade 0.4 of the rows another color. ▶

← Shade 0.3 of the columns one color.

← 0.12 of the squares are shaded by both colors.

Talk About It

▶ How does the shading help you find the product?

▶ Are the sections of each color more than or less than one whole?

▶ How is multiplying 0.3×0.4 different from multiplying 3×4?

Use graph paper. Shade columns and rows to find the product. Write the multiplication sentence.

a. 2 columns
4 rows

b. 6 columns
8 rows

c. 5 columns
7 rows

d. 8 columns
9 rows

Making the Connection

The graph-paper squares show some decimal products. You can also multiply to find decimal products.

Find the product. $0.3 \times 0.5 = n$

Use the graph-paper model.

The product is 15 hundredths. ←

Multiply.

$$\begin{array}{r} 0.5 \\ \times\ 0.3 \\ \hline 0.15 \end{array}$$

Use the model to place the decimal point.

- Is 0.5 greater than or less than one whole?

- Is 0.3 greater than or less than one whole?

- Is the product of 0.3×0.5 greater than or less than either factor?

Multiply. Use the model to help you place the decimal point.

1.

$0.2 \times 0.8 = n$

2.

$0.9 \times 0.5 = n$

3.

$0.6 \times 0.3 = n$

Talk About It

▶ In Exercise **2**, what part of the whole does 0.5 cover? What part of the 0.9 does the 0.5 cover?

▶ When you multiply tenths times tenths, is the product greater than or less than either factor? Explain.

Checking Understanding

Use 10-by-10 sections of graph paper to show each product. Write the multiplication sentence.

4. 6 columns and 4 rows   **5.** 3 columns and 8 rows   **6.** 7 columns and 4 rows

Use multiplication to find each product.

7. $0.9 \times 0.2 = n$ **8.** $0.7 \times 0.8 = n$ **9.** $0.1 \times 0.6 = n$

More Practice, Lesson 8.3, page H62

MULTIPLYING DECIMALS

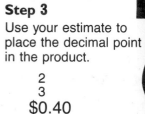

Emily located a center that recycles aluminum cans. In a week she collected 5.8 pounds of aluminum cans. If she earned $0.40 for each pound, how much money did she earn for the week?

Multiply. $5.8 \times 0.40 = n$ Estimate. $6 \times 0.40 = 2.40$

Step 1 Multiply by the tenths.	**Step 2** Multiply by the ones. Add.	**Step 3** Use your estimate to place the decimal point in the product.
$\begin{array}{r} 3 \\ \$0.40 \\ \times\ \ 5.8 \\ \hline 320 \end{array}$ Think: 0.8×0.40	$\begin{array}{r} 2 \\ 3 \\ \$0.40 \\ \times\ \ 5.8 \\ \hline 320 \\ +\ 2000 \\ \hline \$2320 \end{array}$ Think: 5×0.40 ← Remember to place a zero here.	$\begin{array}{r} 2 \\ 3 \\ \$0.40 \\ \times\ \ 5.8 \\ \hline 320 \\ +\ 2000 \\ \hline \$2.32\cancel{0} \end{array}$ Round money to the nearest cent.

So, Emily earned $2.32 for the week.

• How does the answer compare to the estimate?

You can use a calculator to multiply.

      `.` `4` `0` `×` `5` `.` `8` `=`   `2.32`

• Why does the calculator display only two decimal places?

Talk About It

▶ What relationship do you see between the number of decimal places in the product and the total number of decimal places in the factors?

▶ How many decimal places are in the product of 1.86×0.43?

▶ What can you write about this relationship?

Check for Understanding

Estimate. Then find the product.

| 1. $\begin{array}{r} 0.8 \\ \times 0.7 \end{array}$ | 2. $\begin{array}{r} 2.41 \\ \times\ \ 0.8 \end{array}$ | 3. $\begin{array}{r} \$12.36 \\ \times\ \ \ \ 1.5 \end{array}$ | 4. $\begin{array}{r} 0.7 \\ \times 0.6 \end{array}$ | 5. $\begin{array}{r} 32.8 \\ \times 0.95 \end{array}$ |

Idea Bank, page 464, Exercise 5

Practice

Estimate. Then find the product.

6. 0.9
 × 0.8

7. 0.6
 × 0.7

8. 6.2
 × 3.1

9. 5.43
 × 3.8

10. 9.26
 × 4.9

11. 7.89
 × 4.2

12. 32.5
 × 0.95

13. $45.60
 × 5.5

14. 856.4
 × 0.84

15. 602.74
 × 2.8

16. $0.7 \times 0.9 = n$

17. $8.5 \times 2.7 = n$

18. $5.9 \times 6.3 = n$

19. $4.95 \times 1.6 = n$

20. $8.25 \times 1.3 = n$

21. $713.2 \times 8.9 = n$

Compare. Write $<$, $>$, or $=$ for ●.

22. 2.5×3.1 ● 0.25×31

23. 0.8×4.5 ● 1.4×4.4

24. 2.4×0.8 ● 2.5×0.6

Mixed Applications

25. The recycling center pays $0.44 a pound for aluminum. Owen has collected 75.5 pounds of aluminum. How much will he earn?

26. Every recycled ton of paper saves 17 trees. If 850 trees are saved, how many tons of paper were recycled?

27. A recycled ton of glass saves 37 liters of oil. If people recycle 4,575 tons of glass each day, how many liters of oil are saved?

28. **Number Sense** Both factors are the same number. The product is 420.25. Use a calculator to find the number.

PATTERNS AND RELATIONSHIPS

Tell whether each number is multiplied by a *decimal* or by a *whole number*, and complete the pattern.

29. 2.1, 4.2, 8.4, ■, ■

30. 1.5, 7.5, 37.5, ■, ■

31. 50, 25, 12.5, ■, ■

32. 12, 18, 27, ■, ■

33. 3.4, 10.2, 30.6, ■, ■

34. 10, 25, 62.5, ■, ■

How do you know where to place the decimal point in the product of two decimals?

WRAP UP...

In one month Gordon collected $540.45 from his paper route. Of this amount, he paid $433.50 to the newspaper company. He saved $20.85 toward a new bicycle and put $30.50 in his savings account. The rest was his to spend. How much spending money did he have that month?

Decide which method of computation you should use to solve the problem.

▶ **UNDERSTAND**

What are you asked to find?

What facts are given?

▶ **PLAN**

How can you decide which method of computation to use?

Think about the methods you have used in problem solving.

- If an exact answer is not needed, try estimation.
- If mental math is too difficult, choose between paper and pencil or a calculator.

▶ **SOLVE**

How will you carry out the plan?

Subtract to find the amount Gordon kept for himself.

⎡5⎤⎡4⎤⎡0⎤⎡.⎤⎡4⎤⎡5⎤⎡−⎤⎡4⎤⎡3⎤⎡3⎤⎡.⎤⎡5⎤⎡0⎤⎡M+⎤ ⎢ᴹ 106.95⎥

Add to find the amount he set aside for the bicycle and his savings account.

⎡2⎤⎡0⎤⎡.⎤⎡8⎤⎡5⎤⎡+⎤⎡3⎤⎡0⎤⎡.⎤⎡5⎤⎡0⎤⎡M−⎤ ⎢ᴹ 51.35⎥ ← The ⎡M−⎤ key subtracts the sum from the value already in memory.

Press the memory recall key to find the difference.

⎡MRC⎤ ⎢ᴹ 55.6⎥ ← Remember to place a zero here.

So, Gordon had $55.60 for spending money that month.

▶ **LOOK BACK**

How can you check your solution?

WHAT IF... ... Gordon decided to save $5 extra toward the bicycle and put $2.50 extra into his savings account? How much spending money would he have left?

Apply

Choose a method of computation and solve.

1 The Lopez family spent $48.50 each night for 3 nights on its vacation. The family spent $27.89, $48.25, $32.95, and $41.30 on meals and $52.50 for admissions to parks. About how much did the family spend on its vacation?

2 The Jacksons spent $17.98 for gasoline the first day of their vacation. Their meals cost $13.67 and $25.76. Their motel room cost $55.00. If they brought $500.00 for their vacation, how much money is left?

Mixed Applications

STRATEGIES

- Make a Table
- Work Backward
- Use Estimation
- Write a Number Sentence
- Guess and Check
- Find a Pattern

Choose a strategy and solve.

3 The Nelsons traveled 242 miles the first day of their trip and 285 miles the second day. If they drove about 60 miles per hour, about how many hours did they spend driving?

4 Pearl has saved $90. She received half of this money on her birthday. She earned the rest from her paper route. If she has worked 3 weeks, how much did she earn each week?

5 Sammy has 140 papers to deliver. If he can deliver 10 papers in 5 minutes, how long will it take him to deliver all the papers?

6 Laura needs $130 to buy a coat. She has $45. If she saves $5 each week, how many weeks will it take her to save enough money?

7 One week Ruben earned money doing chores around the house. For vacuuming and washing windows, he earned $1.00 per job. He earned $2.50 for cleaning the garage and $1.75 for washing the kitchen floor. How much did he earn?

8 Paco figured how much he spent for meals during his vacation. On Friday he spent $1.89, $2.49, and $6.75. On Saturday he spent $2.29, $2.10, and $6.50. On Sunday he spent $2.45, $3.05, and $5.80. On which day did he spend the most for meals?

1. Barbara bought a radio-controlled car for $38.95. She bought a battery for $5.98 and used it for the transmitter. She needed 8 more batteries for the car. The batteries were sold in packages of 4 for $5.29. What was the total cost of the car and batteries?

2. Tikaya compared her sales of radio-controlled cars during a four-month period. The totals sold in each of the four months were 35, 28, 45, and 42. She sold the fewest cars in April and the most in July. If she sold more than 40 cars in May, how many did she sell in June?

3. Richard compared speeds of radio-controlled cars Big Bandit, Cyclone, White Lion, and Prancer. The speeds of the cars were 4, 7, 8, and 12 miles per hour. White Lion did not go less than 10 miles per hour, and Prancer did not go more than 5 miles per hour. If Cyclone had a speed of 7 miles per hour, what was the speed of Big Bandit?

4. Brian went to the store and bought 2 packages of batteries for $4.98 each and a radio-controlled truck for $27.95. He had about $15.00 when he returned home. About how much did he have when he started?

I can make a table to solve a problem.

Order from least to greatest.

5. 1,789; 179; 1,798; 178

6. 25,465; 24,456; 24,465

7. 45.02; 4.50; 45.20; 4.52

8. 6.578; 60.508; 6.057; 6.508

Use mental math to find the product.

9. 40 × 6

10. 500 × 5

11. 800 × 3

12. 3,000 × 9

13. 8,000 × 5

Are the figures similar? Write yes or no.

14.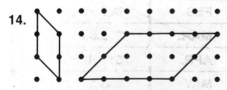

15.

16.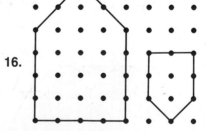

Find the quotient.

17. 3)471

18. 6)549

19. 8)969

20. 36)728

21. 42)4,209

22. 13)2,613

Find the range, mode, median, and mean.

23. 87, 93, 90, 93, 82

24. 325, 250, 175, 275, 175

Spotlight ON
PROBLEM SOLVING

Make Predictions

Sometimes, you can use the information provided in a problem, graph, or table to make predictions about what will happen in the future. These predictions are based on information that has been collected.

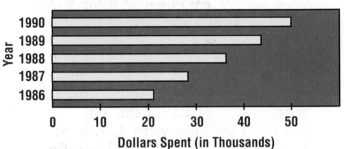

Streetlight Expenses for Plant City

Study the graph. It displays the money Plant City paid for streetlight expenses during a five-year period.

Talk About It

Work with a partner, and use the graph to answer the questions.

■ About how much more did Plant City spend on streetlights in 1990 than in 1986?

■ What pattern do you observe in the graph?

■ What would you predict for streetlight expenses in 1991? in 1992?

Apply

Use the table to decide whether the predictions may be correct. Write *yes* or *no*. Justify your answer.

1. The Snack Shack uses more electricity in the summer months.

2. The hotter the weather, the more air-conditioning is used.

3. The electric expenses for November will be more than $30.

4. Gather some data about the electric bill in your home or school. Collect information from at least three billings. Make a graph or table of the data, and make a prediction based on the information collected.

Snack Shack Electric Costs

Month	Cost
JAN.	$19.97
FEB.	$19.50
MAR.	$19.85
APR.	$19.92
MAY	$33.19
JUNE	$52.35
JULY	$67.50
AUG.	$79.10
SEPT.	$45.30
OCT.	$19.74

USING MENTAL MATH
to Divide Decimals

Ramona has saved her money for several months. Her goal is to save $375.50. This amount is 10 times more than she has saved already. How much money has Ramona saved?

You can use a calculator to divide. $375.50 \div 10 = n$

| 3 | 7 | 5 | . | 5 | 0 | ÷ | 1 | 0 | = | | 37.55 |

So, Ramona has saved $37.55 toward her goal.

Divide. $132 \div 100 = n$

132 ÷ 100 = | 1.32 |

Divide. $2,416 \div 1,000 = n$

2,416 ÷ 1,000 = | 2.416 |

- What happens to the position of the decimal point when you divide by 10? by 100? by 1,000?

Mental math can be as fast as a calculator when you divide by 10, 100, or 1,000.

$372 \div 10 = 37.2$	$2,418 \div 10 = 241.8$	$40 \div 10 = 4.0$
$372 \div 100 = 3.72$	$2,418 \div 100 = 24.18$	$40 \div 100 = 0.4$
$372 \div 1,000 = 0.372$	$2,418 \div 1,000 = 2.418$	$40 \div 1,000 = 0.04$

Talk About It

▶ What pattern do you see in the placement of the decimal point?

▶ Why do you need to write zeros in the quotient?

▶ Why is dividing by 10, 100, and 1,000 easy to compute mentally?

Check for Understanding

Use mental math to complete the pattern.

1. $14 \div 10 = 1.4$
   $14 \div 100 = n$
   $14 \div 1,000 = 0.014$

2. $250 \div 10 = 25$
   $250 \div 100 = 2.5$
   $250 \div 1,000 = n$

3. $1,354 \div 10 = n$
   $1,354 \div 100 = 13.54$
   $1,354 \div 1,000 = 1.354$

Practice

Use mental math to complete each pattern.

4. $24 \div 10 = n$
$24 \div 100 = 0.24$

5. $2.5 \div 10 = n$
$2.5 \div 100 = 0.025$

6. $654 \div 10 = 65.4$
$654 \div 100 = n$

7. $34.5 \div 10 = 3.45$
$34.5 \div 100 = n$

8. $61.9 \div 10 = 6.19$
$61.9 \div 100 = n$

9. $128 \div 100 = n$
$128 \div 1,000 = 0.128$

Divide each number by 10, 100, and 1,000.

10. 45   **11.** 106   **12.** 295   **13.** 3,872   **14.** 13,912

Divide.

15. $6.8 \div 10 = n$ **16.** $49 \div 10 = n$ **17.** $148 \div 100 = n$

18. $19.7 \div 100 = n$ **19.** $895 \div 100 = n$ **20.** $425 \div 1,000 = n$

Mixed Applications

21. Davie has deposited $555.00 in his savings account. If he made 10 equal deposits, how much was each deposit?

22. Juana bought a sweater for $18.95 and a pair of jeans for $16.99. If she paid a sales tax of $0.06 for each dollar of her purchase, how much did she pay in sales tax?

23. Each week Nina saves $9.75 from her pay. In 12 weeks, how much money will she have saved?

24. Albert has collected 1,372 pennies. How much money does he have in dollars and cents?

MIXED REVIEW

Find the sum or difference.

1. 4.567
$+ 5.443$

2. 12.906
$- 9.879$

3. 8.952
$+ 5.139$

4. 25.475
$- 18.685$

5. 39.654
$+ 14.048$

Divide.

6. $12 \overline{)99}$ **7.** $14 \overline{)784}$ **8.** $25 \overline{)955}$ **9.** $32 \overline{)992}$ **10.** $48 \overline{)866}$

How will the position of the decimal point change if you divide by 10,000? by 100,000?

WRAP UP...

EXPLORING
Decimal Division

WORK TOGETHER

Building Understanding

You can use base-ten blocks to explore dividing with decimals.

Divide. $5.36 \div 4 = n$

Work with a partner. Model 5.36 using base-ten blocks. If you let the flat represent 1, you can make the following chart.

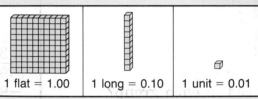

| 1 flat = 1.00 | 1 long = 0.10 | 1 unit = 0.01 |

- What blocks can you use to model 5.36?

- How many flats can be sorted evenly into 4 groups?

Regroup.
- How many longs are there now?

- How many longs can be sorted evenly into each of the 4 groups?

Regroup.
- How many units are there now?

- How many units can be sorted evenly into each of the 4 groups?

- Are there any flats left over?

- What regrouping can be made?

- Are there any longs left over?

- What regrouping can be made to use the other long?

- Did you use all of the blocks?

- What blocks are in each of the 4 groups?

Talk About It
▶ What decimal number represents the amount in each of the 4 equal groups?

▶ How can you compare division to this sorting process?

Making the Connection

The base-ten blocks can help you divide a decimal into groups to find the amount in each group. The steps are the same as when you divide with whole numbers. Remember, the values of the base-ten blocks are different for decimals.

Divide. $9.51 \div 3 = n$

Base-Ten Blocks	Recording

Show 9.51 as 9 flats, 5 longs, 1 unit.

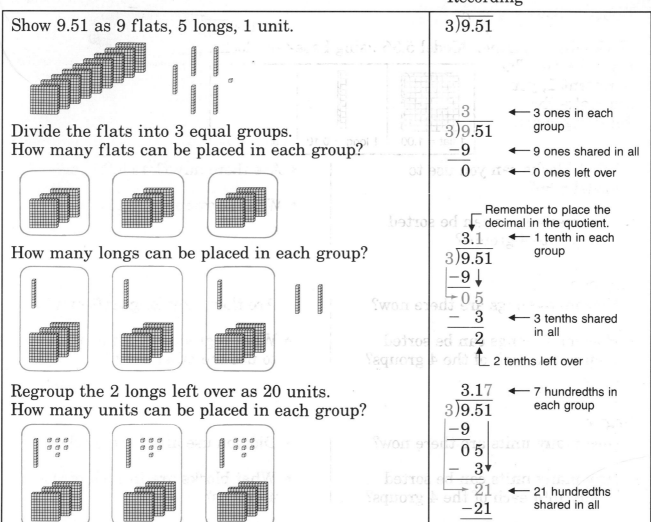

$3\overline{)9.51}$

Divide the flats into 3 equal groups.
How many flats can be placed in each group?

$$\begin{array}{r} 3 \\ 3\overline{)9.51} \\ -9 \\ \hline 0 \end{array}$$
← 3 ones in each group
← 9 ones shared in all
← 0 ones left over

How many longs can be placed in each group?

Remember to place the decimal in the quotient.

$$\begin{array}{r} 3.1 \\ 3\overline{)9.51} \\ -9\downarrow \\ \hline 05 \\ -3 \\ \hline 2 \end{array}$$
← 1 tenth in each group
← 3 tenths shared in all
← 2 tenths left over

Regroup the 2 longs left over as 20 units.
How many units can be placed in each group?

$$\begin{array}{r} 3.17 \\ 3\overline{)9.51} \\ -9 \\ \hline 05 \\ -3 \\ \hline 21 \\ -21 \\ \hline 0 \end{array}$$
← 7 hundredths in each group
← 21 hundredths shared in all
← 0 left over

Checking Understanding

Divide. Use base-ten blocks to model each problem. Then record.

1. $3.74 \div 2 = n$ **2.** $5.16 \div 3 = n$ **3.** $2.10 \div 6 = n$ **4.** $6.24 \div 4 = n$

More Practice, Lesson 8.9, page H64

263

DIVIDING DECIMALS
by Whole Numbers

Joan and 3 classmates bought some food to share. The total bill was $25.40. If they share the bill equally, how much will each owe?

First estimate. $4\overline{)25.40}$

Think: $4 \times n = 24$
$4 \times 6 = 24$

$\begin{array}{r} 6.00 \\ 4\overline{)24.00} \end{array}$

Divide. $25.40 \div 4 = n$

Step 1	Step 2	Step 3
Divide as with whole numbers. Since the estimate is 6 dollars, put the decimal point after the 6.	Continue to divide.	Check.
$\begin{array}{r} 6. \\ 4\overline{)\$25.40} \\ -24 \\ \hline 1 \end{array}$	$\begin{array}{r} \$6.35 \\ 4\overline{)\$25.40} \\ -24 \downarrow \\ \hline 1\,4 \\ -1\,2 \downarrow \\ \hline 20 \\ -20 \\ \hline 0 \end{array}$	$\begin{array}{r} \$6.35 \\ \times \quad 4 \\ \hline \$25.40 \end{array}$

So, each one will owe $6.35 for a share of the food.

More Examples

A. $\begin{array}{r} 60.5 \\ 7\overline{)423.5} \\ -42 \\ \hline 03 \\ -\ 0 \\ \hline 3\,5 \\ -3\,5 \\ \hline 0 \end{array}$ There are 0 ones, so place a zero in the ones place.

B. $\begin{array}{r} 0.07 \\ 21\overline{)1.47} \\ -0 \\ \hline 1\,4 \\ -\ 0 \\ \hline 1\,47 \\ -1\,47 \\ \hline 0 \end{array}$ There are 0 ones and 0 tenths, so place a zero in the ones and tenths places.

- Why do you write zero in the quotient in Example **A**? in Example **B**?

Check for Understanding

Divide.

1. $5\overline{)19.75}$ 2. $6\overline{)276.48}$ 3. $23\overline{)25.07}$ 4. $37\overline{)51.06}$ 5. $42\overline{)3.612}$

Practice

Estimate the cost for one item.

6. 5 bars of soap for $1.47   **7.** 6 apples for $1.25   **8.** 6 boxes of raisins for $1.79

9. 3 bags of popcorn for $1.00   **10.** 4 onions for $0.25   **11.** 4 oranges for $0.99

Find the quotient.

12. $3\overline{)1.8}$ **13.** $4\overline{)2.0}$ **14.** $6\overline{)0.24}$ **15.** $5\overline{)3.5}$ **16.** $8\overline{)8.72}$

17. $7\overline{)1.47}$ **18.** $3\overline{)3.69}$ **19.** $9\overline{)83.7}$ **20.** $4\overline{)44.8}$ **21.** $6\overline{)49.26}$

22. $8\overline{)56.8}$ **23.** $6\overline{)54.48}$ **24.** $2\overline{)19.62}$ **25.** $8\overline{)496.16}$ **26.** $41\overline{)438.7}$

27. $15\overline{)52.5}$ **28.** $24\overline{)115.2}$ **29.** $36\overline{)442.8}$ **30.** $12\overline{)902.4}$ **31.** $19\overline{)1.026}$

Mixed Applications

Use the price list for Exercises 32–35.

32. Estimate the cost of 1 pound of potatoes.

33. Evan bought a dozen eggs and 2 loaves of bread. How much did he spend?

34. **Making Choices** If you need one gallon of milk, would 2 half-gallon containers or 1 one-gallon container be less expensive?

35. **Write a Question** Use the price list to write a question.

Price List	
5-pound bag potatoes	$2.39
half-gallon milk	$0.99
gallon milk	$1.89
dozen eggs	$0.79
bread	$0.89

CALCULATOR

Use your calculator to complete each pattern.

36. $8.5 \div 0.1 = n$
$8.5 \div 0.01 = n$
$8.5 \div 0.001 = n$

37. $12.4 \div 0.2 = n$
$12.4 \div 0.02 = n$
$12.4 \div 0.002 = n$

38. $12.5 \div 0.5 = n$
$1.25 \div 0.5 = n$
$0.125 \div 0.5 = n$

39. $21.6 \div 0.3 = n$
$2.16 \div 0.3 = n$
$0.216 \div 0.3 = n$

How is division with decimals like division with whole numbers? How is it different?

WRAP UP...

PROBLEM Solving

Chuck spent $10.11 for 3 audiocassettes. The price was $1.00 more than he wanted to pay. Carolee spent $5.12 for 2 audiocassettes. Did Chuck or Carolee pay less money for a single audiocassette?

Sometimes, a problem may contain more information than you need to answer a question. **Relevant** means that something is important in the situation. **Irrelevant** means that something is not important in the situation.

▶ **UNDERSTAND**

What are you asked to find?

What facts are given?

▶ **PLAN**

What information is irrelevant to the question?

The statement that Chuck paid $1.00 more than he wanted to pay is irrelevant in solving the problem.

What information is needed to solve the problem?

You can use the number of audiocassettes and the amount spent for both purchases.

▶ **SOLVE**

How will you carry out the plan?

Use the relevant information to find the solution.

Divide.

	Amount of Purchase		Number of Audiocassettes Purchased		Amount Paid for Each Audiocassette
Chuck	$10.11	÷	3	=	$3.37
Carolee	$ 5.12	÷	2	=	$2.56

So, Carolee paid less money for a single audiocassette.

▶ **LOOK BACK**

How can you check your solution?

WHAT IF... ... Chuck paid $7.77 for the 3 audiocassettes? Who would have made the better buy?

Apply

List the relevant information and solve.

1 Sara Ann wants to buy 2 new video games. At a store 4.5 miles from her house, she can buy 2 games for $39.98. At a store 2 miles from her house, the games are $21.95 each. What is the difference in cost for a video game?

2 Cesar receives an allowance of $3.75 a week. He says that most of his friends receive between $2.00 and $5.00. His friend Alfred receives $3.25. If Cesar saves all his allowance, how much will he have in 4 weeks?

Mixed Applications

STRATEGIES
- Make a Table
- Write a Number Sentence
- Guess and Check
- Use Estimation

Choose a strategy and solve.

3 Daphne bought oranges and grapefruits at the grocery store. She bought a total of 12 pieces of fruit for $3.36. If oranges cost $0.24 each and grapefruits cost $0.36 each, how many of each type of fruit did Daphne buy?

4 Nancy made a phone call that cost $2.00 for the first minute and $0.45 for each additional minute. If she was on the phone for 5 minutes, what was the cost of the phone call?

5 Jared and his brother have been saving baseball cards for 4 years. Jared has 1,123 cards, and his brother has 792 cards. If they continue to save at the same rate over the next 4 years, about how many cards will they have?

6 Ralph buys a package of meat that weighs 1.20 pounds and costs $2.25 per pound. How much change will he receive from $5.00?

WRITER'S CORNER

7 Write a question about a purchase you made recently. The question should contain more information than needed to solve the problem.

More Practice, Lesson 8.11, page H65

CHAPTER REVIEW

Vocabulary Check

Choose a word or words from the box to complete each sentence.

decimal point
irrelevant
relevant
zero

1. Sometimes you need to write a ⎯?⎯ in the product to place the decimal point. *(page 254)*

2. Information given in a problem that is not important for solving the problem is ⎯?⎯ information. *(page 266)*

3. Information that is needed to solve a problem is ⎯?⎯ information. *(page 266)*

4. When you divide by 10, the ⎯?⎯ moves one place to the left. *(page 260)*

Concept Check

Copy each exercise. Place the decimal point in the product. *(pages 244, 250)*

> An estimate helps me place the decimal point in the product.

5.	6.	7.	8.
$\begin{array}{r} 0.32 \\ \times\ \ \ 10 \\ \hline 0320 \end{array}$	$\begin{array}{r} 0.045 \\ \times\ \ \ 100 \\ \hline 004500 \end{array}$	$\begin{array}{r} 0.68 \\ \times\ \ \ 100 \\ \hline 06800 \end{array}$	$\begin{array}{r} 0.279 \\ \times\ \ \ 1,000 \\ \hline 0279000 \end{array}$

9.	10.	11.	12.
$\begin{array}{r} 0.02 \\ \times\ \ \ 5 \\ \hline 010 \end{array}$	$\begin{array}{r} 0.07 \\ \times\ \ \ 4 \\ \hline 028 \end{array}$	$\begin{array}{r} 0.005 \\ \times\ \ \ 6 \\ \hline 0030 \end{array}$	$\begin{array}{r} 0.404 \\ \times\ \ \ 5 \\ \hline 2020 \end{array}$

Choose the best estimate. Write **a, b,** or **c.** *(page 246)*

13. 18×4.9 **a.** 100   **b.** 800   **c.** 1,000

14. 31×6.3 **a.** 18   **b.** 180   **c.** 210

15. 48×3.8 **a.** 120   **b.** 200   **c.** 2,000

Use mental math to complete the pattern. *(pages 244, 260)*

16. $10 \times 0.07 = 0.7$
    $100 \times 0.07 = 7$
    $1,000 \times 0.07 = n$

17. $10 \times 0.24 = 2.4$
    $100 \times 0.24 = n$
    $1,000 \times 0.24 = 240$

18. $10 \times 1.4 = 14$
    $100 \times 1.4 = 140$
    $1,000 \times 1.4 = n$

19. $12 \div 10 = 1.2$
    $12 \div 100 = n$
    $12 \div 1,000 = 0.012$

20. $145 \div 10 = n$
    $145 \div 100 = 1.45$
    $145 \div 1,000 = 0.145$

21. $1,756 \div 10 = 175.6$
    $1,756 \div 100 = n$
    $1,756 \div 1,000 = 1.756$

Skill Check

Find each product. *(page 244)*

22. $10 \times 0.5 = n$ **23.** $10 \times 2.8 = n$ **24.** $100 \times 0.7 = n$

25. $100 \times 5.6 = n$ **26.** $1{,}000 \times 0.75 = n$ **27.** $1{,}000 \times 0.123 = n$

Estimate each product. *(page 246)*

28. 4.7
$\times\ 12$

29. 6.9
$\times\ 23$

30. 18.5
$\times\ \ 32$

31. 1.72
$\times\ \ 58$

32. 3.9
$\times\ 86$

Find the product. *(pages 248, 250, 252, 254)*

33. 1.8
$\times\ \ 6$

34. \$12.48
$\times\ \ \ \ \ 15$

35. 0.985
$\times\ \ \ \ 27$

36. 0.8
$\times\ 0.4$

37. 1.9
$\times\ 0.6$

38. 2.5
$\times\ 3.8$

39. 4.52
$\times\ \ 3.2$

40. 0.08
$\times\ 0.05$

41. 0.52
$\times\ \ 0.6$

42. 0.455
$\times\ \ \ \ 0.4$

Find the quotient. *(pages 260, 262, 264)*

43. $4.9 \div 10 = n$ **44.** $75 \div 10 = n$ **45.** $14.8 \div 100 = n$

46. $72.5 \div 100 = n$ **47.** $632 \div 100 = n$ **48.** $3{,}180 \div 1{,}000 = n$

49. $6\overline{)28.8}$ **50.** $13\overline{)282.1}$ **51.** $21\overline{)787.50}$ **52.** $32\overline{)540.8}$ **53.** $23\overline{)646.99}$

Problem-Solving Check   *(pages 256, 266)*

54. A merchant bought 6 pairs of skis for \$45.50 a pair, 3 pairs of poles for \$8.50 a pair, 8 pairs of boots for \$38.00 a pair, and 5 parkas for \$29.00 each. How much did he pay for the skis?

55. Amy is comparing breakfast cereals. A box of Brand A has 10 grams of sugar, weighs 13 ounces, and sells for \$2.08. A box of Brand B has 12 grams of sugar, weighs 14 ounces, and sells for \$2.10. Which cereal costs less per ounce?

56. Janell bought 2 shirts for \$11.98 each, a sweater for \$18.95, and 3 pairs of socks for \$2.05 a pair. About how much did all of these items cost?

57. Each week for 6 weeks Harry deposited his check of \$74.28 into his bank. He also deposited \$25.00 he received as a gift. How much did Harry deposit during the 6 weeks?

CHAPTER TEST

Estimate each product.

1. 5.2
× 9

2. 1.78
× 18

3. 4.7
× 52

4. 19.3
× 76

Find the product.

5. 7.6
× 10

6. 1.85
× 100

7. 14.95
× 1,000

8. 0.635
× 24

9. 6.5
× 3.2

10. 0.48
× 4.1

11. 0.08
× 0.5

12. 0.004
× 8

Find the quotient.

13. $8.2 \div 10 = n$

14. $95 \div 10 = n$

15. $14.6 \div 100 = n$

16. $318.4 \div 100 = n$

17. $473 \div 1,000 = n$

18. $1,214 \div 1,000 = n$

19. $48.2 \div 2 = n$

20. $302.4 \div 14 = n$

21. $805.77 \div 21 = n$

Solve.

22. Ed bought 2 books for $3.95 each, a magazine for $2.50, and 2 bookmarks for $1.55 each. If he paid a sales tax of $0.06 on each dollar of his purchase, how much sales tax did he pay?

23. Sonia's parents paid a fee of $150.00 so she could attend a computer camp for 3 weeks. While she was there, Sonia paid $29.50 for books and $12.25 for supplies. What was the fee for one week at the camp?

24. Bobbie bought some sporting supplies. She bought 6 tennis balls at $3.95 for each 3-ball can, a tennis racket for $18.99, and a tennis skirt for $9.95. How much did the tennis balls cost?

25. Hilda drove 4.8 miles to work and then back home each day for 5 days. On Saturday morning her odometer read 36,417 miles, and on Sunday night it read 36,479 miles. About how many miles did she drive for the week?

I can work backward to solve a problem.

Make a Graph

Suppose your class wants to keep track of money earned from a recycling project. The goal is to earn $250 by collecting aluminum cans for recycling. The recycling center pays $0.45 a pound for aluminum cans. With your teammates, decide on the number of weeks for the project, and make a frequency table to show the amount earned each week.

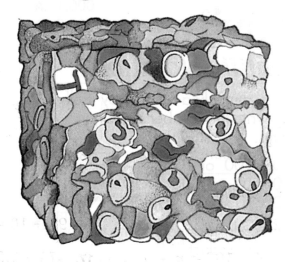

Decide

Work with your team. Talk about what kind of graph you can use to display the data on your frequency table.

Do

Decide on a title, labels, and a scale, and make your graph. Each week, compute the amount of money earned. To do this, multiply the number of pounds collected by the amount paid by the recycling center for each pound. Add this amount each week to the previous week's total, and continue marking your graph until the goal is reached.

Share

Let other teams study your graph. Discuss whether your graph clearly shows the progress made each week.

TALK ABOUT IT

- What type of graph did you use?

- How could you use your graph to find the amount of money earned each week?

- How is the graph helpful in keeping track of the progress in reaching the goal?

- In your everyday activities, what other situations require multiplication and division with decimals?

NUMBER THEORY AND FRACTIONS

Did you know . . .

. . . that Dutch growers produce nearly 2,000 varieties of tulips? Tulips grow from bulbs, and the leaves, stems, and flowers grow directly out of the bulb.

Talk About It

Janie Chang plants tulips of different colors in her garden. Of the tulips in her garden, $\frac{1}{16}$ are red, $\frac{5}{16}$ are orange, $\frac{1}{4}$ are yellow, and $\frac{3}{8}$ are pink. How can Janie compare the parts of her garden that are different colors?

EXPLORING

Least Common Multiples

Mr. Hamilton wants to plant one row with tulip bulbs and another row with an equal number of crocus bulbs. Tulip bulbs come 3 to a box. Crocus bulbs come 4 to a box. If all the bulbs from all the boxes are used, what is the least number of bulbs he can put in each row?

Knowing about **multiples** can help you find the answer.

A **multiple** is the product of two or more numbers. → Multiples of 2: 2, 4, 6, 8, . . .
Multiples of 3: 3, 6, 9, 12, . . .

WORK TOGETHER

Building Understanding

Use geometric shapes and what you know about multiples to help determine the least number Mr. Hamilton can plant in each row.

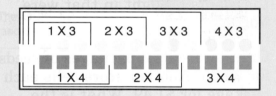

- Line up a row of 3 circle shapes to represent one box of tulip bulbs.
- Line up a row of 4 square shapes to represent one box of crocus bulbs.
- Compare the rows to find the row that has more shapes.

- Place groups of 3 circles in the circle row and groups of 4 squares in the square row until both rows have the same number of shapes.

> **Talk About It**

▶ If Mr. Hamilton wants the least number of bulbs in each row, how many bulbs should he plant in each row?

▶ Name some multiples of 3 greater than 0.

▶ Name some multiples of 4 greater than 0.

▶ Which multiples of 3 are also multiples of 4?

Multiples of one number that are also multiples of another number are called **common multiples**. The smallest number that is a common multiple is called the **least common multiple** (LCM).

▶ What is the least common multiple of 3 and 4? How does this compare to the number of bulbs Mr. Hamilton should plant in each row?

Making the Connection

Some multiples of 2 and of 8 that are greater than 0 are shown on the number line.

Some common multiples are 8 and 16. The smallest number that is a common multiple is 8. So, 8 is the least common multiple of 2 and 8.

Talk About It

▶ How are using the number line and lining up shapes alike?

▶ How can you find the least common multiple of two numbers without using a number line or lining up shapes?

Checking Understanding

Use geometric shapes, draw a number line, or list multiples to solve.

1. What is the least common multiple of 6 and 9?

2. What is the least common multiple of 8 and 3?

3. Paving stones come in boxes. Mr. Hamilton will use triangular and rectangular patio stones for a sidewalk, and he will use all the stones he buys. If he uses the same number of each shape, how many stones will be in the shortest sidewalk he makes?

4. If Mr. Hamilton uses the same number of circular and triangular stones, how many stones will be in the sidewalk he makes?

5. If Mr. Hamilton uses the same number of circular, triangular, and rectangular stones, how many stones will be in the sidewalk he makes?

shape of stone	number in a box
◯	6
◺	3
▭	5

More Practice, Lesson 9.8, page H68

COMPARING FRACTIONS

Mr. Sigman planted flower seeds in $\frac{2}{3}$ of the garden. Mrs. Sigman planted $\frac{3}{9}$ of the garden with herbs. Is more of the garden planted with flowers or herbs?

You can compare numerators or use fraction bars to compare fractions with like denominators. Which is greater, $\frac{2}{5}$ or $\frac{4}{5}$?

| $\frac{1}{5}$ | $\frac{1}{5}$ | $\frac{1}{5}$ | $\frac{1}{5}$ | $\frac{1}{5}$ |

| $\frac{1}{5}$ | $\frac{1}{5}$ | $\frac{1}{5}$ | $\frac{1}{5}$ | $\frac{1}{5}$ |

The fraction bar shows that $\frac{4}{5}$ is longer. Also, $4 > 2$. So, $\frac{4}{5} > \frac{2}{5}$.

You can use fraction bars to compare fractions with unlike denominators.

| $\frac{1}{3}$ | $\frac{1}{3}$ | $\frac{1}{3}$ |

| $\frac{1}{9}$ | $\frac{1}{9}$ | $\frac{1}{9}$ | $\frac{1}{9}$ | $\frac{1}{9}$ | $\frac{1}{9}$ | $\frac{1}{9}$ | $\frac{1}{9}$ | $\frac{1}{9}$ |

The fraction bars show that $\frac{2}{3}$ is longer. So, $\frac{2}{3} > \frac{3}{9}$. More of the garden is planted with flowers.

Another Method

Compare $\frac{2}{3}$ and $\frac{3}{9}$ by renaming them as fractions with like denominators.

Step 1 Find the least common multiple (LCM) of 3 and 9.	**Step 2** Write an equivalent fraction. Use the LCM as the denominator.	**Step 3** Compare the numerators.
3: 3, 6, 9 9: 9	$\dfrac{2 \times 3}{3 \times 3} = \dfrac{\blacksquare}{9} \qquad \dfrac{2}{3} = \dfrac{6}{9}$	$\dfrac{6}{9} > \dfrac{3}{9}$ So, $\dfrac{2}{3} > \dfrac{3}{9}$.

- Why do you change fractions to have like denominators?

Check for Understanding

Compare. Write the greater fraction in each pair.

1. $\frac{5}{7}, \frac{6}{7}$ 2. $\frac{3}{4}, \frac{5}{8}$ 3. $\frac{5}{6}, \frac{2}{4}$ 4. $\frac{1}{2}, \frac{3}{8}$ 5. $\frac{3}{12}, \frac{7}{24}$ 6. $\frac{5}{15}, \frac{3}{5}$

Practice

Compare. Write $<$, $>$, or $=$ for ⬤.

7. $\dfrac{2}{4}$ ⬤ $\dfrac{3}{4}$

8. $\dfrac{1}{4}$ ⬤ $\dfrac{1}{8}$

9. $\dfrac{2}{3}$ ⬤ $\dfrac{5}{6}$

10. $\dfrac{7}{8}$ ⬤ $\dfrac{5}{6}$

11. $\dfrac{5}{6}$ ⬤ $\dfrac{3}{4}$

12. $\dfrac{1}{2}$ ⬤ $\dfrac{3}{6}$

13. $\dfrac{5}{8}$ ⬤ $\dfrac{2}{3}$

14. $\dfrac{6}{8}$ ⬤ $\dfrac{3}{4}$

15. $\dfrac{3}{4}$ ⬤ $\dfrac{5}{8}$

16. $\dfrac{1}{8}$ ⬤ $\dfrac{1}{6}$

17. $\dfrac{1}{2}$ ⬤ $\dfrac{3}{8}$

18. $\dfrac{2}{3}$ ⬤ $\dfrac{4}{6}$

Mixed Applications

19. Anna used $\frac{2}{3}$ pound of fertilizer for her apple trees and $\frac{4}{6}$ pound for her pear trees. Did she use more fertilizer for her apple trees or for her pear trees?

20. Derek made some fruit sauce for his pancakes. He used $\frac{3}{4}$ cup of strawberries and $\frac{7}{8}$ cup of blueberries. Did he use more strawberries or more blueberries?

21. The members of the garden club are purchasing seeds. One catalog advertises $\frac{5}{6}$ pound of pumpkin seeds for $1, and another catalog offers $\frac{7}{8}$ pound of pumpkin seeds for $1. Which is the better buy?

22. Brent planted $\frac{1}{3}$ of his garden with tomato plants, and Jill planted $\frac{2}{5}$ of her garden with tomato plants. Who has more tomato plants if both the gardens have the same number of plants?

23. Rhonda bought a total of 12 packages of seeds, 4 packages of which were flower seeds. Write in simplest form the fraction that were flower seeds.

24. **Write a Question** Using the fractions $\frac{1}{2}$ and $\frac{3}{5}$, write a question in which the fractions are compared.

MIXED REVIEW

Find the range, mode, median, and mean.

1. 75, 80, 80, 100, 90

2. $14.40; $15.75; $15.75

3. 425, 505, 375, 425, 350

Find the product.

4. 6.7
   × 5

5. 12.8
   × 9

6. 6.32
   × 1.4

7. 12.93
   × 12

8. 10.95
   × 21

Describe how to compare fractions with unlike denominators.

WRAP UP...

ORDERING FRACTIONS

Lynette plants $\frac{1}{6}$ of the garden with vegetables. Larry plants $\frac{1}{2}$ of the garden with flowers, and Jeff plants $\frac{1}{3}$ of the garden with strawberries. How can they find who plants the greatest and the least amounts of space in the garden?

You can compare the amounts of garden space by using fraction bars to order from least to greatest.

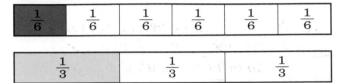

The fraction bars show that $\frac{1}{6} < \frac{1}{3} < \frac{1}{2}$. So, Larry plants the greatest amount of garden space, and Lynette plants the least amount of garden space.

Another Method

Another way to compare is to use the least common multiple to rename the fractions so they have like denominators.

$\frac{1}{2} \rightarrow$ 2: 2, 4, 6
$\frac{1}{3} \rightarrow$ 3: 3, 6, 9
$\frac{1}{6} \rightarrow$ 6: 6

The least common multiple of 2, 3, and 6 is 6.

Step 1
Write equivalent fractions with like denominators.

$\frac{1}{6} = \frac{1}{6}$ $\frac{1}{3} = \frac{\blacksquare}{6}$ $\frac{1}{2} = \frac{\blacksquare}{6}$

$\frac{1}{3} = \frac{2}{6}$ $\frac{1}{2} = \frac{3}{6}$

Step 2
Compare the numerators.

$\frac{1}{6}$ ● $\frac{2}{6}$ ● $\frac{3}{6}$

So, $\frac{1}{6} < \frac{1}{3} < \frac{1}{2}$.

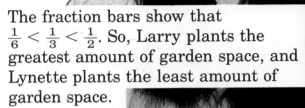

Check for Understanding

Use like denominators to rename the fractions. Order the fractions from least to greatest. You may use a number line if you want.

1. $\frac{2}{4}, \frac{1}{3}, \frac{3}{8}$

2. $\frac{2}{10}, \frac{8}{12}, \frac{2}{5}$

3. $\frac{2}{3}, \frac{3}{9}, \frac{3}{27}$

Practice

Write in order from least to greatest.

4. $\frac{3}{4}, \frac{2}{8}, \frac{1}{2}$

5. $\frac{1}{3}, \frac{2}{3}, \frac{1}{6}$

6. $\frac{6}{8}, \frac{1}{8}, \frac{2}{4}$

Write in order from greatest to least.

7. $\frac{3}{8}, \frac{2}{4}, \frac{5}{16}$

8. $\frac{2}{3}, \frac{3}{15}, \frac{4}{5}$

9. $\frac{1}{2}, \frac{3}{4}, \frac{7}{12}$

Mixed Applications

10. Alfonso made punch for a party. The recipe called for $\frac{1}{2}$ gallon of orange juice, $\frac{3}{4}$ gallon of pineapple juice, and $\frac{4}{5}$ gallon of grape juice. List the ingredients in order from greatest to least.

11. Cara used a recipe calling for $\frac{3}{4}$ cup of cherries, $\frac{5}{8}$ cup of water, and $\frac{1}{2}$ cup of honey. List the ingredients in order from the least amount used to the greatest amount used.

Use the price list for Exercises 12–14.

12. Esther bought each of the items listed. Write the fractions in order from least to greatest.

Item	Price
$\frac{1}{2}$ pound trail mix	$1.89
$\frac{1}{8}$ pound California mix	$0.50
$\frac{1}{4}$ pound pistachios	$1.75

13. Logical Reasoning Is a pound of trail mix or a pound of pistachios more expensive?

14. Analyze Data If Esther bought each of the items listed, did she have enough left over from $6.00 to buy another $\frac{1}{2}$ pound of trail mix?

VISUAL THINKING

15. Copy the number line. At the correct place, write each fraction.

$\frac{1}{4}, \frac{5}{12}, \frac{2}{3}, \frac{1}{3}, \frac{3}{4}, \frac{1}{6}$

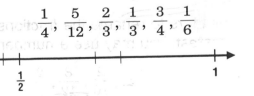

0      $\frac{1}{2}$ 1

16. Which is greater, $\frac{5}{12}$ or $\frac{1}{2}$?

17. Which is less, $\frac{1}{4}$ or $\frac{1}{6}$?

What skill for comparing numbers is needed to order unlike fractions?

WRAP UP...

USING FRACTIONS

Did you know ...

... that a scene designer for the theater begins by making a sketch and a model for each set before the construction actually begins?

Talk About It

Kevin is painting scenery for a play. He needs $3\frac{1}{2}$ gallons of paint. He already had $1\frac{3}{4}$ gallons of paint when he bought $1\frac{1}{2}$ more gallons of paint. How can Kevin find out if he needs more paint and how much more he may need?

Fraction circles are helpful when you are estimating the value of fractions. It is easy to think about fractions as being close to 0, $\frac{1}{2}$, or 1.

$\frac{1}{12}$ is about 0.

$\frac{3}{8}$ is about $\frac{1}{2}$.

$\frac{5}{6}$ is about 1.

You can compare the numerator with the denominator to estimate sums and differences of fractions.

A. Estimate. $\frac{3}{8} + \frac{1}{5} \approx n$

$\frac{3}{8}$ The numerator is about one half the denominator. $\frac{3}{8}$ is close to $\frac{1}{2}$. ⟶ $\frac{1}{2}$

$\frac{1}{5}$ The numerator is much less than the denominator. $\frac{1}{5}$ is close to 0. ⟶ 0

So, $\frac{3}{8} + \frac{1}{5}$ is close to $\frac{1}{2}$.

B. Estimate. $\frac{11}{12} - \frac{7}{8} \approx n$

$\frac{11}{12}$ The numerator is about the same as the denominator. $\frac{11}{12}$ is close to 1. ⟶ 1

$\frac{7}{8}$ The numerator is about the same as the denominator. $\frac{7}{8}$ is close to 1. ⟶ 1

So, $\frac{11}{12} - \frac{7}{8}$ is close to 0.

Talk About It

▶ Without fraction circles, how do you know when a fraction is close to $\frac{1}{2}$?

▶ How do you know when a fraction is close to 0?

▶ What can you say about the numerator and denominator when a fraction is close to 1?

▶ Does $\frac{1}{4}$ round to 0 or $\frac{1}{2}$? Explain.

Check for Understanding

Estimate whether each fraction is closer to 0, $\frac{1}{2}$, or 1.

1. $\frac{1}{10}$

2. $\frac{3}{7}$

3. $\frac{5}{8}$

4. $\frac{8}{9}$

5. $\frac{7}{15}$

6. $\frac{2}{11}$

Practice

Estimate the sum or difference.

7. $\frac{9}{10}$
   $+ \frac{3}{5}$

8. $\frac{8}{9}$
   $- \frac{7}{8}$

9. $\frac{5}{11}$
   $+ \frac{6}{13}$

10. $\frac{1}{12}$
    $+ \frac{2}{15}$

11. $\frac{7}{15}$
    $- \frac{1}{14}$

12. $\frac{8}{14}$
    $+ \frac{1}{11}$

13. $\frac{8}{9} + \frac{2}{13} \approx n$

14. $\frac{9}{10} - \frac{6}{7} \approx n$

15. $\frac{4}{9} + \frac{10}{12} \approx n$

Mixed Applications

16. There are 11 members in a band. If 3 members play guitar and 2 other members play keyboard, what fraction of the band plays guitar and keyboard?

17. **Mental Math** Ann practiced for about $\frac{9}{10}$ hour on Monday, about $\frac{4}{5}$ hour on Tuesday, and about $\frac{5}{6}$ hour on Wednesday. For about how long did she practice altogether?

18. The first band class completed about $\frac{7}{8}$ of the book, and the second band class completed about $\frac{3}{5}$ of the book. Estimate the difference in the amounts completed by the first and second band classes.

19. Callie has practiced about $\frac{3}{4}$ of a new song. Bryan has practiced about $\frac{1}{2}$ of it. If Lorrie has practiced more than Bryan but less than Callie, write a fraction that shows about how much of the song Lorrie has practiced.

LOGICAL REASONING

Use any four of the digits 1 through 5. Write a fraction for each.

20. a sum close to 1

21. a difference close to 0

How can you determine that a fraction is close to 1?

WRAP UP...

In a jazz band, $\frac{3}{8}$ of the musicians play trumpets, and $\frac{2}{8}$ play trombones. Trumpets and trombones are brass instruments. What fraction of the musicians in the band play these brass instruments?

Add. $\quad \frac{3}{8} + \frac{2}{8} = n$

Step 1	**Step 2**	**Step 3**
Compare the denominators. They are the same.	Add the numerators mentally.	Write the sum over the denominator.
$\begin{array}{r}\frac{3}{8}\\[4pt]+\frac{2}{8}\\\hline\end{array}$	**Think:** $\begin{array}{r}\frac{3}{8}\leftarrow 3 \text{ eighths}\\[4pt]+\frac{2}{8}\leftarrow +2 \text{ eighths}\\\hline\end{array}$	$\begin{array}{r}\frac{3}{8}\\[4pt]+\frac{2}{8}\\\hline\frac{5}{8}\leftarrow 5 \text{ eighths}\end{array}$

So, $\frac{5}{8}$ of the musicians in the band play these brass instruments.

Subtract. $\quad \frac{7}{8} - \frac{5}{8} = n$

Step 1	**Step 2**	**Step 3**
Compare the denominators. They are the same.	Subtract the numerators mentally.	Write the difference over the denominator.
$\begin{array}{r}\frac{7}{8}\\[4pt]-\frac{5}{8}\\\hline\end{array}$	**Think:** $\begin{array}{r}\frac{7}{8}\leftarrow 7 \text{ eighths}\\[4pt]-\frac{5}{8}\leftarrow -5 \text{ eighths}\\\hline\end{array}$	$\begin{array}{r}\frac{7}{8}\\[4pt]-\frac{5}{8}\\\hline\frac{2}{8}\end{array}$ Remember to write the answer in simplest form. **Think:** $\frac{2}{8}=\frac{2\div 2}{8\div 2}=\frac{1}{4}$

Check for Understanding

Find the sum or difference. Write the answer in simplest form.

1. $\begin{array}{r}\frac{5}{6}\\[4pt]-\frac{4}{6}\\\hline\end{array}$

2. $\begin{array}{r}\frac{2}{9}\\[4pt]+\frac{1}{9}\\\hline\end{array}$

3. $\begin{array}{r}\frac{7}{8}\\[4pt]-\frac{2}{8}\\\hline\end{array}$

4. $\begin{array}{r}\frac{3}{10}\\[4pt]+\frac{4}{10}\\\hline\end{array}$

5. $\begin{array}{r}\frac{8}{12}\\[4pt]-\frac{4}{12}\\\hline\end{array}$

Practice

Write an addition or a subtraction sentence for each drawing.

6.

7.

8.

Use mental math to find the sum or difference. Write the answer in simplest form.

9. $\frac{1}{8}$
$+\frac{5}{8}$

10. $\frac{6}{10}$
$-\frac{1}{10}$

11. $\frac{5}{9}$
$-\frac{2}{9}$

12. $\frac{1}{6}$
$+\frac{2}{6}$

13. $\frac{3}{5}$
$-\frac{1}{5}$

14. $\frac{3}{7}$
$-\frac{2}{7}$

15. $\frac{5}{12} + \frac{3}{12} = n$

16. $\frac{1}{8} + \frac{4}{8} + \frac{2}{8} = n$

17. $\frac{2}{9} + \frac{4}{9} + \frac{3}{9} = n$

18. $\frac{5}{12} + \frac{4}{12} = n$

19. $\frac{9}{15} - \frac{4}{15} = n$

20. $\frac{9}{16} + \frac{7}{16} = n$

Mixed Applications

21. A jazz band is made up of $\frac{1}{3}$ trumpets, $\frac{1}{9}$ trombones, and $\frac{2}{9}$ clarinets. List the instruments in order from the greatest number to the least number.

22. Make Up a Problem A jazz band has 1 piano, 1 string bass, 1 drum, 3 trumpets, 2 trombones, and 4 saxophones. Use fractions to write an addition problem.

MIXED REVIEW

Identify the angle. Write *right, acute,* or *obtuse.*

1.

2.

3.

4.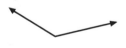

Divide.

5. $18\overline{)365}$

6. $25\overline{)5,075}$

7. $31\overline{)9,308}$

8. $46\overline{)31,510}$

When you add like fractions, what parts of the fractions are computed?

WRAP UP...

EXPLORING
Unlike Fractions

Bill and Juan constructed part of the outdoor stage for the school orchestra. In the morning they built $\frac{1}{4}$ of the stage, and in the afternoon they built $\frac{3}{8}$ of the stage.

WORK TOGETHER

Building Understanding

Use fraction bars to show $\frac{1}{4} + \frac{3}{8} = n$.

1 whole

$\frac{1}{4}$	$\frac{1}{8}$	$\frac{1}{8}$	$\frac{1}{8}$

Talk About It

▶ What do you notice about the fraction pieces?

▶ Which like fraction bars can be used to match the length of both $\frac{1}{4} + \frac{3}{8}$?

▶ How many eighth pieces does it take to show $\frac{1}{4}$?

▶ Use the fraction bars to find the sum. What number sentence do the bars represent?

▶ How much of the stage did they build?

Use fraction bars to show $\frac{7}{10} - \frac{1}{5} = n$.

1 whole

$\frac{1}{10}$	$\frac{1}{10}$	$\frac{1}{10}$	$\frac{1}{10}$	$\frac{1}{10}$	$\frac{1}{10}$	$\frac{1}{10}$

▢	$\frac{1}{5}$

Talk About It

▶ Which like fraction bars will fit exactly over the unknown length?

▶ How many tenth pieces does it take to show $\frac{1}{5}$?

▶ Use the fraction bars to find the difference. What number sentence do the bars represent?

Making the Connection

To find the sum or difference of fractions with *unlike* denominators, you first need to change the fractions to *like* fractions, which have a common denominator.

When you added fourths and eighths, the sum was expressed in eighths.

$$\frac{1}{4} + \frac{3}{8} = \frac{2}{8} + \frac{3}{8} = \frac{5}{8}$$

When you subtracted fifths from tenths, the difference was expressed in tenths.

$$\frac{7}{10} - \frac{1}{5} = \frac{7}{10} - \frac{2}{10} = \frac{5}{10}$$

One unlike denominator may be a multiple of the other.

$\frac{1}{4}$ and $\frac{1}{8}$ → 8 is a multiple of 4.

$\frac{1}{5}$ and $\frac{1}{10}$ → 10 is a multiple of 5.

$\frac{1}{4}$ and $\frac{1}{9}$ → 9 is not a multiple of 4.

$\frac{1}{6}$ and $\frac{1}{7}$ → 7 is not a multiple of 6.

Talk About It
▶ Are sixths multiples of thirds? Explain.

▶ Name another multiple of 3.

Checking Understanding

Tell whether one number is a multiple of the other. Write *yes* or *no*.

1. 5, 15　　　**2.** 3, 9　　　**3.** 4, 16　　　**4.** 7, 15　　　**5.** 2, 20

Tell whether one denominator is a multiple of the other. Write *yes* or *no*.

6. $\frac{1}{5}, \frac{2}{10}$　　　**7.** $\frac{1}{4}, \frac{3}{8}$　　　**8.** $\frac{2}{3}, \frac{3}{5}$　　　**9.** $\frac{5}{6}, \frac{3}{12}$

Use fraction bars to find the sum or difference.

10. $\frac{2}{5} + \frac{3}{10} = n$　　　**11.** $\frac{3}{4} - \frac{1}{8} = n$　　　**12.** $\frac{1}{6} + \frac{2}{3} = n$　　　**13.** $\frac{2}{3} - \frac{4}{9} = n$

EXPLORING

Unlike Fractions

Alida and Gwen made a drapery skirt to put across the stage for the school orchestra. The first piece covered $\frac{1}{2}$ of the stage. The second piece covered $\frac{2}{5}$ of the stage.

WORK TOGETHER

Building Understanding

Use fraction bars to show $\frac{1}{2} + \frac{2}{5} = n$.

1 whole		
$\frac{1}{2}$	$\frac{1}{5}$	$\frac{1}{5}$

Talk About It
► Are fifths multiples of halves? Explain.

► Which like fraction bars will fit exactly over the $\frac{1}{2}$ and the $\frac{2}{5}$ lengths?

► Use the fraction bars to find the sum. What number sentence do the bars represent?

► How much of the stage did the two pieces cover?

Use fraction bars to show $\frac{1}{2} - \frac{1}{3} = n$.

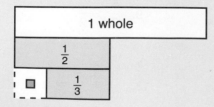

Talk About It
► Which like fraction bars can be used to cover exactly both $\frac{1}{2}$ and $\frac{1}{3}$?

► How many of these pieces fill the space that shows $\frac{1}{2} - \frac{1}{3}$?

► Use the fraction pieces to find the difference. What number sentence do the bars represent?

Making the Connection

These fraction bars show that $\frac{1}{6}$ and $\frac{3}{4}$ match 11 of the twelfths pieces.

1 whole			
$\frac{1}{6}$	$\frac{1}{4}$	$\frac{1}{4}$	$\frac{1}{4}$
$\frac{1}{12}$ $\frac{1}{12}$ $\frac{1}{12}$ $\frac{1}{12}$ $\frac{1}{12}$ $\frac{1}{12}$ $\frac{1}{12}$ $\frac{1}{12}$ $\frac{1}{12}$ $\frac{1}{12}$ $\frac{1}{12}$			

So, $\frac{1}{6}$ can be expressed as $\frac{2}{12}$ and $\frac{3}{4}$ as $\frac{9}{12}$.

You can find the sum or difference of fractions with unlike denominators in another way. First you need to find a common denominator and then use it to rewrite the fractions.

To add $\frac{1}{6}$ and $\frac{3}{4}$, first find the common multiples. Since 6 is not a multiple of 4, search for common multiples of 4 and 6.

Multiples of 6:   6, 12, 18, 24, 30, 36, . . .
Multiples of 4:   4, 8, 12, 16, 20, 24, 28, 32, 36, . . .

Three common multiples of 6 and 4 are 12, 24, and 36. The least common multiple of 6 and 4 is 12. Use the least common multiple as the **least common denominator,** or **LCD.**

Talk About It
▶ What is the least common multiple of 5 and 3? 5 and 4?

▶ How does knowing the least common multiple help you find the least common denominator?

Checking Understanding

Use fraction bars to find the sum or difference.

1. $\frac{2}{3} + \frac{1}{5} = n$

2. $\frac{3}{6} - \frac{1}{9} = n$

3. $\frac{1}{2} + \frac{2}{10} = n$

4. $\frac{7}{10} - \frac{1}{4} = n$

Find the least common multiple.

5. 5, 7

6. 4, 10

7. 9, 6

8. 2, 5

Find the least common denominator.

9. $\frac{1}{5}, \frac{2}{3}$

10. $\frac{3}{4}, \frac{4}{10}$

11. $\frac{2}{9}, \frac{5}{6}$

12. $\frac{1}{2}, \frac{4}{5}$

More Practice, Lesson 10.4, page H70

EXPLORING

Adding Mixed Numbers

Dimitri was in a play. The first week he learned $2\frac{3}{4}$ pages of his part. The second week he learned $2\frac{1}{2}$ pages. How many pages did he learn in the two weeks?

WORK TOGETHER

Building Understanding

The numbers $2\frac{3}{4}$ and $2\frac{1}{2}$ are called mixed numbers. Each is a number written as a whole number and a fraction.

Add. $2\frac{3}{4} + 2\frac{1}{2} = n$

Estimate. $2\frac{3}{4}$ is close to 3. $\longrightarrow 3 + 2\frac{1}{2} = 5\frac{1}{2}$

You can use fraction squares to help you add mixed numbers.

$2\frac{3}{4}$ $+2\frac{1}{2}$

 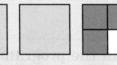

- What happens when you join the partial squares?

- What fraction names the amount that is more than the whole?

- How many whole fraction squares are there now?

So, Dimitri learned $5\frac{1}{4}$ pages in the two weeks.

Talk About It

▶ What happened when $\frac{3}{4}$ and $\frac{1}{2}$ were joined?

▶ How did the sum of $\frac{3}{4}$ and $\frac{1}{2}$ affect the sum of the whole numbers?

▶ How does the sum compare with the estimate? Is the sum reasonable?

Making the Connection

Sometimes you need to rename mixed numbers before you can add. Compare this with regrouping in the addition of whole numbers.

A. Add. $15 + 78 = n$

Step 1 Add the ones. Regroup 1 ten.	**Step 2** Add the tens.
$\begin{array}{r} \overset{1}{} \\ 78 \\ +15 \\ \hline 3 \end{array}$ 13 = 1 ten 3 ones	$\begin{array}{r} \overset{1}{} \\ 78 \\ +15 \\ \hline 93 \end{array}$

B. Add. $5\frac{3}{4} + 2\frac{3}{4} = n$

Step 1 Add the fractions. Rename $\frac{6}{4}$.	**Step 2** Regroup 1 whole. Add the ones. Write in simplest form.
$\begin{array}{r} 5\dfrac{3}{4} \\ +2\dfrac{3}{4} \\ \hline \dfrac{6}{4} = 1\dfrac{2}{4} \end{array}$	$\begin{array}{r} \overset{1}{5}\dfrac{3}{4} \\ +2\dfrac{3}{4} \\ \hline 8\dfrac{2}{4} = 8\dfrac{1}{2} \end{array}$

Talk About It

▶ In Exercise **A**, why do you need to regroup?

▶ In Exercise **B**, why do you need to rename?

▶ What happens when the sum of two fractions is greater than one?

▶ How can you rename $1\frac{6}{5} + \frac{6}{5}$?

Checking Understanding

Use fraction squares to find the sum.

1. $\begin{array}{r} 3\frac{2}{3} \\ +2\frac{2}{3} \\ \hline \end{array}$

2. $\begin{array}{r} 4\frac{2}{5} \\ +3\frac{3}{5} \\ \hline \end{array}$

3. $\begin{array}{r} 2\frac{3}{4} \\ +1\frac{3}{8} \\ \hline \end{array}$

4. $\begin{array}{r} 1\frac{5}{6} \\ +5\frac{2}{3} \\ \hline \end{array}$

Tell whether or not you need to rename the sum. Write *yes* or *no*.

5. $\begin{array}{r} 4\frac{3}{5} \\ +3\frac{1}{5} \\ \hline \end{array}$

6. $\begin{array}{r} 5\frac{2}{7} \\ +1\frac{6}{7} \\ \hline \end{array}$

7. $\begin{array}{r} 3\frac{5}{8} \\ +5\frac{3}{4} \\ \hline \end{array}$

8. $\begin{array}{r} 8\frac{1}{6} \\ +\ \frac{2}{3} \\ \hline \end{array}$

EXPLORING

Subtracting Mixed Numbers

Paige played the piano for the school play. She played $5\frac{1}{4}$ minutes of music during the first half of the play. During the second half, she played for $2\frac{3}{4}$ minutes. For how much longer did she play in the first half?

WORK TOGETHER

Building Understanding

Estimate.

$5\frac{1}{4}$ is close to 5. → 5

$-2\frac{3}{4}$ is close to 3. → $\frac{-3}{2}$

A. Use fraction circles to help you subtract $2\frac{3}{4}$ from $5\frac{1}{4}$.

This is one way to model $5\frac{1}{4}$.

This is another way to model $5\frac{1}{4}$.

> **Talk About It**
>
> ▶ What fraction is shaded in the first picture? in the second picture?
>
> ▶ How is the second picture different from the first picture?
>
> ▶ Which model of the larger fraction can be used so that $2\frac{3}{4}$ can be removed?
>
> ▶ What is left when you subtract $2\frac{3}{4}$?
>
> ▶ For how much longer did Paige play in the first half?
>
> ▶ How does the difference compare with the estimate?

B. Use fraction circles to subtract $1\frac{1}{3}$ from 4.

• How can you model the whole number, 4, so that $1\frac{1}{3}$ can be removed?

• How can you subtract a mixed number from a whole number?

Making the Connection

Sometimes you need to rename mixed numbers before you can subtract. Compare this with regrouping in the subtraction of whole numbers.

A. Subtract. $46 - 19 = n$

Step 1	**Step 2**
Since $9 > 6$, regroup 4 tens 6 ones as 3 tens 16 ones.	Subtract.

$$\begin{array}{r} 3\ 16 \\ \cancel{4}\ \cancel{6} \\ -1\ 9 \\ \hline \end{array}$$

$$\begin{array}{r} 3\ 16 \\ \cancel{4}\ \cancel{6} \\ -1\ 9 \\ \hline 2\ 7 \end{array}$$

B. Subtract. $3\frac{2}{8} - 1\frac{5}{8} = n$

Step 1	**Step 2**
Since $\frac{5}{8} > \frac{2}{8}$, rename 3 ones $\frac{2}{8}$ as 2 ones $\frac{10}{8}$.	Subtract.

$$\begin{array}{r} 3\frac{2}{8} \\ -1\frac{5}{8} \\ \end{array}$$
Think:
$2 + \frac{8}{8} + \frac{2}{8} = 2\frac{10}{8}$

$$\begin{array}{r} 2\frac{10}{8} \\ -1\frac{5}{8} \\ \hline 1\frac{5}{8} \end{array}$$

> **Talk About It**
>
> ▶ In Example **A**, why do you need to regroup?
>
> ▶ In Example **B**, why do you need to rename the mixed number?
>
> ▶ How can you rename the larger fraction to find $5\frac{1}{5} - 3\frac{4}{5}$?
>
> ▶ Do you need to rename $4\frac{5}{6} - 3\frac{1}{6}$? Explain.

Checking Understanding

Use fraction circles to find the difference. Write the answer in simplest form.

1. $\begin{array}{r} 4\frac{1}{4} \\ -2\frac{3}{4} \\ \hline \end{array}$
2. $\begin{array}{r} 3\frac{3}{8} \\ -\frac{3}{4} \\ \hline \end{array}$
3. $\begin{array}{r} 5 \\ -1\frac{7}{8} \\ \hline \end{array}$
4. $\begin{array}{r} 2\frac{2}{3} \\ -1\frac{5}{6} \\ \hline \end{array}$
5. $\begin{array}{r} 2\frac{1}{2} \\ -\frac{5}{6} \\ \hline \end{array}$

Tell whether you need to rename. Write *yes* or *no*.

6. $3 - 2\frac{1}{3} = n$

7. $2\frac{3}{8} - 1\frac{1}{8} = n$

8. $8\frac{2}{5} - 5\frac{3}{5} = n$

9. $10\frac{1}{2} - 7\frac{1}{2} = n$

Mrs. Hsing is adding a step to the platform for the chorus performance. She needs to nail together two boards to go across the front tier. One board measures $7\frac{5}{16}$ feet, and another measures $8\frac{3}{4}$ feet. How long will the two boards together measure?

Add. $7\frac{5}{16} + 8\frac{3}{4} = n$ Estimate. $7\frac{1}{2} + 9 = 16\frac{1}{2}$

Step 1	Step 2	Step 3
The fractions are unlike. Find the least common denominator (LCD).	Rename each fraction. Use the LCD. Add.	Rename the sum.
16: **16**, 32 4: 4, 8, 12, **16**	$\begin{aligned}7\frac{5}{16} &= 7\frac{5}{16}\\ +8\frac{3}{4} &= +8\frac{12}{16}\\ \hline &\quad 15\frac{17}{16}\end{aligned}$	$15\frac{17}{16}$ Think: $= 15 + \frac{16}{16} + \frac{1}{16}$ $16\frac{1}{16}$
The LCM of 16 and 4 is 16, so the LCD is sixteenths.		

So, the two boards together will measure $16\frac{1}{16}$ feet.

Subtract. $16\frac{1}{6} - 4\frac{3}{8} = n$ Estimate. $16 - 4\frac{1}{2} = 11\frac{1}{2}$

Step 1	Step 2	Step 3
Rename the fractions. Use the LCD.	Decide if you can subtract. $\frac{6}{16} > \frac{1}{16}$ Rename to subtract.	Subtract.
$\begin{aligned}16\frac{1}{16} &= 16\frac{1}{16}\\ -4\frac{3}{8} &= -4\frac{6}{16}\\ \hline\end{aligned}$	$16\frac{1}{16}$ Think: $15\frac{16}{16} + \frac{1}{16} = 15\frac{17}{16}$ $-4\frac{6}{16}$	$\begin{aligned}15\frac{17}{16}\\ -4\frac{6}{16}\\ \hline 11\frac{11}{16}\end{aligned}$
The LCD is sixteenths.		

• How do the solutions compare with the estimates?

Check for Understanding

Find the sum or difference. Write the answer in simplest form.

1. $10\frac{1}{3} - 6\frac{2}{5} = n$ 2. $12\frac{5}{6} + 9\frac{3}{4} = n$ 3. $15\frac{1}{8} - 6\frac{3}{8} = n$

Practice

Estimate the sum or difference.

4. $6\frac{1}{2} + 1\frac{3}{4} \approx n$ **5.** $5\frac{6}{7} + 1\frac{1}{14} \approx n$ **6.** $3\frac{7}{8} + 2\frac{1}{3} \approx n$

7. $12\frac{1}{14} - 1\frac{2}{7} \approx n$ **8.** $11\frac{4}{5} - 3\frac{2}{15} \approx n$ **9.** $25\frac{2}{9} - 16\frac{3}{5} \approx n$

Add or subtract. Write the answer in simplest form.

10. $5\frac{3}{8}$ $+4\frac{3}{4}$ **11.** $6\frac{2}{3}$ $+4\frac{3}{4}$ **12.** $4\frac{7}{20}$ $+2\frac{4}{5}$ **13.** $4\frac{1}{2}$ $+1\frac{3}{5}$

14. $6\frac{3}{4}$ $-1\frac{7}{8}$ **15.** $4\frac{2}{3}$ $-1\frac{5}{6}$ **16.** $10\frac{1}{5}$ $-3\frac{3}{10}$ **17.** $5\frac{1}{8}$ $-2\frac{3}{4}$

18. $4\frac{5}{6}$ $+4\frac{2}{3}$ **19.** $3\frac{11}{12}$ $+2\frac{1}{4}$ **20.** $8\frac{3}{15}$ $+2\frac{4}{5}$ **21.** $9\frac{1}{10}$ $-6\frac{2}{15}$

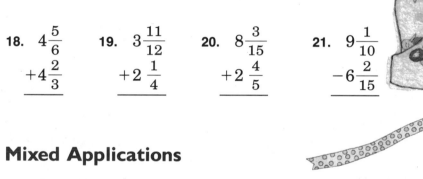

Mixed Applications

22. The chorus practiced for $2\frac{3}{4}$ hours on Saturday and $3\frac{2}{3}$ hours on Sunday. Was the total time practiced more or less than 6 hours? How do you know?

23. Carey has $2\frac{7}{8}$ yards of material. The dress she is making requires $3\frac{1}{4}$ yards. How much more material does she need?

Use the table for Exercises 24–26.

24. Charlene bought fabric for costumes. How many total yards of cotton, felt, and metallic fabric did she buy?

Fabrics Purchased			
Amount	$3\frac{2}{3}$ yards	$1\frac{1}{2}$ yards	$\frac{3}{4}$ yard
Type	Cotton	Felt	Metallic

25. **Write a Question**   Use the information in the table to write a question with fractions.

26. How much more cotton than felt did Charlene buy?

How do you rename $8\frac{11}{6}$?

WRAP UP...

Jerome went to his first orchestra concert. He found a diagram of the orchestra and a table of the instruments in the program for the concert.

Jerome liked the violins during the concert. How can he find what fractional part of the orchestra is violins?

▶ **UNDERSTAND**

What are you asked to find?

What facts are given?

▶ **PLAN**

What strategy can you use?

You can *make a table* that shows the number of each type of instrument.

▶ **SOLVE**

How will you carry out the plan?

Make a table of the information from the diagram.

Orchestra Instruments (52)			
Percussion (4)	**Brass (11)**	**Woodwinds (11)**	**Strings (26)**
Bass Drum (1)	Tuba (1)	Bassoon (2)	Violin (7 + 6)
Snare Drum (1)	Trombone (3)	Clarinet (3)	Viola (5)
Kettledrum (1)	Trumpet (4)	Oboe (2)	Cello (3)
Cymbals (1)	Horn (3)	Flute (4)	Harp (1)
			Bass (4)

Expressed as fractions, the violins make up $\frac{7}{52}$ and $\frac{6}{52}$, or $\frac{13}{52}$, of the orchestra.

So, $\frac{13}{52}$, or $\frac{1}{4}$, of the orchestra is violins.

▶ **LOOK BACK**

Does your answer seem reasonable?

WHAT IF... ...only the strings, woodwinds, and 2 drums were playing during part of the concert? What fraction of the orchestra was playing?

Apply

Use the diagram of the orchestra on page 328 to make a table of the instruments for Exercises 1–4.

1. What fraction of the brass section is made up of horns?

2. What fraction of the woodwind section does not play the flute?

3. Does the string section or all the other sections of the orchestra make up the greater fraction of the orchestra?

4. What fraction of the orchestra is the brass section?

Mixed Applications

STRATEGIES
- Make a Model • Guess and Check
- Write a Number Sentence

Choose a strategy and solve.

5. Kimiko went to symphony performances in Washington and New York. The table shows the fraction of each section in each orchestra. What fraction of the orchestra in Washington was strings? If the symphonies were the same size, which symphony had more string players?

Symphony Orchestras		
Section	New York	Washington
Percussion	$\frac{1}{10}$	$\frac{2}{9}$
Brass	$\frac{1}{5}$	$\frac{1}{6}$
Woodwinds	$\frac{1}{5}$	$\frac{1}{6}$
Strings	$\frac{1}{2}$	

6. Claudio bought tickets to the school play for his family. If children's tickets were $1.50 less than adults' tickets and Claudio paid $11.00 for 2 adults' and 2 children's tickets, how much was each of the tickets?

7. Dolores bought 9 yards of material to make costumes for Lenno and Betty. If Lenno needs $4\frac{1}{4}$ yards for his costume and Betty needs $4\frac{1}{3}$ yards for her costume, how much material will be left over?

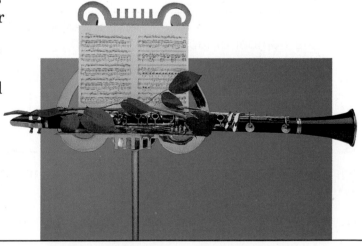

WRITER'S CORNER

8. Use the diagram of the orchestra to make up problems with fractions. Write at least one addition problem and one subtraction problem.

REVIEW AND MAINTENANCE

1. Two high schools each have a chorus with the same number of singers. The table shows the part of each chorus singing soprano, tenor, bass, and alto. What fraction of the West High chorus sings alto? Which chorus has more students singing alto?

Chorus		
Singer	East High	West High
Soprano	$\frac{2}{5}$	$\frac{3}{8}$
Tenor	$\frac{1}{5}$	$\frac{1}{4}$
Bass	$\frac{1}{10}$	$\frac{1}{8}$
Alto	$\frac{3}{10}$	■

2. There are 75 people in a chorus. There are 35 singing soprano, 20 singing tenor, 15 singing alto, and 5 singing bass. What fraction of the chorus is tenors?

3. Greta went to see an orchestra that had 81 instruments. There were 36 in the string section, 7 in percussion, 18 in brass, and 20 in woodwind. What fraction of the orchestra was brass?

I can draw a picture to solve a problem.

Find the sum or difference.

4. 456.85
  + 837.45

5. 9.057
  + 9.943

6. 18.73
  − 14.84

7. 8.095
  − 6.986

Estimate.

8. 395
  × 5

9. 880
  × 9

10. 1,032
  × 7

11. 9,845
  × 8

Write the number of faces for each solid figure.

12. rectangular prism

13. hexagonal pyramid

14. cube

Find the range, mode, median, and mean.

15. 75; 80; 100; 95; 80

16. 200; 150; 220; 180; 220

Divide.

17. 8)$\overline{49.6}$

18. 5)$\overline{139.05}$

19. 12)$\overline{57.6}$

20. 21)$\overline{115.5}$

Write each fraction as a whole or mixed number.

21. $\frac{18}{9}$

22. $\frac{9}{6}$

23. $\frac{12}{7}$

24. $\frac{24}{3}$

330

Spotlight ON PROBLEM SOLVING

Make Inferences

Sometimes when you analyze a problem, you can think of an idea that is related to the problem but is not stated in the problem. When you use this kind of thinking, you are making an **inference.**

Sally and Warren were leaders of their own bands. They kept track of the number of band performances during January, February, and March.

Number of Band Performances

	Sally's Band	Warren's Band
January	3	6
February	5	7
March	8	8

Talk About It

■ Which band performed more often during the three months?

■ What inference can you make about which band made more money during the three months?

■ Which band probably had more performances in April, May, and June? Explain.

■ Can you make an inference as to how many band members are in Sally's band? in Warren's band?

■ Would you infer that there will be more or fewer performances in April, May, and June? Why?

Apply

State an inference from the information given.

1 A music student is thinking about taking drum, trumpet, or piano lessons. The drum course requires 20 lessons. The trumpet requires 35 lessons, and the piano requires more than 75 lessons.

2 The members of the Wings Drum and Bugle Corps practiced five times a week during September, October, and November. In December they practiced only three times a week.

331

Did you know . . .

... that Scouting began in 1907? Today there are over 15 million young people and Scout leaders belonging to Scouting units in nearly 120 countries.

A Boy Scout troop is constructing rafts for a project. The leader needs to buy enough wood to build 3 rafts. If each board measures 6 in. wide and the rafts will be 5 ft wide, how can the leader determine how many boards he should buy for the project?

Kimiko and Nat must choose a unit to measure their model ship.

Units of Length
1,000 millimeters (mm) = 1 meter (m)
100 centimeters (cm) = 1 meter
10 decimeters (dm) = 1 meter
1 kilometer (km) = 1,000 meters

1 meter is about the width of a doorway.

1 centimeter is about the width of a large paper clip.

1 millimeter is about the thickness of a dime.

The model ship is smaller than a meter. Centimeters can be used to measure objects smaller than a meter.

So, it is reasonable to measure the model ship in centimeters.

Talk About It

▶ Which units are smaller than a meter? larger than a meter?

▶ Which unit would you use to measure the height of your desk? Explain why you think your choice is reasonable.

▶ What objects in your classroom would you measure in meters? Explain why you think your choices are reasonable.

Check for Understanding

Choose the most reasonable unit of measure. Write *mm, cm, m,* or *km.*

1. thickness of paper   **2.** distance to the next town

Write **a, b,** or **c** to tell which measurement is the most reasonable.

3. 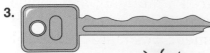   **a.** 6 dm   **b.** 6 cm   **c.** 60 m

4.   **a.** 15 m   **b.** 15 cm   **c.** 15 mm

Practice

Choose the most reasonable unit of measure. Write *mm, cm, m,* or *km.*

5. length of a spelling book

6. distance from the earth to the moon

7. height of a chalkboard

8. distance around a baseball field

9. thickness of a dime

10. length of a piece of chalk

11. length of a bus

12. distance from your home to school

Write **a, b,** or **c** to tell which measurement is the most reasonable.

13. width of a window | **a.** 10 cm | **b.** 10 dm | **c.** 10 km

14. diameter of a ring | **a.** 15 mm | **b.** 15 cm | **c.** 15 km

15.  length of a crayon | **a.** 8 mm | **b.** 8 cm | **c.** 8 dm

16.  length of a car | **a.** 4 dm | **b.** 4 m | **c.** 4 km

Mixed Applications

17. **Write a Question** Chin measured his plant's growth on each of seven days. By the seventh day his plant had grown 21 mm.

18. Franklin and Candy cut 12 pieces of wire that were each 20.5 cm long. How many centimeters of wire did they cut?

19. Mildred kept track of rainfall during four weeks for her science project. She measured 1.4 cm the first week, 2.1 cm the second week, 1.8 cm the third week, and 2.9 cm the fourth week. How many centimeters of rain fell during four weeks?

20. Greta and Mario measured the length of the chalkboard. Greta said it measured 3 dm long, and Mario said it measured 3 m long. Whose measurement was more reasonable?

How can you compare the length of a centimeter with the length of a meter?

WRAP
UP...

EXPLORING
with Metric Units

WORK TOGETHER

Building Understanding

To measure length, you can use a meterstick or a metric ruler. Both may be marked to show millimeters and centimeters. A decimeter is equal to 10 centimeters. A meterstick is marked to show decimeters.

Find the marks that represent each unit on your ruler.

1mm ⊢ 1cm ⊢——⊣ 1dm ⊢————————————————————⊣

Use a metric ruler. Measure the length of an index card in cm.

Talk About It ▸ How can you find the length of the index card in mm? in dm?

Measure the length of your desk with a metric ruler. When you reach the end of the ruler, use chalk to mark the spot on your desk.

Slide the ruler to the right. Line it up with your chalk mark.

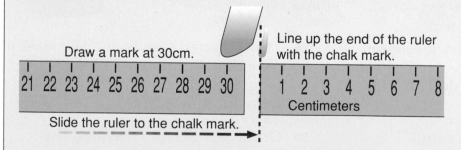

Draw a mark at 30cm.

21 22 23 24 25 26 27 28 29 30

Slide the ruler to the chalk mark. →

Line up the end of the ruler with the chalk mark.

1 2 3 4 5 6 7 8
Centimeters

Measure and mark the rest of the length of your desk. Add the measurements to find the length of your desk.

• What metric measuring instrument would have made measuring your desk as easy as measuring the index card?

• How many mm long is your metric ruler? How many cm? How many dm?

• How many mm long is your meterstick? How many cm? How many dm?

Making the Connection

The reason you have for measuring an object will determine the unit of measure you use. The smaller the unit you use, the more precise your measurement will be. When you measure an object, you measure to the nearest unit.

Measuring to the nearest unit is like rounding numbers.

Measure

10mm=1cm

Round 473

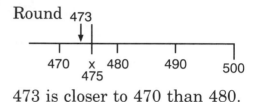

473 is closer to 470 than 480.

The length of the nail is closer to 3 cm than 4 cm.

It is about 3 cm.

Measure the nail in mm to find a more precise measure.

The length of the nail is 32 mm.

Measure each side of the rectangle to the nearest cm. Add the measurements. This is the perimeter of the rectangle.

Checking Understanding

Write the measure to the nearest cm and then write a more precise measure.

1.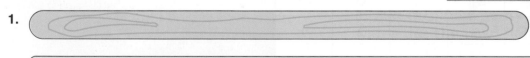

2.

Measure each side of the rectangle to the nearest cm. Add the measurements to find the perimeter.

3.

4.

Use a metric ruler. Draw a line to show each length.

5. 25 cm   **6.** 58 mm   **7.** 2 dm   **8.** 153 mm

METRIC
Units of Mass

Linda wants to know the mass of a nickel and a pair of men's shoes. She remembered that the mass of a paper clip is about 1 gram. She can estimate the mass of each object by comparing it to the mass of a paper clip.

Units of Mass
1,000 milligrams (mg) = 1 gram (g)
1,000 grams = 1 kilogram (kg)

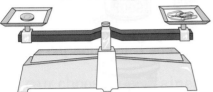

What is the mass of the nickel?

It takes 5 paper clips to balance a nickel. So, 1 nickel has a mass of about 5 g.

It takes 1,000 paper clips to balance a pair of men's shoes. So, a pair of men's shoes has a mass of 1,000 grams, or about 1 kg.

■ Choose five objects of different sizes and weights.
■ Label each object as shown.
■ Estimate the mass of each object. Put the objects in order from least mass to greatest mass. Copy the table and record the order.
■ Use a metric scale. Find the mass of each object in grams. Write *yes* or *no* to tell whether the mass is more than a kilogram.

Object	A	B	C	D	E
Mass in grams	■	■	■	■	■
More or less than a kilogram	?	?	?	?	?

Talk About It

▶ Which objects were the most difficult to estimate? Why?

▶ Which objects in your classroom would you measure in kilograms? in grams?

Check for Understanding

Choose the most reasonable unit. Write *kg*, *g*, or *mg*.

1. a full box of cereal

2. a grain of rice

3. a loaf of bread

4. an iron

Practice

Choose the most reasonable unit. Write *kg, g,* or *mg.*

5. a full suitcase   **6.** a cat   **7.** a pencil   **8.** a grain of salt

9. a cookie   **10.** a snowflake   **11.** a book   **12.** a bag of oranges

Choose the more reasonable estimate of mass. Write **a** or **b**.

13.

a. 30 mg
b. 30 g

14.

a. 10 g
b. 10 kg

15.

a. 1 mg
b. 1 kg

16.

a. 15 g
b. 15 kg

17.

a. 4 mg
b. 4 g

18.

a. 200 g
b. 200 kg

19.

a. 500 mg
b. 500 kg

20.

a. 10 g
b. 10 kg

Mixed Applications

For Exercises 21–24, write how many servings can be made from each item.

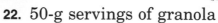

21. 25-g bags of peanuts   **22.** 50-g servings of granola

23. 20-g servings of popcorn   **24.** 60-g bags of peanuts

25. For a cooking project, Hoshie bought 3 bags of nuts for $1.29 each, 1 bag of flour for $1.69, and 2 bags of coconut for $0.95 each. How much did he spend for all the items?

26. Peggy is using a recipe that makes 12 cookies. Would the mass of the cookies be greater or less than a kilogram?

Name some items that are usually measured in grams and kilograms.

WRAP UP...

THE METRIC SYSTEM

The Math Club members worked on a project, using only units from the **metric system.** They used metric units of length, capacity, and mass. They discovered that the same prefixes are used with the different base units to name all the other units in the system. The prefixes relate to place value.

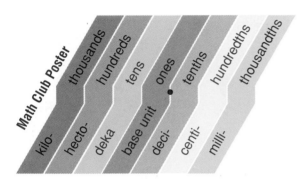

Metric units use a <u>prefix</u> and a base unit.

<u>centi</u> *meter* <u>milli</u> *liter* <u>kilo</u> *gram*

You can change each measurement to the base unit.

Prefix	Base Unit	Measurement
kilo-	gram	1,000 grams
centi-	meter	0.01 meter
milli-	liter	0.001 liter

A. 7 kilograms = ▦ grams
   Think: 1 kilogram = 1,000 grams
   7 × 1,000 = 7,000
   7 kilograms = 7,000 grams

B. 4 centimeters = ▦ meter
   Think: 1 centimeter = 0.01 meter
   4 × 0.01 = 0.04
   4 centimeters = 0.04 meter

C. 3 milliliters = ▦ liter
   Think: 1 milliliter = 0.001 liter
   3 × 0.001 = 0.003
   3 milliliters = 0.003 liter

Talk About It

▶ Which prefixes indicate units smaller than the base units?

▶ Which prefix indicates a unit 1,000 times greater than the base unit?

Check for Understanding

Write each measurement as a decimal, using the base unit.

1. 4 cm   **2.** 5 mg   **3.** 7 L   **4.** 6 mm   **5.** 8 cm

Practice

Choose the smaller unit of measure. Write **a** or **b**.

6. a. milliliter
   b. liter

7. a. gram
   b. milligram

8. a. kilometer
   b. meter

Choose the larger unit of measure. Write **a** or **b**.

9. a. gram
   b. kilogram

10. a. milliliter
    b. liter

11. a. decimeter
    b. centimeter

Give the decimal meaning for each prefix.
Write **a**, **b**, **c**, or **d** for Exercises 12–15.

12. milli-
13. deci-
14. kilo-
15. centi-

   a. tenth
   b. thousand
   c. hundredth
   d. thousandth

Use the place-value chart on page 358. Change each measurement to the base unit.

16. 5 dm
17. 3 mL
18. 8 g
19. 2 mm
20. 9 mg

21. 2 mL
22. 13 mL
23. 6 cm
24. 12 mg
25. 25 mg

Mixed Applications

26. Ricardo is painting his display board. He already has 0.25 L of paint. If the board requires 1.5 L of paint, how much more paint does he need?

27. Kristen and Sara need string for their projects. Kristen needs 2.5 m of string, and Sara needs 3.4 m of string. How much string do both girls need?

28. For her science project, Lois needs a board that is 1 m long. Alex needs a board that is 1 dm long. Who needs a longer board?

29. Cornelius is using an object that weighs 1 kg. Mark is using an object that weighs 1 mg. Who is using the lighter object?

How can you tell that a decimeter is longer than a centimeter?

CHANGING METRIC UNITS

The directions say Suki's model will be 2.4 meters long. Her ruler has only centimeter units. How can she find the number of centimeters in 2.4 meters?

Changing units in the metric system is like moving from one place-value position to another.

kilo- thousands	hecto- hundreds	deka- tens	base- ones	deci- tenths	centi- hundredths	milli- thousandths

×10 (between each, to the right)
÷10 (between each, to the left)

To change larger units to smaller units, multiply by 10 for each place you move to the right.

km thousands	hm hundreds	dam tens	m ones	dm tenths	cm hundredths	mm thousandths

×10 ×10

2.4 m = ■ cm
2.4 × 100 = 240

To change meters to centimeters, move two places to the right, so multiply by 100.

Suki can multiply by 100 to change 2.4 m to 240 cm.

To change smaller units to larger units, divide by 10 for each place you move to the left.

km thousands	hm hundreds	dam tens	m ones	dm tenths	cm hundredths	mm thousandths

÷10 ÷10

200 cm = ■ m
Divide. 200 ÷ 100 = 2
200 cm = 2 m

To change centimeters to meters, move 2 places to the left, so divide by 100.

Talk About It

▶ If you change 7 meters to centimeters, does the number become greater or lesser?

▶ Why do you multiply to change 7 kilograms to grams?

▶ Why do you divide to change meters to kilometers?

▶ How can you determine how many times you must multiply or divide by 10 to change units in the metric system?

Check for Understanding

1. Is a gram larger or smaller than a kilogram?

2. How many grams are equal to 9 kg?

3. Do you multiply or divide to change 9.5 kg to g?

Practice

Complete.

4. 3 kg = 3,000 _?_

5. 50 km = 50,000 _?_

6. 4.309 L = 4,309 _?_

7. 9.813 kg = 9,813 _?_

8. 6,200 g = 6.2 _?_

9. 760 mL = 0.760 _?_

10. 5.8 m = 580 _?_

11. 50 m = 5,000 _?_

12. 5,850 mm = 5.85 _?_

Write *multiply* or *divide* for each exercise. Then solve.

13. 5.2 cm = ▉ mm

14. 80 mm = ▉ cm

15. 4.5 m = ▉ cm

16. 15 L = ▉ mL

17. 25,000 mL = ▉ L

18. 120 L = ▉ mL

19. 4,000 mg = ▉ g

20. 6.52 g = ▉ mg

21. 23,000 mg = ▉ g

22. 3.75 m = ▉ cm

23. 50 mm = ▉ dm

24. 8.754 g = ▉ mg

Mixed Applications

25. Thelma poured 0.5 L of water into a beaker. During an experiment, she added 200 mL of water. How much water was in the beaker at the end of the experiment?

26. While doing a science project, Roberto learned that weather balloons burst at an altitude of 27 km. What is this altitude in meters?

27. Marvin had a piece of wire that was 2.7 m long. He cut the wire into 3 equal pieces. Was each piece of wire greater than or less than 1 m?

28. **Analyze Data** Darlene and Jason collected rocks for science class. Darlene's rock weighed 0.3 kg, and Jason's rock weighed 350 g. Whose rock weighed more?

Why do you multiply to change kilometers to meters?

Mandy used a Fahrenheit thermometer to find the difference between the high and low temperatures on Monday.

In the customary system, temperature is measured in degrees **Fahrenheit (°F).** This is a Fahrenheit thermometer. It shows room temperature at 68°F.

The low temperature on Monday was 10 degrees below zero, or ⁻10°F. The high temperature was 29°F.

You can find the difference in temperature by comparing the starting temperature with the number of degrees it rises or falls.

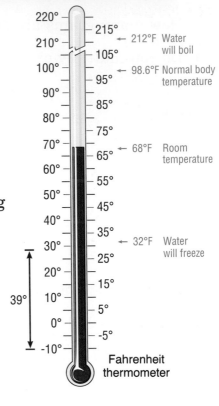

Starting Temperature	Change in Temperature
⁻10°F	from ⁻10° to 0° → 10° from 0° to 29° → +29° _____ 39°

The temperature rose 39°F.

In the metric system, temperature is recorded in degrees **Celsius (°C).** This is a Celsius thermometer. It shows room temperature at 20°C.

On Tuesday the high temperature was 15°C. The low temperature was ⁻5°C.

Starting Temperature	Change in Temperature
15°C	from 15° to 0° → 15° from 0° to ⁻5° → + 5° _____ 20°

The temperature fell 20°C.

Check for Understanding

Use the thermometers. Find the difference in temperature.

1. high 25°F, low ⁻7°F
2. high 20°C, low ⁻5°C
3. high 33°C, low 20°C
4. high 68°F, low 32°F

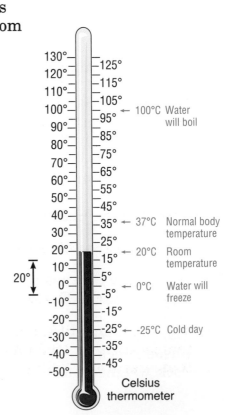

Practice

Use the starting temperature on each thermometer to find the new temperature.

5. 12° colder **6.** 56° warmer **7.** 8° colder **8.** 15° warmer

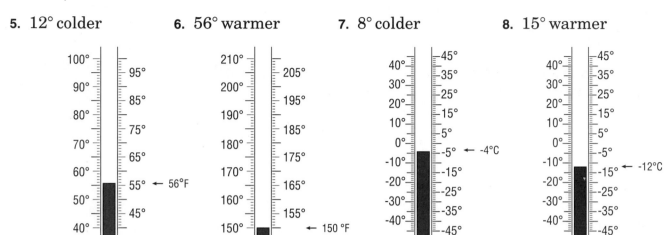

Copy and complete the table. Use the thermometers on page 362.

Starting Temperature	62°F	**10.**	10°C	45°C
Change in Temperature	rose 10°	rose 15°	fell 12°	**12.**
Final Temperature	**9.**	52°F	**11.**	32°C

Mixed Applications

13. The highest temperature ever recorded in the United States was 134°F in Death Valley in 1913. The lowest temperature was ⁻80°F in Prospect Creek, Alaska, in 1971. What is the difference between the highest and the lowest temperatures?

14. Rosalinda recorded the afternoon temperature in her backyard for 5 days. On Monday the temperature was 16°C. On Tuesday and Wednesday the temperature was 18°C. On Thursday it was 17°C, and on Friday it was 16°C. What was the average temperature for these 5 days?

Use the graph for Exercises 15–17.

15. What was the coldest time of the day?

16. How many degrees did the temperature rise between 8:30 A.M. and noon?

17. What was the difference between the temperature at 10:00 A.M. and the temperature at 3:30 P.M.?

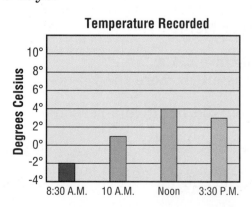

What are the units on a customary and a metric thermometer?

Tom measured the 24 bookshelves in his classroom. Each shelf was 105 cm long. When his teacher asked how many meters of bookshelves there were, Tom said 5 meters. Did Tom give a reasonable answer?

▶ UNDERSTAND

What are you asked to find?

What facts are given?

▶ PLAN

What strategy can you use?

You can estimate the total number of meters in 24 bookshelves. Then compare.

▶ SOLVE

How can you solve the problem?

Round 105 to 100. ◀——— cm length of 1 shelf
Multiply:
   $100 \times 24 = 2,400$ ◀— cm length of 24 shelves

Compare your estimate of 2,400 cm with 5 m.

$5\ m = 500\ cm$
500 cm is much less than 2,400 cm.

Another Method

$2,400\ cm = 24\ m$
24 m is much more than 5 m.

So, Tom did not give a reasonable answer.

▶ LOOK BACK

What is another way to solve the problem?

WHAT **IF...** . . . there were 35 bookshelves 90 cm long and Tom told his teacher there were 3.5 m of bookshelves? Did Tom give a reasonable answer?

Apply

1 Geraldo walks a total of 3 km to and from school each day. At the end of the 180-day school year, Geraldo said, "I have walked 540 m to and from school this year." Is this reasonable? Explain.

2 The mass of 1 granola bar is 100 grams. When Francine's friend asked her what the mass of 12 granola bars was, Francine answered it was more than 1 kg. Was her answer reasonable? Explain.

3 If it rained 2 cm on Monday, 1 cm on Tuesday, 2.5 cm on Wednesday, 3.5 cm on Thursday, and 2 cm on Friday, is it reasonable to say that more than a decimeter of rain fell in 5 days? Explain.

4 Ming Chin poured 4 cups of water into a container. Each cup held 250 mL of water. Is it reasonable to say that the container held 10 L of water? Explain.

> **Mixed Applications**

STRATEGIES	• Find a Pattern • Work Backward • Make a Table • Make a Diagram

Choose a strategy and solve.

5 Ken, Michael, Marcia, and Larry each did a science project on a different topic. The topics were electricity, sea life, space, and weather. Ken did his project on space. Michael did not do his project on sea life. Larry did his project on electricity. What project did each person do?

6 Students in the industrial arts class had a choice of making a planter, bookends, or a shelf. Of the students, $\frac{1}{2}$ chose to make a planter, $\frac{1}{3}$ chose to make bookends, and $\frac{1}{6}$ chose to make a shelf. If 5 of the students chose to make a shelf, how many students are in the class?

7 A student listed a temperature of 85°F at 1:00 P.M., 82°F at 3:00 P.M., 78°F at 5:00 P.M., and 73°F at 7:00 P.M. If this pattern continued, what was the temperature at 11:00 P.M.?

8 Cristina spent half of her project money for a display board. Then she spent half of what was left for paint. After that she had $2.50 left. How much did she have at the start?

1. Of the rooms in Zachary's house, $\frac{1}{2}$ are white, $\frac{1}{3}$ are yellow, and $\frac{1}{6}$ are blue. If there is one blue room in Zachary's house, how many yellow rooms are in his house?

2. Linda's garden is $\frac{2}{5}$ tomato plants, $\frac{1}{2}$ green vegetable plants, and $\frac{1}{10}$ strawberry plants. If she has 4 strawberry plants, how many tomato plants does she have?

3. The window in Yosi's room is 1.5 m wide. Yosi tells the salesclerk he needs a window shade 15 cm wide. Is this reasonable? Explain.

4. Emily's cat weighs about 3 kg. She told her friend that her cat weighs 300 g. Is this reasonable? Explain.

Write the amount as a decimal form of the whole unit.

5. 6 dimes   6. 7 dm   7. 4 tenths   8. 5 pennies

Think about the meaning of the prefix to decide if a metric measure is reasonable.

Solve.

9. $8,230 \times 0 =$

10. $(3 \times$ ▪$) \times 5 = 75$

11. $20 \times (3 \times 2) =$ ▪

12. $2,380 \times$ ▪ $= 2,380$

Trace each figure. Draw all the lines of symmetry for each shape.

13.    14.   15.    16.

Estimate the quotient.

17. $4\overline{)79}$ 18. $8\overline{)231}$ 19. $18\overline{)395}$ 20. $28\overline{)1,470}$

Use the graph for Exercises 21–23.

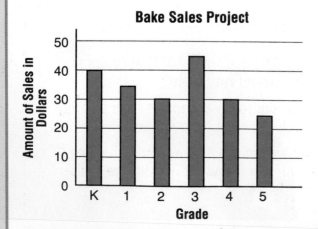

Bake Sales Project

21. How much did the kindergarten earn in bake sales?

22. How much more did the first grade earn than the fifth grade?

23. How much did all the grades earn in bake sales?

Spotlight ON
PROBLEM SOLVING

Observe Relationships

Some fifth graders are making bird feeders as a class project. In the first week, they constructed 3 bird feeders. They plan to get more helpers each week in order to double the number of bird feeders they construct in each of the next 4 weeks. How many bird feeders will they construct in 5 weeks?

Talk About It

■ How could making a table or a list help you solve this problem?

■ How many bird feeders will be constructed in each week?

■ What relationship do you see in the number constructed each week?

■ What is the total number of bird feeders the class will construct in 5 weeks?

■ It cost $3.50 to build each bird feeder. The class sold all the bird feeders for $5.00 each. How much was their profit?

Apply

Solve. Be prepared to describe the relationships you found.

1. The temperature was 17°C at 3:00 P.M., 15°C at 6:00 P.M., and 13°C at 9:00 P.M. If this pattern continued, what was the temperature at midnight?

2. Sandy walked 90 km in 5 days. Each day Sandy walked 6 km more than the day before. How many kilometers did she walk each day?

3. Dee made 42 bracelets in 6 weeks. Each week she made 2 more than the week before. If she kept making bracelets at the same rate, how many did she make in week 12?

12

PERIMETER, AREA, AND VOLUME

Did you know . . .

. . . that the building with the largest area of land under one roof is a building in the Netherlands? The building measures 2,546 ft x 1,794 ft.

Talk About It

Matt and his sister are planning to build a doghouse for their dog, Rex. They want the doghouse to measure 5 ft long by $3\frac{3}{4}$ ft wide. How can you find the area of the doghouse?

13

RATIO, PERCENT, AND PROBABILITY

Did you know ...

... that there are over 44,000 miles of highway in the United States interstate system?

Talk About It

Jan draws a map to record the places she visits on her summer vacation. The scale on Jan's map shows that 1 inch stands for 25 miles. So far, Jan has recorded 5 inches of travel on her map. How can Jan compare the distance on the map with the miles she has actually traveled?

In Mrs. Appleton's class, 3 of the 5 students who ride bicycles to school ride red bicycles. In Mr. Brown's class, 4 of the 6 students who ride bicycles to school ride red ones. In Ms. Chester's class, 2 students ride bicycles to school. They both ride red bicycles.

WORK TOGETHER

Building Understanding

You can compare the number of students who ride red bicycles to the total number of students who ride bicycles to school for each class.

Mrs. Appleton	Mr. Brown	Ms. Chester
3 to 5	4 to 6	2 to 2

You can use counters to show comparisons and explore ratio. Work with a partner for this activity.

• Use counters to represent all five students in Mrs. Appleton's class who ride bicycles to school. Each counter represents one student.

○ ○ ○ ○ ○

• Turn the red side of the counters up to represent the number of students with red bicycles.

● ● ● ○ ○

• Use counters to represent Mr. Brown's class and Ms. Chester's class. Show the comparison of the number of students who ride red bicycles with all students who ride bicycles for each class.

Talk About It

▶ How many students who ride bicycles do *not* ride red bicycles in Mrs. Appleton's class? in Mr. Brown's class? in Ms. Chester's class?

▶ Compare the total number of students who ride bikes to the total number who ride red bikes.

Making the Connection

You can use a **ratio** to compare two numbers. A ratio can be written in any one of three ways. The ratio of students in Mrs. Appleton's class who ride red bicycles to all students who ride bicycles can be written in these three ways.

3 to 5   3:5 $\frac{3}{5}$

Read each ratio "three to five."

You can use ratios to make other comparisons about the students who ride bicycles in Mrs. Appleton's class.

The counters that represent Mrs. Appleton's class show three relationships.

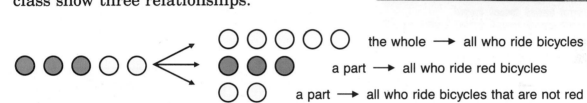

the whole → all who ride bicycles

a part → all who ride red bicycles

a part → all who ride bicycles that are not red

Here are other ratios for Mrs. Appleton's class.

part:whole	whole:part	part:part
not red:all	all:red	red:not red
2:5	5:3	3:2

Talk About It

▶ For Mrs. Appleton's class, what does the ratio $\frac{5}{2}$ describe?

▶ Is the ratio $\frac{5}{2}$ the same as $\frac{2}{5}$? Explain.

Checking Understanding

In Exercises 1–3, write each ratio in three ways.

1. stars to circles   **2.** circles to all shapes   **3.** all shapes to stars

For Exercises 4–6, write *part to whole, whole to part,* or *part to part* for each description in Exercises 1–3.

4. ___?___   **5.** ___?___   **6.** ___?___

EQUIVALENT RATIOS

Hector rents canoes and rowboats at Spring Lake Park. On Thursday he rented 2 canoes and 3 rowboats. On Friday he rented 4 canoes and 6 rowboats. On Saturday he rented 6 canoes and 9 rowboats.

You can draw pictures to show the relationship of canoes to rowboats rented.

Let ⬛ represent a canoe and ▱ represent a rowboat.

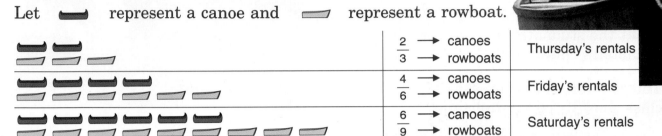

$\dfrac{2}{3}$ → canoes → rowboats	Thursday's rentals
$\dfrac{4}{6}$ → canoes → rowboats	Friday's rentals
$\dfrac{6}{9}$ → canoes → rowboats	Saturday's rentals

You can make a ratio table to show the relationship of canoes to rowboats rented.

Canoes	2	4	6
Rowboats	3	6	9

You can multiply or divide both terms of a ratio by the same number to show the relationship of canoes to rowboats rented.

$$\frac{2}{3} \overset{\times 2}{\underset{\times 2}{=}} \frac{4}{6} \qquad \frac{2}{3} \overset{\times 3}{\underset{\times 3}{=}} \frac{6}{9}$$

So, the ratios of canoes to rowboats rented were equivalent, or had the same relationship, each day.

Talk About It

▶ How can you use multiplication to find a ratio equivalent to $\frac{1}{4}$?

▶ How can you use division to find a ratio equivalent to $\frac{10}{15}$?

▶ Name two other ratios equivalent to $\frac{2}{3}$.

Check for Understanding

Draw pictures to show whether these ratios are equivalent. Write *yes* or *no*.

1. $\frac{1}{3}, \frac{2}{6}, \frac{3}{9}$

2. $\frac{1}{4}, \frac{2}{8}, \frac{3}{9}$

3. $\frac{1}{8}, \frac{2}{16}, \frac{3}{24}$

4. $\frac{1}{6}, \frac{2}{12}, \frac{3}{18}$

Write three ratios that are equivalent to the given ratio.

5. $\frac{3}{4}$

6. $\frac{1}{2}$

7. $\frac{1}{5}$

8. $\frac{2}{3}$

Practice

Tell whether the ratios are equivalent. Write *yes* or *no*.

9. $\frac{2}{3}$ and $\frac{3}{4}$

10. 1:4 and 3:12

11. 3 to 5 and 6 to 10

12. Use multiplication to write two ratios that are equivalent to $\frac{2}{5}$.

13. Use division to write two ratios that are equivalent to $\frac{6}{12}$.

Write two ratios that are equivalent to the given ratio.

14. 1:6

15. 4:5

16. 4:6

17. 3:5

18. $\frac{8}{12}$

Mixed Applications

19. **Logical Reasoning** Find two numbers between 20 and 25 that have a ratio equivalent to 7:8.

20. John worked for 2 hours and earned $7. For how many hours must he work to earn $35?

21. There are 4 children and 2 adults in the car. There are 6 children and 4 adults in the van. Are the ratios of children to adults the same in both vehicles?

22. On Sunday Hector rented 2 more rowboats than canoes. He rented 14 boats in all. How many canoes did he rent?

MIXED REVIEW

Multiply. Write the answer in simplest form.

1. $\frac{2}{5} \times \frac{1}{2} = n$

2. $\frac{1}{3} \times \frac{3}{4} = n$

3. $\frac{5}{6} \times \frac{2}{3} = n$

4. $\frac{1}{6} \times \frac{3}{8} = n$

Complete.

5. $2.54 \text{ m} = \blacksquare \text{ cm}$

6. $55 \text{ g} = \blacksquare \text{ mg}$

7. $3{,}000 \text{ mL} = \blacksquare \text{ L}$

8. $17{,}000 \text{ mm} = \blacksquare \text{ m}$

Explain how you can multiply to find the missing number. $\frac{3}{4} = \frac{n}{20}$

WRAP UP...

EXPLORING

Scale Drawings

On their vacation trip to the Florida Keys, Jared and his family drove on the Overseas Highway from Key Largo to Key West. They discussed how many kilometers it is from Plantation to Long Key.

KEY LARGO

PLANTATION

ISLAMORADA

LONG KEY

KEY WEST

MARATHON

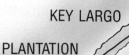

LEGEND
⬆ STATE PARKS
🏛 STATE MONUMENTS

km	0	10	20	30	40	50	60
cm	0	1	2	3	4	5	6

WORK TOGETHER

Building Understanding

You can use a map and a ruler to explore scale drawings and to estimate distances.

Copy and complete the table. On the map, measure to the nearest centimeter the number of centimeters between the cities.

Cities	Distance on Map (in cm)
Key Largo and Islamorada	■
Key Largo and Long Key	■
Key Largo and Marathon	■
Key Largo and Key West	■

Talk About It

▶ What is an estimate of the distance between Plantation and Long Key?

▶ Is the distance greater between Marathon and Key West or between Key Largo and Marathon? How do you know?

Making the Connection

A ratio that compares the distance on the map with the actual distance is a **scale**.

The scale of the map on page 426 is 1 cm : 10 km.

The scale tells you that 1 centimeter on the map represents an actual distance of 10 kilometers.

You can use equivalent ratios to find the actual distance between the cities listed in the table on page 426.

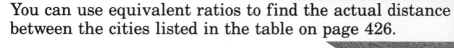

distance on map in cm ⟶
actual distance in km ⟶
$$\frac{1}{10} = \frac{3}{30} \frac{\text{cm}}{\text{km}}$$

So, the actual distance from Plantation to Long Key is about 30 kilometers.

Checking Understanding

1. Add a third column to the table you made on page 426.

2. Use "Actual Distance (in km)" as the heading at the top of the column.

Cities	Distance on Map (in cm)	Actual Distance (in km)
Key Largo and Islamorada		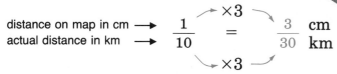
Key Largo and Long Key		
Key Largo and Marathon		
Key Largo and Key West		

3. Use equivalent ratios to find the actual distances between the cities in the table.

SOCIAL STUDIES CONNECTION

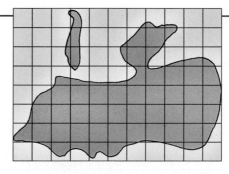

In scale drawings, dimensions are sometimes enlarged and sometimes reduced.

This map of Key West has been drawn on graph paper. Each square on the graph paper is 0.5 cm by 0.5 cm.

4. Enlarge the map of Key West by drawing it on graph paper on which each square is 1 cm by 1 cm.

5. What size graph paper can be used to reduce the map of Key West?

EXPLORING

Percent

You can use colored markers or crayons and graph paper with 10-by-10 grids to explore percent. Work with a partner for these activities.

WORK TOGETHER

Building Understanding

Activity 1 On a 10-by-10 grid, color some squares blue. Then color all the other squares on the grid red.

Talk About It

▶ How many squares are on the grid?

▶ How many squares are blue? How many are red?

▶ What is the ratio of blue squares to all the squares on the grid? of red squares to all the squares on the grid?

▶ How can you shade a grid to show a ratio of blue squares to all squares of 75 to 100? 23:100? $\frac{50}{100}$?

Activity 2
On a 10-by-10 grid, color all the squares blue. On another 10-by-10 grid, do not color any squares.

▶ Look at the first grid. How many squares are blue?

▶ What is the ratio of blue squares to all squares?

▶ Look at the other grid. How many squares are blue?

▶ What is the ratio of blue squares to all squares?

▶ How can you shade a grid to show a ratio of red squares to all squares of 100:100?

428

Making the Connection

Percent is a ratio of some number to 100. Percent means "per hundred." The symbol for percent is %.

Look at this 10-by-10 grid.

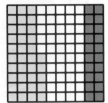

The ratio of blue squares to all squares is 35 to 100.

Thirty-five percent of the grid is blue.

- What percent of the grid is red?

- What percent of the grid is not colored?

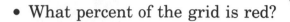

Percent is often used with money.

Think of $1.00 as 100 pennies with each penny, or counter, in a square of a 10-by-10 grid.

35% of $1.00 is $0.35.

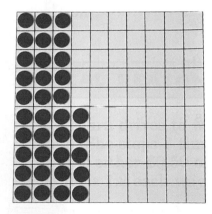

> **Talk About It**
>
> ▶ What is 50% of $1.00? 10% of $1.00? 36% of $1.00?
>
> ▶ What part of a dollar do you have if you have 0% of it? 100% of it?
>
> ▶ What does 200% of a number mean?

Checking Understanding

1. Color a 10-by-10 grid so that it is 25% blue, 50% red, and 25% yellow. How much of the grid is colored? What is the sum of the three percents?

2. Suppose you have $1.00 in your wallet. What percent of your money is $1.00? is $0.75? is $0.50? is $0.25? is $0.00?

Ahmed is planning to travel from England to France. He can leave on Monday or on Wednesday. He can go to France by airplane, or he can cross the English Channel by Hovercraft or by auto ferry. How many travel choices does he have?

Sometimes you can solve a problem by *making an organized list* of the information.

▶ UNDERSTAND

What are you asked to find?

What facts are given?

▶ PLAN

What strategy can you use?

You can *make an organized list*, or a **tree diagram,** to list all the choices Ahmed has for traveling to France.

▶ SOLVE

How can you solve the problem?

You can make a tree diagram showing both days and each type of transportation given in the problem. List all the possibilities Ahmed can choose.

Days	Transportation	Possibilities
Monday	Airplane	Monday/Airplane
	Hovercraft	Monday/Hovercraft
	Auto ferry	Monday/Auto ferry
Wednesday	Airplane	Wednesday/Airplane
	Hovercraft	Wednesday/Hovercraft
	Auto ferry	Wednesday/Auto ferry

So, Ahmed has six choices for traveling to France.

▶ LOOK BACK

How can you check your answer?

WHAT IF... ...a tunnel to France is open for train travel on Monday and Wednesday? How many choices does Ahmed have for traveling to France?

Idea Bank, page 465, Exercises 10–11

Apply

Make an organized list and solve.

1 Norman packed green pants, black pants, and blue pants. He packed a white shirt, a yellow shirt, and a red shirt. How many different outfits can he make?

2 For lunch Winsie may order a sandwich with chicken, tuna fish, or peanut butter. She can have the sandwich on white bread, wheat bread, rye bread, or a roll. How many choices does she have?

Mixed Applications

STRATEGIES
- Make a Table
- Work Backward
- Write a Number Sentence
- Use a Formula

Choose a strategy and solve.

3 Elston is staying in a hotel that is 14 blocks from the Empire State Building. If Elston can walk 2 blocks in 5 min, how long will it take him to walk from his hotel to the Empire State Building?

4 Pepita left her hotel at 8:00 A.M. She spent 1 hr 20 min eating breakfast, 30 min traveling to a museum, and 3 hr 45 min at the museum. If it took Pepita 35 min to get back to the hotel, at what time did she arrive back at the hotel?

5 Percy rode his bicycle once around the perimeter of Central Park. The park is $2\frac{1}{2}$ mi long and $\frac{1}{2}$ mi wide. How far did Percy ride his bicycle?

6 On Tuesday, Wednesday, and Thursday, Caroline visited a different museum in Paris each day. The museums were the Louvre, the Orsay Museum, and the Museum of Man. She did not visit the Louvre on Tuesday, and she did visit the Museum of Man on Wednesday. On which day did she visit each museum?

WRITER'S CORNER

7 Imagine that you can ask one person to take a trip with you. Choose three people with whom you might travel and three places you might visit. Make a diagram to show the different possibilities.

REVIEW AND MAINTENANCE

1. Maria can use either Red Avenue, Main Street, or Elm Street to get to school. She can ride her bicycle, walk, or ride in the car. In how many different ways can she go to school?

2. Both the school and the city bus systems drop off students at the main entrance, the cafeteria, and the parking lot. In how many different ways can a student arrive at school by bus?

3. Julia walked around a square city block. If each side of the block is 500 ft long, how far did Julia walk?

4. Paul went camping at a state park that was about $1\frac{1}{2}$ mi long and $\frac{3}{4}$ mi wide. About how many square miles is the area of the state park?

Multiply.

5. 542
   × 8

6. 1,793
   × 6

7. 68
   × 17

8. 405
   × 24

I can use a formula to solve a problem.

Write *slide, flip,* or *turn* to indicate how each figure was moved.

9.

10.

11.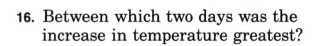

Find the quotient.

12. $3\overline{)2,981}$

13. $4\overline{)9,860}$

14. $13\overline{)957}$

15. $24\overline{)1,370}$

Use the graph for Exercises 16–17.

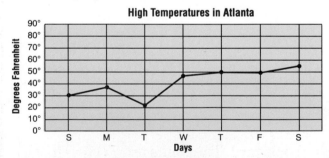

High Temperatures in Atlanta

16. Between which two days was the increase in temperature greatest?

17. What was the difference in the high temperature on Sunday and the high temperature on Saturday?

Write the greatest common factor for each pair of numbers.

18. 6, 9

19. 10, 35

20. 4, 14

21. 8, 24

22. 12, 20

23. 8, 12

Add or subtract. Write the answer in simplest form.

24. $2\frac{1}{3}$
    $+1\frac{1}{6}$

25. $4\frac{5}{8}$
    $-2\frac{1}{4}$

26. $10\frac{4}{5}$
    $-3\frac{2}{3}$

Spotlight ON PROBLEM SOLVING

Understand
Plan
Solve
Look Back

Choose the Method for the Solution

When you plan the solution to a problem, you should consider all possible solutions.

Every day, Samantha sees the same three cars parked in the school parking lot. A blue car is in front, a red car is next, and a green car is parked at the end of the line. In how many different ways can these three cars be parked?

 **Talk About It** ● ● ● ● ● ● ● ● ● ● ● ● ● ● ● ●

Work with a partner. Be prepared to share your answers with the class.

● Name some ways you can solve the problem.

● Choose a method, and find the solution. In how many different ways can the cars be parked?

● Find the solution by using another method.

● Which method was the easier way to find the solution?

Apply

Solve. Use at least two different methods for each problem. Be prepared to discuss how you solved each problem.

1. Suppose Samantha sees the same three cars, plus a yellow car. In how many different ways could the cars be parked?

2. Ed has a model train with five cars. The engine is always first in line, and the caboose is always last. In how many different ways can Ed order the cars?

3. Mary can win a trip if she can arrange the digits of a number to read the same forward and backward. The digits are 73171. How can she find a solution?

4. Sarah parks five cars in a row. The owner of the red car always wants his car parked directly in back of the blue car and directly in front of the green car. In how many different positions can Sarah park the red car?

EXPLORING

Probability

You can do a coin-tossing experiment to explore probability and to learn how to make good predictions.

When you toss a coin, the coin can land in two possible ways. It can land heads up or tails up. These are the **possible outcomes** of tossing one coin.

For this experiment you will
• predict the results of tossing two coins at one time.
• compare your results with your predictions.

Building Understanding

Step 1 Copy the table. The possible outcome HH means that the first coin landed heads up and the second coin landed heads up.

Coin-Tossing Experiment				
Possible Outcomes	Prediction for 5 Tosses	Result for 5 Tosses	Prediction for 50 Tosses	Result for 50 Tosses
HH				
HT				
TH				
TT				

• What does the outcome TH mean?

Step 2 Predict the number of times you think each outcome will occur for 5 tosses and then for 50 tosses.

Step 3 Toss the 2 coins 5 times. Use tally marks to record your results in the table.

Step 4 Now toss the two coins 50 times. Record your results.

Talk About It

▶ Describe how you made your predictions.

▶ How did your results for the 5 tosses and for the 50 tosses compare with your predictions?

▶ How many times do you think each outcome would occur if you tossed the coins 100 times? 1,000 times?

▶ Combine your results with those of all others in your class. How does this total compare to your results?

Making the Connection

The chance of something happening is called **probability**.

Probability is a ratio.

When you toss a coin, there are two possible outcomes: heads and tails. There is 1 chance in 2 of tossing heads.

The probability can be written as a fraction.

$$\text{Probability} = \frac{\text{number of favorable outcomes (heads)}}{\text{number of possible outcomes (heads, tails)}} = \frac{1}{2}$$

Talk About It

▶ When you toss two coins at one time, how many possible outcomes are there? List the possible outcomes.

▶ What is the probability of the result being HH? HT? TH? TT?

▶ For how many possible outcomes is there at least 1 heads? What is the probability of tossing heads?

▶ For how many possible outcomes is there 1 heads and 1 tails? What is the probability of tossing 1 heads and 1 tails?

Checking Understanding

Suppose this spinner is used in the experiment.

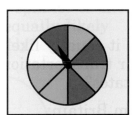

1. How many equivalent sections does the spinner have?

2. What are the possible outcomes of spinning the spinner?

3. What is the probability of the spinner landing on yellow? on blue? on red?

4. If you spin the spinner eight times, how many times do you think it will land on yellow? on blue? on red?

5. On what color will the spinner probably land most often? Why?

PROBLEM *Solving*

Mrs. Wooldridge must choose a student for a part in a play. Four students are equally qualified. How can a choice be made so that each student has an equal chance of being selected?

Student 1	→	Brett
Student 2	→	Linda
Student 3	→	Renee
Student 4	→	David

▶ UNDERSTAND

What are you asked to find?

What facts are given?

▶ PLAN

What process can you use?

You can choose the student by drawing numbers from a bag.
- On each of four slips of paper, write a student's number. Put the slips in a bag.
- Without looking, select one slip of paper. Make a tally mark next to the student's number in a table. Return the slip to the bag.
- Repeat this activity 50 times. The number selected most often will determine Mrs. Wooldridge's choice.

▶ SOLVE

How can you conduct a simulation?

You can use a computer program to simulate the experiment.

This BASIC program will generate the digits 1–4 at random 50 times.

```
10 REM THIS PROGRAM PRINTS
20 REM 50 RANDOM NUMBERS
30 REM BETWEEN 1 AND 4
40 PRINT "THE 50 RANDOM NUMBERS ARE:"
50 FOR I = 1 TO 49
60 X = INT ( RND (1) * 4) + 1
70 PRINT X; ",";
80 NEXT I
90 PRINT INT ( RND (1) * 4) + 1
100 END
```

On one computer run, these numbers were generated.

2,4,4,2,4,2,2,3,1,3,3,3,4,4,
2,4,3,2,4,2,3,3,4,1,4,3,1,4,
3,2,4,1,2,1,1,2,4,4,2,1,1,3,
4,2,1,2,3,3,1,1

Summary: 1 = 11
2 = 13
3 = 12
4 = 14

So, student number 4, David, was the choice.

▶ LOOK BACK

If you repeat the activity, will you get the same results?

... there are five students who are equally qualified? How will the computer program have to be changed?

Apply

1 A program generates the digits 1–5 at random 100 times. Write a problem that this program could simulate.

2 If a program generates the digits 1–4 at random 100 times, about how many times would you expect each number to occur?

Mixed Applications ➔ **STRATEGIES** • Make a Diagram • Work Backward • Use a Table • Guess and Check • Solve a Simpler Problem

Choose a strategy and solve.

3 When Saki got back to her hotel after a day of sightseeing, she had $32.45. She had spent $9.50 on food, $14.80 on souvenirs, $13.75 on admission tickets, and $4.50 on transportation. How much money did she have at the beginning of the day?

4 Mrs. Berry assigned 38 students to do a report on England, France, Spain, Germany, or Italy. One half of the class chose to do a report on Spain, Germany, or Italy. France was chosen 5 more times than England. How many students did a report on France?

5 Six girls plan to go to the beach during the summer. If each goes to the beach once with each of the other girls, what will be the total number of trips made to the beach by the six girls?

6 Mr. Aviles asked his students if they would rather take a trip to Florida, Hawaii, or Canada. Of the students, $\frac{1}{2}$ chose Hawaii, $\frac{2}{5}$ chose Florida, and $\frac{1}{10}$ chose Canada. If 3 students chose Canada, how many students chose Hawaii?

Use the table for Exercise 7.

7 In which month does Paris have the greatest difference between its average high and low temperatures?

Average Temperatures in Paris		
Month	**High**	**Low**
January	42°F	32°F
April	60°F	41°F
July	76°F	55°F
October	59°F	44°F

Vocabulary Check

Choose a word or words from the box to complete each sentence.

equivalent
ratios
scale
percent
probability
ratio
scale drawing
tree diagram

1. You can use a __?__ to compare two numbers. *(page 423)*

2. If you want to show enlarged or reduced parts of an object, you can make a __?__. *(page 427)*

3. A ratio of some number to 100 is a __?__. *(page 429)*

4. A ratio that compares the distance on a map with the actual distance is a __?__. *(page 427)*

5. A ratio that gives the chance that something will happen is a __?__. *(page 437)*

6. A diagram that is an organized list is a __?__. *(page 432)*

7. Ratios that show the same relationships are __?__. *(page 424)*

You can use a ratio to compare two numbers.

Concept Check

Write the ratio for each comparison. *(page 422)*

8. triangles to circles

9. squares to all shapes

10. all shapes to triangles

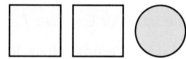

Write the ratio in three ways. *(page 422)*

11. the ratio of red hats to all hats

12. the ratio of red hats to green hats

Use the map for Exercises 13–14. *(page 426)*

13. What is the distance on the map between points *A* and *B*?

14. Use the map scale to find the actual distance between points *A* and *B*.

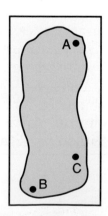

Scale 1 cm: 100 km

Use the grid for Exercises 15–16. *(page 428)*

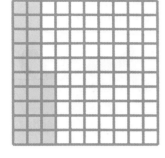

15. What percent of the grid is blue?

16. What percent of the grid is not colored?

Write the amount of money for each. *(page 428)*

17. 25% of $1.00 **18.** 100% of $1.00 **19.** 200% of $1.00

Write each as a percent, a decimal, and a fraction in simplest form. *(page 430)*

20. 4 percent

21. thirteen per hundred

22. 26 hundredths

Skill Check

Write a ratio equivalent to the given ratio. *(page 424)*

23. 1:3 **24.** 2 to 5 **25.** $\frac{3}{2}$ **26.** 10:12 **27.** $\frac{15}{10}$

Use the spinner for Exercises 28–30. *(pages 436, 438)*

28. What are the possible outcomes of spinning the spinner?

29. What is the probability of the spinner landing on red?

30. What is the probability of the spinner landing on green?

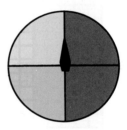

Problem-Solving Check *(pages 432, 440)*

31. A program generates 25 random numbers for the digits 1–3. Write a problem that this program could simulate.

32. If a computer program generates 100 random numbers for the digits 1–3, about how many times would you expect each digit to occur?

33. Jon can travel from Rutland to Simon by car, bus, or train. He can travel from Simon to Titan by boat or jet. In how many different ways can he travel from Rutland to Simon to Titan?

34. Becky can paint the walls in her room yellow, pink, or blue. She can paint the trim white, tan, or green. In how many different ways can Becky paint her room?

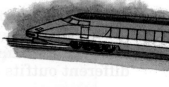

COMPUTER
Connection

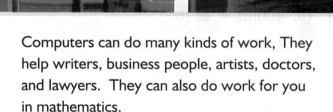

Computers can do many kinds of work, They help writers, business people, artists, doctors, and lawyers. They can also do work for you in mathematics.

In this section you will explore LOGO, use a word processor, make a spreadsheet, and build a data base. You will be using the kinds of computer programs that many people use at their jobs and at home.

▶▶▶▶▶▶▶▶▶

Table of Contents

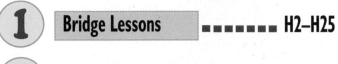

Student **H**andbook

CHAPTER I

Numbers to Thousands

In this lesson you will explore how ones, tens, hundreds, and thousands are related.

WORK TOGETHER

Building Understanding

Use graph paper to make place-value models.

Color 1 square, and label it *one*.

Color 10 squares in a row, and label them *ten*.

Color 100 squares in 10 rows of 10, and label them *one hundred.*

Since □ = 1, then = 10, and 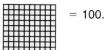 = 100.

one   ten   one hundred

Use graph paper to make models for 40, 90, 200, and 600.

Talk About It

▶ How many hundreds are in each number?

▶ How many tens are in each number? How many ones?

Since = 100, then 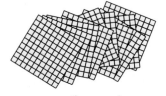 = 1,000.

one hundred   one thousand

▶ How many hundreds are in 1,000? How many tens? How many ones?

Numbers can be expressed in different ways.

Standard Form: 600
Expanded Form: $(6 \times 100) + (0 \times 10) + (0 \times 1)$
Word Form: six hundred

• How can you express 657 in two other forms?

Practice

Here are some statements about 1,000. Write *true* or *false*.

1. There are more than 1,000 books in the classroom.

2. A line of one thousand squares (■) would reach from the classroom door to the principal's office.

3. One thousand equals 10 hundreds.

Use place-value models to show each number. Then write how many thousands, hundreds, tens, or ones you used.

4. 846 = ■ hundreds, ■ tens, ■ ones

5. 406 = ■ hundreds, ■ tens, ■ ones

6. 8,374 = ■ thousands, ■ hundreds, ■ tens, ■ ones

7. 30 = ■ tens, ■ ones

8. 866 = ■ hundreds, ■ tens, ■ ones

9. 5,559 = ■ thousands, ■ hundreds, ■ tens, ■ ones

What kind of container would hold 1,000 pencils?

What item could you buy with 1,000 pennies?

From the front door of the school, where would you be if you took 1,000 steps?

Write two other forms for each number.

10. (4 × 100) + (8 × 10) + (5 × 1)

11. twenty-nine

12. (9 × 10) + (3 × 1)

13. eight hundred three

14. three hundred fifty-three

15. 675

16. (2 × 100) + (0 × 10) + (4 × 1)

17. 700

18. five thousand, forty-seven

19. 6,110

20. (6 × 1,000) + (0 × 100) + (0 × 10) + (3 × 1)

Write the value of the underlined digit.

21. 34<u>5</u>

22. <u>1</u>6

23. 1,0<u>7</u>5

24. <u>5</u>89

25. <u>7</u>,900

26. 2,43<u>9</u>

27. 90<u>0</u>

28. 6,0<u>9</u>8

29. 4<u>3</u>5

30. 8,4<u>5</u>2

Solve.

31. I am a number greater than 99 but less than 101. What am I?

32. I am a number less than 1,050 but greater than 1,048. What am I?

Patterns in Addition and Subtraction

Counting On	
$5 + 3 = 8$	$5 \leftarrow$ addend
Think: 5 . . . 6, 7, 8	$+3 \leftarrow$ addend
	$\overline{8} \leftarrow$ sum
Zero	8
$8 + 0 = 8$	$+0$
	$\overline{8}$
Doubles	4
$4 + 4 = 8$	$+4$
	$\overline{8}$
Doubles Plus One	6
$6 + 5 = 11$	$+5$
Think: 1 more than 5 + 5	$\overline{11}$

When one of the addends is 1, 2, or 3, *count on* to find the sum.

When you add *zero* to a number, the sum is that number.

If both addends are the same, you are adding *doubles*.

When one addend is one more than the other, you can use *doubles plus one* to find the sum.

You can use the addition methods to find patterns in the table.

- Use the *zero* method to find sums on the addition table. What pattern do you notice?

- Use the *doubles* method to find sums on the addition table. What pattern do you notice?

- Use the *doubles plus one* method to find sums on the addition table. What pattern do you notice?

Since addition and subtraction are opposite operations, you can use the addition table to subtract.

Example: $10 - 6 = 4$

Begin at 6 in the first row.

Move down the column to 10.

From 10, move left to the first column to find the difference.

+	0	1	2	3	4	5	6	7	8	9
0	0	1	2	3	4	5	6	7	8	9
1	1	2	3	4	5	6	7	8	9	10
2	2	3	4	5	6	7	8	9	10	11
3	3	4	5	6	7	8	9	10	11	12
4	4	5	6	7	8	9	10	11	12	13
5	5	6	7	8	9	10	11	12	13	14
6	6	7	8	9	10	11	12	13	14	15
7	7	8	9	10	11	12	13	14	15	16
8	8	9	10	11	12	13	14	15	16	17
9	9	10	11	12	13	14	15	16	17	18

+	0	1	2	3	4	5	6	7	8	9
0	0	1	2	3	4	5	6	7	8	9
1	1	2	3	4	5	6	7	8	9	10
2	2	3	4	5	6	7	8	9	10	11
3	3	4	5	6	7	8	9	10	11	12
4	4	5	6	7	8	9	10	11	12	13
5	5	6	7	8	9	10	11	12	13	14
6	6	7	8	9	10	11	12	13	14	15
7	7	8	9	10	11	12	13	14	15	16
8	8	9	10	11	12	13	14	15	16	17
9	9	10	11	12	13	14	15	16	17	18

Practice

Find the sum. Name the addition method.

1. $4 + 5 =$ ▨

2. $6 + 0 =$ ▨

3. $7 + 2 =$ ▨

4. $7 + 8 =$ ▨

5. $8 + 8 =$ ▨

6. $3 + 4 =$ ▨

7. $12 + 0 =$ ▨

8. $9 + 3 =$ ▨

9. $1 + 9 =$ ▨

10. $4 + 0 =$ ▨

11. $2 + 3 =$ ▨

12. $3 + 7 =$ ▨

13. $6 + 2 =$ ▨

14. $4 + 4 =$ ▨

15. $1 + 4 =$ ▨

16. $7 + 7 =$ ▨

17. $6 + 6 =$ ▨

18. $5 + 3 =$ ▨

19. $8 + 0 =$ ▨

20. $5 + 6 =$ ▨

21. $9 + 1 =$ ▨

22. $\begin{array}{r} 7 \\ +6 \\ \hline \end{array}$
23. $\begin{array}{r} 3 \\ +5 \\ \hline \end{array}$
24. $\begin{array}{r} 2 \\ +9 \\ \hline \end{array}$
25. $\begin{array}{r} 6 \\ +0 \\ \hline \end{array}$
26. $\begin{array}{r} 8 \\ +9 \\ \hline \end{array}$

27. $\begin{array}{r} 3 \\ +6 \\ \hline \end{array}$
28. $\begin{array}{r} 1 \\ +8 \\ \hline \end{array}$
29. $\begin{array}{r} 2 \\ +6 \\ \hline \end{array}$
30. $\begin{array}{r} 5 \\ +5 \\ \hline \end{array}$
31. $\begin{array}{r} 0 \\ +4 \\ \hline \end{array}$

Find the missing addend. Write a subtraction sentence.

32. $6 +$ ▨ $= 13$

33. $3 +$ ▨ $= 8$

34. $9 +$ ▨ $= 13$

35. $8 +$ ▨ $= 14$

36. $5 +$ ▨ $= 10$

37. $6 +$ ▨ $= 12$

38. $9 +$ ▨ $= 16$

39. $3 +$ ▨ $= 5$

40. $3 +$ ▨ $= 10$

Add or subtract.

41. $\begin{array}{r} 15 \\ -\ 7 \\ \hline \end{array}$
42. $\begin{array}{r} 7 \\ +7 \\ \hline \end{array}$
43. $\begin{array}{r} 9 \\ +3 \\ \hline \end{array}$
44. $\begin{array}{r} 14 \\ -\ 4 \\ \hline \end{array}$
45. $\begin{array}{r} 13 \\ -\ 5 \\ \hline \end{array}$

Solve.

46. Claire waited 6 minutes for Mark at the baseball game. Then she waited 5 minutes for Cherie. How long did Claire wait for Mark and Cherie?

47. Robbie won 4 stuffed bears and 5 stuffed rabbits. How many stuffed animals did Robbie win?

Adding 2- and 3-Digit Numbers

A basketball team scored 27 points in the first half of a game and 35 points in the second half. How many points did the team score in all?

You can add to find how many points the team scored in all.

Add: 27 + 35 = ▆

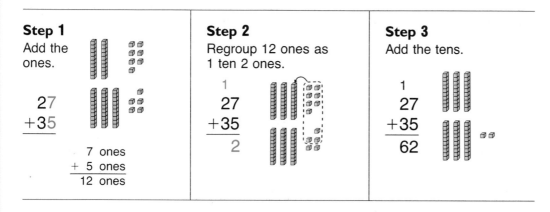

Step 1 Add the ones.	**Step 2** Regroup 12 ones as 1 ten 2 ones.	**Step 3** Add the tens.

Step 1
Add the ones.

$$\begin{array}{r} 27 \\ +35 \\ \hline \end{array}$$

$$\begin{array}{r} 7 \text{ ones} \\ + 5 \text{ ones} \\ \hline 12 \text{ ones} \end{array}$$

Step 2
Regroup 12 ones as 1 ten 2 ones.

$$\begin{array}{r} \overset{1}{} \\ 27 \\ +35 \\ \hline 2 \end{array}$$

Step 3
Add the tens.

$$\begin{array}{r} \overset{1}{} \\ 27 \\ +35 \\ \hline 62 \end{array}$$

So, the team scored 62 points in all.

More Examples

A. $\begin{array}{r} 47 \\ +32 \\ \hline 79 \end{array}$ **B.** $\begin{array}{r} 1 \\ 35 \\ +59 \\ \hline 94 \end{array}$ **C.** $\begin{array}{r} 83 \\ +65 \\ \hline 148 \end{array}$ **D.** $\begin{array}{r} 1 \\ 58 \\ +74 \\ \hline 132 \end{array}$

• What columns were regrouped in Examples B, C, and D?

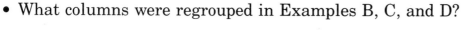

You can use what you know about adding two-digit numbers to help you add three-digit numbers.

Add: 154 + 167 = ▆

Step 1	**Step 2**

Step 1
Add the ones.
Regroup 11 ones as
1 ten 1 one.

$$\begin{array}{r} \overset{1}{} \\ 154 \\ +167 \\ \hline 1 \end{array}$$

$$\begin{array}{r} 4 \text{ ones} \\ + 7 \text{ ones} \\ \hline 11 \text{ ones} \end{array}$$

Step 2
Add the tens.
Regroup 12 tens as
1 hundred 2 tens.
Add the hundreds.

$$\begin{array}{r} \overset{11}{} \\ 154 \\ +167 \\ \hline 321 \end{array}$$

$$\begin{array}{r} 1 \text{ ten} \\ 5 \text{ tens} \\ + 6 \text{ tens} \\ \hline 12 \text{ tens} \end{array}$$

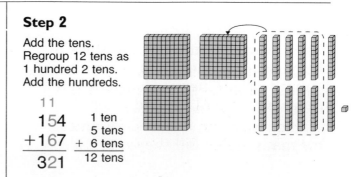

Practice

Find the sum. In Exercises 1–15, circle the columns in which you regrouped.

1. $52 + 9$

2. $15 + 6$

3. $14 + 9$

4. $63 + 12$

5. $21 + 19$

6. $13 + 47$

7. $18 + 17$

8. $65 + 39$

9. $24 + 16$

10. $44 + 28$

11. $38 + 69$

12. $69 + 36$

13. $27 + 46$

14. $33 + 39$

15. $54 + 18$

Find the sum.

16. $72 + 19 = $ ▪

17. $29 + 32 = $ ▪

18. $66 + 28 = $ ▪

19. $33 + 64 = $ ▪

20. $48 + 65 = $ ▪

21. $69 + 37 = $ ▪

22. $98 + 89 = $ ▪

23. $13 + 79 = $ ▪

24. $45 + 39 = $ ▪

25. $58 + 77 = $ ▪

26. $34 + 79 = $ ▪

27. $17 + 56 = $ ▪

Find the sum. In Exercises 28–37, circle the columns in which you regrouped.

28. $169 + 26$

29. $213 + 94$

30. $462 + 318$

31. $610 + 297$

32. $337 + 145$

33. $318 + 198$

34. $422 + 278$

35. $197 + 413$

36. $276 + 935$

37. $479 + 460$

Find the sum.

38. $399 + 211 = $ ▪

39. $255 + 546 = $ ▪

40. $483 + 118 = $ ▪

41. $855 + 295 = $ ▪

42. $469 + 545 = $ ▪

43. $633 + 749 = $ ▪

44. $909 + 321 = $ ▪

45. $594 + 398 = $ ▪

46. $212 + 727 = $ ▪

Solve.

47. The Oak Street School band traveled 38 miles to the game. On the return trip, they went a different way and traveled 29 miles. How many miles did they travel?

48. On Thursday 293 tickets were sold for the game. On Friday 428 tickets were sold for the game. How many tickets were sold in all?

Subtracting 2- and 3-Digit Numbers

There were 43 students at the swim meet on Wednesday. There were 19 students at the swim meet on Thursday. How many more students were at the swim meet on Wednesday than on Thursday?

To find how many more students were at the swim meet on Wednesday than on Thursday, subtract.

Subtract: $43 - 19 = n$

Step 1	**Step 2**	**Step 3**
Decide whether to regroup. Since $9 > 3$, regroup 4 tens 3 ones as 3 tens 13 ones.	Subtract the ones.	Subtract the tens.
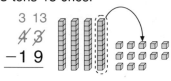		

So, 24 more students were at the swim meet.

You can use what you know about subtracting two-digit numbers to help you subtract three-digit numbers.

Subtract: $243 - 197 = n$

Step 1	**Step 2**	**Step 3**
Decide whether to regroup. Since $7 > 3$, regroup 4 tens 3 ones as 3 tens 13 ones. Subtract the ones.	Since $9 > 3$, regroup 2 hundreds 3 tens as 1 hundred 13 tens. Subtract the tens.	Subtract the hundreds.
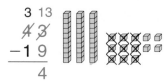		

- How would you have estimated the difference?
- How can you check your subtraction?

Practice

Find the difference. In Exercises 1–15, circle the columns in which you regrouped.

1. 99
    -23

2. 36
    -12

3. 43
    -34

4. 67
    -27

5. 80
    -49

6. 78
    -19

7. 56
    -27

8. 22
    -13

9. 75
    -57

10. 41
    -29

11. 56
    -28

12. 31
    -18

13. 47
    -18

14. 95
    -76

15. 80
    -35

Find the difference.

16. $33 - 26 = n$ 17. $98 - 47 = n$ 18. $60 - 39 = n$

19. $56 - 27 = n$ 20. $87 - 49 = n$ 21. $39 - 25 = n$

Find the difference. In Exercises 22–36, circle the columns in which you regrouped.

22. 465
    -124

23. 688
    -317

24. 975
    -461

25. 738
    -527

26. 437
    -218

27. 971
    -337

28. 396
    -218

29. 882
    -713

30. 452
    -126

31. 532
    -346

32. 213
    $- 98$

33. 435
    -146

34. 582
    -394

35. 732
    -545

36. 848
    -459

Find the difference.

37. $313 - 234 = n$ 38. $463 - 372 = n$ 39. $898 - 789 = n$

40. $244 - 198 = n$ 41. $749 - 568 = n$ 42. $900 - 699 = n$

Solve.

43. Last year the team won 17 basketball games. This year they won 24 basketball games. How many more basketball games did they win this year than last year?

44. On Thursday morning there were 182 tickets to be sold. At the end of the day, 114 tickets had not been sold. How many tickets were sold during the day?

CHAPTER 3

Multiplying 2-Digit Numbers

Meg McNeil likes to make sun catchers. She uses 16 pieces of colored plastic for each flower. How many pieces of plastic does she need to make 4 flowers?

Estimate. Front-end: $4 \times 10 = 40$

Rounding: $4 \times 20 = 80$

Use place-value blocks to model 4×16.
Then compare your model with this method.

Step 1	**Step 2**	**Step 3**
Multiply the ones. 4×6 ones $= 24$ ones	Regroup 24 ones as 2 tens 4 ones. Record the 2 tens above the 1 ten.	Multiply the tens. Then add the regrouped tens. 4 tens + 2 tens = 6 tens
$\begin{array}{r} 16 \\ \times\ 4 \\ \hline \end{array}$	$\begin{array}{r} 2 \\ 16 \\ \times\ 4 \\ \hline 4 \end{array}$	$\begin{array}{r} 2 \\ 16 \\ \times\ 4 \\ \hline 64 \end{array}$

So, Meg needs 64 pieces of plastic. Since 64 is close to 80, the answer is reasonable.

Talk About It

▶ Compare the method shown at the right with the shorter method shown above. Explain how the methods differ.

▶ Explain why the 40 is not shown in the problem above.

▶ How does your estimate help you determine whether your answer is reasonable?

T	**O**
1	6
×	4
2	4
4	0
6	4

Practice

Estimate the product.

1. $2 \times 32 = n$ **2.** $3 \times 26 = n$ **3.** $2 \times 37 = n$

4. $3 \times 12 = n$ **5.** $6 \times 23 = n$ **6.** $3 \times 28 = n$

Find the product.

7. $\begin{array}{r} 18 \\ \times\ 4 \\ \hline \end{array}$
8. $\begin{array}{r} 23 \\ \times\ 3 \\ \hline \end{array}$
9. $\begin{array}{r} 34 \\ \times\ 6 \\ \hline \end{array}$
10. $\begin{array}{r} 43 \\ \times\ 7 \\ \hline \end{array}$
11. $\begin{array}{r} 52 \\ \times\ 8 \\ \hline \end{array}$

12. $\begin{array}{r} 79 \\ \times\ 4 \\ \hline \end{array}$
13. $\begin{array}{r} 45 \\ \times\ 2 \\ \hline \end{array}$
14. $\begin{array}{r} 54 \\ \times\ 4 \\ \hline \end{array}$
15. $\begin{array}{r} 28 \\ \times\ 3 \\ \hline \end{array}$
16. $\begin{array}{r} 29 \\ \times\ 5 \\ \hline \end{array}$

17. $\begin{array}{r} 28 \\ \times\ 5 \\ \hline \end{array}$
18. $\begin{array}{r} 62 \\ \times\ 7 \\ \hline \end{array}$
19. $\begin{array}{r} 37 \\ \times\ 4 \\ \hline \end{array}$
20. $\begin{array}{r} 52 \\ \times\ 6 \\ \hline \end{array}$
21. $\begin{array}{r} 43 \\ \times\ 8 \\ \hline \end{array}$

22. $\begin{array}{r} 35 \\ \times\ 2 \\ \hline \end{array}$
23. $\begin{array}{r} 78 \\ \times\ 8 \\ \hline \end{array}$
24. $\begin{array}{r} 19 \\ \times\ 8 \\ \hline \end{array}$
25. $\begin{array}{r} 24 \\ \times\ 5 \\ \hline \end{array}$
26. $\begin{array}{r} 67 \\ \times\ 9 \\ \hline \end{array}$

27. $\begin{array}{r} 43 \\ \times\ 5 \\ \hline \end{array}$
28. $\begin{array}{r} 32 \\ \times\ 3 \\ \hline \end{array}$
29. $\begin{array}{r} 97 \\ \times\ 4 \\ \hline \end{array}$
30. $\begin{array}{r} 62 \\ \times\ 3 \\ \hline \end{array}$
31. $\begin{array}{r} 40 \\ \times\ 7 \\ \hline \end{array}$

32. $\begin{array}{r} 77 \\ \times\ 3 \\ \hline \end{array}$
33. $\begin{array}{r} 21 \\ \times\ 5 \\ \hline \end{array}$
34. $\begin{array}{r} 36 \\ \times\ 6 \\ \hline \end{array}$
35. $\begin{array}{r} 87 \\ \times\ 8 \\ \hline \end{array}$
36. $\begin{array}{r} 14 \\ \times\ 9 \\ \hline \end{array}$

37. $\begin{array}{r} 45 \\ \times\ 4 \\ \hline \end{array}$
38. $\begin{array}{r} 31 \\ \times\ 7 \\ \hline \end{array}$
39. $\begin{array}{r} 67 \\ \times\ 5 \\ \hline \end{array}$
40. $\begin{array}{r} 54 \\ \times\ 6 \\ \hline \end{array}$
41. $\begin{array}{r} 13 \\ \times\ 8 \\ \hline \end{array}$

42. $7 \times 64 = n$ **43.** $5 \times 48 = n$ **44.** $3 \times 86 = n$

45. $6 \times 17 = n$ **46.** $9 \times 56 = n$ **47.** $8 \times 43 = n$

48. $3 \times 39 = n$ **49.** $4 \times 42 = n$ **50.** $5 \times 27 = n$

51. $3 \times 72 = n$ **52.** $6 \times 35 = n$ **53.** $4 \times 59 = n$

Solve.

54. Leon sold 27 sun catchers. Pete sold twice as many as Leon. How many sun catchers did Pete sell?

55. Maria sold 4 sun catchers for $12 each. How much money did she receive for the sun catchers?

CHAPTER 4

Exploring Plane Figures and Polygons

Some plane figures are polygons.

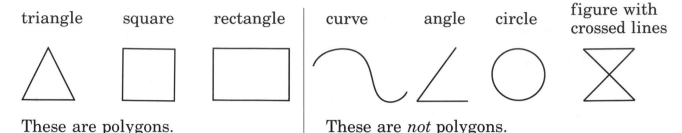

| triangle | square | rectangle | curve | angle | circle | figure with crossed lines |

These are polygons. | These are *not* polygons.

Polygons are made up of line segments that do not cross.

WORK TOGETHER

Use string to model plane figures.

Cut a piece of string about 6 feet long. Lay the string on a flat table or a desk top. Make sure that the ends do not touch. This is an **open figure.**

Talk About It

▶ How do you know that the string forms a plane figure?

▶ How can you make a closed figure with the string?

Tie the ends of the string. Now, have three people in the group each hold a point on the string. Each point shows where two line segments meet and is called a **vertex.**

▶ What is the figure that you made? Is it a closed figure?

▶ Is the figure a plane figure? How do you know?

▶ If one person lifts up a point, will the figure be in a different plane?

▶ Is the figure a polygon? What is this polygon called?

▶ What makes a polygon different from other plane figures?

▶ Why are curves, angles, and circles not polygons?

Practice

Use string to make a model of each of these polygons. Then make two different examples of each type of polygon, and draw them.

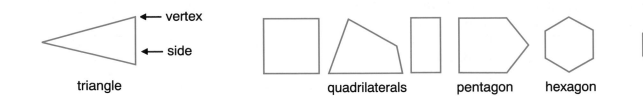

triangle   quadrilaterals   pentagon   hexagon   octagon

Write *true* or *false.*

1. A quadrilateral can be a rectangle, a square, or a figure with four sides that are not parallel.

2. The point where the sides meet is called the vertex.

3. A circle is a polygon.

4. All plane figures are polygons.

Write *yes* or *no* to tell whether the figure is a polygon. Give a reason for your answer.

5.

6.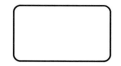

7.

8.

9.

10.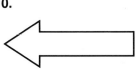

11.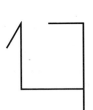

12.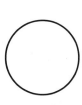

Name each figure.

13.

14.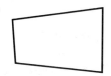

15.

16.

17. a polygon with four sides

18. a quadrilateral with four equal sides

CHAPTER 5

Exploring Division

WHBJ-TV produces 52 children's programs per season on their 3 soundstages. Each soundstage can handle about the same number of programs. How many programs are produced on each soundstage?

Divide: $52 \div 3 = n$ $\qquad 3\overline{)52}^{\,n}$

Building Understanding

Use place-value blocks to model the problem. Record the numbers as you complete each step.

Step 1
Draw 3 circles. Show 52 as 5 tens 2 ones.

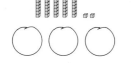

Record:

$3\overline{)52}$

Step 2
Place an equal number of tens into each circle.

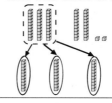

Record:
$$\begin{array}{r} 1 \\ 3\overline{)52} \\ -3 \\ \hline 2 \end{array}$$
← 1 ten in each group
← 3 tens used
← 2 tens left

Step 3
Regroup the 2 tens left over into ones.

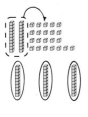

Record:
$$\begin{array}{r} 1 \\ 3\overline{)52} \\ -3\downarrow \\ \hline 22 \end{array}$$
← bring down ones

Step 4
Place an equal number of ones into each circle. Record the remainder.

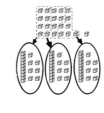

Record:
$$\begin{array}{r} 17 \ \ r1 \\ 3\overline{)52} \\ -3\downarrow \\ \hline 22 \\ -21 \\ \hline 1 \end{array}$$

So, 17 programs are produced on each of 2 soundstages and 18 programs are produced on 1 soundstage.

Talk About It

▸ In Step 2, why did you put only 1 ten in each circle?

▸ Why did you have to regroup the 2 leftover tens?

▸ Why must you bring down the ones before you can divide again?

▸ After Step 4, how many blocks are in each circle?

Practice

Use place-value blocks to model each problem. Then find the quotient.

1. $2\overline{)46}$
2. $3\overline{)48}$
3. $2\overline{)38}$
4. $3\overline{)42}$
5. $4\overline{)34}$

6. $4\overline{)57}$
7. $6\overline{)89}$
8. $8\overline{)29}$
9. $3\overline{)74}$
10. $5\overline{)73}$

Find the quotient.

11. $5\overline{)75}$
12. $2\overline{)52}$
13. $3\overline{)57}$
14. $4\overline{)72}$
15. $6\overline{)78}$

16. $2\overline{)59}$
17. $4\overline{)79}$
18. $7\overline{)66}$
19. $5\overline{)47}$
20. $3\overline{)32}$

21. $8\overline{)96}$
22. $3\overline{)87}$
23. $6\overline{)78}$
24. $4\overline{)39}$
25. $9\overline{)24}$

26. $7\overline{)96}$
27. $7\overline{)51}$
28. $2\overline{)93}$
29. $3\overline{)77}$
30. $6\overline{)43}$

31. $90 \div 7 = n$
32. $88 \div 5 = n$
33. $81 \div 4 = n$

34. $36 \div 7 = n$
35. $82 \div 3 = n$
36. $33 \div 8 = n$

37. $41 \div 5 = n$
38. $42 \div 4 = n$
39. $65 \div 3 = n$

40. $67 \div 2 = n$
41. $56 \div 5 = n$
42. $75 \div 8 = n$

43. $35 \div 2 = n$
44. $85 \div 7 = n$
45. $39 \div 8 = n$

Solve.

46. A science program showed a total of 21 experiments in 5 days. If on each day except one the program showed the same number of experiments, how many experiments were shown each day?

47. Gary videotaped 3 programs on a 90-minute tape. If each program was the same length, how long was each program?

48. In one episode of the television show, *Dandy Lions,* Dandy and his 2 friends are building a clubhouse. The materials will cost $54. If they share the cost equally, how much will each person pay?

49. In another episode, Dandy has to pack 68 books into boxes. Each box will hold 8 books. How many boxes will Dandy need to pack all the books?

CHAPTER 7

Collecting Data

Angela and Eric took a survey for a social studies project. They asked students to name their favorite restaurant at the Maple Mall. They used tally marks (/) to record the data and then made a frequency table. How can they find the total number of people who participated in the survey?

Restaurant	Tallies
Burger World	⊞ IIII
Taco-Ria	⊞ ⊞ III
Hot Dog Haven	⊞
Julie's Pizza	⊞ ⊞ ⊞
Sizzling Subs	⊞
Pasta Factory	III

Tally Table

Restaurant Choice	Number of Votes Frequency
Burger World	9
Taco-Ria	13
Hot Dog Haven	5
Julie's Pizza	15
Sizzling Subs	5
Pasta Factory	3

Frequency Table

A **frequency table** is a table that shows how often an item occurs.

You can add to find the total number of people surveyed.

$$9 + 13 + 5 + 15 + 5 + 3 = \boxed{50.}$$

So, 50 people were surveyed in all.

Talk About It

▸ What do you need to think about when you plan a survey?

▸ How many votes does each tally mark (/) represent?

▸ How was the data displayed for this project?

▸ How do you know what numbers to put in the frequency table?

Practice

Use the tally table for Exercises 1–5.

Favorite Fruit Juices

Juice	Tally
Orange	~~HHH~~ ~~HHH~~ I
Grape	III
Apple	~~HHH~~ ~~HHH~~ ~~HHH~~
Pineapple	~~HHH~~ II

1. Which juice is most popular?

2. Which juice is least popular?

3. How many people like apple or orange juice?

4. Change the tally table into a frequency table.

5. How many people participated in this survey?

Use the frequency table for Exercises 6–8.

Stan's Juice Stand	
Day	**Bottles Sold**
Monday	120
Tuesday	194
Wednesday	239
Thursday	248
Friday	219

6. On which day did Stan sell the most bottles of juice?

7. How many more bottles of juice did he sell on Thursday than on Wednesday?

8. How many bottles of juice did Stan sell in all?

Use the frequency table for Exercises 9–11.

9. On which days did Mona sell the same number of salads?

10. How many more salads did Mona sell on Friday than on Tuesday?

11. How many salads did Mona sell in all?

Mona's Health Salads	
Day	**Salads Sold**
Monday	56
Tuesday	38
Wednesday	70
Thursday	38
Friday	63

CHAPTER 9

Fractions in Simplest Form

$\frac{8}{24}$

8 out of 24

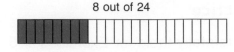

Chandra has 24 plants in her garden. Of these plants, 8 are tomato plants. What is the simplest form of a fraction that tells the part of Chandra's garden that is planted in tomato plants?

$\frac{4}{12}$

4 out of 12

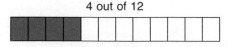

Look at the fraction bars. Find the fraction bar with the largest piece that is the same size as $\frac{8}{24}$. This shows the **simplest form** of the fraction.

$\frac{2}{6}$

2 out of 6

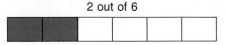

The $\frac{1}{3}$ piece of the fraction bar is the same size as $\frac{8}{24}$. So, $\frac{1}{3}$ is the simplest form of $\frac{8}{24}$.

$\frac{1}{3}$

1 out of 3

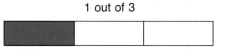

To **simplify** a fraction, divide the numerator and the denominator by the same number. This number is a **common factor.**

More Examples

A.

$\frac{3}{12} = \frac{1}{4}$

A common factor of 3 and 12 is 3.

B.

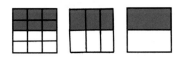

$\frac{6}{12} = \frac{3}{6} = \frac{1}{2}$

Both 2 and 3 are common factors of 6 and 12.

C.

$\frac{1}{13}$

The only common factor of 1 and 13 is 1. So, $\frac{1}{13}$ is in simplest form.

Talk About It

▶ How can you test whether a fraction is in its simplest form?

▶ Why does dividing both the numerator and the denominator by the same number not change the value of the fraction?

▶ What is the largest number you can use to divide the numerator and the denominator of $\frac{6}{12}$?

Practice

Complete.

1.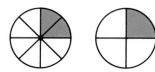

$$\frac{2}{8} = \frac{\blacksquare}{4}$$

2.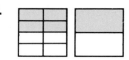

$$\frac{4}{8} = \frac{\blacksquare}{2}$$

3.

$$\frac{6}{8} = \frac{\blacksquare}{4}$$

4.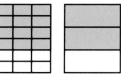

$$\frac{12}{\blacksquare} = \frac{\blacksquare}{3}$$

5.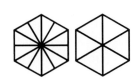

$$\frac{4}{16} = \frac{\blacksquare}{\blacksquare}$$

6.

$$\frac{\blacksquare}{\blacksquare} = \frac{\blacksquare}{\blacksquare}$$

7.

$$\frac{6}{16} = \frac{\blacksquare}{\blacksquare}$$

8.

$$\frac{10}{\blacksquare} = \frac{\blacksquare}{6}$$

9.

$$\frac{\blacksquare}{\blacksquare} = \frac{\blacksquare}{\blacksquare}$$

10. $\dfrac{6}{9} = \dfrac{6 \div 3}{9 \div 3} = \dfrac{\blacksquare}{\blacksquare}$

11. $\dfrac{12}{14} = \dfrac{12 \div 2}{14 \div 2} = \dfrac{\blacksquare}{\blacksquare}$

12. $\dfrac{4}{12} = \dfrac{4 \div 4}{12 \div 4} = \dfrac{\blacksquare}{\blacksquare}$

13. $\dfrac{9}{12} = \dfrac{9 \div 3}{12 \div 3} = \dfrac{\blacksquare}{\blacksquare}$

14. $\dfrac{6}{10} = \dfrac{6 \div 2}{10 \div 2} = \dfrac{\blacksquare}{\blacksquare}$

15. $\dfrac{15}{30} = \dfrac{15 \div 15}{30 \div 15} = \dfrac{\blacksquare}{\blacksquare}$

Write in simplest form.

16. $\dfrac{2}{4}$

17. $\dfrac{3}{9}$

18. $\dfrac{4}{12}$

19. $\dfrac{4}{16}$

20. $\dfrac{6}{12}$

21. $\dfrac{3}{15}$

22. $\dfrac{5}{10}$

23. $\dfrac{4}{6}$

24. $\dfrac{2}{6}$

25. $\dfrac{2}{16}$

26. $\dfrac{8}{18}$

27. $\dfrac{12}{36}$

28. $\dfrac{10}{24}$

29. $\dfrac{14}{16}$

30. $\dfrac{30}{60}$

Solve.

31. Helene works in her garden 2 hours every day. What is the simplest form of a fraction that tells the part of a day Helene works in her garden?

32. Robert is in school 6 hours each day. What is the simplest form of a fraction that tells the part of a day Robert is in school?

Metric Units

These pictures of animals will help you think about **metric** units for measuring length.

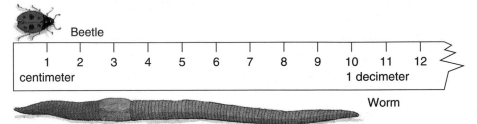

Beetle

1 centimeter 1 2 3 4 5 6 7 8 9 10 11 12

1 decimeter

Worm

- The beetle is about 1 centimeter long and the worm is about 1 decimeter long. What other living creatures are about 1 centimeter long? 1 decimeter long?

Here is a table of metric units.

A **centimeter** is about the width of your index finger.

| 1 cm |

Metric Units		
10 centimeters (cm)	=	1 decimeter (dm)
10 decimeters (dm)	=	1 meter (m)
100 centimeters (cm)	=	1 meter (m)
1,000 meters (m)	=	1 kilometer (km)

A **decimeter** is about the width of an adult's hand.

| 1 dm |

- Which unit is equal to 10 cm? 100 cm?

A meter is about the distance from one hand to the other when your arms are stretched out.

A kilometer is about how far you can walk in 15 minutes.

Talk About It

▶ If you and a partner stand side by side and measure your outstretched arms, about how far do your arms reach?

▶ If you walk around Palm Lake for 30 minutes, about how many kilometers will you walk?

Practice

Write the unit that is longer.

1. 1 cm or 1 dm
2. 1 km or 1 m
3. 1 dm or 1 m
4. 4 dm or 4 cm
5. 5 m or 5 cm
6. 700 dm or 700 km
7. 2 km or 2 m
8. 30 cm or 2 dm
9. 10 dm or 2 m

Use your index finger to measure each. Label in centimeters.

10. |————————|

11. |——————————|

12. |————————————————|

13. |——————————————————|

Name the longer unit.

14. 4 dm or 4 cm
15. 5 m or 5 cm
16. 700 dm or 700 km
17. 2 km or 2 m

Choose the appropriate unit for each. Write *cm, dm, m,* or *km.*

18. length of a ladybug
19. distance a car travels in 1 hour
20. width of a garage door
21. length of the classroom
22. distance you can walk in 40 minutes
23. height of a classroom wall
24. width of a table
25. height of a garbage can
26. length of a window
27. width of a sheet of paper
28. width of a book
29. length of a pencil
30. length of your index finger
31. length of a playground

Draw a line of each length.

32. 5 cm
33. 1 dm
34. 12 cm
35. 2 dm

Solve.

36. Corky says she has a bookmark that is 9 dm long. Is this reasonable? Explain.

37. Holly wants to tie a ribbon in her hair. Would she need 25 cm or 25 dm?

38. Patti walked 1 km on a hike. Then she walked 500 m farther to a new trail. Pam walked 2 km on a hike. Who walked farther? How many meters farther?

39. Mr. Cruz drove 57 km to Elk City and 72 km to St. Cloud. Estimate the total distance that he drove.

CHAPTER 11

Length in Customary Units

These pictures of things Ryan found in his desk will help you think about customary units for measuring length.

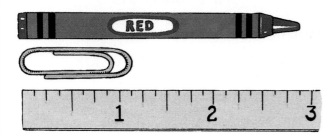

Talk About It

▶ About how long is the paper clip?

▶ About how long is the crayon?

Here is a table of customary units.

Customary Units	
12 inches (in.)	= 1 foot (ft.)
3 feet	= 1 yard (yd)
36 inches	= 1 yard
5,280 feet	= 1 mile (mi)
1,760 yards	= 1 mile

An **inch** is about the length of your thumb from the first knuckle to the tip.

1 in.

A **yard** is about the length of a baseball bat.

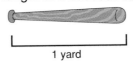

1 yard

A **foot** is about the length of a man's shoe.

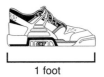

1 foot

A **mile** is about the distance you can walk in 20 minutes.

1 mile

Talk About It

▶ Which unit is most appropriate to measure the length of a football field? the length of a pencil?

▶ Which part of your hand can you use to help you estimate 10 in.?

▶ How many baseball bats laid end to end measure about 12 yds?

Practice

Write the unit that is longer.

1. 2 yd or 2 ft

2. 72 in. or 72 ft

3. 1 yd or 1 mi

4. 5,000 mi or 5,000 ft

5. 10 yd or 10 ft

6. 33 ft or 33 in.

Choose the appropriate unit. Write *in., ft, yd,* or *mi.*

7. The distance from the floor to the chalkboard is about 3 __?__ .

8. Mrs. McBee bought 4 __?__ of fabric to make a dress.

9. The length of a fishing pole is about 5 __?__ .

10. A football player rushed for 10 __?__ in the last game.

11. The height of a skyscraper is about 1,000 __?__ .

12. The distance from home to the supermarket is about 3 __?__ .

13. The length of a table is about 8 __?__ .

14. The height of a dog is about 24 __?__ .

15. The length of a bus is about 20 __?__ .

16. The width of a piece of notebook paper is about 9 __?__ .

17. The width of a toy boat is 5 __?__ .

18. The height of a desk is 25 __?__ .

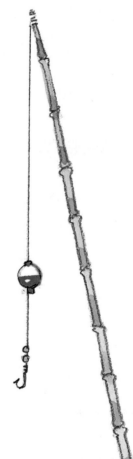

Draw a line of each length.

19. 4 in.

20. 7 in.

21. 10 in.

Solve.

22. Nathan rides his bike 5,000 ft to school. Teri rides 1 mi to school. Who rides the greater distance?

23. Bonnie's room is 4 yd long. Carol's room is 11 ft long. Whose room is longer?

24. Nan's desk measures 38 in. long. Jennifer's desk measures 3 ft in length. Who has the longer desk?

25. John walks 1 mi to school every day. Gary walks 2,000 yards. Who has the longer walk to school?

CHAPTER 12

Connecting Geometry and Measurement

Geometric figures can be one-dimensional, two-dimensional, or three-dimensional. Sort the figures in the picture by drawing them on a table.

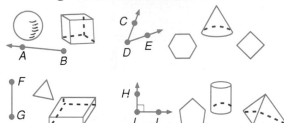

One-Dimensional	Two-Dimensional	Three-Dimensional

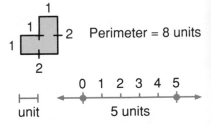

Perimeter = 8 units

- A line segment is one-dimensional. You can use a *unit* to measure the perimeter of a figure.

- A polygon is two-dimensional. You can use a *square unit* to measure the area of a polygon.

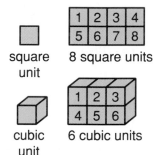

square unit   8 square units

cubic unit   6 cubic units

- A solid figure is three-dimensional. You can use a *cubic unit* to measure the volume of a three-dimensional figure.

What three dimensions do you use to find the volume of a rectangular prism?

_____

Use 18 connecting cubes. Make as many different-shaped prisms as you can. In a table, record the results.

Measuring Volume			
Length	Width	Height	Volume
9	2	1	18 cubic units

Talk About It

▶ What is the volume of each model you made?

▶ If the length of one model is 18 units, what are the other two measurements?

▶ How can you use multiplication to find the volume of a prism?

▶ If a prism is 2 units in length, 6 units in width, and 4 units in height, what is the volume?

Practice

Find the volume. Use connecting cubes to help you.

1.

2.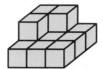

3.

4.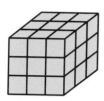

5.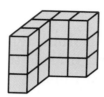

6.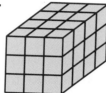

Write a multiplication sentence to find the volume of each.

7.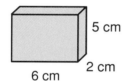
5 cm
2 cm
6 cm

8.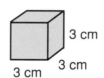
3 cm
3 cm
3 cm

9.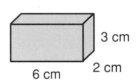
3 cm
2 cm
6 cm

10.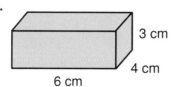
3 cm
4 cm
6 cm

11.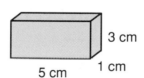
3 cm
1 cm
5 cm

12.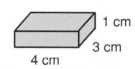
1 cm
3 cm
4 cm

Complete this table for rectangular prisms.

	Length	Width	Height	Volume
13.	2 cm	3 cm	1 cm	
14.	5 cm	3 cm	2 cm	
15.	3 cm	2 cm		18 cubic cm
16.	4 cm		1 cm	8 cubic cm
17.		4 cm	3 cm	60 cubic cm

CHAPTER 1

Place Value: Whole Numbers and Decimals

Project: Plan a Meal

Use a grocery store receipt with a total of at least $15.00. Circle at least three items that total about $5.00. Record your choices. Use a calculator. Compare your estimate to the actual cost of the items.

Now Try This

Create a breakfast, lunch, or dinner menu from items on your grocery store receipt. Plan a meal with foods that cost about $5.00 by estimating the cost of each item.

Example

eggs	$0.89
milk	$1.79
cheese	$1.89
bread	$0.99
juice	$0.89
napkins	$2.19
meat	$2.49

Breakfast

eggs → $1.00
bread → $1.00
juice → $1.00
meat → $2.00

CHAPTER 2

Adding and Subtracting Whole Numbers and Decimals

Application: Comparing Field Dimensions

Modern field hockey is played on a field that is 100 yards long by 55 yards wide.

A football field is 120 yards long by 53.3 yards wide.

How much longer is a football field than a hockey field?

$120 - 100 = 20$
It is 20 yards longer.

How much wider is a football field than a hockey field?

$55 - 53.3 = 1.7$
It is 1.7 yards wider.

Now Try This

Find the length and width of a soccer field. Compare these dimensions to those of football and hockey fields.

CHAPTER 3

Multiplying Whole Numbers

Application: Using a Lattice to Multiply

You can use a lattice to multiply two numbers.
Follow these steps to multiply 531×274.

1. Write 531 along the top of the lattice, and 274 down the right side.

2. For each small box, multiply the number at the top of its column by the number at the right of its row. Write one digit of the product in each half of the box.

3. Add along the diagonals. Start in the lower right corner. Regroup to the next diagonal. Write the sums along the edges of the lattice.

4. Read the product, moving down the left side and across the bottom.

Now Try This

Use lattice multiplication to find these products.

1. 421×265 **2.** 205×156 **3.** 951×607 **4.** 123×456

. . . .

CHAPTER 4

Geometry

Project: Design a Moon House

Architecture is the art of designing buildings. An architect uses geometric ideas and shapes to design and create structures.

Now Try This

Design a house you might build on the moon. Use a combination of solid shapes and the geometric ideas of congruence and symmetry. Make a model of your moon house.

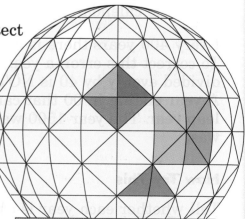

CHAPTER 9

Number Theory and Fractions

Project: Sketch a Garden Plan

Gardening is a popular hobby. You can gather information about gardening from books, seed catalogs, plant dealers, or your county agricultural extension agent. Some gardeners sketch a plan before they select or plant seeds. This sketch shows that $\frac{3}{8}$ of the garden will be planted with leaf lettuce, $\frac{1}{8}$ with tomatoes, $\frac{1}{8}$ with spinach, $\frac{2}{8}$, or $\frac{1}{4}$, with carrots, and $\frac{1}{8}$ with snap beans.

Now Try This

Sketch a garden plan. Determine what fraction of your garden you want to plant with each type of seed you select. You may wish to plant the garden.

leaf lettuce	
leaf lettuce	
tomatoes	
spinach	
leaf lettuce	
carrots	
carrots	
snap beans	

CHAPTER 10

Using Fractions

Project: Design a Costume

Madame Barbara Karinska designed and made the costumes for a New York City Ballet production of *The Nutcracker*. *The Nutcracker* is the story of a nutcracker that comes to life during the winter holiday season. This is one costume design for the character of the Nutcracker.

Now Try This

Sketch your own costume design for the Nutcracker. Suppose your design requires $2\frac{1}{2}$ yards of fabric. Find the number of yards of fabric you would need to make 4 identical costumes.

CHAPTER 11

Measurement

Project: Make a Weighing Device

One nickel weighs about 5 grams. You can use nickels, cardboard, paper clips, a paper fastener, a paper punch, glue, scissors, a marker, and a heavy object like a washer or a rock to make a weighing device.

Large versions of these three pieces can be found in *Learning Resources*, page H101. Use carbon paper to trace them onto cardboard. Cut out the pieces and punch out the holes as shown. Cut out a 2-cm by 2-cm square of cardboard. Glue the square between B and C. Attach B and C on either side of A with a paper fastener. Put the fastener through the holes marked X.

Use a paper clip to fasten a heavy object to A at the hole marked Y. Use a paper clip at the hole marked Z to hold things you want to weigh. You may want to attach a plastic cup to the paper clip.

To mark your device, first mark the position when nothing is hanging from the paper clip. Then hang from 1–10 nickels and mark where the arrow points for 5 to 50 grams. You can use a set of standard weights to mark your device if it is available.

Now Try This

Estimate the weight of an object. Then weigh it on your weighing device.

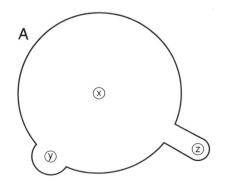
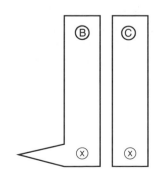

CHAPTER I

Lesson 1.1 *(pages 2–3)*

Complete.

1. $10 \times 10 = $ ◼

2. 10 ◼ $= 1,000$

3. $10^5 = $ ◼

	Number Name	Number	Multiplication	Power of Ten
4.	◼	10	10×1	10^1
5.	hundred	100	◼	10^2
6.	thousand	1,000	$10 \times 10 \times 10$	◼
7.	ten thousand	◼	$10 \times 10 \times 10 \times 10$	10^4
8.	◼	100,000	◼	10^5

Lesson 1.2 *(pages 4–5)*

Write two other forms for each number.

1. $800,000 + 3,000 + 60 + 5$ **2.** six thousand, thirty   **3.** 50,312

Write the value of each underlined digit.

4. $\underline{3}1,254$ **5.** $\underline{2}19,005$ **6.** $67,\underline{4}91$ **7.** $429,2\underline{9}3$

Lesson 1.3 *(pages 6–7)*

Write the value of each underlined digit.

1. $\underline{2},756,489$ **2.** $7,0\underline{6}3,495$ **3.** $1\underline{8},487,003$ **4.** $\underline{3}96,652,105$

Lesson 1.4 *(pages 8–9)*

Write $<$, $>$, or $=$ for ●.

1. 2,967 ● 2,769   **2.** 84,817 ● 84,987   **3.** 4,298,178 ● 4,298,178

4. 14,670 ● 13,760   **5.** 423,470 ● 424,370   **6.** 7,425,367 ● 7,425,367

Order from least to greatest.

7. 4,298; 4,098; 3,980   **8.** 29,600; 27,860; 29,060   **9.** 630,030; 603,300; 630,300

Lesson 1.5 *(pages 10–11)*

Round to the nearest ten.

1. 643 **2.** 789 **3.** 399 **4.** 884 **5.** 2,121

Round to the nearest hundred.

6. 574 **7.** 316 **8.** 974 **9.** 6,498 **10.** 1,951

Round to the nearest thousand.

11. 4,289 **12.** 7,030 **13.** 9,800 **14.** 8,154 **15.** 18,550

Round to the nearest ten thousand.

16. 47,260 **17.** 69,982 **18.** 364,531 **19.** 745,715

Round to the nearest hundred thousand.

20. 582,263 **21.** 787,060 **22.** 549,200 **23.** 675,800

24. 463,975 **25.** 723,842 **26.** 976,590 **27.** 14,672,400

Round to the nearest million.

28. 8,781,200 **29.** 10,821,700 **30.** 92,989,432

31. 82,398,114 **32.** 15,786,456 **33.** 672,899,243

Lesson 1.6 *(pages 12–13)*

Make a table and answer the questions.

In a recycling contest, Mrs. Reed's class collected 99 cans the first week, 80 cans the second week, and 118 cans the third week. Mr. Mason's class collected 207 cans the first week, 170 cans the second week, and 244 cans the third week. Mrs. Jenner's class collected 197 cans the first week, 95 cans the second week, and 102 cans the third week.

1. Which class collected the most cans the first week? the second week?

2. How many more cans did Mr. Mason's class collect than Mrs. Reed's class?

3. How many more cans did Mr. Mason's class collect than Mrs. Jenner's class?

4. How many cans were collected in all?

CHAPTER 2

Lesson 2.1 *(pages 38–39)*

Write a missing-addend sentence for each.

1. $63 - 15 = \blacksquare$ **2.** $31 - 19 = \blacksquare$ **3.** $72 - 59 = \blacksquare$ **4.** $123 - 48 = \blacksquare$

Write the inverse operation sentence for each. Solve.

5. $16 + \blacksquare = 93$ **6.** $112 + \blacksquare = 139$ **7.** $\blacksquare + 13 = 27$ **8.** $109 = 45 + \blacksquare$

Lesson 2.2 *(pages 40–41)*

Estimate each sum. Tell which method you used.

1. 58	**2.** 32	**3.** 510	**4.** 326	**5.** 7,019
+17	+41	+293	+569	+ 895

6. 43	**7.** 75	**8.** 207	**9.** 362	**10.** 1,293
78	12	629	517	6,742
61	93	341	721	2,140
+34	+34	+537	+542	+3,291

Lesson 2.3 *(pages 42–43)*

Estimate the sum. If the estimated sum is greater than 10,000, find the sum.

1. 634	**2.** 207	**3.** 6,407	**4.** 34,413
+329	+ 84	+2,317	+14,793

5. 34,507	**6.** 47,598	**7.** 82,730	**8.** 60,320
+16,894	+61,423	+ 5,896	+29,798

Complete the table.

Number Sentence	Estimate		Sum	
$6,212 + 5,324 = \blacksquare$	**9.**	$\blacksquare$	**10.**	$\blacksquare$
$3,104 + 828 = \blacksquare$	**11.**	$\blacksquare$	**12.**	$\blacksquare$
$1,212 + 10,462 = \blacksquare$	**13.**	$\blacksquare$	**14.**	$\blacksquare$
$16,412 + 3,892 = \blacksquare$	**15.**	$\blacksquare$	**16.**	$\blacksquare$
$12,142 + 30,912 = \blacksquare$	**17.**	$\blacksquare$	**18.**	$\blacksquare$

Lesson 2.4 (pages 44–45)

Write a number sentence and solve.

1. At basketball practice Manuel made 21 baskets, Nathan made 19 baskets, and Lucas made 8 more than Nathan. How many baskets did the three boys make?

2. Kaitlin bought 2 pairs of soccer shoes that cost $42 a pair. The store ran a special, $21 off the price of a second pair of shoes. How much did Kaitlin pay for both pairs of shoes?

Lesson 2.5 (pages 46–47)

Estimate the difference.

1. 525
   −214

2. 829
   −416

3. 920
   −186

4. 791
   − 57

5. 3,512
   − 219

6. 4,692
   −1,921

7. 38,192
   −17,893

8. 16,412
   − 9,843

Lesson 2.6 (pages 48–49)

Complete the table.

Number Sentence	Estimate		Difference	
36,129 − 13,208 = n	1.	▮	2.	▮
82,929 − 40,127 = n	3.	▮	4.	▮
47,291 − 19,260 = n	5.	▮	6.	▮
76,928 − 23,619 = n	7.	▮	8.	▮

Lesson 2.7 (pages 50–51)

Find the difference.

1. 700
   −264

2. 1,007
   − 698

3. 30,000
   −18,534

4. 60,009
   −53,874

5. 4,500
   − 692

6. 3,007
   −1,689

7. 400
   −265

8. 940
   −679

9. 8,400
   − 625

10. 12,001
    − 436

11. 60,002
    −25,913

12. 73,004
    −39,425

CHAPTER 3

Chapter 3.1 (pages 76–77)

Solve. Identify the property used.

1. $4,298 \times \blacksquare = 0$
2. $123 \times 1 = \blacksquare$
3. $7 \times 42 = \blacksquare \times 7$
4. $(3 \times \blacksquare) \times 40 = 3 \times (6 \times 40)$
5. $9 \times 16 = \blacksquare \times 9$
6. $(12 \times 2) \times \blacksquare = 12 \times (2 \times 30)$

Solve.

7. $3,924 \times 0 = \blacksquare$
8. $1,118 \times \blacksquare = 3 \times 1,118$
9. $1,294 \times \blacksquare = 1,294$
10. $(3 \times 4) \times 10 = 3 \times (\blacksquare \times 10)$
11. $74 \times 23 = \blacksquare \times 74$
12. $495 \times \blacksquare = 0$

Lesson 3.2 (pages 78–79)

Use mental math to find the product.

1. $\begin{array}{r} 30 \\ \times\ 4 \\ \hline \end{array}$
2. $\begin{array}{r} 500 \\ \times\ 8 \\ \hline \end{array}$
3. $\begin{array}{r} 600 \\ \times\ 2 \\ \hline \end{array}$
4. $\begin{array}{r} 2,000 \\ \times\ 9 \\ \hline \end{array}$
5. $\begin{array}{r} 8,000 \\ \times\ 3 \\ \hline \end{array}$

6. $\begin{array}{r} 7,000 \\ \times\ 7 \\ \hline \end{array}$
7. $\begin{array}{r} 9,000 \\ \times\ 6 \\ \hline \end{array}$
8. $\begin{array}{r} 600 \\ \times\ 5 \\ \hline \end{array}$
9. $\begin{array}{r} 1,000 \\ \times\ 8 \\ \hline \end{array}$
10. $\begin{array}{r} 10,000 \\ \times\ 9 \\ \hline \end{array}$

Complete each number sentence by using mental math.

11. $500 \times 4 = n$
12. $300 \times 7 = n$
13. $n \times 60 = 360$
14. $3 \times n = 2,700$
15. $8 \times n = 5,600$
16. $900 \times n = 8,100$

Multiply each number by 10, 100, and 1,000.

17. 3
18. 6
19. 8
20. 10

Lesson 3.3 (pages 80–81)

Estimate each product. Tell which method you used.

1. $\begin{array}{r} 46 \\ \times\ 5 \\ \hline \end{array}$
2. $\begin{array}{r} 82 \\ \times\ 4 \\ \hline \end{array}$
3. $\begin{array}{r} 192 \\ \times\ 6 \\ \hline \end{array}$
4. $\begin{array}{r} 599 \\ \times\ 2 \\ \hline \end{array}$

5. $\begin{array}{r} 2,921 \\ \times\ 3 \\ \hline \end{array}$
6. $\begin{array}{r} 1,134 \\ \times\ 6 \\ \hline \end{array}$
7. $\begin{array}{r} 12,921 \\ \times\ 3 \\ \hline \end{array}$
8. $\begin{array}{r} 17,547 \\ \times\ 9 \\ \hline \end{array}$

Lesson 3.4 *(pages 82–83)*

Complete. Find each product.

1. Find 6×34.
   $6 \times 30 = n$
   $6 \times 4 = n$
   Add.
   $180 + 24 = n$
   $6 \times 34 = n$

2. Find 4×62.
   $4 \times 60 = n$
   $4 \times 2 = n$
   Add.
   $240 + 8 = n$
   $4 \times 62 = n$

3. Find 8×29.
   $8 \times 20 = n$
   $8 \times 9 = n$
   Add.
   $160 + 72 = n$
   $8 \times 29 = n$

Lesson 3.5 *(pages 84–85)*

Solve. Use counters to model each regrouping.

1. $5 \times 23 = n$

2. $9 \times 37 = n$

3. $3 \times 56 = n$

4. $4 \times 83 = n$

5. $7 \times 29 = n$

6. $5 \times 43 = n$

7. $6 \times 48 = n$

8. $8 \times 92 = n$

9. $7 \times 68 = n$

Estimate each product by rounding. If the estimate is greater than 1,000, find the product.

10. 42×5

11. 87×3

12. 294×6

13. 819×2

14. 119×4

15. $1{,}123 \times 7$

16. $3{,}175 \times 3$

17. $6{,}543 \times 5$

18. 593×2

19. $2{,}403 \times 6$

Lesson 3.6 *(pages 86–87)*

Solve.

1. Mrs. Lee ordered 15 copies of *Introduction to the Microscope* at $8 each. She bought 23 pamphlets about starfish at $4 each. How much money did she spend on books and pamphlets?

2. Felipe bought 2 sets of microscope slides at $22 per set and a lab manual for $8. He paid for his purchases with two $50 bills. How much change did he receive?

3. Elliot bought 4 toy trucks at $2 each and 3 action figures at $3 each. How much money did he have left if he started with $25?

4. Danielle had $45. She bought 2 compact discs at $14 each and a calculator at $12. How much money did she have left after her purchases?

Lesson 3.7 *(pages 90–91)*

Use mental math to find the product.

$$
\begin{array}{cccccccccc}
\textbf{1.} & 40 & \textbf{2.} & 30 & \textbf{3.} & 200 & \textbf{4.} & 600 & \textbf{5.} & 500 \\
& \times 20 & & \times 30 & & \times\ 60 & & \times\ 30 & & \times\ 10 \\
\end{array}
$$

$$
\begin{array}{cccccccccc}
\textbf{6.} & 700 & \textbf{7.} & 1{,}000 & \textbf{8.} & 900 & \textbf{9.} & 4{,}000 & \textbf{10.} & 8{,}000 \\
& \times\ 50 & & \times\ \ \ 20 & & \times\ \ 10 & & \times\ \ \ 40 & & \times\ \ \ 90 \\
\end{array}
$$

11. $5{,}000 \times 60 = n$ **12.** $80 \times 70 = n$ **13.** $700 \times 30 = n$

14. $7{,}000 \times 40 = n$ **15.** $3{,}000 \times 60 = n$ **16.** $50{,}000 \times 60 = n$

Lesson 3.8 *(pages 92–93)*

Estimate the product.

$$
\begin{array}{cccccccccc}
\textbf{1.} & 59 & \textbf{2.} & 32 & \textbf{3.} & 68 & \textbf{4.} & 47 & \textbf{5.} & 55 \\
& \times 24 & & \times 61 & & \times 17 & & \times 86 & & \times 62 \\
\end{array}
$$

$$
\begin{array}{cccccccccc}
\textbf{6.} & 76 & \textbf{7.} & 493 & \textbf{8.} & 738 & \textbf{9.} & 949 & \textbf{10.} & 563 \\
& \times 34 & & \times\ 17 & & \times\ 25 & & \times\ 94 & & \times\ 81 \\
\end{array}
$$

11. $79 \times 293 \approx n$ **12.** $32 \times 687 \approx n$ **13.** $16 \times 827 \approx n$

14. $56 \times 473 \approx n$ **15.** $23 \times 842 \approx n$ **16.** $14 \times 921 \approx n$

Lesson 3.9 *(pages 94–95)*

Find the product.

$$
\begin{array}{cccccccccc}
\textbf{1.} & 18 & \textbf{2.} & 48 & \textbf{3.} & 29 & \textbf{4.} & 192 & \textbf{5.} & 438 \\
& \times 33 & & \times 17 & & \times 43 & & \times\ 14 & & \times\ 16 \\
\end{array}
$$

$$
\begin{array}{cccccccccc}
\textbf{6.} & 509 & \textbf{7.} & 224 & \textbf{8.} & 250 & \textbf{9.} & 619 & \textbf{10.} & 423 \\
& \times\ 15 & & \times\ 17 & & \times\ 54 & & \times\ 92 & & \times\ 75 \\
\end{array}
$$

11. $64 \times 17 = n$ **12.** $43 \times 291 = n$ **13.** $13 \times 964 = n$

14. $32 \times 456 = n$ **15.** $67 \times 949 = n$ **16.** $43 \times 608 = n$

17. $83 \times 127 = n$ **18.** $45 \times 350 = n$ **19.** $95 \times 435 = n$

Lesson 3.10 *(pages 96–97)*

Estimate the product.

1. 421 ×192	**2.** 294 ×623	**3.** 609 ×302	**4.** 521 ×347	**5.** 732 ×121
6. 1,293 × 550	**7.** 6,529 × 143	**8.** 927 ×314	**9.** 4,293 × 617	**10.** 2,654 × 692

Find the product.

11. 320 ×403	**12.** 780 ×680	**13.** 348 ×627	**14.** 647 ×432	**15.** 427 ×806
16. 5,423 × 143	**17.** 8,234 × 203	**18.** 9,615 × 981	**19.** 4,530 × 705	**20.** 2,746 × 825
21. 8,743 × 403	**22.** 5,090 × 672	**23.** 4,302 × 430	**24.** 3,487 × 226	**25.** 6,821 × 376

Lesson 3.11 *(pages 98–99)*

Solve.

1. A custodian at the zoo cleaned the bird cages on August 4, 7, and 10. He cleaned the monkey cages on August 11, 15, and 19. If the custodian continues the same cleaning pattern, what is the next date he will clean the bird cages? What is the next date he will clean the monkey cages?

2. An animal trainer was teaching a monkey to catch a ball. When he stood 3 feet from the monkey, the monkey caught 6 of 8 balls. When he stood 4 feet from the monkey, the monkey caught 5 of 8 balls. At 5 feet the monkey caught every other ball. If the pattern continues, how many balls will the monkey catch at a distance of 8 feet?

3. The snakes were fed on July 1, 9, and 17. The tigers were fed on July 7, 9, and 11. If the same pattern of feeding continues, what is the next date the snakes will be fed? What is the next date the tigers will be fed?

4. The zoo closes early every third day so the trainers can exercise the animals. If it closes early on Monday, on what other day of the week will it close early?

CHAPTER 4

Lesson 4.1 *(pages 108–110)*

Choose the sentence or sentences that describe the relationship of the lines. Write **a, b,** or **c.**

1.

a. $\overleftrightarrow{FG}$ is parallel to $\overleftrightarrow{HI}$.

b. $\overleftrightarrow{FG}$ is perpendicular to $\overleftrightarrow{HI}$.

c. $\overleftrightarrow{FG}$ intersects $\overleftrightarrow{HI}$.

2.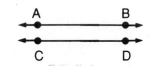

a. $\overleftrightarrow{AB}$ is not parallel to $\overleftrightarrow{CD}$.

b. $\overline{AB}$ intersects $\overline{CD}$.

c. $\overleftrightarrow{AB}$ is parallel to $\overleftrightarrow{CD}$.

3.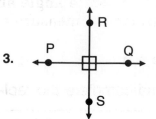

a. $\overleftrightarrow{PQ}$ is parallel to $\overleftrightarrow{RS}$.

b. $\overleftrightarrow{PQ}$ is perpendicular to $\overleftrightarrow{RS}$.

c. $\overleftrightarrow{PQ}$ intersects $\overleftrightarrow{RS}$.

Lesson 4.2 *(pages 112–113)*

Identify the angle. Write *right*, *acute*, or *obtuse*.

1.

2.

3.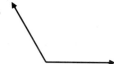

Use the figure for Exercises 4–6.

4. Name two acute angles.   **5.** Name an obtuse angle.

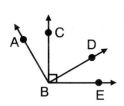

6. Name a right angle.

Lesson 4.3 *(pages 114–115)*

Trace each angle. First, estimate the angle measure. Then, use a protractor to measure each angle. You may need to extend the rays.

1.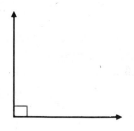

2.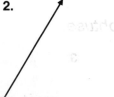

3.

Use a protractor to solve.

4. Use a protractor to draw an angle of 70°.

5. Draw an acute angle and an obtuse angle. Use a protractor to measure each angle. Record the measures.

Lesson 4.4 *(pages 116–117)*

Copy and complete the table.

Polygons		
Name of Polygon	**Number of Sides**	**Number of Angles**
Rectangle	1. ▨	2. ▨
Quadrilateral	3. ▨	4. ▨
Pentagon	5. ▨	6. ▨
Octagon	7. ▨	8. ▨

Write *true* or *false*.

9. A sixagon has six angles and six sides.

10. A pentagon has five angles and five sides.

11. All polygons are quadrilaterals.

12. All quadrilaterals are polygons.

Lesson 4.5 *(pages 118–119)*

Identify the triangle. Write *equilateral*, *isosceles*, or *scalene*.

1.

2.

3.
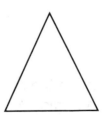

4.

Lesson 4.6 *(pages 120–121)*

Name each triangle. Write *right*, *acute*, or *obtuse*.

1.
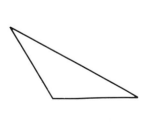

2.

3.

4.
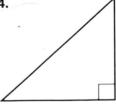

CHAPTER 6

Lesson 6.1 (pages 180–181)

Find the quotient.

1. $40 \div 20 = n$
2. $100 \div 10 = n$
3. $320 \div 40 = n$
4. $480 \div 60 = n$
5. $2,700 \div 90 = n$
6. $25,000 \div 50 = n$

7. $20\overline{)20}$
8. $10\overline{)70}$
9. $7\overline{)70}$
10. $30\overline{)600}$

11. $20\overline{)400}$
12. $30\overline{)180}$
13. $70\overline{)420}$
14. $90\overline{)810}$

15. $60\overline{)3,600}$
16. $20\overline{)8,000}$
17. $50\overline{)3,500}$
18. $30\overline{)30,000}$

Lesson 6.2 (pages 182–183)

Write two pairs of compatible numbers for each. Give two possible estimates.

1. $214 \div 35 \approx n$
2. $490 \div 77 \approx n$
3. $176 \div 27 \approx n$
4. $353 \div 57 \approx n$
5. $1,192 \div 28 \approx n$
6. $4,192 \div 77 \approx n$

Estimate the quotient.

7. $18\overline{)203}$
8. $23\overline{)217}$
9. $42\overline{)827}$
10. $46\overline{)519}$

11. $29\overline{)192}$
12. $37\overline{)856}$
13. $82\overline{)396}$
14. $11\overline{)743}$

15. $46\overline{)483}$
16. $92\overline{)789}$
17. $34\overline{)265}$
18. $21\overline{)189}$

Lesson 6.3 (pages 184–185)

Divide. Check with multiplication.

1. $15\overline{)46}$
2. $41\overline{)57}$
3. $21\overline{)93}$
4. $16\overline{)37}$

5. $32\overline{)82}$
6. $22\overline{)74}$
7. $19\overline{)49}$
8. $23\overline{)97}$

9. $80 \div 14 = n$
10. $54 \div 23 = n$
11. $76 \div 12 = n$

12. $75 \div 17 = n$
13. $64 \div 13 = n$
14. $98 \div 16 = n$

15. $87 \div 14 = n$
16. $74 \div 12 = n$
17. $95 \div 15 = n$

Lesson 6.4 *(pages 186–187)*

Choose the correct estimate to use in the quotient. Write **a** or **b**.

1. $16\overline{)298}$ **a.** 20   **b.** 10   6. $23\overline{)610}$ **a.** 30   **b.** 40

2. $48\overline{)176}$ **a.** 2   **b.** 3   7. $82\overline{)318}$ **a.** 5   **b.** 4

3. $35\overline{)314}$ **a.** 8   **b.** 7   8. $71\overline{)349}$ **a.** 4   **b.** 5

4. $23\overline{)160}$ **a.** 6   **b.** 7   9. $52\overline{)411}$ **a.** 8   **b.** 9

5. $41\overline{)290}$ **a.** 7   **b.** 6   10. $59\overline{)477}$ **a.** 7   **b.** 8

Divide.

11. $11\overline{)63}$ 12. $14\overline{)76}$ 13. $23\overline{)60}$ 14. $52\overline{)482}$

15. $74\overline{)449}$ 16. $34\overline{)256}$ 17. $79\overline{)239}$ 18. $84\overline{)342}$

Lesson 6.5 *(pages 188–189)*

Estimate. Then find the quotient.

1. $42\overline{)938}$ 2. $52\overline{)851}$ 3. $16\overline{)763}$ 4. $38\overline{)892}$

Find the quotient.

5. $78\overline{)957}$ 6. $40\overline{)873}$ 7. $39\overline{)897}$ 8. $17\overline{)357}$

9. $21\overline{)532}$ 10. $56\overline{)712}$ 11. $28\overline{)576}$ 12. $63\overline{)748}$

13. $30\overline{)938}$ 14. $48\overline{)495}$ 15. $54\overline{)973}$ 16. $78\overline{)712}$

17. $939 \div 44 = n$ 18. $589 \div 28 = n$ 19. $267 \div 34 = n$

Lesson 6.6 *(pages 190–191)*

Tell whether an exact answer is needed. Solve.

1. A teacher ordered a kit for $57.60, microscope slides for $5.12, and a microscope for $298.97. She had $375.00 to spend. Did she have enough money? How much did she spend?

2. About four students can work at each science center. Estimate how many centers are needed if there are 38 students in the Science Club.

Lesson 6.7 (pages 194–195)

Choose the correct answer. Write **a, b,** or **c.**

1. $15\overline{)2{,}453}$ a. 153   b. 163 r8   c. 162 r8

2. $17\overline{)1{,}263}$ a. 74 r5   b. 64 r5   c. 75

3. $32\overline{)7{,}808}$ a. 245   b. 244   c. 246

4. $43\overline{)1{,}384}$ a. 33   b. 31   c. 32 r8

5. $33\overline{)5{,}697}$ a. 173   b. 172 r21   c. 173 r27

6. $27\overline{)8{,}954}$ a. 331   b. 332   c. 331 r17

Estimate. Then find the quotient.

7. $58\overline{)4{,}128}$ 8. $24\overline{)1{,}968}$ 9. $50\overline{)3{,}361}$ 10. $62\overline{)5{,}420}$

11. $22\overline{)1{,}631}$ 12. $21\overline{)1{,}327}$ 13. $31\overline{)1{,}742}$ 14. $47\overline{)3{,}359}$

Divide.

15. $82{,}736 \div 38 = n$ 16. $15{,}398 \div 93 = n$ 17. $59{,}099 \div 64 = n$

18. $67{,}032 \div 39 = n$ 19. $19{,}047 \div 85 = n$ 20. $63{,}019 \div 54 = n$

21. $72{,}097 \div 45 = n$ 22. $13{,}946 \div 78 = n$ 23. $58{,}215 \div 93 = n$

Lesson 6.8 (pages 196–197)

Divide.

1. $20\overline{)400}$ 2. $14\overline{)420}$ 3. $17\overline{)685}$ 4. $19\overline{)2{,}098}$

5. $18\overline{)3{,}080}$ 6. $13\overline{)6{,}552}$ 7. $18\overline{)5{,}526}$ 8. $13\overline{)7{,}838}$

9. $3{,}131 \div 31 = n$ 10. $5{,}382 \div 26 = n$ 11. $3{,}888 \div 36 = n$

12. $13{,}150 \div 36 = n$ 13. $23{,}410 \div 57 = n$ 14. $37{,}050 \div 61 = n$

15. $14{,}649 \div 47 = n$ 16. $56{,}094 \div 34 = n$ 17. $48{,}201 \div 93 = n$

18. $19{,}040 \div 42 = n$ 19. $89{,}405 \div 31 = n$ 20. $53{,}200 \div 62 = n$

21. $12{,}090 \div 22 = n$ 22. $56{,}002 \div 91 = n$ 23. $18{,}004 \div 19 = n$

Find the quotient.

24. $34{,}921 \div 18 = n$ **25.** $27{,}090 \div 36 = n$ **26.** $50{,}325 \div 74 = n$

27. $40{,}029 \div 29 = n$ **28.** $60{,}387 \div 92 = n$ **29.** $89{,}048 \div 53 = n$

30. $30{,}847 \div 48 = n$ **31.** $59{,}048 \div 57 = n$ **32.** $47{,}408 \div 81 = n$

33. $49{,}028 \div 63 = n$ **34.** $71{,}049 \div 41 = n$ **35.** $40{,}913 \div 66 = n$

Lesson 6.9 *(pages 198–199)*

Use a calculator to divide. Then find the remainder.

1. $17 \overline{)48{,}192}$ **2.** $81 \overline{)62{,}109}$ **3.** $15 \overline{)75{,}623}$ **4.** $43 \overline{)29{,}815}$

5. $43 \overline{)30{,}628}$ **6.** $29 \overline{)62{,}517}$ **7.** $91 \overline{)43{,}218}$ **8.** $21 \overline{)64{,}582}$

9. $14{,}261 \div 14 = n$ **10.** $79{,}216 \div 58 = n$ **11.** $46{,}987 \div 39 = n$

12. $36{,}257 \div 17 = n$ **13.** $37{,}842 \div 36 = n$ **14.** $48{,}634 \div 56 = n$

15. $53{,}845 \div 52 = n$ **16.** $42{,}946 \div 63 = n$ **17.** $98{,}024 \div 43 = n$

18. $66{,}029 \div 14 = n$ **19.** $77{,}215 \div 79 = n$ **20.** $88{,}358 \div 51 = n$

21. $41{,}806 \div 25 = n$ **22.** $52{,}934 \div 84 = n$ **23.** $35{,}914 \div 19 = n$

24. $59{,}882 \div 86 = n$ **25.** $23{,}841 \div 21 = n$ **26.** $12{,}054 \div 35 = n$

Lesson 6.10 *(pages 200–201)*

Choose a strategy and solve.

1. On her birthday, Annie received $10 from her grandparents, $10 from an aunt, and $15 from her parents. She now has $70. How much money did Annie have before her birthday?

2. The sum of the ages of a mother and a daughter is 50. The difference between their ages is 22 years. How old is the mother?

3. The total number of reporters and photographers who work at the *Daily Herald* is 30. There are 12 more reporters than photographers. How many reporters work at the *Daily Herald*?

4. A zookeeper cleans the bear cage on August 2, 9, and 16. If the same pattern of cleaning continues, what is the next date the zookeeper will clean the bear cage?

CHAPTER 7

Lesson 7.1 *(pages 210–211)*

Tell which sample group would better predict the choice of fifth graders. Defend your answer.

Soccer Team Sample Group	
Favorite Sport	
Sport	**Number of Students**
Football	10
Soccer	24
Gymnastics	3
Tennis	8

Random Sample Group	
Favorite Sport	
Sport	**Number of Students**
Football	25
Soccer	9
Gymnastics	10
Tennis	6

Lesson 7.2 *(pages 212–213)*

Find the range, mean, median, and mode.

1. 67, 23, 129, 83, 83

2. 40, 50, 22, 68, 40, 35, 60

3. 85, 40, 131, 94, 85

4. 43, 60, 88, 72, 55, 88, 77

5. 18, 25, 15, 29, 18

6. 103, 109, 113, 110, 110

7. $196, $181, $196

8. 48, 72, 48, 83, 49

9. 496, 321, 480, 496, 397

10. $86, $93, $73, $42, $86

Lesson 7.3 *(pages 214–215)*

Use the pictograph for Exercises 1–7.

1. Which month had the most rainfall?

2. How much rain fell in April?

3. How much rain fell in July?

4. Which months had the same amount of rain?

5. How much more rain fell in April than in January?

6. How much more rain fell in July than in October?

7. How many symbols would represent 7 in. of rain?

Rainfall for Charleston, S.C.
Jan. ☂
April ☂ ☂ ☂
July ☂ ☂ ☂
Oct. ☂
Each ☂ stands for 2 inches

Lesson 7.4 *(pages 216–217)*

Use the bar graph for Exercises 1–6.

1. In which years were there more than 50 inches of snow?

2. In which years were there fewer than 50 inches of snow?

3. How many inches of snow fell in 1987?

4. How many more inches of snow fell in 1982 than in 1977?

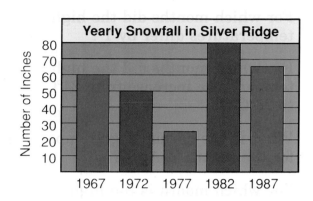

5. How many inches of snow fell in 1967 and 1972 altogether?

6. How much more snow fell in 1967 than in 1972?

Lesson 7.5 *(pages 218–219)*

Choose the most reasonable scale for the set of data.
Write **a, b,** or **c.**

Favorite Pets	
Pet	**Number of Students**
Fish	10
Dog	35
Cat	40
Bird	5

a.
```
100
 80
 60
 40
 20
  0
```

b.
```
50
45
40
35
30
25
20
15
10
 5
 0
```

c.
```
10
 9
 8
 7
 6
 5
 4
 3
 2
 1
 0
```

Lesson 7.6 *(pages 220–221)*

Make a table and solve.

1. There are 450 report cards to distribute to fifth graders. If one teacher can give 30 students their report cards every 15 minutes, how long will it take her to distribute all of them?

2. The Art Club has orders for 300 ceramic vases. If the club can make 15 vases in one day, how many days will it take to fill the orders?

CHAPTER 8

Lesson 8.1 *(pages 244–245)*

Multiply each number by 10, 100, and 1,000.

1. 0.6   **2.** 4.2   **3.** 1.79   **4.** 0.23   **5.** 51.6

6. 21.64   **7.** 0.519   **8.** 1.654   **9.** 0.073   **10.** 39.083

Find each product.

11. $10 \times 0.5 = n$ **12.** $100 \times 0.8 = n$ **13.** $100 \times 5.3 = n$

14. $100 \times 36.82 = n$ **15.** $1,000 \times 0.76 = n$ **16.** $1,000 \times 0.097 = n$

17. $100 \times 8.976 = n$ **18.** $10 \times 59.29 = n$ **19.** $1,000 \times 36.907 = n$

Lesson 8.2 *(pages 246–247)*

Estimate each product.

1. $\begin{array}{r} 6.7 \\ \times\ 12 \\ \hline \end{array}$ **2.** $\begin{array}{r} 4.2 \\ \times\ 48 \\ \hline \end{array}$ **3.** $\begin{array}{r} 9.8 \\ \times\ 42 \\ \hline \end{array}$ **4.** $\begin{array}{r} 2.5 \\ \times\ 25 \\ \hline \end{array}$ **5.** $\begin{array}{r} 1.8 \\ \times\ 97 \\ \hline \end{array}$

6. $\begin{array}{r} 7.4 \\ \times 2.8 \\ \hline \end{array}$ **7.** $\begin{array}{r} 9.65 \\ \times\ \ 42 \\ \hline \end{array}$ **8.** $\begin{array}{r} 5.33 \\ \times\ \ 29 \\ \hline \end{array}$ **9.** $\begin{array}{r} 2.94 \\ \times\ \ 19 \\ \hline \end{array}$ **10.** $\begin{array}{r} 7.03 \\ \times\ \ 11 \\ \hline \end{array}$

11. $2.9 \times 92 \approx n$ **12.** $6.57 \times 72 \approx n$ **13.** $36.2 \times 81 \approx n$

14. $92 \times 4.76 \approx n$ **15.** $7.31 \times 48 \approx n$ **16.** $8.4 \times 49 \approx n$

Lesson 8.3 *(pages 248–249)*

Use 10-by-10 sections of graph paper to show each product.
Write the multiplication sentence.

1. 4 rows and 8 columns   **2.** 5 rows and 5 columns   **3.** 3 rows and 6 columns

Use multiplication to find each product.

4. $0.8 \times 0.7 = n$ **5.** $0.6 \times 0.5 = n$ **6.** $0.2 \times 0.9 = n$

7. $0.4 \times 0.9 = n$ **8.** $0.7 \times 0.9 = n$ **9.** $0.4 \times 0.6 = n$

10. $0.6 \times 0.6 = n$ **11.** $0.5 \times 0.9 = n$ **12.** $0.7 \times 0.6 = n$

13. $0.8 \times 0.6 = n$ **14.** $0.6 \times 0.9 = n$ **15.** $0.9 \times 0.9 = n$

Lesson 8.4 *(pages 250–251)*

Place the decimal point in the product.

1. $\begin{array}{r} 6.3 \\ \times\ \ 4 \\ \hline 252 \end{array}$
2. $\begin{array}{r} \$2.19 \\ \times\ \ \ \ 6 \\ \hline \$1314 \end{array}$
3. $\begin{array}{r} \$1.95 \\ \times\ \ \ 15 \\ \hline \$2925 \end{array}$
4. $\begin{array}{r} 5.19 \\ \times\ \ 32 \\ \hline 16608 \end{array}$
5. $\begin{array}{r} 27.45 \\ \times\ \ \ 23 \\ \hline 63135 \end{array}$

Estimate. Then find the product.

6. $\begin{array}{r} 1.8 \\ \times\ \ 2 \\ \hline \end{array}$
7. $\begin{array}{r} 4.2 \\ \times\ \ 7 \\ \hline \end{array}$
8. $\begin{array}{r} 2.1 \\ \times\ \ 9 \\ \hline \end{array}$
9. $\begin{array}{r} 3.19 \\ \times\ \ 22 \\ \hline \end{array}$
10. $\begin{array}{r} \$43.29 \\ \times\ \ \ \ \ 4 \\ \hline \end{array}$

11. $\begin{array}{r} \$73.99 \\ \times\ \ \ \ 13 \\ \hline \end{array}$
12. $\begin{array}{r} 0.673 \\ \times\ \ \ 17 \\ \hline \end{array}$
13. $\begin{array}{r} 5.62 \\ \times\ \ 61 \\ \hline \end{array}$
14. $\begin{array}{r} 6.714 \\ \times\ \ \ 58 \\ \hline \end{array}$
15. $\begin{array}{r} \$619.29 \\ \times\ \ \ \ \ 26 \\ \hline \end{array}$

Lesson 8.5 *(pages 252–253)*

Estimate. Then find the product.

1. $\begin{array}{r} 1.7 \\ \times 0.9 \\ \hline \end{array}$
2. $\begin{array}{r} 0.8 \\ \times 0.6 \\ \hline \end{array}$
3. $\begin{array}{r} 6.7 \\ \times 9.1 \\ \hline \end{array}$
4. $\begin{array}{r} 6.35 \\ \times\ 7.4 \\ \hline \end{array}$
5. $\begin{array}{r} 3.41 \\ \times\ 6.8 \\ \hline \end{array}$

6. $\begin{array}{r} 63.9 \\ \times\ 7.5 \\ \hline \end{array}$
7. $\begin{array}{r} 25.8 \\ \times 0.46 \\ \hline \end{array}$
8. $\begin{array}{r} 19.97 \\ \times\ \ 3.2 \\ \hline \end{array}$
9. $\begin{array}{r} 573.1 \\ \times\ 0.64 \\ \hline \end{array}$
10. $\begin{array}{r} 209.47 \\ \times\ \ \ \ 3.6 \\ \hline \end{array}$

11. $0.5 \times 0.9 = n$
12. $6.7 \times 3.2 = n$
13. $815.6 \times 8.6 = n$

Lesson 8.6 *(pages 254–255)*

Copy each exercise. Place the decimal point in each product.
Write zeros if they are needed.

1. $\begin{array}{r} 0.09 \\ \times\ 0.3 \\ \hline 0027 \end{array}$
2. $\begin{array}{r} 0.28 \\ \times\ 0.5 \\ \hline 014 \end{array}$
3. $\begin{array}{r} 0.1 \\ \times 0.7 \\ \hline 007 \end{array}$
4. $\begin{array}{r} 4.2 \\ \times 3.6 \\ \hline 1512 \end{array}$
5. $\begin{array}{r} 0.324 \\ \times\ \ \ 57 \\ \hline 18468 \end{array}$

Find the product.

6. $\begin{array}{r} 0.07 \\ \times\ 0.9 \\ \hline \end{array}$
7. $\begin{array}{r} 15.7 \\ \times 0.36 \\ \hline \end{array}$
8. $\begin{array}{r} 0.002 \\ \times\ \ \ 49 \\ \hline \end{array}$
9. $\begin{array}{r} 4.36 \\ \times\ 7.2 \\ \hline \end{array}$
10. $\begin{array}{r} 7.285 \\ \times\ \ \ \ 9 \\ \hline \end{array}$

11. $5.67 \times 29.6 = n$
12. $1.78 \times 0.6 = n$
13. $396 \times 0.89 = n$

14. $0.03 \times 0.9 = n$
15. $0.94 \times 0.1 = n$
16. $27 \times 0.003 = n$

Lesson 8.7 (pages 256–257)

Choose a method of computation and solve.

1. The Akido family spent $5.95 each for 2 adult movie tickets and $3.50 for each of 3 children's tickets. They also spent $19.78 on snacks and $3.98 on parking. About how much did the Akido family spend?

2. The Akido family went out to dinner. Mr. Akido's meal cost $13.95, and Mrs. Akido's meal cost $16.95. Each of the 3 children ordered a buffet that cost $9.95. If they gave the cashier $100.00, how much money is left from their $100.00?

Lesson 8.8 (pages 260–261)

Divide each number by 10, 100, and 1,000.

1. 34	2. 109	3. 496	4. 2,924	5. 16,523
6. 63,214	7. 39,880	8. 54,080	9. 23,712	10. 19,030

Divide.

11. $7.2 \div 10 = n$

12. $64 \div 10 = n$

13. $137 \div 100 = n$

14. $16.5 \div 100 = n$

15. $674 \div 100 = n$

16. $463 \div 1,000 = n$

17. Adam wants to save $650.00 for his summer vacation. If he has 10 months left to save, how much should he save each month?

18. Adam began saving for his vacation by counting a jar of pennies he had saved. He counted 2,094 pennies. How much money does he have in dollars and cents?

Lesson 8.9 (pages 262–263)

Divide. Use base-ten blocks to model each problem.
Then record.

1. $6.82 \div 2 = n$

2. $2.76 \div 3 = n$

3. $7.56 \div 6 = n$

4. $10.25 \div 5 = n$

5. $5.20 \div 8 = n$

6. $1.53 \div 3 = n$

7. $6.24 \div 4 = n$

8. $8.75 \div 7 = n$

9. $6.75 \div 5 = n$

10. $7.84 \div 4 = n$

11. $8.73 \div 3 = n$

12. $9.68 \div 8 = n$

13. $14.98 \div 7 = n$

14. $9.25 \div 5 = n$

15. $16.02 \div 2 = n$

Lesson 8.10 *(pages 264–265)*

Estimate the cost for one item.

1. 3 pairs of socks for $8.88

2. 5 pounds of bananas for $2.45

3. 4 tennis lessons for $29.96

4. 1 dozen muffins for $10.68

5. 6 rolls of film for $12.90

6. 5 pencils for $0.95

7. 5 apples for $2.55

8. 7 balloons for $15.75

9. 2 pizzas for $19.99

10. 4 bottles of juice for $3.89

Find the quotient.

11. $4\overline{)7.6}$

12. $5\overline{)3.0}$

13. $7\overline{)0.42}$

14. $8\overline{)5.6}$

15. $4\overline{)4.16}$

16. $7\overline{)19.6}$

17. $12\overline{)2.4}$

18. $9\overline{)22.86}$

19. $3\overline{)44.55}$

20. $4\overline{)70.88}$

21. $48\overline{)599.04}$

22. $39\overline{)304.2}$

23. $16\overline{)9.44}$

24. $87\overline{)94.83}$

25. $11\overline{)807.4}$

26. $3\overline{)799.02}$

27. $8\overline{)208.4}$

28. $6\overline{)709.8}$

29. $4\overline{)54.08}$

30. $20\overline{)650.20}$

Solve.

31. A human heart pumps 42.3 liters of blood in 9 minutes. How many liters per minute is this?

32. The heart of a cocker spaniel pumps 10.4 liters of blood in 5 minutes. How many liters of blood per minute is this?

Lesson 8.11 *(pages 266–267)*

List the relevant information and solve.

1. Beginning aerial performers train for 7 months before their first performance. They earn $3,000 for each month that they work. Experienced aerial performers earn $14,000 for each month that they work. How much more do experienced aerial performers earn than beginning performers?

2. The red unit of the Hiho Circus has 250 members. It traveled 187 miles from New York City to Baltimore. Then it traveled 246 miles from Baltimore to Pittsburgh. How many miles did the red unit travel in all?

CHAPTER 9

Lesson 9.1 *(pages 276–277)*

Write the fraction for the part that is shaded.

1.

2.

3.

4.

Draw two pictures for each fraction. Show part of a whole with one picture and part of a group with the other picture.

5. $\dfrac{4}{6}$

6. $\dfrac{4}{5}$

7. $\dfrac{3}{7}$

8. $\dfrac{2}{3}$

Lesson 9.2 *(pages 278–279)*

Write two equivalent fractions for each pair of pictures.

1.

2.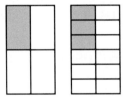

3.

Draw two pictures to find an equivalent fraction.

4. $\dfrac{6}{20}$

5. $\dfrac{9}{18}$

6. $\dfrac{4}{5}$

7. $\dfrac{15}{25}$

8. $\dfrac{4}{16}$

Lesson 9.3 *(pages 280–281)*

Find the missing numerator or denominator.

1. $\dfrac{3}{5} = \dfrac{\blacksquare}{10}$

2. $\dfrac{1}{2} = \dfrac{\blacksquare}{8}$

3. $\dfrac{2}{3} = \dfrac{6}{\blacksquare}$

Which fraction is *not* equivalent to the given fraction?
Write **a, b,** or **c.**

4. $\dfrac{4}{5}$ a. $\dfrac{8}{10}$ b. $\dfrac{6}{12}$ c. $\dfrac{12}{15}$

5. $\dfrac{6}{8}$ a. $\dfrac{7}{9}$ b. $\dfrac{3}{4}$ c. $\dfrac{12}{16}$

6. $\dfrac{2}{3}$ a. $\dfrac{4}{6}$ b. $\dfrac{6}{9}$ c. $\dfrac{4}{9}$

7. $\dfrac{10}{15}$ a. $\dfrac{2}{3}$ b. $\dfrac{2}{5}$ c. $\dfrac{40}{60}$

Lesson 9.4 *(pages 282–283)*

Act out the problem and solve.

1. Misha's necklace has 25 beads. The first bead is red, the second is blue, and the third is white. If this pattern continues, what color is the last bead?

2. You must design a necklace that will have 19 beads. You have 7 purple beads, 7 yellow beads, and 7 gold beads. If you start the pattern as one purple, one yellow, one gold, what color bead will be last? What beads will be left?

3. Amy's necklace has 4 beads. The red bead comes after the yellow bead. The green bead comes before the yellow bead. The blue bead comes between the green bead and the yellow bead. Which bead comes first?

4. You want to design a bracelet to wear with your necklace. The bracelet will have 10 beads. You have 4 purple beads, 4 yellow beads, and 4 gold beads. If you start the pattern as one yellow, one purple, and one gold, what color bead will be the last? What beads will be left?

Lesson 9.5 *(pages 286–287)*

Write *prime* or *composite* for each number.

1. 14   2. 7   3. 24   4. 17   5. 22

6. 2   7. 13   8. 15   9. 3   10. 51

11. 27   12. 10   13. 53   14. 19   15. 18

16. 25   17. 11   18. 91   19. 75   20. 29

Lesson 9.6 *(pages 288–289)*

List the factors of each number.

1. 9   2. 20   3. 15   4. 30   5. 27

6. 33   7. 48   8. 18   9. 8   10. 13

11. 45   12. 6   13. 39   14. 66   15. 21

List the factors of each number. Write the greatest common factor for each pair of numbers.

16. 10, 20   17. 12, 16   18. 18, 21   19. 15, 25

20. 27, 36   21. 9, 18   22. 16, 24   23. 7, 63

24. 8, 10   25. 6, 9   26. 12, 20   27. 5, 15

Lesson 9.7 (pages 290–291)

Tell whether the fraction is in simplest form. Write *yes* or *no*.

1. $\dfrac{8}{12}$ 2. $\dfrac{3}{5}$ 3. $\dfrac{7}{11}$ 4. $\dfrac{3}{12}$ 5. $\dfrac{5}{20}$

Write in simplest form.

6. $\dfrac{8}{12}$ 7. $\dfrac{14}{16}$ 8. $\dfrac{4}{10}$ 9. $\dfrac{10}{15}$ 10. $\dfrac{10}{20}$

11. $\dfrac{16}{32}$ 12. $\dfrac{6}{9}$ 13. $\dfrac{24}{27}$ 14. $\dfrac{18}{32}$ 15. $\dfrac{8}{16}$

16. $\dfrac{6}{8}$ 17. $\dfrac{12}{16}$ 18. $\dfrac{15}{45}$ 19. $\dfrac{12}{30}$ 20. $\dfrac{15}{60}$

21. $\dfrac{18}{40}$ 22. $\dfrac{20}{24}$ 23. $\dfrac{28}{42}$ 24. $\dfrac{14}{16}$ 25. $\dfrac{10}{35}$

Lesson 9.8 (pages 292–293)

Find the least common multiple.

1. $2, 3$ 2. $3, 4$ 3. $4, 5$ 4. $5, 8$ 5. $6, 7$

6. $6, 8$ 7. $10, 25$ 8. $12, 20$ 9. $10, 15$ 10. $8, 12$

11. $20, 50$ 12. $12, 15$ 13. $30, 45$ 14. $15, 25$ 15. $20, 16$

16. $16, 40$ 17. $10, 14$ 18. $24, 9$ 19. $12, 18$ 20. $12, 28$

Lesson 9.9 (pages 294–295)

Compare. Write <, >, or = for ●.

1. $\dfrac{2}{5} ● \dfrac{7}{8}$ 2. $\dfrac{1}{2} ● \dfrac{3}{4}$ 3. $\dfrac{5}{6} ● \dfrac{3}{4}$ 4. $\dfrac{2}{3} ● \dfrac{5}{9}$

5. $\dfrac{2}{3} ● \dfrac{9}{15}$ 6. $\dfrac{1}{5} ● \dfrac{1}{3}$ 7. $\dfrac{7}{10} ● \dfrac{8}{15}$ 8. $\dfrac{3}{4} ● \dfrac{4}{5}$

9. $\dfrac{1}{2} ● \dfrac{4}{8}$ 10. $\dfrac{3}{4} ● \dfrac{1}{9}$ 11. $\dfrac{2}{3} ● \dfrac{4}{6}$ 12. $\dfrac{3}{7} ● \dfrac{2}{5}$

Lesson 9.10 (pages 296–297)

Write in order from least to greatest.

1. $\dfrac{1}{2}, \dfrac{1}{4}, \dfrac{1}{3}$ 2. $\dfrac{4}{9}, \dfrac{1}{3}, \dfrac{3}{6}$ 3. $\dfrac{2}{3}, \dfrac{1}{9}, \dfrac{5}{6}$

Write in order from greatest to least.

4. $\dfrac{2}{5}, \dfrac{3}{10}, \dfrac{9}{15}$ 5. $\dfrac{3}{6}, \dfrac{8}{12}, \dfrac{1}{3}$ 6. $\dfrac{2}{7}, \dfrac{5}{14}, \dfrac{1}{2}$

Lesson 9.11 *(pages 298–300)*

Write a whole number or a mixed number for each picture.

1.   2. 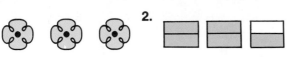 3. 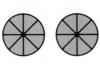 4.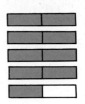

Rename each as a mixed number or a whole number.

5. $\dfrac{6}{5}$ 6. $\dfrac{11}{5}$ 7. $\dfrac{11}{8}$ 8. $\dfrac{15}{3}$

9. $\dfrac{5}{2}$ 10. $\dfrac{11}{3}$ 11. $\dfrac{13}{5}$ 12. $\dfrac{20}{4}$

13. $\dfrac{7}{6}$ 14. $\dfrac{22}{7}$ 15. $\dfrac{32}{8}$ 16. $\dfrac{17}{4}$

Rename each as a fraction.

17. $1\dfrac{5}{8}$ 18. $3\dfrac{5}{6}$ 19. $6\dfrac{3}{4}$ 20. $4\dfrac{2}{3}$ 21. $6\dfrac{3}{5}$

22. $2\dfrac{1}{5}$ 23. $4\dfrac{1}{2}$ 24. $8\dfrac{1}{3}$ 25. $5\dfrac{1}{4}$ 26. $4\dfrac{4}{7}$

Arrange in order from least to greatest.

27. $4\dfrac{2}{3};\ 4\dfrac{5}{9};\ 4\dfrac{1}{3}$ 28. $3\dfrac{4}{6};\ 3\dfrac{1}{3};\ 3\dfrac{5}{18}$

Lesson 9.12 *(pages 302–303)*

Draw a picture and solve.

The 24 students in Mr. Sojo's class and the 24 students in Mrs. Olsen's class were asked to name their favorite kind of music.

1. Which class has more students who like country?

2. How many students in each class like rock?

3. How many students in each class like classical music?

4. How many students in each class like jazz?

Favorite Type of Music		
Type of Music	Mr. Sojo's Class	Mrs. Olsen's Class
Rock	$\dfrac{5}{6}$	$\dfrac{5}{8}$
Country	$\dfrac{1}{12}$	■
Classical	$\dfrac{1}{24}$	$\dfrac{1}{6}$
Jazz	$\dfrac{1}{24}$	$\dfrac{1}{12}$

5. Is country or classical music more popular in Mr. Sojo's class?

CHAPTER 10

Lesson 10.1 (pages 312–313)

Estimate the sum or difference.

1. $\dfrac{2}{5}$
$+\dfrac{4}{10}$

2. $\dfrac{7}{12}$
$-\dfrac{1}{6}$

3. $\dfrac{5}{6}$
$+\dfrac{8}{9}$

4. $\dfrac{8}{14}$
$-\dfrac{1}{13}$

5. $\dfrac{5}{7}$
$+\dfrac{13}{14}$

6. $\dfrac{17}{18}$
$-\dfrac{2}{5}$

7. $\dfrac{2}{3} - \dfrac{4}{6} \approx n$

8. $\dfrac{3}{5} + \dfrac{6}{10} \approx n$

9. $\dfrac{13}{14} - \dfrac{3}{5} \approx n$

Lesson 10.2 (pages 314–315)

Write an addition or subtraction sentence for each drawing.

1.

2.

3.

Use mental math to find the sum or difference. Write the answer in simplest form.

4. $\dfrac{3}{6}$
$+\dfrac{2}{6}$

5. $\dfrac{5}{6}$
$-\dfrac{1}{6}$

6. $\dfrac{1}{3}$
$+\dfrac{2}{3}$

7. $\dfrac{2}{12}$
$+\dfrac{9}{12}$

8. $\dfrac{8}{15}$
$-\dfrac{3}{15}$

9. $\dfrac{26}{48}$
$-\dfrac{19}{48}$

10. $\dfrac{7}{9}$
$+\dfrac{1}{9}$

11. $\dfrac{9}{11}$
$-\dfrac{3}{11}$

12. $\dfrac{5}{8}$
$+\dfrac{3}{8}$

13. $\dfrac{3}{4}$
$-\dfrac{1}{4}$

Lesson 10.3 (pages 316–317)

Tell whether one denominator is a multiple of the other. Write *yes* or *no*.

1. $\dfrac{2}{5}, \dfrac{3}{15}$

2. $\dfrac{1}{6}, \dfrac{5}{13}$

3. $\dfrac{1}{2}, \dfrac{5}{8}$

4. $\dfrac{1}{3}, \dfrac{3}{5}$

5. $\dfrac{5}{8}, \dfrac{1}{16}$

Lesson 10.4 (pages 318–319)

Find the least common multiple.

1. $2, 5$

2. $3, 7$

3. $2, 6$

4. $3, 5$

Find the least common denominator.

5. $\dfrac{1}{2}, \dfrac{3}{10}$

6. $\dfrac{3}{4}, \dfrac{5}{6}$

7. $\dfrac{1}{2}, \dfrac{5}{9}$

8. $\dfrac{1}{6}, \dfrac{3}{12}$

More Practice

Lesson 10.5 *(pages 320–321)*

Add or subtract. Write the answer in simplest form.

1. $\frac{2}{3}$
$+\frac{1}{4}$

2. $\frac{1}{2}$
$-\frac{1}{4}$

3. $\frac{5}{6}$
$-\frac{2}{3}$

4. $\frac{1}{2}$
$+\frac{2}{5}$

5. $\frac{3}{5}$
$-\frac{1}{3}$

6. $\frac{3}{5}$
$+\frac{3}{8}$

7. $\frac{1}{4}$
$-\frac{1}{8}$

8. $\frac{9}{16}$
$+\frac{1}{4}$

9. $\frac{1}{2}$
$-\frac{3}{8}$

10. $\frac{7}{12}$
$+\frac{3}{8}$

Lesson 10.6 *(pages 322–323)*

Use fraction squares to find the sum.

1. $4\frac{3}{5}$
$+2\frac{4}{5}$

2. $1\frac{7}{8}$
$+3\frac{5}{8}$

3. $6\frac{1}{2}$
$+1\frac{5}{8}$

4. $2\frac{5}{9}$
$+4\frac{2}{3}$

5. $6\frac{4}{5}$
$+3\frac{1}{3}$

Tell whether you need to rename the sum. Write *yes* or *no*.

6. $2\frac{2}{3}$
$+5\frac{5}{6}$

7. $1\frac{1}{10}$
$+2\frac{3}{5}$

8. $8\frac{1}{4}$
$+2\frac{5}{12}$

9. $1\frac{4}{9}$
$+3\frac{2}{3}$

10. $6\frac{9}{15}$
$+1\frac{3}{5}$

Lesson 10.7 *(pages 324–325)*

Use fraction circles to find the difference. Write the answer in simplest form.

1. $9\frac{1}{4}$
$-2\frac{3}{4}$

2. $3\frac{1}{3}$
$-1\frac{2}{3}$

3. $6\frac{3}{5}$
$-4\frac{4}{5}$

4. $4\frac{2}{7}$
$-3\frac{5}{7}$

5. $11\frac{5}{9}$
$-4\frac{7}{9}$

Tell whether you need to rename. Write *yes* or *no*.

6. $3\frac{3}{8}$
$-1\frac{7}{8}$

7. $6\frac{1}{3}$
$-4\frac{2}{3}$

8. $8\frac{4}{5}$
$-4\frac{1}{5}$

9. $5\frac{3}{4}$
$-1\frac{1}{4}$

10. $10\frac{1}{8}$
$-3\frac{5}{8}$

Lesson 10.8 *(pages 326–327)*

Add or subtract. Write the answer in simplest form.

1. $3\frac{3}{4}$
   $+1\frac{3}{4}$

2. $3\frac{1}{5}$
   $-2\frac{2}{3}$

3. $8\frac{7}{10}$
   $+3\frac{5}{6}$

4. $8\frac{3}{7}$
   $-7\frac{1}{2}$

5. $6\frac{5}{8}$
   $-2\frac{1}{2}$

6. $7\frac{2}{3}$
   $-5\frac{3}{4}$

7. $4\frac{3}{10}$
   $-2\frac{1}{2}$

8. $4\frac{3}{4}$
   $+2\frac{2}{3}$

9. $8\frac{1}{4}$
   $-5\frac{3}{6}$

10. $1\frac{9}{10}$
    $+6\frac{4}{5}$

Lesson 10.9 *(pages 328–329)*

Use the diagram to make a table of the chorus members for Exercises 1–2.

1. What fraction of the chorus is made up of altos?

2. Which group makes up the greater fractional part of the chorus, alto or tenor?

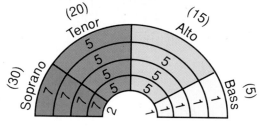

Chorus Members

Lesson 10.10 *(pages 332–333)*

Multiply. Write the product as a whole or mixed number.

1. $\frac{2}{3} \times 4 = n$

2. $7 \times \frac{4}{6} = n$

3. $5 \times \frac{5}{8} = n$

4. $9 \times \frac{2}{4} = n$

5. $6 \times \frac{3}{5} = n$

6. $8 \times \frac{4}{6} = n$

7. $\frac{3}{4} \times 8 = n$

8. $3 \times \frac{5}{6} = n$

Lesson 10.11 *(pages 334–335)*

Multiply. Write the answer in simplest form.

1. $\frac{3}{5} \times \frac{2}{3} = n$

2. $\frac{5}{6} \times \frac{3}{4} = n$

3. $\frac{3}{9} \times \frac{1}{2} = n$

4. $\frac{3}{4} \times \frac{1}{9} = n$

5. $\frac{5}{9} \times \frac{3}{5} = n$

6. $\frac{6}{7} \times \frac{1}{2} = n$

7. $\frac{4}{5} \times \frac{2}{10} = n$

8. $\frac{1}{2} \times \frac{4}{9} = n$

9. $\frac{2}{3} \times \frac{3}{6} = n$

10. $\frac{7}{8} \times \frac{2}{5} = n$

11. $\frac{3}{5} \times \frac{4}{7} = n$

12. $\frac{2}{3} \times \frac{3}{10} = n$

13. $\frac{7}{8} \times \frac{5}{7} = n$

14. $\frac{1}{10} \times \frac{5}{6} = n$

15. $\frac{1}{8} \times \frac{4}{7} = n$

16. $\frac{2}{3} \times \frac{3}{8} = n$

Lesson 10.12 *(pages 336–337)*

Draw fraction squares to help you find each product.

1. $3\frac{2}{3} \times \frac{5}{6} = n$

2. $\frac{2}{5} \times 5\frac{1}{2} = n$

3. $2\frac{1}{6} \times \frac{3}{4} = n$

4. $5\frac{1}{3} \times \frac{3}{7} = n$

5. $4\frac{1}{4} \times \frac{2}{3} = n$

6. $\frac{2}{5} \times 5\frac{5}{6} = n$

7. $\frac{3}{4} \times 4\frac{1}{4} = n$

8. $3\frac{1}{2} \times \frac{3}{4} = n$

9. $1\frac{1}{3} \times \frac{1}{3} = n$

10. $\frac{3}{5} \times 6\frac{1}{3} = n$

11. $\frac{3}{4} \times 2\frac{2}{3} = n$

12. $\frac{7}{8} \times 7\frac{1}{4} = n$

Lesson 10.13 *(pages 338–339)*

Complete.

1. How many fives are in twenty-five?

2. How many twos are in sixteen?

3. How many sevens are in thirty-five?

4. How many fours are in thirty-six?

Write a division number sentence for each picture.

5.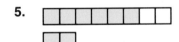

6.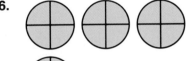

7.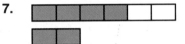

Use your rule for dividing fractions with like denominators.

8. $\frac{7}{2} \div \frac{1}{2} = n$

9. $\frac{10}{3} \div \frac{2}{3} = n$

10. $\frac{7}{8} \div \frac{1}{8} = n$

11. $\frac{28}{9} \div \frac{4}{9} = n$

12. $\frac{48}{4} \div \frac{3}{4} = n$

13. $\frac{48}{8} \div \frac{3}{8} = n$

14. $\frac{18}{3} \div \frac{2}{3} = n$

15. $\frac{20}{6} \div \frac{5}{6} = n$

16. $\frac{24}{3} \div \frac{2}{3} = n$

Lesson 10.14 *(pages 340–341)*

Make a diagram and solve.

1. Of the plants in Josie's garden, $\frac{1}{10}$ are rosebushes, $\frac{1}{2}$ are daisies, and $\frac{2}{5}$ are lilies. There are 3 rose bushes. How many lilies are planted?

2. Of the plants in Jamie's garden, $\frac{1}{4}$ are tomatoes, $\frac{1}{2}$ are lettuce, $\frac{1}{8}$ are cabbage, and $\frac{1}{8}$ are squash. There are 3 cabbage plants. How many vegetable plants were planted in all?

CHAPTER 11

Lesson 11.1 *(pages 350–351)*

Choose the most reasonable unit of measure.
Write *mm, cm, m,* or *km.*

1. the length of a room

2. the height of an apartment building

3. the thickness of a penny

4. the distance between Miami and Dallas

5. the length of a pencil

6. the length of the Mississippi River

Lesson 11.2 *(pages 352–353)*

Write the measure to the nearest cm and then write a more precise measure.

1.

2.

Measure each side of the rectangle to the nearest cm.
Add the measurements to find the perimeter.

3.

4.

Use a metric ruler. Draw a line to show each length.

5. 15 cm

6. 38 mm

7. 1 dm

8. 112 mm

Lesson 11.3 *(pages 354–355)*

Choose the more reasonable unit of measure. Write *mL* or *L.*

1. a jug of apple juice

2. a bottle of shampoo

3. a glass of milk

4. a can of paint

Lesson 11.4 *(pages 356–357)*

Choose the most reasonable unit. Write *kg, g,* or *mg.*

1.

2.

3.

Lesson 11.5 *(pages 358–359)*

Choose the smaller unit of measure. Write **a** or **b**.

1. a. meter
    b. centimeter

2. a. kilogram
    b. milligram

3. a. milliliter
    b. liter

Choose the larger unit of measure. Write **a** or **b**.

4. a. kilometer
    b. meter

5. a. centimeter
    b. decimeter

6. a. kilogram
    b. gram

Use the place-value chart on page 358. Change each measurement to the base unit.

7. 7 dm   **8.** 5 mL   **9.** 10 g   **10.** 4 mm

11. 8 cm   **12.** 14 mg   **13.** 2 mL   **14.** 50 mg

Lesson 11.6 *(pages 360–361)*

Write *multiply* or *divide* for each exercise. Then solve.

1. 4.3 cm = ■ mm   **2.** 60 mm = ■ cm   **3.** 3.2 m = ■ cm

4. 14 L = ■ mL   **5.** 15,000 mL = ■ L   **6.** 16,000 mg = ■ g

Lesson 11.7 *(pages 362–363)*

Use the starting temperature on each thermometer to find the new temperature.

1. 17° warmer   **2.** 6° colder   **3.** 41° warmer   **4.** 11° colder

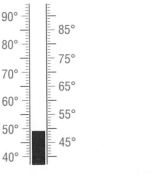

Fahrenheit

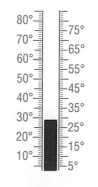
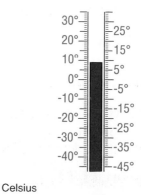

Celsius

Copy and complete the table. Use the thermometers on page 362.

Starting Temperature	80°F	**6.** ■	9°C	64°C
Change in Temperature	fell 32°	rose 14°	fell 12°	**8.** ■
Final Temperature	**5.** ■	74°F	**7.** ■	37°C

Lesson 11.8 *(pages 364–365)*

Solve.

1. Myung drank 500 mL of water in the morning, 500 mL in the afternoon, and another 500 mL in the evening. She estimates she drank 15 liters of water. Is this reasonable? Explain.

2. Sam needs to triple a recipe for beef stew. It calls for 1 lb. of beef, 4 cups of stock, and 2 cups of chopped vegetables. Sam estimates he will need 12 quarts of stock. Is this reasonable? Explain.

Lesson 11.9 *(pages 368–369)*

Find the most precise measurement in inches for each line segment.

1. ――――――――――

2. ――――――――――――――

3. ――――――――――――――――――

Draw a line segment to the given length.

4. $2\frac{7}{8}$ in.   5. $1\frac{5}{16}$ in.   6. $5\frac{1}{2}$ in.   7. $3\frac{3}{4}$ in.

Lesson 11.10 *(pages 370–371)*

Complete.

1. 2 ft = ▨ in.   2. 1,760 yd = ■ ft   3. 10 yd = ■ ft

4. 36 in. = ▨ yd   5. 6 ft = ■ in.   6. 4 mi = ■ ft

Add or subtract.

7.   10 ft 9 in.
   − 8 ft 11 in.

8.   6 yd 2 ft
   +1 yd 2 ft

9.   9 ft 6 in.
   −3 ft 10 in.

10.   3 ft 8 in.
   +7 ft 11 in.

Lesson 11.11 *(pages 372–373)*

Write *multiply* or *divide*. Then complete.

1. 5 gal = ■ qt   2. 3 T = ■ lb   3. 6 pt = ■ c

4. 24 c = ■ fl oz   5. 10 qt = ■ gal   6. 144 oz = ■ lb

7. 18 c = ■ pt   8. $6\frac{1}{2}$ T = ■ lb   9. 22 pt = ■ qt

Lesson 11.12 *(pages 374–375)*

Complete.

1. 2 days = ■ hr
2. 3 min = ■ sec
3. 6 wk = ■ days

4. 240 sec = ■ min
5. 49 days = ■ wk
6. 730 days = ■ yr

7. $\frac{3}{4}$ yr = ■ mo
8. $1\frac{1}{2}$ days = ■ hr
9. 210 min = ■ hr

10. 2 yr = ■ days
11. 96 hr = ■ days
12. 60 mo = ■ yr

13. 156 wk = ■ yr
14. 11 min = ■ sec
15. 5 hr = ■ min

16. 3 hr 15 min = ■ min
17. 160 hr = ■ days ■ hr

Lesson 11.13 *(pages 376–377)*

Compute the time when each event began or ended.

1. The train left at 4:20 P.M.. and arrived 32 min later.

2. Lunch was served at 12:45 P.M. and took 50 min to prepare.

Add or subtract.

3.
```
  3 hr 25 min
+ 2 hr 50 min
```

4.
```
  10 min 45 sec
-  3 min 23 sec
```

5.
```
  4 hr 15 min
- 1 hr 45 min
```

6.
```
  6 hr 10 min
- 4 hr 35 min
```

7.
```
  3 min 29 sec
+ 5 min 43 sec
```

8.
```
  14 hr 50 min
+ 10 hr 25 min
```

9.
```
  7 min 45 sec
- 3 min 50 sec
```

10.
```
  2 hr 25 min
- 1 hr 40 min
```

11.
```
  8 min 35 sec
+ 5 min 55 sec
```

Lesson 11.14 *(pages 378–379)*

Use the schedule for Exercises 1–3.

1. At what time does Flight 57 arrive in Los Angeles?

2. At what time does Flight 413 leave Sacramento?

3. Joe has an important meeting at 2:00 P.M. in Los Angeles. What is the latest flight he can take?

To Los Angeles		
Leave from Sacramento	Arrive	Flight No.
6:35 A.M.	7:45 A.M.	41
8:25 A.M.	9:28 A.M.	43
1:15 P.M.	2:18 P.M.	413
5:20 P.M.	6:27 P.M.	57

CHAPTER 12

Lesson 12.1 *(pages 388–389)*

Find the perimeter of each figure.

1.

2 cm 2 cm
2 cm 2 cm
2 cm

2.

48 mm 59 mm
34 mm

3.

6 cm
3 cm   3 cm
6 cm

4.

47 mm
45 mm   36 mm
62 mm

5.

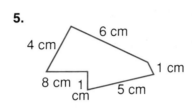

6.

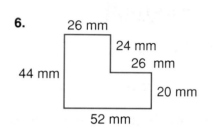

Lesson 12.2 *(pages 390–391)*

Find the perimeter of each figure.

1.

6 m

2.

9 ft
2 ft

3.

16 mm
6 mm   10 mm
8 mm   8 mm
8 mm

4.

20 cm
8 cm

5.

6.

5 m

Find the missing length in each figure.

7.

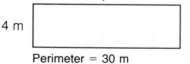

?
4 m
Perimeter = 30 m

8.

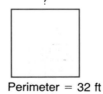

?
Perimeter = 32 ft

9.

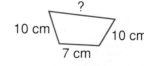

?
10 cm   10 cm
7 cm
Perimeter = 40 cm

10.

?
Perimeter = 25 cm

11.

6 cm   ?
3 cm
Perimeter = 15 cm

12.

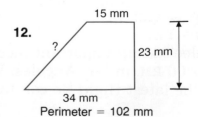

15 mm
?   23 mm
34 mm
Perimeter = 102 mm

Lesson 12.3 *(pages 392–393)*

Find the circumference. Round to the nearest tenth.

1.
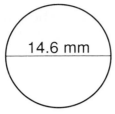
14.6 mm

2.
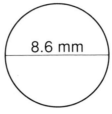
8.6 mm

3.

11.5 mm

Find the diameter. Round to the nearest tenth.

4. $C = 72.9$ mm

5. $C = 28.2$ cm

6. $C = 124.9$ in.

7. $C = 69.8$ cm

8. $C = 87.6$ in.

9. $C = 172.5$ cm

Lesson 12.4 *(pages 394–395)*

Find each area. Each square equals 1 cm².

1.
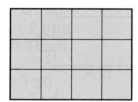

2.
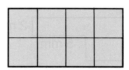

3.
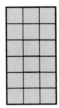

Use the formula to find the area of each rectangle.

4.
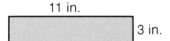
11 in.
3 in.

5.
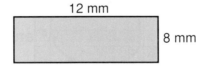
12 mm
8 mm

6.
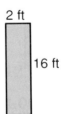
2 ft
16 ft

Lesson 12.5 *(pages 396–397)*

Find the area of each figure.

1.
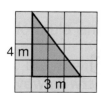
4 m
3 m

2.
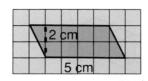
2 cm
5 cm

3.
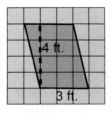
4 ft.
3 ft.

4. Triangle:
$b = 7$ m
$h = 3.5$ m

5. Rectangle:
$b = 14$ in.
$h = 33$ in.

6. Triangle:
$b = 2.7$ cm
$h = 9.4$ cm

CHAPTER 13

Lesson 13.1 (pages 422–423)

Write each ratio in three ways.

1. cardinals to blue jays   2. penguins to flamingos   3. eagles to nests

Write a fraction to show each ratio.

4. 3 to 4   5. 1 to 5   6. 7:10   7. 6 to 3

8. 10 to 13   9. 9 to 4   10. 4:9   11. 8 to 1

12. 143:100   13. 180:5   14. 50:200   15. 4:9

Lesson 13.2 (pages 424–425)

Tell whether the ratios are equivalent. Write *yes* or *no.*

1. $\dfrac{3}{4}$ and $\dfrac{9}{12}$ 2. $\dfrac{5}{12}$ and $\dfrac{7}{14}$ 3. $\dfrac{1}{2}$ and $\dfrac{15}{30}$

4. $\dfrac{4}{15}$ and $\dfrac{20}{75}$ 5. $\dfrac{8}{7}$ and $\dfrac{16}{21}$ 6. $\dfrac{2}{15}$ and $\dfrac{10}{50}$

7. $\dfrac{3}{15}$ and $\dfrac{6}{30}$ 8. $\dfrac{4}{8}$ and $\dfrac{11}{22}$ 9. $\dfrac{1}{5}$ and $\dfrac{4}{10}$

Write two ratios that are equivalent to the given ratio.

10. 6:14   11. 7:10   12. 1:4   13. $\dfrac{2}{3}$ 14. 1 to 3

Solve.

15. The ratio of scenic backdrops to solid-color backdrops in Lisa's studio is 2 to 5. If she has 4 scenic backdrops, how many solid-color backdrops does she have?

16. The ratio of setting changes to light-meter readings is 1 to 12. Lisa took 24 light-meter readings. How many setting changes did she make?

17. Lisa can make 3 slides for every 5 pictures she develops. If she develops 30 pictures, how many slides can she make?

18. The ratio of individual poses to group poses is 3 to 2. If Lisa takes 24 group poses, how many individual poses did she take?

Lesson 13.3 *(pages 426–427)*

Use the scale drawing for Exercises 1–12.

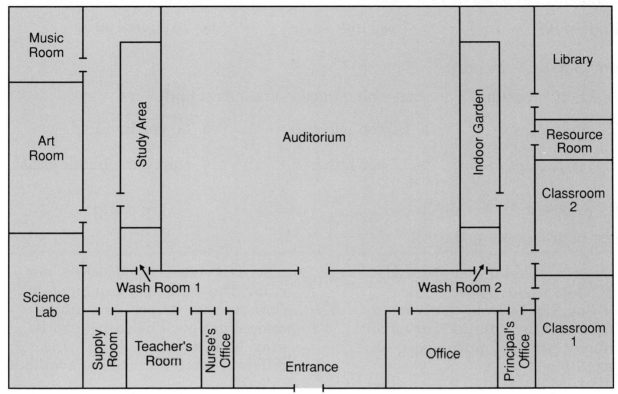

Scale: 1 cm = 4 m

Measure the drawing. Find the dimensions of these rooms.

1. Teachers' Room
2. Classroom 1
3. Art Room
4. Principal's Office
5. Study Area
6. Science Lab
7. Washroom 1
8. Resource Room
9. Auditorium
10. Nurse's Office
11. Classroom 2
12. Music Room

Lesson 13.4 *(pages 428–429)*

Write the percent that tells what part is shaded.

1.
2.
3.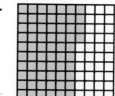
4.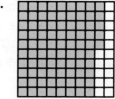

Write the percent for each ratio.

5. 6 out of 100

6. 3 out of 100

7. 24 out of 100

8. 63 per 100

9. 2 per 100

10. 55 per 100

11. 50 out of 100

12. 1 per 100

13. 75 out of 100

Lesson 13.5 *(pages 430–431)*

Write each as a percent, a decimal, and a fraction in simplest form.

1. six hundredths

2. fifteen percent

3. 30 per hundred

4. seventy percent

5. 17 per hundred

6. thirty-one hundredths

Lesson 13.6 *(pages 432–433)*

Make an organized list and solve.

1. Desmond is making muffins. He can make whole wheat or corn muffins. They can have raisins, blueberries, or walnuts. How many different kinds of muffins can he make?

2. Suki will choose the decor for her room. The wallpaper can be pink flowers, blue stripes, or a multi-colored design. The carpet can be gray, blue, or white. How many different combinations are available to her?

Lesson 13.7 *(pages 436–437)*

Use the spinner for Exercises 1–6.

1. How many sections does the spinner have?

2. What are the possible outcomes of spinning the spinner?

3. What is the probability of landing on red? on brown? on blue?

4. What is the probability of *not* landing on green?

5. What is the probability of *not* landing on red?

6. What is the probability of landing on green or blue?

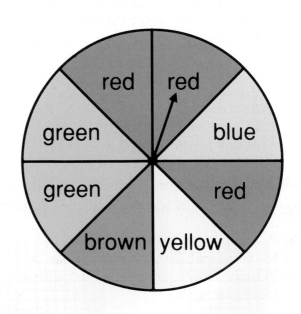

Lesson 13.8 *(pages 438–439)*

Write a fraction for the probability of picking each kind of flower.

1. a rose

2. an iris

3. a petunia

4. a tulip

5. a daisy

6. not a rose

7. a rose or a daisy

8. not a tulip

9. not a daisy

10. a tulip or a rose

Use the spinner for Exercises 11–16.

11. What are the possible outcomes of spinning the spinner?

12. On which number(s) is the spinner most likely to land?

13. What is the probability of the spinner landing on 2?

14. What is the probability of the spinner landing on 5?

15. What is the probability of the spinner landing on an odd number?

16. What is the probability of the spinner landing on an even number?

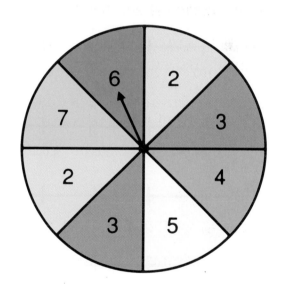

Lesson 13.9 *(pages 440–441)*

Write a problem that each program could simulate.

1. A computer program generates 75 random numbers for 1–4.

2. A computer program generates 25 random numbers for 4–9.

Use the results of one computer run to find the probability of a coin landing on heads or tails when tossed 100 times.

3. A computer program generated these possibilites for coin tosses. Which event occurred most often, heads or tails?

Toss the Coin 100 Times
HTTTTTTTHHTHHHHTHTTHTTHHT
HHHTHHTTTHHHHHTHTHHHTHHHT
THTHHTTTHTTHHTHTTTTHHHTHT
THTTHTHTHTTHTTHTTHTHHHHHT

Learning Resources

The Learning Resources can be traced, colored, and cut out. These resources can be used as tools to help you understand math concepts and solve problems.

Number Lines

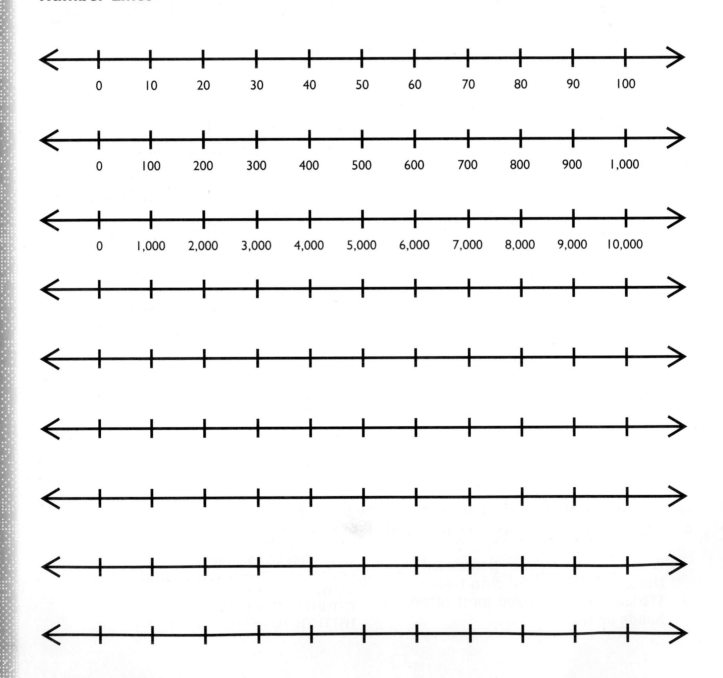

Regular Polygons

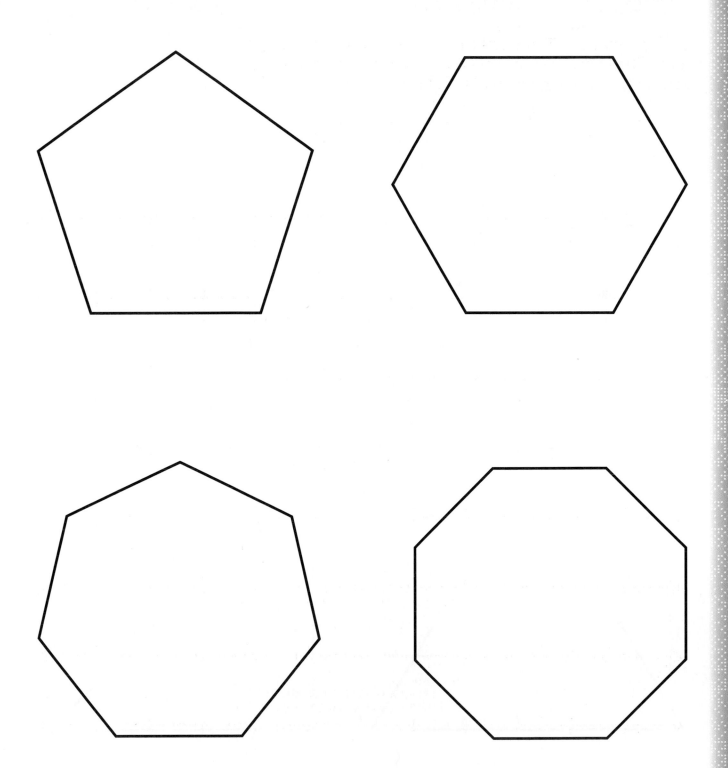

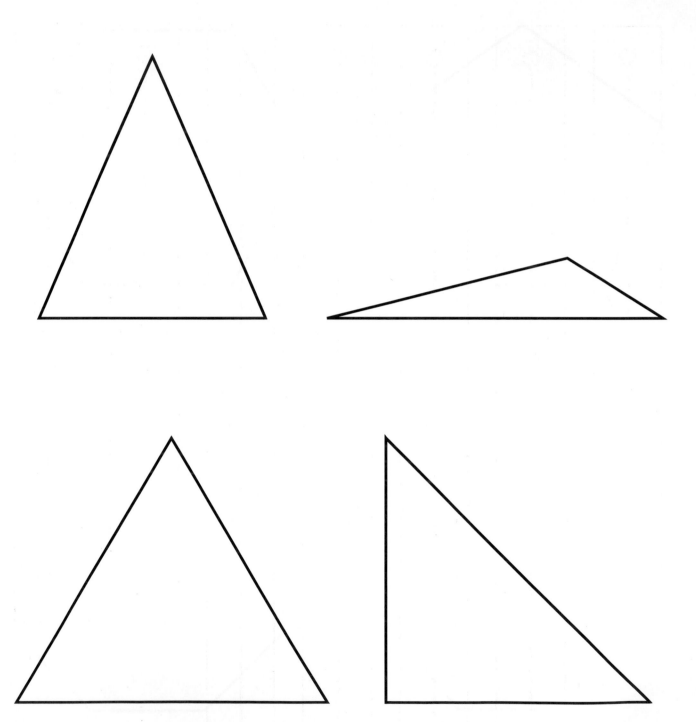

Geostrips

The number on each strip represents the distance (in cm) between the end holes.

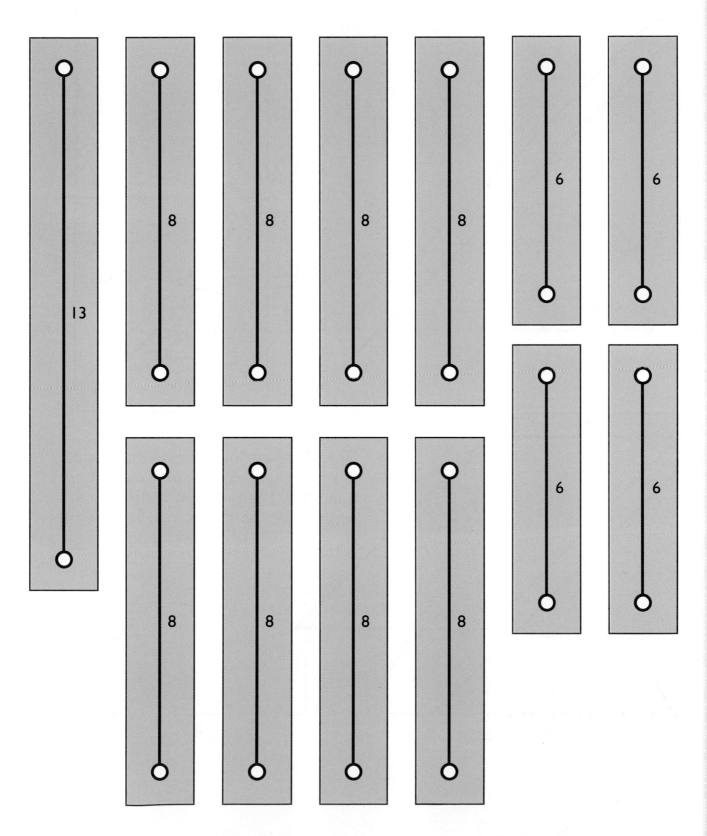

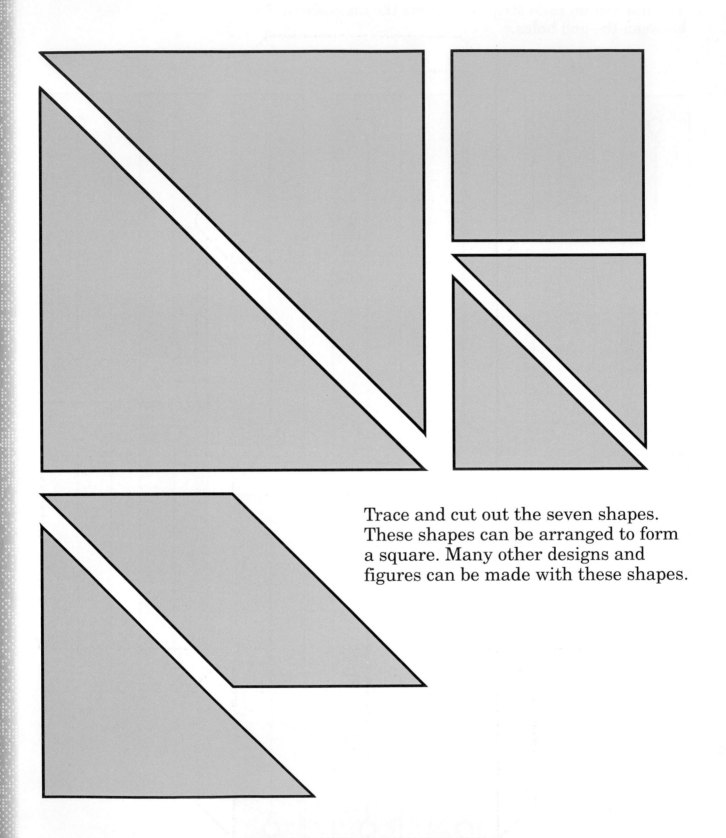

Trace and cut out the seven shapes. These shapes can be arranged to form a square. Many other designs and figures can be made with these shapes.

Solid Geometric Shape

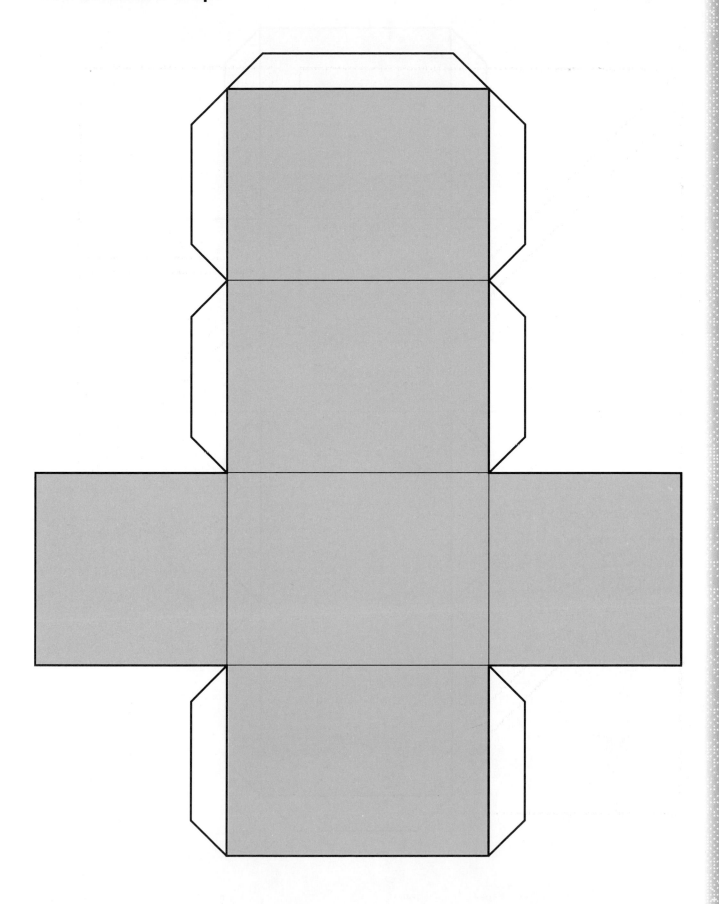

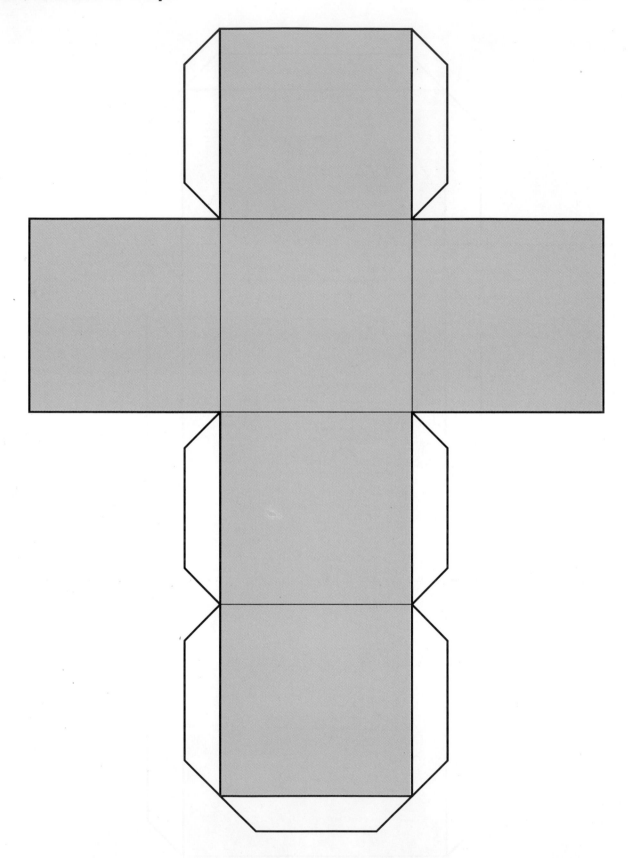

Solid Geometric Shape

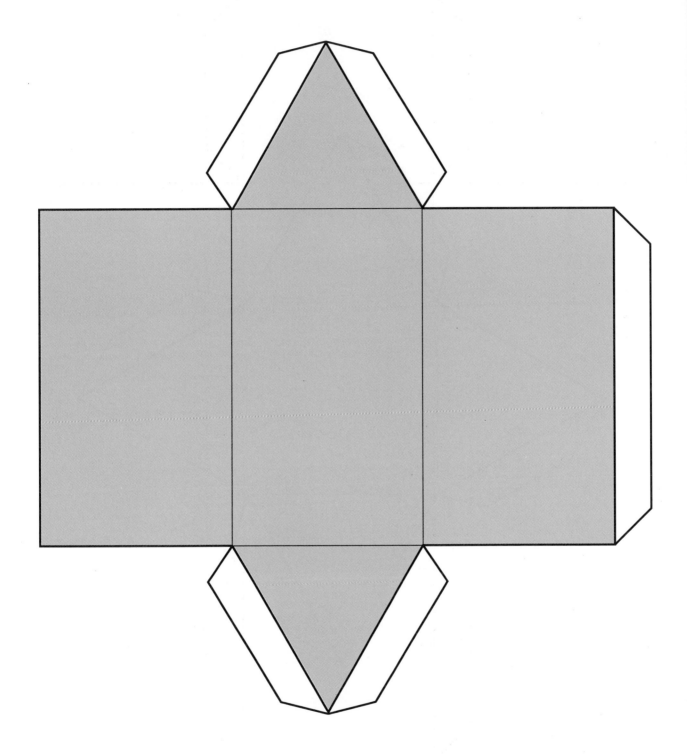

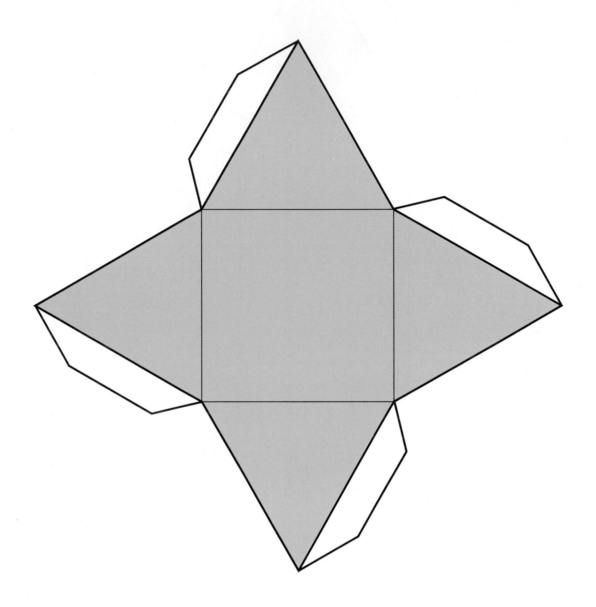

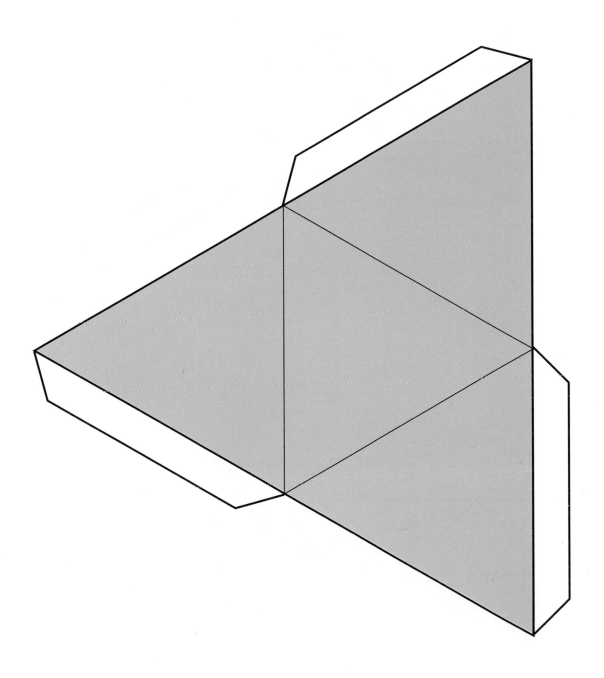

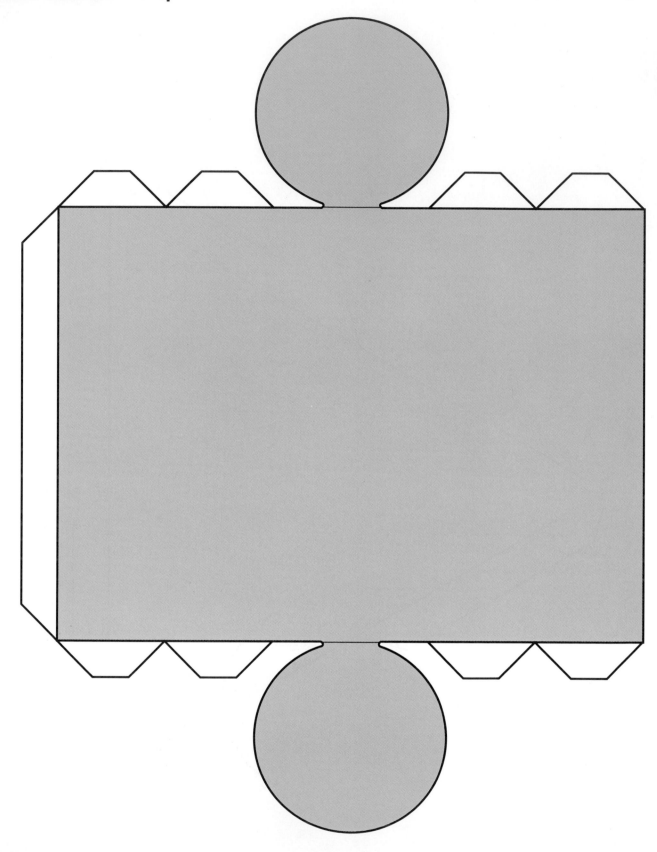

Solid Geometric Shape

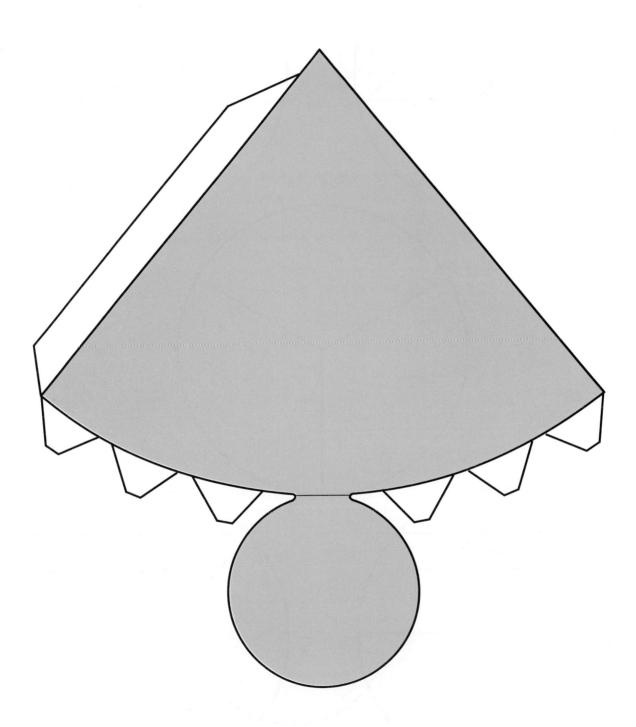

Fraction Circles

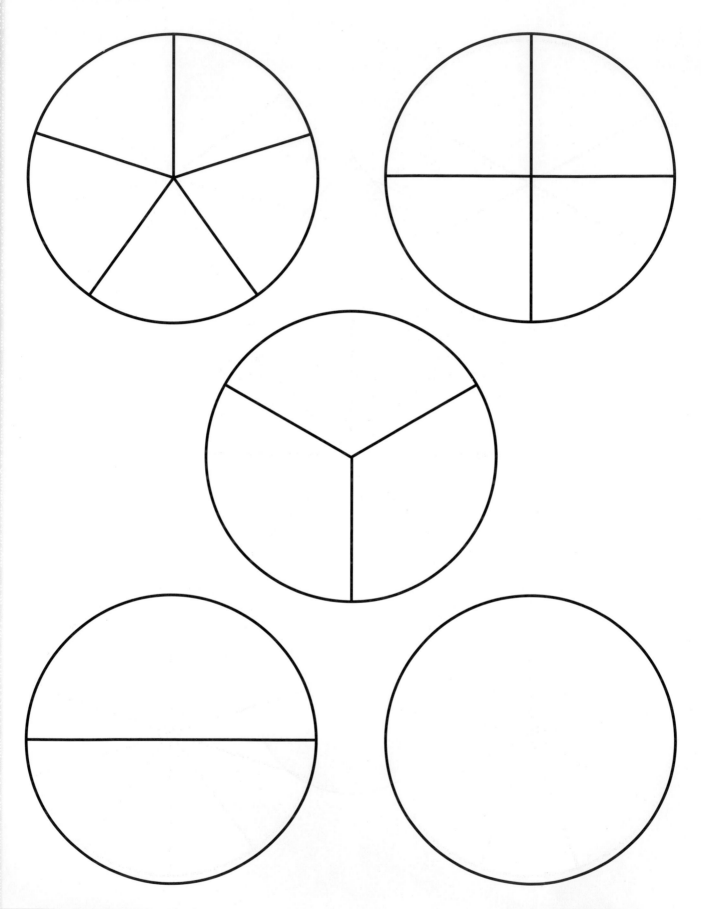

Fraction Circles

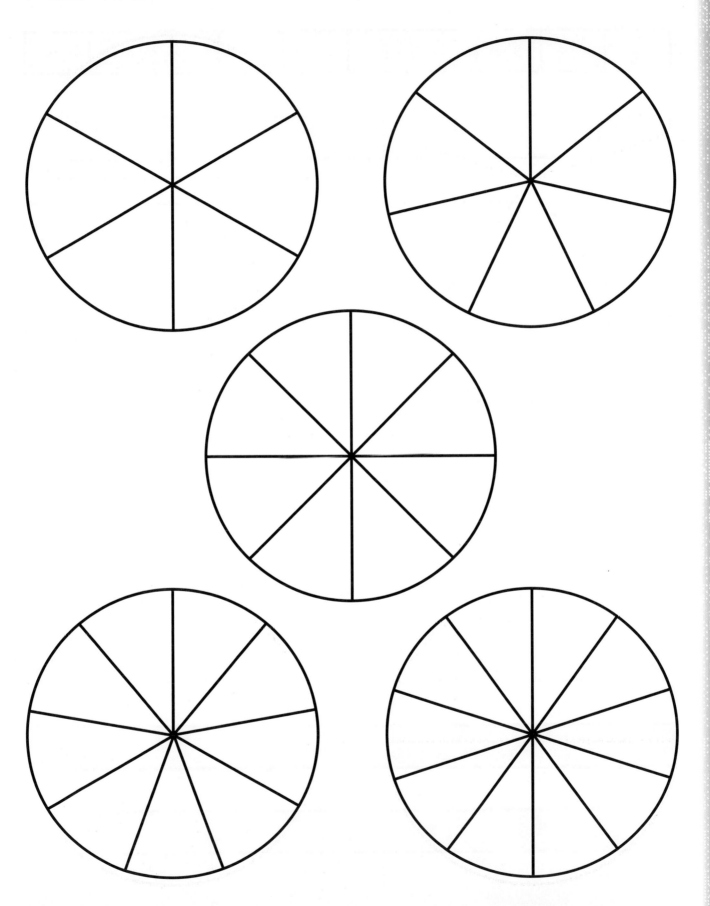

Fraction Bars

$\frac{1}{10}$									

$\frac{1}{9}$								

$\frac{1}{8}$							

$\frac{1}{7}$						

$\frac{1}{6}$					

$\frac{1}{5}$				

$\frac{1}{4}$			

$\frac{1}{3}$		

$\frac{1}{2}$	

1

Weighing Device

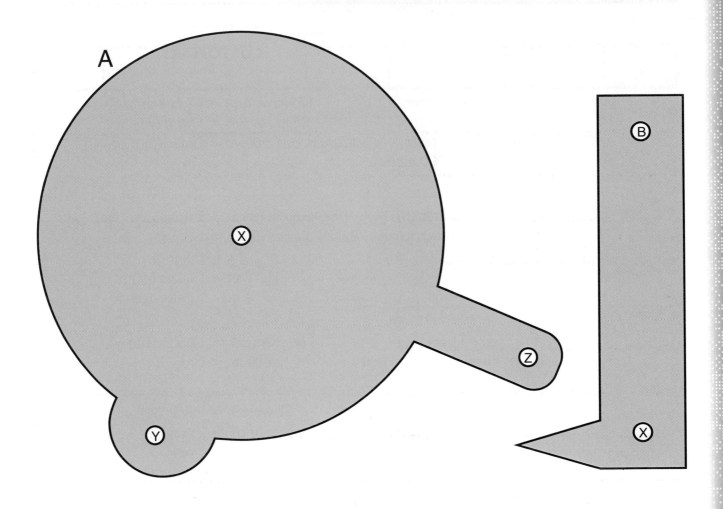

A

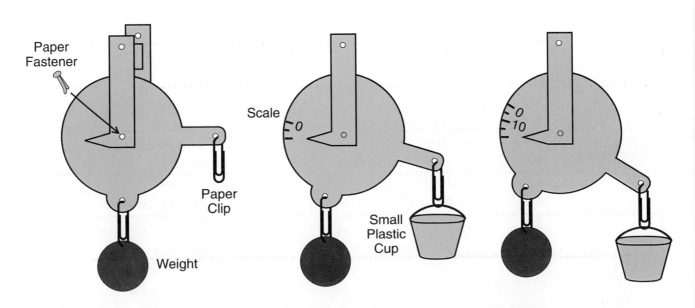

Paper Fastener

Paper Clip

Weight

Scale

Small Plastic Cup

Table of Measures

METRIC

Length
1,000 millimeters (mm) = 1 meter (m)
100 centimeters (cm) = 1 meter
10 decimeters (dm) = 1 meter
1 kilometer (km) = 1,000 meters

Capacity
1,000 milliliters (mL) = 1 liter (L)
250 milliliters = 1 metric cup

Mass/Weight
1,000 milligrams (mg) = 1 gram (g)
1,000 grams = 1 kilogram (kg)

Time
60 seconds (sec) = 1 minute (min)
60 minutes = 1 hour (hr)
24 hours = 1 day
7 days = 1 week (wk)

CUSTOMARY

Length
12 inches (in.) = 1 foot (ft)
36 in., or 3 ft = 1 yard (yd)
5,280 ft, or 1,760 yd = 1 mile (mi)

Capacity
1 tablespoon (tbsp) = 3 teaspoons (tsp)
8 fluid ounces (fl oz) = 1 cup (c)
2 c = 1 pint (pt)
2 pt = 1 quart (qt)
4 qt = 1 gallon (gal)

Mass/Weight
16 ounces (oz) = 1 pound (lb)
2,000 lb = 1 ton (T)

Time
52 weeks = 1 year (yr)
12 months (mo) = 1 year
365 days = 1 year
366 days = 1 leap year

Formulas

Perimeter of rectangle $P = (2 \times l) + (2 \times w)$

Perimeter of square $P = 4 \times s$

Circumference $C = \pi \times d$

Area of Rectangle $A = l \times w$

Area of Triangle $A = \frac{1}{2} \times b \times h$

Volume of prism $V = l \times w \times h$

Symbols

$=$	is equal to	$\overline{AB}$	line segment AB
$>$	is greater than	$\angle ABC$	angle ABC
$<$	is less than	$\triangle ABC$	triangle ABC
10^4	ten to the fourth power	π	pi (3.14)
$\approx$	is approximately equal to	$\circ$	degree
1:3	ratio of 1 to 3	°C	degree Celsius
$\overrightarrow{AB}$	ray AB	°F	degree Fahrenheit
$\overleftrightarrow{AB}$	line AB	(2,3)	ordered pair 2,3

Glossary

acute angle An angle that has a measure less than 90° *(page 112)*

angle A figure formed by two rays that meet at a common endpoint *(page 112)*

area The number of square units needed to cover a surface *(page 394)*

Associative Property of Addition The property which states that when adding three or more addends, any two of the addends can be joined, and the remaining addends may then be added to their sum without changing the total sum *(page 58)*
Example: $(7 + 5) + 6 = 7 + (5 + 6)$
$12 + 6 = 7 + 11$
$18 = 18$

Associative Property of Multiplication The property which states that when multiplying three or more factors, any two of the factors can be multiplied, and the remaining factors may then be multiplied without changing the total product *(page 76)*
Example: $(3 \times 4) \times 5 = 3 \times (4 \times 5)$
$12 \times 5 = 3 \times 20$
$60 = 60$

average The number found by dividing the sum of a set of numbers by the number of addends *(page 168)*

bar graph A graph which uses bars of different heights or lengths to show and compare information *(page 230)*

base A side of a polygon or a face of a solid figure by which the figure is measured or named *(page 136)*
Example:

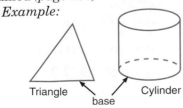

Triangle   Cylinder
base

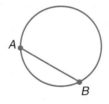

capacity The amount of liquid a container can hold *(page 354)*

category A type of information in a data base, such as names or phone numbers *(page 462)*

cell In a spreadsheet, a block area in which data or formulas can be entered; located by an address consisting of a letter and a number *(page 458)*

centimeter (cm) A unit of length in the metric system
0.01 meter = 1 centimeter *(page 350)*

chord A line segment with endpoints on a circle *(page 135)*
Example:

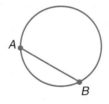

circle A flat, round shape that has all points the same distance from the center point *(page 134)*

circle graph A graph in the shape of a circle that shows fractions, percents, or parts of a whole *(page 230)*

circumference The distance around a circle *(page 392)*
Example:

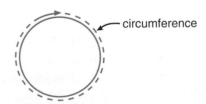

← circumference

closed figure An outline of a shape that begins and ends at the same point *(page 116)*

clustering A method used in estimation when several addends are close to the same number that is easy to compute mentally *(page 55)*

common factor   A number that is a factor of two or more numbers *(page 288)*
  Example: The common factors of 6 and 12 are 1, 2, 3, and 6.

common multiple   A number that is a multiple of two or more numbers *(page 292)*
  Example: A common multiple of 2, 3, 4, and 6 is 24.

Commutative Property of Addition   The property which states that when the order of two addends is changed, the sum is the same *(page 58)*
  Example: $6 + 4 = 4 + 6$
  $10 = 10$

Commutative Property of Multiplication   The property which states that when the order of two factors is changed, the product is the same *(page 76)*
  Example: $5 \times 7 = 7 \times 5$
  $35 = 35$

compatible numbers   Pairs of numbers that are easy to compute mentally *(page 152)*

composite numbers   Numbers that have more than two factors *(page 287)*
  Example: 6 is a composite number since its factors are 1, 2, 3, and 6.

cone   A solid figure that has a flat, round base *(page 138)*

congruent figures   Figures that have the same size and shape *(page 130)*

coordinates   The two numbers in an ordered pair *(page 234)*

cube   A solid figure with six congruent square faces *(page 136)*

cup (c)   A customary unit for measuring capacity
  8 fluid ounces = 1 cup *(page 372)*

cylinder   A solid figure with two faces that are parallel, congruent circles *(page 138)*

· · · · · · **D** · · · · · · ·

data   Information, such as text, formulas, or numbers, that can be organized, sorted, collected, or used in calculations *(page 12)*

data base   A computer program used to organize, sort, and find the kind of information that is normally kept in a list or on file cards *(page 462)*

decimal   A number that uses place value and a decimal point to show values less than one, such as tenths, hundredths, and so on *(page 16)*

decimeter (dm)   A unit of length in the metric system
  10 centimeters = 1 decimeter *(page 350)*

degree (°)   A unit for measuring angles and for measuring temperature *(page 114)*

degree Celsius (°C)   A metric unit for measuring temperature *(page 362)*

degree Fahrenheit (°F)   A unit of the customary system for measuring temperature *(page 362)*

diameter   A line segment that passes through the center of a circle and has its endpoints on the circle *(page 135)*
  Example:

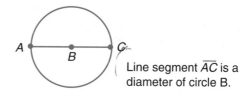
Line segment $\overline{AC}$ is a diameter of circle B.

Distributive Property of Multiplication   The property which states that multiplying a sum by a number is the same as multiplying each addend by the number and then adding the products *(page 83)*
  Example: $3 \times (4 + 2) = (3 \times 4) + (3 \times 2)$
  $3 \times 6 = 12 + 6$
  $18 = 18$

dividend   The number that is to be divided in a division problem *(page 150)*
  Example: $3\overline{)18}$
  The dividend is 18.

divisible   A number is divisible by another number if the result of the division is a whole number and the remainder is zero *(page 150)*
  Example: 18 is divisible by 3.

divisor   The number that divides the dividend *(page 150)*
  Example: $3\overline{)18}$
  The divisor is 3.

document   A file, or a group of information, that is stored on a disk or in a computer's hard drive, used by a computer program *(page 456)*

equally likely Outcomes that have the same chance of occurring *(page 436)*

equilateral triangle A triangle with three congruent sides *(page 118)*

equivalent fractions Fractions that name the same number or amount *(page 279)*
Example: $\frac{3}{4} = \frac{6}{8}$

estimate An answer close to the exact answer, found by rounding, using front-end digits, or by using compatible numbers *(pages 40, 46)*

expanded form A way to write numbers by showing the value of each digit *(page 4)*
Example: $635 = 600 + 30 + 5$ or
$(6 \times 100) + (3 \times 10) + (5 \times 1)$ or
$(6 \times 10^2) + (3 \times 10^1) + (5 \times 10^0)$

exponent A number that tells how many times the base is used as a factor *(page 3)*
Example: $10^3 = 10 \times 10 \times 10$

face A flat surface of a solid figure *(page 136)*

factor A number multiplied by another number to find a product *(page 92)*

field A type of information in a data base, such as names or phone numbers *(page 462)*

file The electronic form of information stored together as a group on a disk or on a computer's hard drive *(page 457)*

flip A move that involves turning a figure across a line of symmetry *(page 130)*
Example:

fluid ounce (fl oz) A customary unit for measuring capacity *(page 372)*

foot (ft) A unit of length in the customary system
12 inches = 1 foot *(page 368)*

formula In a spreadsheet, a set of instructions that tells the computer to calculate a total or to perform a task *(page 458)*

fraction A number that names part of a whole or part of a group *(page 276)*
Example:

$\frac{1}{3}$ of the region is shaded. $\frac{1}{3}$ of the group of pencils is circled.

frequency table A chart used to show how many times each item of data occurs *(page 210)*

front-end estimation A method using only the front-end digits to estimate sums, differences, products, and quotients *(page 40)*

gallon (gal) A customary unit for measuring capacity
4 quarts = 1 gallon *(page 372)*

gram (g) A unit of mass in the metric system
1,000 milligrams = 1 gram *(page 356)*

graphics Art or designs made using the computer *(page 448)*

greatest common factor (GCF) The greatest factor a pair of numbers have in common *(page 289)*
Example: 6 is the GCF of 18 and 30.

grid A set of uniformly-spaced horizontal and vertical lines *(page 234)*

horizontal axis The bottom line of a graph *(page 224)*

inch (in.) A unit of length in the customary system *(page 368)*
Example:

1 inch

intersecting lines   Two lines that cross at exactly one point *(page 109)*
Example:

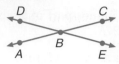

interval   The number of units between equally spaced lines on a graph *(page 214)*

inverse operations   Opposite operations that undo each other; addition and subtraction or multiplication and division are inverse operations *(page 38)*

irregular polygon   A polygon that does not have all sides and all angles congruent *(page 117)*

isosceles triangle   A triangle with at least two congruent sides and two congruent angles *(page 118)*
Example:

······**K**······

kilogram (kg)   A unit of mass in the metric system
1,000 grams = 1 kilogram *(page 356)*

kilometer (km)   A unit of length in the metric system
1,000 meters = 1 kilometer *(page 350)*

······**L**······

least common denominator (LCD)   The smallest common multiple of two or more denominators *(page 319)*

Example: The LCD for $\frac{1}{4}$ and $\frac{5}{6}$ is 12.

least common multiple (LCM)   The smallest number other than zero that is a multiple of two or more given numbers *(page 292)*
Example: The LCM of 6 and 9 is 18.

like fractions   Fractions that have a common denominator *(page 317)*
Example: $\frac{2}{5}$ and $\frac{3}{5}$

line   A straight path extending in both directions with no endpoints *(page 108)*
Example:

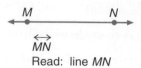
Read: line *MN*

line graph   A graph in which lines are used to show how something changes over a period of time *(page 230)*

line of symmetry   A line that divides a figure so that the two parts of the figure are congruent *(page 128)*

line segment   Part of a line with two endpoints *(page 108)*
Example:

Read: line segment *MN*

liter (L)   A unit for measuring capacity in the metric system
1,000 milliliters = 1 liter *(page 354)*

LOGO   A computer language used primarily to draw graphic designs *(page 450)*

······**M**······

mass   The measure of the quantity of matter of an object *(page 356)*

mean   The number found by dividing the sum of a set of numbers by the number of addends, or the average *(pages 168, 212)*

median   The middle number in a ordered series of numbers *(page 212)*
Example: The median of 1, 3, 4, 6, 7 is 4.

memory keys   Keys on a calculator that store and recall numbers from memory *(page 199)*

meter (m)   A unit of length in the metric system
100 centimeters = 1 meter *(page 350)*

metric system   A measurement system that uses meter as the measure of length; liter as the measure of capacity; gram as the measure of mass; and degree Celsius as the unit of temperature *(page 358)*

mile (mi)   A unit of length in the customary system
  5,280 feet = 1 mile *(page 368)*

milliliter (mL)   A unit for measuring capacity in the metric system
  0.001 L = 1 milliliter *(page 354)*

mixed number   A number that is made up of a whole number and a fraction or a whole number and a decimal *(page 299)*
  Example: $2\frac{1}{2}$, or 2.5

mode   The number that occurs most often in a list of data *(page 212)*
  Example: The mode of 1, 3, 4, 4, 6 is 4.

multiple   A number that is the product of a given number and another whole number *(page 78)*
  Example: Multiples of 3 are 3, 6, 9, 12, 15, . . .

number line   A line with equally spaced points named by numbers *(page 10)*

obtuse angle   An angle that has a measure greater than 90° and less than 180° *(page 112)*

open figure   A set of points that does not completely enclose a region in the same plane *(page 116)*

ordered pair   A pair of numbers used to locate a point on a grid; the first number tells the left-right position and the second number tells the up-down position *(page 234)*

ounce (oz)   A unit for measuring weight in the customary system *(page 372)*

outcome   A possible result in a probability experiment *(page 436)*

parallel lines   Lines in a plane that stay exactly the same distance apart *(page 109)*
  Example:

parallelogram   A quadrilateral with opposite sides parallel and congruent *(page 123)*

partial products   Products that are added together in a multiplication problem to get the final product *(page 94)*

percent   A ratio of some number to 100 *(page 429)*

perimeter   The distance around a figure *(page 388)*

period   Each group of three digits in a number *(page 6)*
  Example: 3,420,071
    The periods are 420 and 071.

perpendicular lines   Two lines that intersect to form right angles *(page 109)*
  Example:

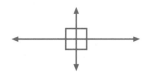

pi (π)   The ratio of the circumference of a circle to the length of its diameter *(page 393)*
  π ≈ 3.14

pictograph   A graph that uses pictures to show and compare information *(page 230)*

pint (pt)   A customary unit for measuring capacity
  2 cups = 1 pint *(page 372)*

plane   A flat surface that extends without end in all directions *(page 108)*

plane figure   A closed figure that lies on a flat surface *(page 116)*

point   An exact location in space *(page 108)*

pound (lb)   A customary unit for measuring weight
  16 ounces = 1 pound *(page 372)*

prime numbers   Numbers that have only two factors, 1 and the number itself *(page 287)*
  Examples: 5, 7, 11, 13, 17, and 19 are all prime numbers.

prism   A solid figure whose ends are congruent, parallel polygons, and whose sides are rectangles *(page 136)*
  Examples:

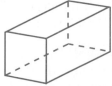

Rectangular Prism   Triangular Prism

Glossary

probability The chance of an event happening *(page 437)*

procedure A set of commands that directs the computer what to do *(page 450)*

Property of One for Multiplication The property which states that the product of any number and 1 is the number *(page 76)*
Examples: $5 \times 1 = 5$
              $16 \times 1 = 16$

pyramid A solid figure with a base that is a polygon and three or more faces that are triangles with a common vertex *(page 137)*
Examples:

Triangular Pyramid   Rectangular Pyramid

·······Q·······

quadrilateral A four-sided polygon *(page 122)*

quart (qt) A customary unit for measuring capacity
2 pints = 1 quart *(page 372)*

quotient The answer in a division problem *(page 150)*
Example:

The quotient is 9.

·······R·······

radius A line segment with one endpoint at the center of a circle and the other endpoint on the circle *(page 135)*
Example:

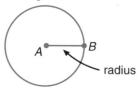

random A method of selection in which each person or item in a group has an equal chance of being chosen *(page 210)*

range A method used in estimation in which a number is rounded high and low; the difference between the greatest and least numbers in a set of data *(pages 41, 212)*

ratio A comparison of two numbers *(page 423)*

ray A part of a line that begins at one endpoint and extends forever in only one direction *(page 112)*
Example:

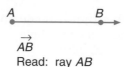
$\overrightarrow{AB}$
Read: ray *AB*

record In a data base, information for one particular person or item *(page 462)*
Example: Joe Rossi, 950 Paces Circle, Jackson, MS (555) 555-1200

rectangle A parallelogram with four right angles *(page 123)*

rectangular prism A solid figure in which the parallel bases are rectangles *(page 136)*

recursion The ability of a procedure to repeat a set of commands by calling itself *(page 454)*

regular polygon A polygon with sides congruent and all angles congruent *(page 117)*
Example:

rhombus A parallelogram with four congruent sides whose opposite angles are congruent *(page 123)*
Example:

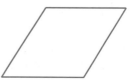

right angle An angle that forms a square corner and measures 90° *(page 112)*

right triangle A triangle with one right angle *(page 120)*
Example:

round To express a number to the nearest thousandth, hundredth, tenth, one, ten, hundred, thousand, and so on *(page 10)*
Examples: 473 rounded to the nearest hundred is 500.
37.85 rounded to the nearest tenth is 37.9.

sample group A number of people or items chosen to be representative of a larger group *(page 210)*

scale The unit length on a line compared with the number it stands for; a ratio that compares the distance on a map with an actual distance *(pages 216, 427)*

scalene triangle A triangle with three unequal angles and whose sides are not congruent *(page 118)*
Example:

short division A short form of division where you multiply and subtract mentally and write the remainders in the dividend *(page 158)*

similar figures Figures that have the same shape but may not have the same size *(page 132)*
Example:

simplest form A fraction that has 1 as the greatest common factor of the numerator and denominator *(page 290)*

slide The movement of a geometric figure to a new position without turning or flipping it *(page 130)*
Example:

sorting A method by which the computer organizes or orders information *(page 460)*

spreadsheet A computer program that organizes information in rows and columns and makes calculations with numbers and formulas *(page 458)*

square A rectangle with four right angles and four congruent sides *(page 123)*

standard form A way to write numbers using the digits 0–9, with each digit having a place value *(page 4)*

survey To ask questions to find the most frequent choice of a group *(page 211)*

tablespoon (tbsp) A customary unit for measuring capacity
3 teaspoons = 1 tablespoon *(page H102)*

ton (T) A customary unit for measuring weight
2,000 pounds = 1 ton *(page 372)*

trapezoid A quadrilateral with only one pair of sides parallel *(page 123)*
Example:

tree diagram An organized list *(page 430)*
Example:

triangle A polygon with three line segments *(page 118)*

turn A move that involves rotating a figure around a point *(page 130)*
Example:

turtle The triangle in the computer language LOGO that is directed to draw graphic designs *(page 450)*

unlike fractions Fractions that have different denominators *(page 317)*

Example: $\frac{3}{4}$ and $\frac{2}{3}$

variable In LOGO, a name by a colon (:) which substitutes a numeric value *(page 450)*

Venn diagram A diagram that uses geometric shapes to show relationships *(page 225)*

vertex The point at which two rays of an angle, two sides of a polygon, or three or more edges of a solid figure meet *(page 112)*

vertical axis The left side of a graph *(page 224)*

volume The measure of space inside a solid figure *(page 406)*

word processor A computer program used to write text, such as letters, reports, word problems, or memos *(page 456)*

yard (yd) A unit of length in the customary system
3 feet = 1 yard *(page 368)*

Zero Property for Addition The property which states that the sum of zero and any number is that number *(page 58)*
Examples: $9 + 0 = 9$
$0 + 12 = 12$

Zero Property for Multiplication The property which states that the product of zero and any number is zero *(page 76)*
Examples: $13 \times 0 = 0$
$0 \times 7 = 0$

PHOTO CREDITS KEY: (t) top; (c) center; (b) bottom; (l) left; (r) right Page iv, (all backgrounds) HBJ/Jerry White; (top and bottom insets) Tim Davis/Photo Researchers; (center inset) R.A. Lee/Superstock; v, Alvin Upitis/The Image Bank; vi, HBJ/J. White; vii, HBJ/Beverly Brosius; viii (t), Royce Bair/The Stock Solution; (b) HBJ/Rob Downey; ix (t) HBJ/J. White; (b) HBJ; x, (t) HBJ/Rob Downey; (b) HBJ/Grey Leary; xi, (t) Lawrence Migdale; (b) Tony Freeman/PhotoEdit; xii, (t) HBJ/Charlie Burton; (b) HBJ/Victoria Bowen; xiii, (t) HBJ/J. White; xiii (b) HBJ/Rob Downey; xiv, (t) HBJ/Richard Haynes; (b) HBJ/ Victoria Bowen; xvi (b), HBJ/J. White; xvi-xvii, HBJ/Terry Sinclair; xvii, (t) HBJ/Earl Kogler; xvii–xxii HBJ/Richard Haynes; xxiii, (t) (b) HBJ/J. White. **CHAPTER 1:** 0–1, (background) Culver Pictures; 0, (INSET) Lee Bolton Photoe, courtesy of Bawne & Co., South Street Seaport Museum; 2, HBJ/Rob Downey; 3, HBJ/Maria Paraskevas; 4, Lawrence Migdale/Photo Researchers; 5, (t) HBJ; (b) H. Armstrong Roberts; 6, (t) (background) HBJ/J. White; (c) (background) HBJ/J. White; (c) (inset) Tim Davis/Photo Researchers; (c) (background) HBJ/J. White; (c) (inset R.A. Lee/Superstock; (b) (background) HBJ/J. White; (b) (inset) Tim Davis/Photo Researchers; 8, HBJ/J. White; 9, George Rose/Gamma-Liaison; 10, Troy Maben/David R. Frazier Photoliray; 12 (background) Wally Hampton Photography; (inset) HBJ/J. White; 16, HBJ/Maria Paraskevas; 17, HBJ/J. White; 18, HBJ/J. White; 20, Steve Vidler/Nawrocki Stock Photo; 22, David R. Frazier Photolibrary; 23, HBJ/J. White; 24, HBJ/Annette Stahl; 25, 26, 28 and 29, HBJ/J. White; 31, L. Willinger/Superstock. **CHAPTER 2:** 36–37, (background) Robert Tringali/SportsChrome; 36, (inset) David Madison/Duomo; 37, (inset) David Madison/Duomo; 38, Bob Daemmrich/TSW; 40, Richard Hutchings/Photo Researchers; 42, Steven E. Sutton/Duomo; 43, Win McNamee/Duomo; 44, Grant LeDuc/Monkmeyer Press; 45, Glennon Donahue/TSW; 46, HBJ/Earl Kogler; 48, David Madison/Duomo; 49, Grafton M. Smith/The Image Bank; 50, Paul Slaughter/The Image Bank; 51, Al Tielemans/Duomo; 54, HBJ/Earl Kogler; 56, (t) HBJ/Earl Kogler; (b) HBJ/J. White; 58, HBJ/Annette Stahl; 59, HBJ/Annette Stahl; 60 Paul Kennedy/Leo deWys, Inc.; 61, HBJ/J. White; 62, HBJ/Maria Paraskevas; 63, HBJ/Rob Downey; 64–65, HBJ/J. White; 66, Alvin Upitis/The Image Bank; 67, Bob Abraham, Pacific Rim Productions/The Stock Market; 69, HBJ/J. White. **CHAPTER 3:** 74–75, (background) James Blank/Stock Imagery; 74, (inset) LaTrobe Barnitz/The Picture Cube; 75, (inset) Stock Imagery; 76, HBJ/Richard Haynes, 78, HBJ/Rob Downey; 79, Ray Pfortner/Peter Arnold, Inc.; 80, Robert V. Eckert, Jr./The Picture Cube; 82, HBJ/Maria Paraskevas; 84, (t) Ann Duncan/Tom Stack & Associates; (b) HBJ/J. White; 86, HBJ/Earl Kogler; 87, Frank P. Rossotto/The Stock Market; 90, (background) David Pollack/The Stock Market; (inset) HBJ/Annette Stahl; 92, HBJ/Richard Haynes; 94, HBJ/Earl Kogler; 95, David Madison/Duomo; 96, Arnold J. Kaplan/Berg & Associates; 98, HBJ/J. White; 99, HBJ/Annette Stahl. **CHAPTER 4:** 106–107, (background) NASA; 106, (inset) Harry J. Przekop/MediChrome-The Stock Shop; 107, (inset) NASA; 108, HBJ/J. White; 109, Comstock; 110, HBJ/J. White; 112, HBJ/J. White; 114, HBJ/Beverly Brosius; 115, HBJ/J. White; 116–117, HBJ/Rodney Jones; 118, HBJ/J. White; 120, HBJ/J. White; 122–123, HBJ/Rob Downey; 124, HBJ/J. White; 125, Helmut Wimmer; 128, HBJ/J. White; 130, HBJ/Rob Downey; 132, (t) and (b) HBJ/J. White; 134, (l) and (r) HBJ/Maria Paraskevas; 135, HBJ/Greg Leary; 136, HBJ/Maria Paraskevas; 137–140, HBJ/J. White; 145, NASA. **CHAPTER 5:** 148–149, (background) Great America Theme Park, Santa Clara, CA.; 148, (inset) HBJ/J. White; 149, (inset) HBJ/Richard Haynes; 150 and 151, HBJ/Beverly Brosius; 152, Bob Daemmrich; 154, (t) HBJ/Richard Haynes; (b) HBJ/Beverly Brosius; 156, Kirk Schlea/Berg & Associates; 158, HBJ/J. White; 160, Bob Daemmrich; 161, HBJ/J. White; 164, David Young-Wolff/Photo Edit; 166, HBJ/Annette Stahl; 168, David R. Frazier Photolibrary; 170 and 174, HBJ/Greg Leary; 175, David Lissy/The Picture Cube. **CHAPTER 6:** 178–179, (background) Ric Ergenbright Photography; 178, (inset) A. Devaney/Devaney Stock Photos; 179, (inset) HBJ/Greg Leary; 180, Royce Bair/The Stock Solution; 182, Jerome F. Shaw/Take Stock; 184, David Lissy/Instock; 186, David Young-Wolff/Photo Edit; 188, (t) and (b) HBJ/Annette Stahl; 190, Gene Cohn/Stock Imagery; 191, (l) Tony Freeman/Photo Edit; (r) HBJ/J. White; 193, HBJ/Charlie Burton; 194, (t) B.J. Adams/Devaney Stock Photos; (b) John Pineda/Miami Herald; 196, (t) HBJ/Chris Lowery; (b) Gale Beery/Stock Imagery; 197, Gale Beery/Stock Imagery; 198, (t) HBJ/Beverly Brosius; 199, (t) and (b) HBJ/Rob Downey; 200, (background) Mark E. and Audrey Gibson/The Stock Market; (inset) HBJ/Greg Leary; 201, HBJ/J. White. **CHAPTER 7:** 208–209, (background and 208, (inset) HBJ/Greg Leary; 210 and 211, HBJ/Richard Haynes; 212 and 213 HBJ/J. White; 214, Tom Myers, 216 and 218, HBJ/Julie Fletcher; 219, Tom Myers; 220, Bob Daemmrich; 224, Richard Hutchings/Info Edit; 226, David Young-Wolff/PhotoEdit; 228, (t) and (b) HBJ/Rob Downey; 229 and 230, HBJ/J. White; 232 and 233, HBJ/ Annette Stahl; 234, (background) Superstock; (inset) HBJ/Greg Leary. **CHAPTER 8:** 242–243, (background) and 242, (inset) HBJ/Charlie Burton; 243, (inset) HBJ/J. White; 244, HBJ/J. White; 246, Dick Wade/Berg & Associates; 248, HBJ/Victoria Bowen; 249, HBJ/Rob Downey; 250, HBJ/Annette Stahl; 252, HBJ/Rodney Jones; 253, Garry Adams/Stock Imagery; 254, David R. Frazier Photolibrary; 256, HBJ/J. White; 257, David Young-Wolff/PhotoEdit; 260, HBJ/J. White; 262, HBJ/Rob Downey; 263, HBJ/Maria Paraskevas; 264, Chris Jones/The Stock Market; 266, HBJ/Charlie Burton; 267, John M. Touscany/Third Coast Stock Source. **CHAPTER 9:** 274–275, (background) Larry Lefever/Grant Heilman Photography; 274, (inset) and 275, (inset) HBJ/Richard Haynes; 276, Dr. E.R. Degginger, FPSA/Color Pic; 278, HBJ/Victoria Bowen; 279, HBJ/Beverly Brosius; 280, HBJ/Charlie Burton; 282, (t) HBJ/Charlie Burton; (b) Walter Chandoha; 283, John Lei/Stock, Boston; 286, HBJ/Victoria Bowen; 287, HBJ/Maria Paraskevas; 288, HBJ/J. White; 289, HBJ/Richard Haynes; 290, HBJ/Greg Leary; 292, HBJ/Victoria Bowen; 293, HBJ/Annette Stahl; 294, Walter Chandoha; 296, (t) David Young-Wolff/PhotoEdit; (b) Walter Chandoha; 298, HBJ/Victoria Bowen; 299, HBJ/Maria Paraskevas; 300, HBJ/Rob Downey; 302, Larry Lefever/Grant Heilman Photography; 303, Christopher Rogers/The Stock Market. **CHAPTER 10:** 310–311, (background) HBJ/Rob/Downey; 310, (inset) HBJ; 311, (inset) HBJ/Charlie Burton; 312, HBJ/J. White; 314, Bob Daemmrich/The Image Works; 316, Bob Daemmrich/The Image Works; 317, HBJ/Richard Haynes; 318 and 319, HBJ/Rob Downey; 320, (t) and (b) HBJ/Annette Stahl; 321, Steve Drexler/ Stockphotos-The Image Bank; 322, HBJ/Maria Paraskevas; 323, HBJ/Richard Haynes; 324, HBJ/Rob Downey; 326, (t) HBJ/Annette Stahl; 328, Joe Sohm/The Image Works, courtesy Utah Symphony; 329, HBJ; 332, HBJ/Charlie Burton; 334, HBJ/J. White; 336, HBJ/Charlie Burton; 338 and 339, HBJ/Rob Downey; 340, Tony Freeman/PhotoEdit; 341,Lawrence Migdale. **CHAPTER 11:** 348–349, (background) Richard Steedman/The Stock Market; 348, (inset) and 349, (inset) HBJ/Greg Leary; 350, HBJ/Charlie Burton; 352, HBJ/Maria Paraskevas; 353, HBJ/Victoria Bowen; 354, 356, and 358, HBJ/J. White; 360, HBJ/Richard Haynes; 364, 365, and 370, HBJ/Charlie Burton; 372 and 374, HBJ/J. White; 376 (t) and (b) and 378, HBJ/Charlie Burton. **CHAPTER 12:** 386, (inset) and 387, (inset) HBJ/Richard Haynes 388, HBJ/Victoria Bowen; 389, HBJ/Beverly Brosius; 390, HBJ/Annette Stahl; 392, HBJ/J. White; 393, HBJ/Beverly Brosius; 394, HBJ/Charlie Burton; 396, HBJ/Richard Haynes; 398, and 399, HBJ/Charlie Burton; 402, HBJ/J. White; 404, HBJ/Maria Paraskevas; 405, HBJ/Rob Downey; 406, HBJ/Victoria Bowen; 407 HBJ/Rob Downey, 408, HBJ/Charlie Burton; 410, HBJ/J. White; 412, (t) and (b) HBJ/J. White; 413, HBJ/Richard Haynes. **CHAPTER 13:** 420–421, (background) HBJ/Greg Leary; 420 (inset) HBJ/Charlie Burton; 421, (inset) HBJ/Richard Haynes; 422 and 423, HBJ/Maria Paraskevas; 424, (t) Wilson Goodrich/Tom Stack & Associates; 424, (b) K.D. McGraw/Stock Imagery; 426 and 427, (t) and (b) HBJ/Maria Paraskevas; 428, (t) and (b) HBJ/Rob Downey; 429, HBJ/Maria Paraskevas; 432, HBJ/Richard Haynes; 433, Milton & Joan Mann/Cameramann International; 436, HBJ/ Rob Downey; 437, HBJ/Victoria Bowen; 438, Chris Sorensen/The Stock Market; 440, HBJ/Richard Haynes; 441 (l), Milton & Joan Mann/Cameramann International; (r) Anita Stonecypher/Berg & Associates; (b) Wendell Metzen/Southern Stock Photos. **COMPUTER CONNECTION:** 448, HBJ/Greg Leary; 448–449, Jay Freis/The Image Bank; 449, Mug Shots/The Stock Market; 462, (t) and (b) Douglas Faulkner/Photo Researchers. **STUDENT HANDBOOK:** All, HBJ Photos.

ILLUSTRATIONS: Michael Adams 175, M8; **Tim Bowers** 14, 30, 32, 52, 68, 70, 88, 100, 102, 126, 142, 144, 172, 174, 202, 204, 236, 238, 268, 270, 304, 306, 342, 344, 380, 382, 414, 416, 442, 444, M1, M16; **Suzanne Clee** 369, 371, 373, 375, 377, 379, 381, 417, 445; **Eldon Doty** 50, 111, 165, 174, 301; **Don Dyen** 71, 89, 103, 153, 157, 159, 163, 167, 173, 337, 355, 357, 361, H82, H85; **Electronic Publishing Center** 215, 231, 234, 235, 251; **Barbara Erickson** H48, H74; **Kathy Hendrickson** 180, 183, 185, 187, 189, 195, 203, 217, 221, 227, 247, 250, 255, 261, 265, 269; **J.A.K. Graphics** 34, 53, 72, 145, 276, 281, 286, 291, 350, 352, 353, 356, 358, 359, 362, 363, 368, 383, 384, 408, 409, 424, 439, 442, 444, H8, H27, H30, H31, H32; **Bryce Lee** 387; **Polly K. Lewis** 15, 33, 287, 295, 297, 313, 321, 327, 333, 335; **Laurie Marks** 307, 308, 401; **Eileen Rosen** 240, 331, 446; **Ed Sauk** 77, 85, 91, 93, 99, 155, 165, 169, 174, 181, 205, 343, 351, 354; **Nancy Schill** 271, 285; **Den Shofield** 431, 443; **Brad Strode** 385, 411, 425, 438; **George Ulrich** 197, 430; **Nina Winters** 7, 21, 27, 28, 127, 367, 418, 435.

Index

A

Activities, 34, 72, 104, 146, 176, 206, 240, 272, 308, 346, 384, 418, 446

Acute angles, 112–113, 115, 120, 122, 451

Acute triangles, 120–121

Addends, 42, 58, 168, H4
  missing, 38–39, H5
  three-digit, H6–H7
  two-digit, H6–H7
  zero as, H4–H5

Addition
  addends, 38–39, 42, 168, H4–H5
  Associative Property, 58–59
  with calculators, 42, H16, H26
  checking sums, 38
  Commutative Property, 58–59
  counting on, H4–H5
  of decimals, 54–59, 64–66, 72
  doubles, H4–H5
  doubles plus one, H4–H5
  estimating sums, 40–43, 54–57, 64–66, 312–313, 322, 326, H26
  of fractions, 312–323, 326–328
  regrouping in, 42, 323, H6–H7
  and subtraction, 38–39
  sums, 168, H4–H5
  tables, H4
  of three-digit numbers, H6–H7
  of two-digit numbers, H6–H7
  with units of measure, 370–371
  with units of time, 376–377
  of whole numbers, 38–45, H4–H7
  Zero Property, 58–59, H4–H5

A.M., 376–379

Analyze data, 15, 33, 47, 51, 65, 81, 89, 127, 129, 169, 187, 217, 225, 227, 231, 281, 297, 333, 361, 371

Angles, 112–115, 451, H12
  acute, 112–113, 115, 120, 122, 451
  exterior, 113
  interior, 113
  measuring, 114–115
  obtuse, 112–113, 115, 120, 122, 451
  of polygons, 116–117
  right, 112–115, 120, 122, 451
  sides of, 112
  straight, 114, 451
  of triangles, 117, 119–120
  vertices of, 112–114

Area, 394–399, 402–403, 412, H32
  estimating, 402–403
  of parallelograms, 396–397
  of rectangles, 394–396, 398–399, 412, 417–418
  surface, 418
  of triangles, 396–397

Associative Property
  of Addition, 58–59
  of Multiplication, 76–77

Average, 71, 168–169, 194, 212
  estimating, 168

B

Bar graphs, 216–217, 223–224, 230–231, 259, 363
  double, 240

Base
  of prisms, 136
  of pyramids, 137

BASIC, 440–441

Bridge Lessons, H2–H25

C

Calculators, 17, 34, 72, 104, 206, 213, 256, 272, 308
  for addition, 42, H16, H26
  Challenge, 34, 72, 104, 206, 272, 308
  for division, 166, 194, 198–199, 260, 265
  memory keys, 78, 199, 256
  for multiplication, 78, 96–97, 244, 247, 252–253
  recall key, 78, 199, 256
  for subtraction, 46, 48, 72

Capacity
  cups, 372–373
  customary system, 372–373
  estimating, 354–355
  fluid ounces, 372–373
  gallons, 372–373
  liters, 354–355, 358–359, 361, 365, 384
  metric cups, 354
  metric system, 354–355, 358–359
  milliliters, 354–355, 358–359
  pints, 372–373
  quarts, 372–373

Celsius, 362–363

Center, 134–135

Centimeters, 16–17, 350–353, 358–361, 364–365, H20–H21

Certainty, 438

Challenges, 34, 72, 104, 146, 176, 206, 240, 272
  Calculator, 34, 72, 104, 206, 272, 308
  Everyday Math, 446
  Logical Reasoning, 308, 346, 418
  Puzzles, 346, 446
  Visual Thinking, 418

Chapter Reviews, 30–31, 68–69, 100–101, 142–143, 172–173, 202–203, 236–237, 268–269, 304–305, 342–343, 380–381, 414–415, 442–443

Chapter Tests, 32, 70, 102, 144, 174, 204, 238, 270, 306, 344, 382, 416, 444

Chords, 135
  diameters, 135

Circle graphs, 228–231

Circles, 132, 134–135, 453–454, H12
  center of, 134–135
  chords, 135
  circumference of, 392–393, 412–413
  diameters, 135, 392–393
  radii, 135

Circumference, 392–393, 412–413

Clocks, 451

Closed figures, 116–123
  circles, 132, 134–135, 392–393, 412
  congruent, 130–131
  polygons, 116–123
  similar, 132–133
  symmetry, 128–129

Clustering, 55

Common factors, 288–291, H18
  greatest, 289–291

Common multiples, 292–294, 319
  least, 292–294, 296, 319–320

Commutative Property
  of Addition, 58–59
  of Multiplication, 76–77

Comparison, 195
  of decimals, 24–25
  of fractions, 277, 294–297, 300, 308
  of whole numbers, 8–9

Compass, 134

Compatible numbers, 40, 152, 182–183, 190

Composite numbers, 287

Computers, 450–465
  data base, 462–465
  LOGO, 450–456, 464
  programs, 440–441
  spreadsheet, 457–461, 464–465
  word processor, 456–457, 464

Hundred thousands, 2–7
Hundredths, 16–24, 26–27, 64, 248–249, 263

Index

MATH FUN MAGAZINE

These brainteasers don't stump me!

Have fun solving these brain teasers!

▶ As you learn
new things this year,
you will be able
to solve problems
that might have
stumped you at first.
So, keep trying!

WALK IN THE PARK

Sometimes you need to see many possibilities to solve a puzzle.

Peak Park has walking paths that form many different triangles.
How many different triangles can you walk around?
List the triangles, using the letters given.

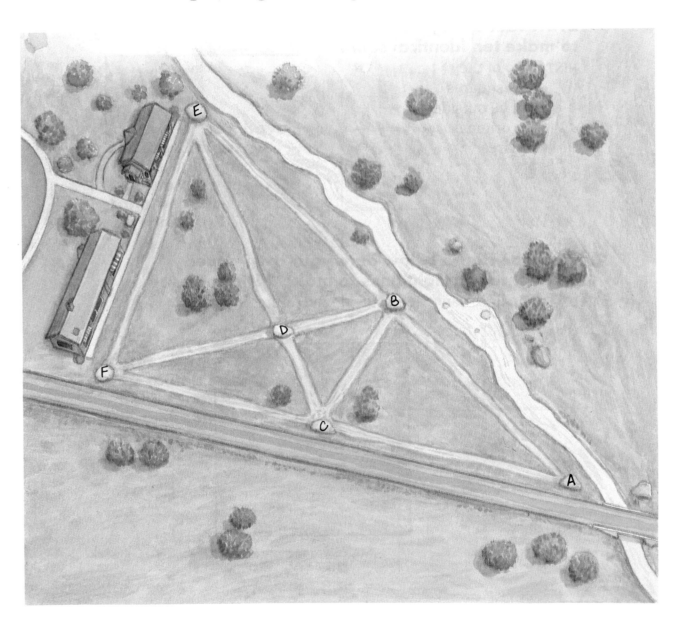

1. Which of these patterns can be folded to make a cube?

A.

B.

C.

D.

E.

F.

G.

H.

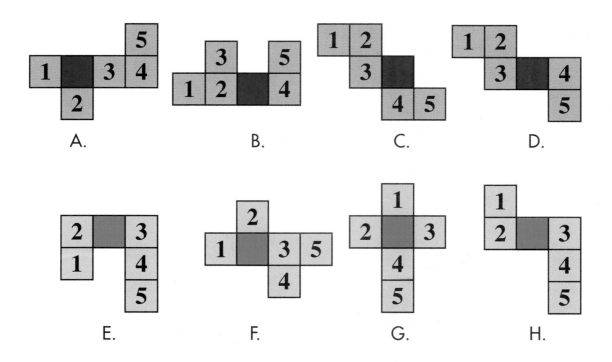

2. Refer to each of the patterns you chose. Think of the shaded face as the bottom of the cube. For each cube, what is the number of the face that would be on top?

In the stack of blocks,
T, E, and *N* in the word *TEN*
can be used to complete the word
in each row of the stack.
Each of the letters *T, E,* and *N*
must be used in each of the rows.
Any of the letters can be used
more than once in each row.
Write each completed word on your own paper.

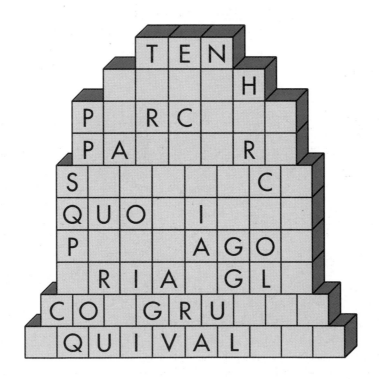

Elementary, My Dear Watson!

Are you a good word detective?
Conduct a word search, and find those fugitive
units of measure.

The table contains the customary and metric units of measure listed.
Copy the table onto graph paper. Fill in each space with the given letter.
Search the table for each word in the list. Circle the hidden words in your table.
You may read the words forward, backward, or diagonally.

C	U	P	C	E	R	U	O	H	E
S	E	C	O	N	D	F	A	C	A
M	I	N	U	T	E	N	N	N	E
L	R	E	T	E	M	O	L	I	K
E	P	I	T	I	L	T	L	E	H
C	O	G	R	A	M	E	T	E	R
N	U	Y	A	R	D	E	L	I	M
U	N	G	U	P	I	N	T	L	M
O	D	E	Q	E	L	I	T	E	R
M	I	L	L	I	L	I	T	E	R

CENTIMETER
CUP
FEET
GRAM
HOUR
INCH
KILOMETER
LITER
METER
MILE
MILLILITER
MINUTE
OUNCE
PINT
POUND
QUART
SECOND
TON
YARD

TIME Traveler

**Draw clock faces on your own paper.
For each time after 7:10 A.M., draw the hands on
a different clock face.**

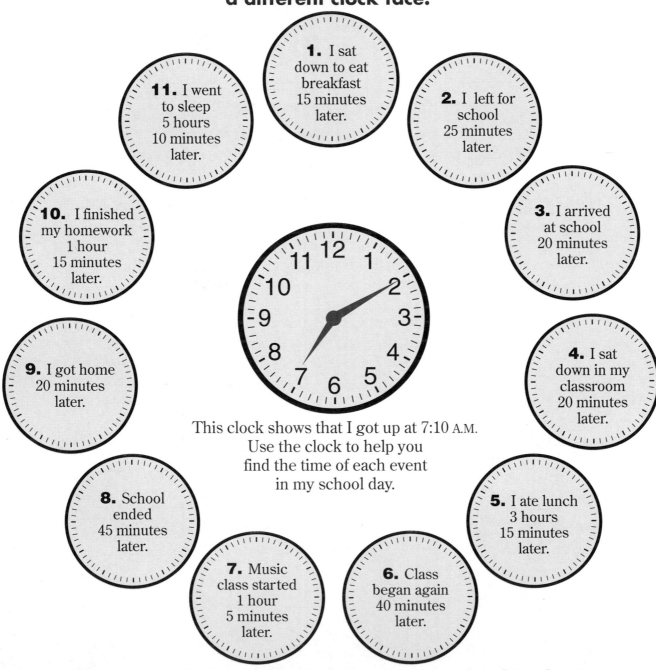

1. I sat down to eat breakfast 15 minutes later.

2. I left for school 25 minutes later.

3. I arrived at school 20 minutes later.

4. I sat down in my classroom 20 minutes later.

5. I ate lunch 3 hours 15 minutes later.

6. Class began again 40 minutes later.

7. Music class started 1 hour 5 minutes later.

8. School ended 45 minutes later.

9. I got home 20 minutes later.

10. I finished my homework 1 hour 15 minutes later.

11. I went to sleep 5 hours 10 minutes later.

This clock shows that I got up at 7:10 A.M.
Use the clock to help you
find the time of each event
in my school day.

How many hours and minutes was I awake that day?

Repeat SHAPE

**When copies of a repeat shape are
laid next to each other,
a similar, but larger, shape is made.**

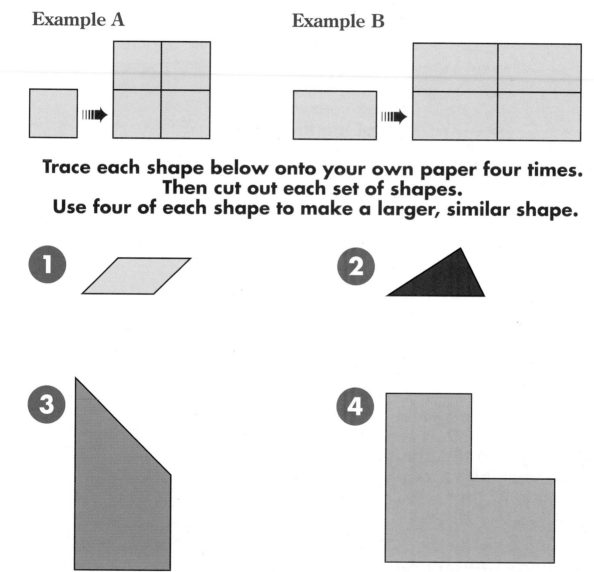

Example A   Example B

**Trace each shape below onto your own paper four times.
Then cut out each set of shapes.
Use four of each shape to make a larger, similar shape.**

1

2

3

4

HAT TRICKS

Others will tip their hats to you when you show them the secrets of these hat trick puzzles.

1. Copy this figure onto your own paper. Write the numbers 1–9 in the circles so that the sum on each of the three sides is the same.

2. Copy this figure onto your own paper. Place the numbers 1–9 in the circles so that the sums of the four numbers on each side of the triangle are equal.

No number may be used more than once.

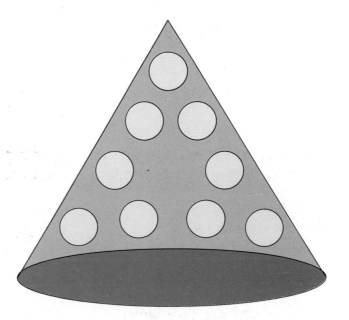

PYRAMID Arithmetic

**Pyramids are built one stone at a time.
Complete each pyramid by finding the missing numbers.
In these pyramids addition is used to find
the number in the top stone.**

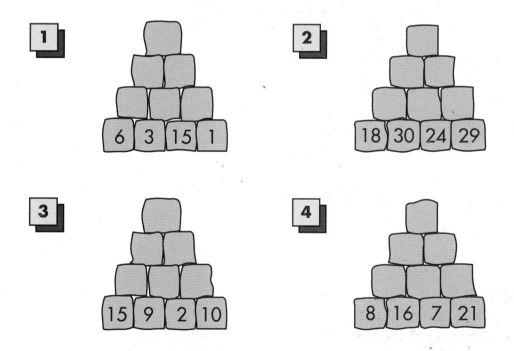

1 6 3 15 1

2 18 30 24 29

3 15 9 2 10

4 8 16 7 21

**Complete each pyramid by finding the missing numbers.
In these pyramids subtraction is used to find each missing number.**

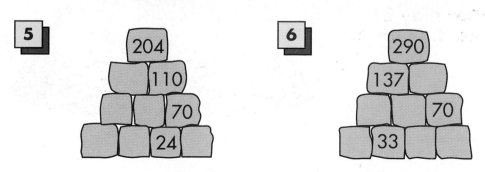

5 204 110 70 24

6 290 137 70 33

Sidewalk of STARS

Perhaps you have noticed the cracks in a sidewalk when you used them as game boundaries or when you tried not to step on them. Sometimes interesting shapes are formed by the cracks. Examine the cracks in this section of sidewalk. How many five-pointed stars can you find?

I solved every problem! Did you?